UNCROWNED

UNCROWNED
ROYAL HEIRS WHO DIDN'T TAKE THE THRONE

ASHLEY MANTLE

AMBERLEY

First published 2023

Amberley Publishing
The Hill, Stroud
Gloucestershire, GL5 4EP

www.amberley-books.com

Copyright © Ashley Mantle, 2023

The right of Ashley Mantle to be identified as the Author of this work has been asserted in accordance with the Copyright, Designs and Patents Act 1988.

All rights reserved. No part of this book may be reprinted or reproduced or utilised in any form or by any electronic, mechanical or other means, now known or hereafter invented, including photocopying and recording, or in any information storage or retrieval system, without the permission in writing from the Publishers.

British Library Cataloguing in Publication Data.
A catalogue record for this book is available from the British Library.

ISBN 978 1 4456 9647 8 (hardback)
ISBN 978 1 4456 9648 5 (ebook)

1 2 3 4 5 6 7 8 9 10

Typesetting by SJmagic DESIGN SERVICES, India.
Printed in the UK

Contents

Acknowledgements		7
A Note on Money		8
Introduction: The Setting Sun		9
1	Robert II, Duke of Normandy	12
2	William Aetheling	28
3	Empress Matilda	36
4	Eustace, Count of Boulogne	47
5	Henry the Young King	55
6	Arthur, Duke of Brittany	66
7	Edward of Woodstock, the Black Prince	78
8	Roger Mortimer, 4th Earl of March	96
9	Edmund Mortimer, 5th Earl of March	104
10	Richard, Duke of York	113
11	Edward of Lancaster	125
12	Edward V	136
13	Edward of Middleham	144
14	John de la Pole, Earl of Lincoln	147
15	Arthur Tudor, Prince of Wales	155
16	Lady Jane Grey	168
17	Lady Catherine Grey, Countess of Hertford	180
18	Lady Mary Grey	189
19	Lady Margaret Clifford, Countess of Derby	195

20	Mary, Queen of Scots	202
21	Henry Frederick, Prince of Wales	221
22	Sophia, Electress of Hanover	231
23	James Francis Edward Stuart	245
24	Frederick Louis, Prince of Wales	259
25	Frederick, Duke of York and Albany	270
26	The Rules of Succession Today	283

Notes	285
Bibliography	304
Index	313

Acknowledgements

Writing this book has been a dream come true and I would like to thank Amberley Publishing and my mentor, Connor Stait, for allowing me the opportunity to do so. I would also like to thank Canterbury Cathedral; Gloucester Cathedral; Tewkesbury Abbey; St Mary of Charity, Faversham; St Laurence's Church, Ludlow; Ludlow Castle; St John the Baptist Church, Cirencester; and the Lewis Walpole Library, Yale University, for their kind permission for me to use the photographs in the plates inside the book.

A special mention must go to Matthew Lewis who has happily answered my numerous questions on the technicalities of writing a book and who also provided me with some of the wonderful photographs for the plates. Your help is much appreciated. Thanks also to Philip Hume for helping me find a depiction of the Mortimer/de Burgh coat of arms as used by Roger and Edmund Mortimer, 4th and 5th Earls of March respectively.

Finally, I would like to thank my family and loved ones who have supported me as I have researched and written this book, particularly Leigh and my mother, Debbie, who proofread the work for me. Any errors that remain are my own.

A Note on Money

For most of the period covered in this book, England employed the pre-decimal system of currency, divided into pounds (£), shillings (s) and pence (d). Before 1279 the only coin in circulation was the silver penny. The penny could be cut in half to make a halfpenny or into quarters to make a farthing. 240 pennies equalled one pound. The pound could be further divided into 20 shillings, each of the value of 12 pence, as well as the silver mark, which equated to 160 pennies.

Over time new denominations were added and others dropped. The reign of Edward I (1272–1307), for instance, saw the introduction of the silver groat, worth 4 pence. Edward III's reign (1327–1377) saw the establishment of the gold noble, valued at 6 shillings and 8 pence, while the reign of the first Tudor monarch, Henry VII (1485–1509), saw the arrival of the shilling as a coin, as well as the gold sovereign that was worth one pound.

From 1663, during the reign of Charles II (1660–1685), the old 'hammered coins' gave way to milled coinage that was pressed by machine. In 1971, the pre-decimal system was superseded by the decimal system that we use today.

I have opted to leave monetary values in their original form rather than attempt to equate them to today's values. For those who wish to do so, the National Archives website has a currency converter (www.nationalarchives.gov.uk/currency-converter) starting from the year 1270.

Introduction

The Setting Sun

The premature death of Henry Frederick, Prince of Wales, the eldest son and heir apparent of King James I of England and VI of Scotland, provoked a massive outpouring of grief. The much-lamented young prince, said to have been 'the glory of his country, and the admiration of all strangers', was aged eighteen, 'in the flower of his age', when he succumbed to typhoid fever on Friday 6 November 1612, never to wear the crown that nature had destined him for.[1] In the wake of his death, an unprecedented swathe of elegies were written in honour of his memory, while in his native Scotland he became the subject of a proverb to console grieving mothers. 'Did not good Prince Henry die?' they would offer as a comfort to the bereaved.[2]

A contemporary, Richard, Earl of Dorset, captures the feeling in a letter he wrote to the English ambassador Sir Thomas Edmondes on 23 November 1612: 'To tell you,' he states, 'that our rising sun is set ere scarcely he had shone, and that with him all our glory lies buried.'[3] Sir Robert Carey, Earl of Monmouth, later noted that 'the loss of him was so grievous to all the subjects of this island that no expression of sorrow could enough manifest their grief'.[4]

The Puritan members of the nation had high hopes for Prince Henry, a devout Protestant who despised popery and who many believed had been chosen by God to restore the true church and destroy Catholic idolatry.[5] Now that hope lay in tatters. Henry would never be able to realise his birthright and rid the country of Catholicism. Unfortunately, the new heir apparent to the throne, Henry's younger brother, the eleven-year-old Charles, Duke of York and future King Charles I, did not possess the same Protestant religious zeal as his elder brother.

Henry Frederick is one of the many kings and queens who never were, the heirs apparent and presumptive who were destined to ascend the thrones of England and, later, Great Britain but never did. Some of these characters, such as Edward of Woodstock, the Black Prince, who fought valiantly at the Battle of Crécy at the tender age of sixteen, and Mary, Queen of Scots, who not only lost the throne of Scotland but also her head, are household names. Others, such as William Aetheling, the son and heir apparent of King

Henry I, whose tragic death in the sinking of the *White Ship* precipitated fourteen years of civil war, are less well known. Their lives invite a series of intriguing 'what ifs' of English history. For instance, had Arthur Tudor, the elder brother of King Henry VIII, survived and become king, would the English Reformation still have taken place? If Henry Frederick had lived, would England still have been engulfed in the civil war that resulted in the abolition of the monarchy and eleven years of the Commonwealth? These are complicated questions and the answers unknowable, but they offer an interesting exercise in speculation. Whatever the case, each of these would-be kings and queens had a discernible impact on English history in both life and death, and their stories are every bit as interesting and illuminating as those of their better-known crowned kin.

It is the intention of this book to briefly trace the lives of these would-be kings and queens who, if fortune's wheel had been more kind, may have reigned illustriously or disastrously over us. We will proceed through nearly 1,000 years of history, starting shortly before the Norman Conquest of 1066 up to the present day. Included among the roster of characters are a few individuals who actually became king or queen. These include Henry the Young King, eldest son of King Henry II and the only heir apparent to be crowned during the lifetime of his father; Edward V, one of the so-called Princes in the Tower; and Lady Jane Grey, England's tragic first queen regnant, who reigned famously for nine days. I have included the Young King as he never 'reigned' in the technical sense and his name will never be found in the regnal lists of our monarchs. Edward V and Lady Jane, likewise, never truly reigned and both were forcibly removed from their thrones. On the other hand, I have opted not to include Edward VIII, who, although never crowned, chose to abdicate the throne after a reign of eleven months in order to marry Wallis Simpson.

Heir Apparent and Heir Presumptive

Before we begin it may be useful to define what we mean by the terms 'heir apparent' and 'heir presumptive'. An heir apparent is an individual whose claim cannot be set aside by the birth of another heir.[6] Until the introduction of the Succession to the Crown Act (2013), only males could be heir apparent to the English throne. In what was a patriarchal society, males took precedence over females and a female heir would be superseded in the order of succession by the birth of a younger brother, meaning that females could only ever be presumptive heirs. Similarly, if a monarch has no children then their heir is their next collateral relation, such as a brother or sister, aunt or uncle. As the collateral relation also has the chance of being supplanted by the birth of a direct heir, they, too, are known as an heir presumptive.

The Rules of Succession

Today, the throne of the United Kingdom is hereditary. The succession is determined by a combination of feudal common-law principles and ancient parliamentary statues.[7] The monarch is said to never die and on their death he or she is automatically succeeded by the heir. The throne descends by primogeniture, in birth order, with the eldest child succeeding their parent regardless of gender. As the gender bias inherent in the succession was only removed in 2013, this only applies to those born since 2011 and male preference still applies to those born before.

While the throne is hereditary, Parliament enjoys the right to subvert the ordinary line of descent if it deems the heir apparent to be ill suited to the role. There are also certain criteria that the heir must meet. He or she must be a descendant of Princess Sophia, Electress of Hanover (see below, chapter 22) and must be in communion with the Church of England. Those who do not meet these requirements are passed over and the next eligible candidate is selected instead.

The rules of succession have not remained static but have evolved over the centuries, from Anglo-Saxon times to the present day. For much of this period there were no codified rules of succession and there is disagreement between historians as to what they constituted at particular times or whether or not clear rules existed. Throughout, we will briefly trace the development of the rules of succession. At the beginning of each chapter is a basic family tree to aid the reader in identifying the subject's place in the succession. You may find it useful to flick back to previous family trees for further clarification.

When quoting from old texts, particularly those from the early modern period, I have modernised the spelling while still retaining the punctuation of the original.

1

Robert II, Duke of Normandy

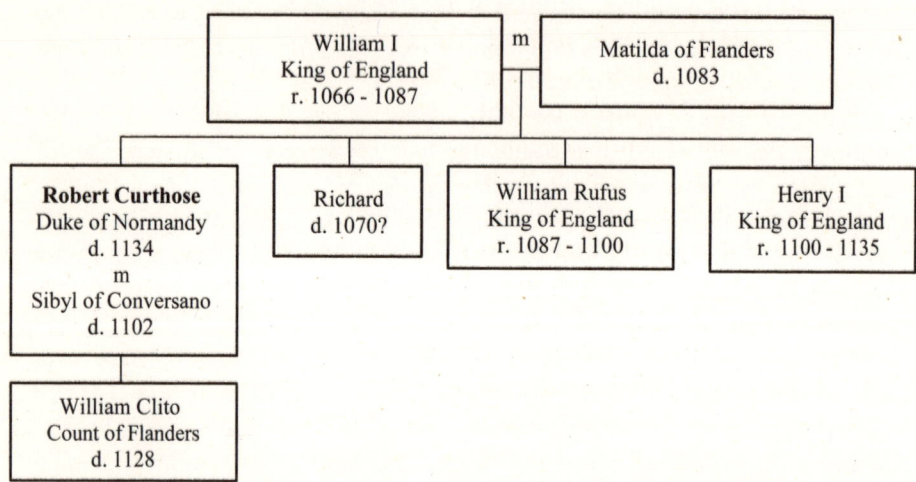

In early September 1087, William I, King of England and Duke of Normandy, better known as William 'the Conqueror', lay dying at the church of Saint-Gervais on the outskirts of Rouen in Normandy. Gathered about his deathbed were his youngest sons, William Rufus and Henry, his physicians and members of the church and nobility. One figure was noticeably absent. Robert 'Curthose', William's eldest son and heir, was in exile at the court of the hated King Philip I of France.

As the end drew near, William announced his intentions regarding the succession to England and Normandy. He granted Robert the duchy of Normandy, but the richer prize of England he bestowed on his second and favourite son, William Rufus. Rufus immediately took leave of his father and hurried to gain possession of the kingdom. Shortly after, the great Conqueror died.

When Robert heard of his father's death he peacefully took charge of Normandy, but his thoughts soon turned to the glittering kingdom across the Channel.

Birth and Early Life

Robert II, Duke of Normandy, or Robert 'Curthose', was the eldest son of William the Conqueror and his queen, Matilda of Flanders. He was likely born at Rouen, the capital of Normandy, sometime between 1050 and 1053.[1] As with most medieval figures, few details survive of Robert's childhood. He would have spent his early years in a nursery, possibly in his mother's household. At the age of six or seven he would have left the care of women and began his formal education, being placed in the charge of a tutor whose role it was to protect and teach him. Robert is recorded as having a tutor, a knight named Hilger, in a charter from 1066.[2] As with all noble children, Robert would have learned how to behave in polite society, to speak, to read and write, to sing and dance, to play an instrument, to hunt, to ride a horse, to joust, and, most importantly for a medieval statesman, to fight.[3] Robert is described by the chronicler William of Malmesbury as being an eloquent speaker and he is purported to have written a poem in Welsh during his later years as a prisoner. He was by all accounts a courageous knight, just like his father, having been raised among the Conqueror's warlike household troops.

At the time of his birth, Robert could look forward to one day becoming Duke of Normandy, the family patrimony which his Viking ancestor, Duke Rollo, had carved from France in 911. There were no settled rules of succession in eleventh-century Normandy. The dukedom was hereditary to the ducal family and the reigning duke would designate his successor and have the barons pay homage to him. The duke could in theory choose any of his sons to succeed him, but it had become ducal tradition to choose the eldest.[4] William continued this tradition and in 1063 he designated Robert as heir apparent to Normandy and to the county of Maine, the first of his conquests.

Then, in September 1066, Robert's prospects changed. That month William invaded England at the head of an army to do battle with King Harold II for the English throne. William claimed that the childless Edward 'the Confessor', the last king of the ancient House of Wessex who had died earlier that year, had designated him as his heir.

Like Normandy, eleventh-century England had no fixed rules of succession. The throne was hereditary – at the start of the century it had been the prerogative of the House of Wessex, the descendants of King Alfred the Great (r. 871–899) who had ruled over a united England since the tenth century. There was no recognised heir apparent – all of the king's sons and brothers were known as Aethelings, a title meaning 'throne-worthy', and were eligible for the kingship. As such, the succession was not automatic and a king would designate his successor. There was usually a tendency to choose the eldest son, or, if a king had no sons, his next brother. There were practical considerations that guided his choice. In a warlike society, adults were preferred to minors and a king's son, if a child, might be passed over in favour of an adult brother. Females, on the other hand, were regarded as being unable to lead armies and as such they were deemed ineligible for the throne.

The king, then, could choose his successor but this did not guarantee that his candidate would succeed. There was an element of election to proceedings as it was the candidate who enjoyed the greatest support of the Witan, the king's council formed by the great magnates and senior members of the church, who was successful. The support of the church was vitally important as it was the church that was responsible for anointing the king at his coronation, transforming him from king-elect into God's anointed, something that made his rule indisputable.[5] In the event that the succession was disputed, the choice of the Witan often carried the day.

Why, then, would an English king choose a Norman duke to be his successor? King Edward was part Norman. His father was the troubled king Aethelred II of England and his mother, Queen Emma, was the daughter of Duke Richard I of Normandy. At the beginning of his reign, King Edward had married Edith, the daughter of Godwine, Earl of Wessex, the most powerful nobleman in the country and the true power behind the throne. However, the marriage proved childless, making the question of Edward's successor an open one throughout his reign. In 1052, Edward is said to have designated his Norman kinsman, Duke William, as his heir. Edward had been raised in Normandy when the English throne had been usurped by a series of four Viking kings (1013–1042) and his designation of William was said to have been made as a token of gratitude. But in 1054, Edward changed his mind. His elder half-brother, King Edmund 'Ironside', who had reigned briefly in 1016, had two baby sons. After his death, the infants had been sent to the safety of Hungary, where one of them, Edward 'the Exile', survived and grew to manhood. In 1054, King Edward invited Edward the Exile to become his heir, but when he arrived in England three years later he soon sickened and died. Edward the Exile had three children who accompanied him to England: Edgar Aetheling, Margaret and Christina. Edgar, as a male descendant of the House of Wessex, was an obvious successor but as he was still young, King Edward's thoughts returned to his Norman kinsman.

In 1064 King Edward is said to have sent Harold Godwinson, the eldest surviving son and successor of Earl Godwine, to Normandy to renew the promise of the throne. Harold is reported to have sworn an oath to help William claim the throne upon Edward's death and agreed to marry one of his daughters. But when Edward eventually died on the night of 5 January 1066, it was not William that he designated as his successor on his deathbed but Earl Harold, who became King Harold II. This was an unprecedented move as Harold did not have the all-important blood of Wessex in his veins. Unfortunately, Edgar Aetheling, who was about fifteen years old, had again been overlooked due to his age. Duke William cried foul. Edward had made him his heir and he was the rightful king. King Harold, he said, was nothing but a perjurer. However, according to English law, a deathbed designation overruled any previous agreement. This did not dissuade Duke William, who first attempted to negotiate with Harold. But when that failed he turned to that other time-tested method of pushing one's claim: conquest.

Before embarking for England, William took the precaution of having the Norman barons once again pay homage and swear fealty to Robert as his heir in the event that he did not return. William, of course, was victorious and was crowned as King William I on 25 December 1066. The following year, the triumphant William returned to Normandy and when he later crossed back to England he left Robert to act as regent of the duchy in conjunction with Matilda and other trusted individuals, in order for him to gain experience in his future role. In 1068, when Matilda travelled to England for her coronation, Robert was left to act as sole regent until her return. Robert would spend most of the remainder of William's lifetime in Normandy and two surviving charters suggest that William may have ceded the duchy to him in the mid to late 1070s.[6] If so, the Conqueror was not willing to let his son wield complete control just yet.

Rebel

As an adult, Robert was short and stocky with a 'projecting belly', prompting his father to bestow upon him the derogatory nickname of 'short boots' or 'Curthose'.[7] As Robert grew, so did his impatience for power. He had been made heir or possibly *de jure* Duke of Normandy but had been given little power or resources with which to support himself. To make matters worse, he was surrounded by the next generation of Norman barons who were eager for his patronage.

In the late 1070s, Robert, now in his mid to late twenties, was urged by his companions to approach his father and demand control of Normandy and Maine or a part of England. William refused. 'I will not abdicate my prerogative in favour of anyone,' the chronicler Orderic Vitalis has him say, 'and no human being shall share my kingdom.'[8] Robert departed in anger and his resentment towards his father grew. Things reached a crisis point when Robert accompanied his father on a military campaign. He was sojourning at a house in the town of l'Aigle when his younger brothers William Rufus and Henry came to see him. The two boys sat upon a gallery that overlooked Robert and his companions on the floor below and played at dice. An argument soon broke out between the three brothers and Rufus and Henry poured a bucket of water over the heads of Robert and his companions. Robert stormed after them, but the clamour drew the attention of King William, who immediately put an end to it. This was the final straw. The following evening, Robert and his friends slipped away and made an unsuccessful attack on Rouen Castle. William ordered the rebels' arrest. Some of them were captured while others managed to cross the border into other provinces where they were granted castles by the king's enemies, from which they harried Normandy. Robert found refuge in Flanders with his uncle, Count Robert the Frisian.

William found his son's actions amusing at first. 'By the resurrection of God, this little Robin Short-boot will be a clever fellow,' he is said to have remarked.[9] He soon awoke to the seriousness of the situation. Robert travelled to the court of King Philip I of France. At this time, the kings of France only had direct control over the Ile-de-France, the area centred on Paris, while the rest of what would become the kingdom of France was divided between petty princes, including King William. These princes tacitly recognised the kings of France as feudal overlord but in reality they paid little attention to their authority. King Philip, jealous of his overmighty vassal, was more than happy to promote strife between father and son. He granted Robert the castle of Gerberoy, situated near the border of Normandy, as a base from which to launch attacks on the duchy. In January 1079, William laid siege to the castle and father and son met in a pitched battle outside the castle walls, during which Robert, unable to identify his father, wounded the ageing Conqueror's arm and knocked him from his horse. It was only the sound of the king's voice that stopped Robert from dealing a deadly blow. In a chivalrous display, Robert offered William his own horse and William took the reins and fled, but not before uttering a curse upon his eldest son. With the intercession of Queen Matilda and members of the nobility and clergy, Robert and William were reconciled and Robert was reconfirmed as William's heir to Normandy.

These good relations came to an end when Queen Matilda, who often acted as a mediator between father and son, died on 2 November 1083. Robert and William soon entered into another argument, and without the queen's staying hand Robert was forced into exile with a few companions. He spent the next four years aimlessly travelling through foreign countries, during which time he acquired the penchant for extravagance that would plague the rest of his life and career. He received gifts and loans from sympathetic nobles, but these he is said to have wasted on 'jugglers, parasites, and harlots'.[10] Robert eventually wound up at the court of King Philip of France and he was there upon his father's death in September 1087.

The Succession

William the Conqueror and Matilda of Flanders had four sons and six daughters. Their second son, Richard, had died young in a tragic hunting accident in the New Forest but their other two sons, William Rufus and Henry, survived to adulthood.

On his deathbed King William granted Normandy and Maine to Robert, but the kingdom of England he bequeathed to his favourite son, William Rufus. This accorded with the succession practice then developing in England and Normandy. The patrimony (Normandy) often went to the eldest son but acquisitions, land that was acquired outside of the main patrimony, could be disposed of as the ruler saw fit and was often granted to younger sons.[11] William could not legally dispossess Robert of Normandy, whom the barons had already recognised as heir and whom he may have already created duke, but England, which he had won by fire and sword, was his to give away as he wished, and he granted it to the ever dutiful Rufus, who was crowned as King William II.

This begs the question – was Robert ever heir to England? There is no record of him being recognised as such, but this does not mean that William had never intended to grant him the kingdom. It had been the practice of previous Norman dukes to pass their entire inheritance, both patrimony and acquisition, to their eldest son and it is possible that William had initially planned to follow custom but his hatred of his eldest son caused him to divide his inheritance. The laws of succession as they then stood gave him a legal basis on which to do so.

To Henry, his third son, he gave the sum of 5,000 silver marks as well as possession of his mother's lands in England.

Duke of Normandy

As soon as William died, law and order broke down in Normandy. The Norman barons turned out the royal garrisons from their castles and gave vent to their pent-up private squabbles with one another. The church and the poor were caught in the middle and their goods plundered. This was a common occurrence upon the death of any ruler, but it was particularly prevalent in Normandy. Orderic Vitalis notes that '[t]he Normans are a turbulent race, and, unless restrained by a firm government, are always ready for mischief'.[12]

Unfortunately, Robert was anything but the firm hand that Normandy needed. His time in exile had seen him become irresolute, lazy and extravagant, qualities unbecoming in a ruler who needed to instil fear in his subjects to keep them in check. He was prodigal and gave away ducal lands and castles, diminishing his power and resources, and in the process he created a set of powerful barons who could flout his command. He would promise justice to those who sought it but was too lenient on offenders and forgave them when bribed, or when enough time had passed. This emboldened them to carry on their depredations without fear of reprisal. He would, on occasion, make a show of ducal authority, but when he had secured the advantage he did not press it and instead returned to inactivity.

Meanwhile, the separation of England from Normandy had produced a set of uncomfortable circumstances for the barons who owned land on both sides of the Channel. They owed homage to two different lords, and when war inevitably broke out between the two brothers they would be stuck between a rock and a hard place – to support one brother ran the risk of losing the lands held by the other. In 1088, William the Conqueror's half-brother Bishop Odo of Bayeux and some of the Norman barons agreed that it would be more prudent to serve just one lord and settled on the easygoing Robert. The barons notified Robert of their intentions and the delighted duke agreed to send a body of troops to help their cause. The barons crossed over to England, fortified their castles and rose in rebellion.

The indolent Robert was slow in following up on his promise, as he had squandered much of his father's treasure on his extravagant lifestyle and had no money left to pay for troops. He was forced to sell the Cotentin, the western part of Normandy, to his brother Henry for the sum of 3,000 silver marks. With these new funds he eventually dispatched an army to England with the intention of following it, but the expedition met with disaster when on approaching the coast, the army was attacked and defeated by the English. Those who survived and attempted to sail away became a laughing stock when their ships were becalmed in the sea. Fearing capture, many of Robert's men jumped into the sea to their deaths. Rufus, meanwhile, laid siege to Bishop Odo's castle at Pevensey, which capitulated after a siege of six weeks and Odo was captured. Rochester soon followed; the rebels were forced to sue for peace and Bishop Odo was exiled from the country forever.

Rufus's Revenge

By 1090 William Rufus was out for revenge, and he set his sights on once again uniting England and Normandy under one ruler. The crafty king used the great treasures of England to bribe many of the barons of eastern Normandy to transfer their allegiance to him. Buoyed by his success, Rufus turned his attention to the great Norman capital of Rouen and bribed a wealthy citizen named Conan to hand the city over to his troops on an appointed day. When Robert learned of Conan's traitorous designs, he summoned help from his adherents. Henry was the first to arrive with a contingent of soldiers and took up residence with Robert at Rouen Castle. On 3 November, Gilbert de l'Aigle, at the head of a troop of horse in support of Robert, crossed the Seine and approached the city's southern gate, while Reynold de Warenne simultaneously arrived at the gate of Caux with 300 men-at-arms backing Rufus. Citizens loyal to Rufus rushed to attack Gilbert and those who supported Robert moved to open the gate of Caux and admit de Warenne.

Robert and Henry sallied forth from the castle and joined the fray, but Robert was convinced by those around him to flee lest he be captured and bring the ducal name into dishonour. He was conveyed out of the east gate and travelled to the village of Emendreville to await the outcome of the battle. Gilbert de l'Aigle, meanwhile, forced entry into the city and, joining forces with Henry, oversaw a great slaughter. The defeated royal soldiers fled for the woods and the duke's men looted the town and threw many of the citizens into jail. Henry seized the traitorous Conan, led him up the tower of Rouen and pushed him out of the window to his death.

Rufus had failed to take Rouen but by early 1091 he felt comfortable enough to launch his own attack on Normandy. He crossed over the Channel and took quarters at the castle of Eu, where he was joined by a large section of the Norman nobility. Robert had little choice but to make peace and in the resultant Treaty of Caen he recognised Rufus's rule over all the areas that had received him. Rufus, in return, promised to help Robert recover all the lands that their father had once owned, including the Cotentin Robert had sold to Henry, and Maine, which had been lost to Count Helias of La Flèche. Most notably, they agreed that if either of them were to die without an heir then the survivor would inherit the others' lands. Both Robert and Rufus were still unmarried and had no legitimate children, making Robert heir presumptive to England.

The only loser in the treaty was Henry, who revolted against his brothers and made a desperate stand at the fortified abbey of Mont-Saint-Michel. Robert and Rufus duly laid siege to the abbey and Henry and his men soon began to run low on water. Henry sent word to Robert, imploring him to allow them sustenance. In a great show of chivalry, the kindly Robert acceded to his brother's request and asked the guards to 'accidentally' allow water to be shepherded into the fortress. Rufus was furious when he found out. 'You well know how to carry on war indeed, who allow your enemies plenty of water: and pray, how shall we subdue them, if we indulge them in food and drink?' he taunted. 'Oh, shame!' Robert replied, 'Should I suffer my brother to die with thirst? and where shall we find another, if we lose him?'[13] After a siege of nearly fifteen days, Henry surrendered and he and his men were allowed to march out of the abbey peacefully. Henry spent the next two years of his life wandering in exile, like Robert before him.

Having dealt with Henry, Robert and Rufus proceeded to England to deal with King Malcolm III of Scotland who had taken advantage of Rufus's absence to invade the north of England. The brothers confronted King Malcolm, their belligerent armies staring each other down across the Firth, but Robert, who, somewhat ironically, was a skilful mediator when it came to other people's problems, managed to secure peace.

Robert was entertained at Rufus's court on their return from Scotland, but he was indignant when he arrived back in Normady to discover that Rufus would not fulfil his part of the treaty and help Robert win back Maine. By Christmas 1093, Robert's patience had worn thin and he sent messengers to Rufus declaring that he would renounce the Treaty of Caen if the king did not adhere to his promise or travel to Normandy to explain himself. The following Lent, Rufus crossed over to Normandy, but the brothers were unable to come to terms. Rufus took mercenaries into his pay and managed to sway more of the Norman nobles to come to his side through bribes and promises, and he garrisoned their castles with his own men. The Treaty of Caen was null and void, and the succession was once again an open question.

Robert joined forces with King Philip of France as his overlord and they marched through Normandy towards Eu with the aim of capturing Rufus, but the French king was lured by Rufus's silver smile and abandoned Robert for France.

Events in England, meanwhile, called Rufus back and in 1095 he placed Henry in charge of the Norman war. Henry returned to Normandy at Lent with great treasure, having reportedly done Robert much harm in both land and men.

The First Crusade

At the council of Clermont, held on 27 November 1095, Pope Urban II preached what would become the First Crusade. The Seljuk Turks had overrun much of Asia Minor (Turkey), land that had been part of the Byzantine Empire, and were encroaching on the Byzantine capital of Constantinople (Istanbul). Most shockingly of all, they had seized Jerusalem and shut its gates to the Christian nations. Pope Urban urged the prelates to rally all Christians to take a pilgrimage to the Holy Land and wage war against the Turks with the ultimate goal of wresting Jerusalem from Muslim occupation. Those who answered God's call would be purged of their sins and also had the opportunity of amassing great riches and achieving fame, glory and honour.

Robert was among the first to join the crusade. His motivation for doing so is unclear. He may have wished to be absolved of his sins against his father or he may have simply been drawn by the promise of adventure. Before he could go, however, Robert had two problems to solve. Firstly, he was still at war with William Rufus; secondly, crusading was an expensive business and Robert's coffers were empty due to his taste for the finer things. Fortunately, Pope Urban stepped in and arranged peace between Robert and Rufus. Rufus agreed to loan Robert 10,000 silver marks for the crusade in exchange for control of Normandy for a period of five years.

Robert set off for the Holy Land in October 1096. He was joined by his uncle, Bishop Odo; his brother-in-law Stephen, Count of Blois, the husband of Robert's sister Adela; his cousin Robert II, Count of Flanders; and an army comprised of Normans, English and Bretons. One of the last crusaders to arrive, on 3 June 1097 Robert joined in the siege of Nicaea (Iznik), which had been invested by the crusaders since May. Amongst those present at the siege were Bohemond of Taranto, Hugh of Vermandois, Godfrey of Bouillon and Raymond, Count of Toulouse. Robert and Stephen of Blois laid siege to the city's eastern gate and shortly after, on 19 June, the city surrendered.

The crusaders handed the city to the Byzantine Emperor, Alexios Komnenos, and departed on 26 June. As they passed through Asia Minor they split into two divisions. On the morning of 1 July, Robert's division was attacked by a much larger Turkish army at Dorylaeum. The mounted Turks launched a deadly shower of arrows upon the crusaders, who began to flee in panic. Seeing this, Robert bravely rallied the army and launched into the enemy, slaying three Turks and reigniting flagging Norman spirits. The battle was nonetheless going decidedly in the favour of the Turks until the second division of the crusaders appeared, at which point the combined force drove off the Turks.

The crusaders arrived at Antioch on 21 October. Antioch was heavily fortified by walls and towers and, in the words of a contemporary, 'fears the attack of no machine and the assault of no man, even if every race of man should come together against it'.[14] It was held under the command of Yaghi Siyan and was reported to have within it 2,000 knights, 4,000 to 5,000 common knights and 10,000 footmen.

The resultant siege proved difficult. It was drawn out over eight long months, during which time the crusaders were not only subject to the dangers of the siege but also to the extremities of winter and famine. At first food was abundant – the area was rich in stocks – but supplies began to run low. By December food was becoming scarce and many began to desert, with Robert's brother-in-law Stephen of Blois shamefully retiring from the crusade. Robert himself received an invitation to help some English sailors who had succeeded in capturing the port of Laodicea, on the coast of Turkey, but were now under threat of attack from marauding bands of Turks. Exhausted by the trying circumstances of the siege, Robert happily obliged. The chronicler Ralph of Caen notes that, in typical fashion, Robert spent his time at Laodicea 'in slumber and idleness'.[15] He was thrice summoned back to the siege and only returned under the threat of excommunication.

Antioch's eventual fall was orchestrated through the machinations of Bohemond of Taranto, who bribed the captain of one of the towers to allow them entry. On 2 June 1098, the army feigned going on a foraging expedition and then returned at midnight, gained entry to the tower via a ladder that had been left for the purpose and opened the gates to let in the army. The town was soon taken, but the castle still held out under the command of Yagi Siyan's son. Yagi Siyan himself managed to flee the city but he was later captured by some Armenians and beheaded.

Robert and the crusaders did not have time to recuperate. Two days later the army of Kerbogha of Mosul, who had been summoned by Yagi Siyan, surrounded the city and the tables turned. Now the crusaders were besieged. Famine reared its head once more, and the crusaders had to resort to eating their horses and donkeys to survive. Miraculously, and somewhat dubiously, in this hour of need the Holy Lance, said to have pierced Jesus's side when he was hanging from the cross, was unearthed in the church of St Peter. Its discovery revitalised the army's spirits and they decided to risk all in battle. On 28 June, the army separated into six divisions, of which Robert had command of the third, and they confronted Kerbogha outside the city and carried the victory. Shortly after, the castle surrendered. Antioch was in Christian hands.

The crusaders decided to postpone the attack on Jerusalem until November due to the dryness of the summer months. During this time, relations between the crusaders began to break down. Bohemond and Count Raymond argued over possession of Antioch. The main army, fearing that the journey to Jerusalem would be postponed, begged Count Raymond to lead them to Jerusalem and threatened to otherwise continue without a leader and trust to the command of God. Raymond agreed and summoned the other leaders to a council at Rugia, where he implored them to join him. Robert and the others were unwilling to do so until Raymond offered to pay them. He promised to pay Robert 10,000 solidi, an offer the duke likely accepted.

The crusaders reached Jerusalem on 7 June 1099. Robert, along with the Count of Flanders, laid siege to the northern wall, near the Church of St Stephen, while Raymond attacked from Mount Zion to the south and Godfrey and his nephew Tancred of Hauteville from the west. On 13 June the crusaders managed to destroy part of the outer wall and some even reached the parapet of the inner wall, where they fought hand to hand with the Turks but made no further progress.

The leaders decided to construct siege engines and launch a fresh attack on 14 July. On the night of the 13th, Duke Robert, Godrey of Bouillon and Robert, Count of Flanders moved their siege engines almost a mile eastward, nearer to the valley of Jehoshaphat where the wall was weaker and the ground was more level and more suitable for moving the machines. The siege began the next day to little avail and through the night the crusaders had to keep guard over the engines lest they be destroyed. The following morning the attack resumed. The crusaders shot burning firebrands, wrapped in cotton, at the enemy and managed to drive them from the wall. Seeing this, Godfrey lowered the drawbridge from the siege tower and breached the wall. His men, led by a knight named Leothold, made it on to the parapet and they swarmed into the city, followed by Godfrey and Tancred. Jerusalem was taken. After ransacking the city, the crusaders prayed at the Holy Sepulchre, having succeeded in their goal.

With Jerusalem captured, the leaders needed to elect one among them to rule the city and prevent it from returning into enemy hands. The other leaders offered Robert this great privilege but the duke, 'through the fear of endless labour', declined.[16] On 22 July, Godfrey of Bouillon accepted the honour.

Rumours soon reached Jerusalem that the Emir Malik al-Afdal was at nearby Ascalon with an army and was threatening battle. He would retake Jerusalem, he said, and afterwards destroy all the holy places within the city so that the Christians would never again have cause to attempt such a rash enterprise. Duke Godfrey went forth to ascertain that the rumours were true and sent word back to those at Jerusalem to make ready for battle. On the morning of 11 August, the crusaders entered a valley by the coast, near Ascalon, where they formed their battle lines. Robert, Tancred and the Count of Flanders were at the centre, while Godfrey commanded the vanguard and Raymond the rearguard beside the sea.

At the beginning of the battle, Robert is said to have spotted al-Afdal's standard, a spear adorned with silver and surmounted by a golden apple, within the ranks of the enemy. He surged forward, carving a path through the enemy, and felled the standard bearer. The rest of the army then attacked, and the enemy was routed and fled.

After the battle, the victorious army pilfered the enemy's tents and then returned laden with booty to Jerusalem. Robert purchased al-Afdal's standard for 20 silver marks and donated it to the Patriarch of the See of Jerusalem as a memento of the victory.

Robert's reputation rests on his role in the First Crusade, and it is as a crusader that he is best remembered. Whatever his other faults, he was undoubtedly a brave and skilled warrior, like his father. He was loyal, acted as a mediator between the feuding leaders and was not self-seeking like some of the other crusaders. He could still be characterised by moments of slothfulness, as in the siege of Antioch, but these were wiped away by his performance in the battles of Ascalon and Dorylaeum.

Having fulfilled their vows, Robert and the other crusaders decided to return home. Robert returned by way of Sicily, where he fell in love with Sibyl, the daughter of Geoffrey de Conversano, and married her in Apulia. Geoffrey granted Robert 10,000 silver marks as Sibyl's dowry, which Robert intended to use to regain Normandy from Rufus. Robert was now in his late forties or early fifties and had not yet produced a legitimate male heir to succeed him. He had illegitimate children, including two sons and a daughter, but as illegitimacy was now a bar to the dukedom he needed a son of legitimate birth.

As Robert made his way back home, accident or fate would change the status quo in England.

Tinchebray

William Rufus had been out hunting in the New Forest on 2 August 1100 when he was accidentally shot and killed with a crossbow bolt fired by his companion Walter Tirel. Rufus was unmarried and childless, and his unexpected and instantaneous death meant that he did not have the opportunity to designate his successor. Robert was still returning from the crusade at this time, but his youngest brother, Henry, was fortuitously present in the New Forest. Henry immediately spurred his horse to Winchester where he demanded the keys to the royal treasury. He was challenged by William de Breteuil, who reminded him that he had previously paid homage to Robert for his lands in Normandy and that God had rewarded the duke with a crown for his role in the crusade. Henry pulled out his sword and declared that no foreigner would lay hand on his father's sceptre. This may sound an odd remark, but Henry was the only one of the Conqueror's sons to be born in England when his parents were king and queen, giving him the distinction of being 'born in the purple'. Breteuil stepped aside. Henry received the treasury and was thereafter elected king by those present. He then made haste for London and on 6 August 1100 was crowned king at Westminster Abbey. Shortly after, he married Matilda, the daughter of King Malcolm III of Scotland and his queen, Saint Margaret. Saint Margaret was the granddaughter of King Edmund Ironside, eldest daughter of Edward 'the Exile' and sister of Edgar Aetheling, and thus a descendant of the House of Wessex.

Rufus had managed to restore order in Normandy in Robert's absence, but his death once again saw chaos unleashed in the duchy. Robert returned in September but soon fell back into old habits. He squandered the money he had received as his wife's dowry on his usual luxuries, Rufus's death having negated the necessity of paying for Normandy's release. The chronicler Orderic Vitalis states that Robert lay in bed until twelve, without going to Mass, and that even the clothes off his back were robbed by the 'idle scamps and loose women' who surrounded him.[17]

Once again, a plot was soon afoot to place Robert on the throne of England. This time the expedition was more successful, and Robert landed at Portsmouth on 1 August 1101 where he was joined by the unscrupulous Robert de Bellême, Earl of Shrewsbury, and William de Warenne, Earl of Surrey, amongst others. Henry raised his own force and the two armies met near Alton, where the brothers came to terms. In the resultant Treaty of Alton, Robert gave up all pretensions to the throne and renounced Henry's homage to him. Henry, for his part, agreed to pay Robert a yearly pension of 3,000 silver marks and to surrender his Norman possessions, save the city of Domfront as he had promised its citizens he would never reliquinsh it. They also agreed, like Robert and Rufus before, that if either of them predeceased the other without a legitimate heir then the surviving brother would inherit the others' lands. Finally, the two brothers also pledged to punish the rebels who had turned them against one another. With peace settled, Robert returned to Normandy two months later laden with gifts.

On 25 October 1102, Sibyl gave birth to a son and heir, William Clito, at Rouen. 'Clito' was the Norman equivalent of an 'aetheling'. The birth of a son secured Robert's possession of Normandy and also offered the possibility that he could one day inherit England. Earlier that year, Queen Matilda had provided Henry with a daughter, named Matilda, but as female rule was unknown in England, the barons would probably opt to give Robert or William the throne in the event of Henry's death. The joyous birth was marred by tragedy as Sibyl died shortly afterwards, reputedly after being given bad advice by a midwife.

Henry, in the meantime, had been true to his word and he had meted out punishment to some of the rebels. In 1102, he summoned Robert de Bellême to court to stand trial for a list of offences but the fiery earl, realising that he could not clear himself of the charges, rebelled against him. Henry laid siege to Bellême's castle of Arundel and sent word to Duke Robert to attack his lands in Normandy as per the Treaty of Alton. Robert duly laid siege to the earl's castle at Vignats but fled when one of his traitorous nobles set fire to the camp. Henry, meanwhile, having taken Arundel, laid siege to Bridgnorth Castle in Shropshire. The garrison surrendered after a siege of three months and Henry then headed for Shrewsbury. As he approached the town he was met by a submissive Robert de Bellême, who handed over the keys to the town. Bellême was stripped of his English possessions and exiled from the country. He returned indignant to Normandy, where he unleashed his wrath upon those who had joined Robert in attacking Vignats. At some point, Robert met the earl in battle at Challoux but suffered a humiliating defeat and was forced to make peace.

William de Warenne, Earl of Surrey, had also been deprived of his earldom by Henry and he begged Robert to speak to the king and reconcile them. Robert agreed and sometime during 1103 he foolishly arrived in England unannounced. Henry was furious and had to be dissuaded from throwing Robert into prison. He had him conveyed into his presence and berated him for not adhering to his side of the Treaty of Alton, pointing out that he had failed to punish the rebels in Normandy, in particular Robert de Bellême. Robert promised that he would address Henry's grievances once he went home. The treaty was reconfirmed and Henry returned the earldom of Surrey to William de Warenne. Robert was allowed to leave for Normandy but not before Queen Matilda persuaded him to drop his yearly pension.

Characteristically, Robert failed to act on his promise and in 1104 Henry returned to Normandy. He summoned a conference with Robert where he accused the duke of breaking the Treaty of Alton and of failing to govern the duchy properly. Robert had little choice but to agree to hand over the county of Évreux to Henry. Satisfied by this, the king returned home. As soon as he left, the duchy returned to its usual state of anarchy.

The following year, when Robert FitzHaimon, one of Henry's adherents, was captured by the duke's supporters, the king once again visited Normandy. He was met at Carentan by Serlo, Bishop of Sèez, who pleaded with the king to take action and restore order in the duchy. Henry, taking counsel with those present, resolved to do as the bishop asked. He burned the town of Bayeux and also took Caen before returning to England in August.

Uncrowned

In the early months of 1106, Robert travelled to England to demand back the land that Henry had taken from him and met the king at Northampton for this purpose. Robert's pleas fell on deaf ears – Henry was by now determined to conquer Normandy. Robert returned to the duchy, knowing that battle was coming. In July, Henry crossed over to Normandy. Many of the nobles submitted to him, all except Robert de Bellême, William, Count of Mortain and a few others. In autumn that year, Henry laid siege to the Count of Mortain's castle of Tinchebray, near Domfront.

William, Count of Mortain requested Robert's aid and the duke duly arrived with an army. Robert demanded that Henry either lift his siege of the castle or face battle. Henry offered Robert a proposition: cede half of Normandy and control of its government to him and he would pay Robert the revenues of his half of the duchy from the English treasury and work hard to bring peace while Robert enjoyed a life of repose. Robert held a meeting with his counsellors and they dissuaded him from accepting the offer. If Henry were to rule the duchy, it would put an end to their enterprise. Robert declared that there would be no truce and that battle was to be met. On 28 September 1106, forty years to the day since William the Conqueror had landed in England in order to fight King Harold, the King of England fought against the Duke of Normandy on Norman soil.

Robert's army was divided into three 'battles'. The vanguard was commanded by Earl William, the main by Robert himself and the rearguard by Robert de Bellême. On Henry's side the vanguard was commanded by Ranulf of Bayeux, the main by Robert, Count of Meulan and the rear by William de Warrene. Stationed nearby but not in the main battle was Count Helias of Maine with an army of Manceaux and Bretons.

The resultant battle, known as the Battle of Tinchebray, was short and details of its proceedings are meagre. As the battle horns sounded, Duke Robert's men 'repulsed the royal line with awesome strength'.[18] Things quickly turned sour for the duke, however. Helias and his men, mounted on horseback, charged into the flank of the duke's army and slew 250 men. Robert de Bellême, taking stock of the situation, fled without striking a blow. The duke's army was routed and Robert was captured by Baudri, one of Henry's chaplains, and brought before the victorious king.

Robert was conciliatory in defeat, confessing that he had been led astray by evil counsel. He handed over to the king the castle of Falaise, which housed his young son, William Clito. Henry took pity on the frightened boy, who was almost four years old, and placed him in the care of Helias de St Saëns, the husband of Robert's illegitimate daughter.

Henry and Robert travelled to Rouen where Robert released the barons of their fealty to him, which was transferred to Henry. The disgraced duke was then sent to England where he would remain a prisoner for the last twenty-seven years of his life. He was kept in comfortable confinement, first at Wareham and then at the castle of Devizes, where he was in the custody of Roger, Bishop of Salisbury. Eventually he was placed with Henry I's illegitimate son Robert, Earl of Gloucester, who first held him at Bristol and then at Cardiff Castle. Robert died in February 1134, aged around eighty-four, and was buried at the church of St Peter at Gloucester, now Gloucester Cathedral. In the thirteenth century, a wooden effigy of Robert, which shows an idealised version of the Conqueror's eldest son, was produced to mark the location of his burial.[19]

The question remains – would Robert have made a successful king of England? His track record of rule in Normandy would suggest otherwise, and England may have seen the same kind of turbulence as the duchy if he had been king. Robert was undoubtedly a great warrior, but his laziness and love of pleasure made him ill suited to the demands of government. The chronicler William of Malmesbury, in summing up Robert's character, states that 'through the easiness of his disposition, was he ever esteemed unfit to have the management of the state'.[20]

2

William Aetheling

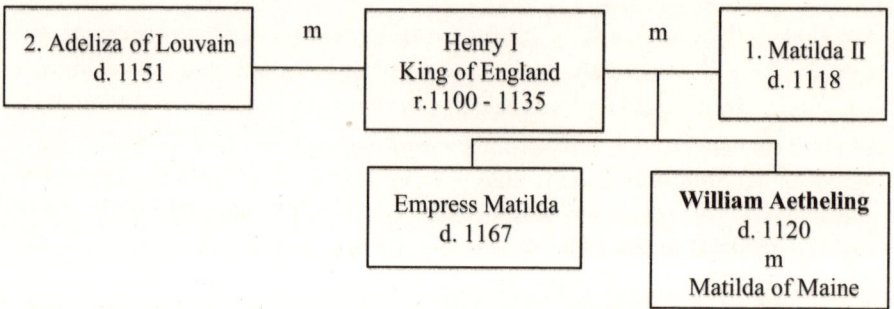

When Edward the Confessor lay dying in his bed at Westminster Palace in early January 1066, he is reported to have had a prophetic dream in which two monks he had known in his youth in Normandy warned him of the Norman conquest of England. Edward asked the monks when England's sorrows were to end, to which they mysteriously replied, 'When a green tree, if cut down in the middle of its trunk, and the part cut off carried the space of three furlongs from the stock, shall be joined again to its trunk, by itself and without the hand of man or any sort of stake, and begin once more to push leaves and bear fruit from the old love of its uniting sap, then first can a remission of these great ills be hoped for.'[1]

By the reign of Henry I the 'green tree prophecy' had come to be understood: the green tree symbolised the kings of the House of Wessex, who were cut in half when King Harold II took over the kingdom. The three acres represented the reigns of Harold, William I and William II, and the tree returned to its original trunk when the English royal line returned to the throne in the shape of King Henry I's marriage to Matilda II, a descendant of the House of Wessex. The fruit the marriage would bear, the children they would conceive, would unite the blood of England and Normandy and bring peace to England.[2]

William of Malmesbury notes that William Aetheling, the only son born to King Henry I and Queen Matilda, was regarded as the fulfilment of the prophecy. 'The hopes of England,' he reports, 'like the tree cut down, would, through this youth, again blossom and bring forth fruit, and thus put an end to her sufferings.'[3] Unfortunately, William would not be the saviour that England sought. His early death, aged just seventeen, would lead to a succession crisis and see the country plunged into fourteen years of civil war known as the Anarchy.

Birth and Early Life

King Henry I succeeded in his bid to seize the throne of England on the death of William Rufus, but the crown did not rest easily upon his head. He knew that it would only be a matter of time before his brother, Duke Robert II of Normandy, would pursue his own claim and that he would be supported by much of the nobility. He therefore took some measures to endear himself to the English population. He restored the laws of Edward the Confessor (although he retained some amendments made by his father), recalled to England Anselm, Archbishop of Canterbury, who had been exiled during the previous reign, and most importantly he married Matilda, the daughter of King Malcolm III of Scotland. This was a match calculated to gratify the English as Matilda was a descendant of the House of Wessex through her mother, Margaret, the eldest granddaughter of King Edmund Ironside and daughter of Edward the Exile. It is not certain if Henry was aware of the green tree prophecy, and there is some suggestion that the marriage was actually a love match, but the politic Henry knew that uniting with the old English royal line would help legitimise both his rule and, more importantly, that of his children.

The prospective marriage was met with controversy. Matilda had been brought up and educated by her aunt, Christina, in a convent of nuns at Romsey and she had often been seen wearing the black veil of a nun. Rumours were rife that she had been consecrated a nun and was therefore unable to marry. This was a cause of concern for Henry; if the marriage was considered to be unlawful then any children born from it would be illegitimate and unable to inherit the throne. Matilda protested to Archbishop Anselm that she had been forced to wear the veil by her aunt in order to ward off the lustful advances of the Normans. If she removed the veil in her aunt's presence, she confided, her aunt would scold her but as soon as her aunt left she would tear the veil from her head and trample upon it in anger. To prove her sincerity, Matilda agreed to bring the case before a church court. At the resultant assembly, held at Lambeth, witnesses were interrogated and the council came to the conclusion that Matilda had never been a nun and that she was free to marry. On Sunday 11 November 1100, Matilda and Henry were married by Archbishop Anselm and she was afterwards consecrated queen.

The first child born to the couple was a daughter named Matilda, in 1102. Henry was no doubt disappointed at the birth of a daughter. Female succession was not known at this time in England and it was a son that he badly craved to guarantee the future of his dynasty. Henry's fears deepened in October 1102 when Duke Robert's son, William Clito, was born. This invited the unsavoury prospect that if Henry were to die, Robert or his son would inherit England and Normandy, undoing all of Henry's hard work. Fortunately, his next child proved to be a son.

William Aetheling was born sometime between June and August 1103 and he was baptised by Gundulf, Bishop of Rochester, who also stood as the boy's godfather.[4] Henry's relief at the birth of a male heir is indicated in a letter he received from Pope Paschal II congratulating him on the birth of the 'male issue you so much desired, by your noble and religious consort'.[5]

William's position as heir was made apparent by the granting of the Anglo-Saxon title of Aetheling, which also marked him out as the rightful heir of the House of Wessex. Unfortunately, details of William's life are meagre. On leaving the nursery he and Matilda were placed under the care of Archbishop Anselm, under whose direction he was carefully educated for the station that fate had chosen for him.[6] At some stage, no later than 1109 when Anselm died, he was placed under the tutelage of Othere, the half-brother of Richard, Earl of Chester.

Henry adored his son and spent lavishly on him. We have a brief description of William in Henry of Huntingdon's *On Contempt for the World*, in which he is painted as arrogant, proud and spoilt. Henry tells us that he witnessed William at some unspecified date 'dressed in silken garments stitched with gold, surrounded by a crowd of household attendants and guards, and gleaming in an almost heavenly glory'.[7] The chronicler Wace relates that William was highly esteemed and much loved by the people, who had high hopes in him, and portrays him as an obedient and dutiful son who 'did what his father asked and avoided what his father forbade'.[8]

Henry and Matilda never had any more children. William of Malmesbury states that Matilda was satisfied at having produced a child of either sex and decided that she did not want any more. This seems unlikely. One of the main roles of a queen consort was to produce heirs, and with the high mortality rate of children in medieval times, the more the better. It may have been that she was unable to conceive and Henry, who is infamous for fathering many illegitimate children, was content with his mistresses. It is also possible that the king, mindful of his own conflicts with his brothers, did not want to risk his children fighting over their inheritance.

In 1110 William had to say goodbye to his eight-year-old sister Matilda when she was shipped off to Germany to marry Emperor Heinrich V. It would be the last time that he would ever see her; she would not return to England until 1126, by which time he was long dead.

As William grew older he began to be involved in the running of the kingdom to educate him in his future role as king. He attested his first charter in 1113, when he is recorded as witnessing the grant of a manor to the monastery of St Mary of Bec and St Neot of Eynulfisbury.[9] In 1115, aged twelve, he joined his mother as vice-regent of England while Henry was absent in Normandy, and he briefly became sole regent in 1118 following his mother's death.

Normandy

England remained at peace for most of Henry's reign but his seizure of Normandy brought him into conflict with the duchy's neighbours on the continent. Henry's greatest enemy was King Louis VI of France, better known as Louis *'le Gros'* or 'the fat', who succeeded King Philip I in 1108. Louis was eager to have his authority as King of France recognised in the wider French kingdom and he deemed Henry to be his vassal in his capacity as Duke of Normandy. He demanded that Henry perform homage but the proud and haughty king did not want to be seen to condescend to someone whom he considered his inferior. It was a dangerous policy for Henry to take as it would likely cause Louis to throw his support behind Duke Robert's son, William Clito, and attempt to deprive Henry of the duchy.

In 1111, King Louis formed a coalition against Henry alongside Fulk V, Count of Anjou, the crusading hero Robert II, Count of Flanders, and some turbulent Norman barons, including Robert de Bellême. The Angevins were old enemies of the Normans and Fulk, who had recently acquired the county of Maine through marriage, resented the fact that he had to pay homage to Henry for the pleasure and instead opted to wage war. Henry soon began to break up the coalition. In 1112 he summoned Robert de Bellême to his court and arrested him for acting illegally against his lord. Bellême was first held at Cherbourg but later sent to England, where he was incarcerated at Wareham Castle in Norfolk for the rest of his life. Robert, Count of Flanders was killed in a skirmish while in February 1113 Henry secured peace with Count Fulk. Henry and Fulk met at Pierre-Percee in Alençon where the count performed homage for the country of Maine. William Aetheling, as heir to England and Normandy, provided an effective bargaining tool and he was betrothed to Fulk's daughter Matilda of Maine, with Fulk granting him Maine as her dowry. For Henry, the match placated a hostile neighbour and invited the possibility of Maine once again falling into his hands, while for Fulk it could mean that one of his descendants may one day take the English throne and inherit Normandy, Maine and Anjou. As a result, King Louis found himself deprived of support and he was forced to sue for peace.

It was during this time that Henry made a costly mistake. He sent Robert de Beauchamp, Viscount of Arques, to Saint-Saëns to seize William Clito before he could become a focus for rebellion. Helias de Saint-Saëns, the boy's governor, was not present at the time but those in the castle quickly roused William from his slumber and managed to conceal him. On Helias's return, he took hold of his charge and headed across the border to find others willing to rally to the boy's cause. After wandering from place to place for several years, William Clito and Helias found refuge with Baldwin VII, Count of Flanders, the son and successor of the deceased Count Robert. William Clito and Baldwin were kinsmen through William's grandmother Queen Matilda of Flanders, and he promised to help the exile reclaim his inheritance. They requested the help of King Louis and the king was so moved by William's predicament that he granted him Normandy and swore to help him retrieve it from Henry.

As a consequence, Henry had the barons of Normandy pay homage and swear fealty to William Aetheling as heir to the duchy in a ceremony at Rouen in 1115. He had come up with a solution to the problem of the homage: he would grant William Normandy and have him perform it in his stead. He offered Louis money if he would receive William's homage and cease his support of William Clito. Louis considered the offer and accepted the money but he was dissuaded by William II, Count of Nevers who reminded him of the pledge he had formerly made to William Clito.

Later that year, Henry's nephew Theobald IV, Count of Blois, the second son of Henry's sister Adela and the disgraced crusader Stephen, Count of Blois, captured the Count of Nevers as he returned home from Louis's court. Louis demanded Nevers's release, and when Theobald refused he had him excommunicated by the church and waged war against him. Henry naturally supported his nephew and before embarking for Normandy he took the unprecedented step of having the magnates swear allegiance and perform homage to William as his successor at Salisbury in March 1116, thereby designating him as heir to England.

In 1118 a new coalition was formed between Louis, Fulk and Baldwin while rebellion also broke out in Normandy in support of William Clito. Henry was at first hard pressed by his enemies but soon things began to go in his favour. Baldwin was mortally wounded while laying siege to Eu and he later died of his injury. Baldwin had no children and he was succeeded by his cousin, Charles the Good, who made peace with Henry. In early 1119, Henry once again made peace overtures towards Fulk and he found the count receptive. He renewed the proposed marriage of William and Fulk's daughter Matilda and in May Henry summoned William to Normandy and the couple were married at Lisieux in June. The marriage, as the chronicler Orderic Vitalis notes, 'gave needful repose to hostile nations'.[10] With Fulk and Baldwin out of the equation, Henry turned his attention to Louis. On 20 August he met Louis in battle on the open plain of Brémule, situated between Les Andely, St Clair and the castle of Noyon. Henry placed his nobles in the vanguard while he himself took command of the main along with his household. He placed his illegitimate sons Robert (later Earl of Gloucester) and Richard, along with a host of foot soldiers, in the rearguard. None of the chronicles state that William took part in the battle but he is noted by Orderic Vitalis as being present in its aftermath so it is possible that he did so and was stationed in the rearguard with his half-brothers.

Louis, meanwhile, placed the vanguard under the command of William Clito while the king himself was situated in the main. The reckless Louis rushed into battle without any plan. The French rearguard launched an attack on Henry's van and managed to disperse them, but on meeting Henry's main host was itself sent running. The royal lines then clashed and William Crispin, who had fought with Duke Robert at Tinchebray, struck Henry twice across the head with his sword, forcing his hauberk slightly into his head and drawing blood. The king struck him back with such force that he knocked horse and rider to the ground and Crispin was immediately captured. Then the rearguard, possibly including William, rushed into battle from the other side, lances levelled, and the French were routed. King Louis escaped the battle but found himself lost in the woods of Andely. He happened upon a peasant who, unaware of his identity, led him safely to Les Andelys.

The following day, Henry returned Louis's horse and all his equipment and he likewise had William Aetheling return William Clito's horse as well, along, we are told, with 'other presents serviceable to an exile'.[11]

Pope Calixtus mediated peace and a conference between the two kings then took place. Louis recognised William Aetheling as heir to Normandy, but in order that he did not break the oath he had sworn to William Clito he had William pay homage to his eldest son and heir, Philip. Henry was jubilant. He had finally succeeded in having Louis recognise his right to the duchy without having to deign to pay homage himself. He had secured his son's possession of Normandy and had forced William Clito into exile. He had the barons of Normandy once again perform homage to William and then arranged to return to England, the land he had not seen for four years.

The *White Ship* Disaster

On 25 November 1120, preparations were being made at Barfleur to transport Henry, his sons, his household and members of the nobility across the Channel. The king was approached by a captain named Thomas who claimed that his father had commanded the ship that had brought William the Conqueror to England in September 1066. He offered his services to Henry, explaining that he had a vessel called the *Blanche-Nef*, or the *White Ship*, which was perfectly equipped to convey the royal party safely across the Channel. The *White Ship*, according to the chronicler William of Malmesbury, 'was of the best construction, and recently fitted with new materials'.[12] Henry accepted Thomas's services but said that he had already chosen a suitable ship for the journey. Instead, he would entrust Thomas with conveying his sons and members of the nobility across the Channel.

Many of the young nobles did not need to be told twice to board the ship. They 'eagerly hastened from all quarters', hoping to procure the future king's favour by demonstrating their devotion to him.[13] There were around 300 passengers on board, including fifty rowers and an armed marine force. Also on board were Henry's illegitimate children Richard and Matilda, Countess of Perche, as well as Richard, Earl of Chester and William's tutor, Othere.

The sailors asked William if they could be given something to drink and the young man gladly acceded. Soon, all on board were drunk. The young nobles mocked and drove away the priests who came on board to bless them amid laughter and jeering. '[T]hey were speedily punished for their mockery,' Orderic Vitalis notes.[14] It was night by the time the *White Ship* eventually set sail. King Henry and the rest of the fleet had already gone ahead and all would arrive safely in England the following morning. The intoxicated passengers on board the *White Ship* challenged Thomas to overtake the royal fleet and the captain accepted, confident in his crew and ship and with the hubris that alcohol brings, boasting 'that he would soon leave behind him all the ships that had started before them'.[15] The rowers took their stations and they departed. The ship, weighed down only by the passengers, wine and the king's treasure stowed on board, glided effortlessly through the water. Orderic tells us that the moon was full that night and visibility good, 'so that all objects on the surface of the sea were clearly visible to the sailors'.[16]

The drunken helmsman steered the ship off course and it struck a rock on its starboard bow side. The impact damaged two planks and the ship began to take on water. Some of the crew endeavoured to force the ship free from the rock by the use of boathooks, but their exertions failed.

As the ship sank, passengers and crew were washed away by the waves, while those below decks were drowned by the rising water. William was placed aboard a ship's boat and could have safely reached the shore but the night was pierced by the screams of his illegitimate sister, the Countess of Perche, who was still aboard the sinking vessel. William had the oarsmen turn the boat around and he gallantly went to rescue his sibling, but his kindness was to prove his undoing; the boat was swarmed by others desperate to preserve their lives and the weight and the commotion caused it to capsize.

William was consumed by the deep. Orderic tells us that as he went underwater, his tutor, Othere, took him into his arms and they sank together.[17] Captain Thomas, on hearing of William's disappearance, chose to drown rather than face Henry's wrath. Of the 300 passengers on board, only one survived. Berold, a butcher from Rouen, had managed to cling to the mast of the stricken vessel. He was rescued in the morning by fishermen who took him to land. He soon revived and would live for another twenty years.

King Henry, having safely reached England, was none the wiser as to his children's fate. He had heard the distant screams of the passengers but nobody knew what it had meant. Rumours of the disaster soon spread and reached the ears of Count Theobald and other members of Henry's court. Nobody wanted to be the one to tell the king the devastating news. Eventually, Theobald sent a young boy into Henry's presence who fell weeping at the king's feet. Henry asked him what was wrong and the boy divulged all. Henry 'instantly fell to the ground', then, being conducted to his private chambers, 'gave free course to the bitterness of his grief'.[18]

After word spread of the wreck, local people scouted the coast to look for any bodies in the hope of claiming a reward. Richard, Earl of Chester and several others were found washed up on the shore and were only identified by the clothes that they wore. William and Othere's bodies were never found, consumed by the deep.

William's death was both a personal and political disaster for King Henry. He had centered all his hopes for his dynasty on William and he had failed to sire the obligatory spare male heir as a contingency. His only other legitimate child was a daughter, but as female rule was unknown in England and Normandy it was likely that people would look to William Clito, the next male in the direct male line, as Henry's successor. With William's death went the hopes of the people. The green tree prophecy would not be fulfilled for another thirty-four years, when William's nephew, Henry II, ascended the throne in 1154.

3

Empress Matilda

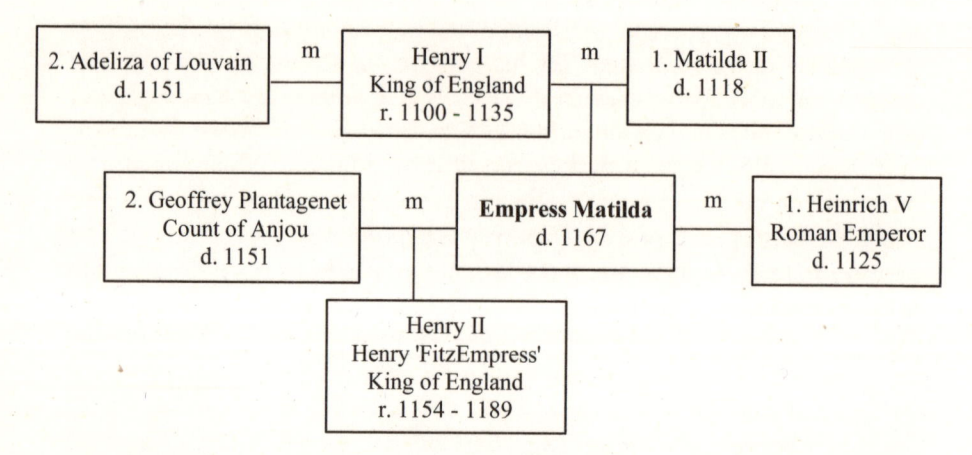

```
2. Adeliza of Louvain — m — Henry I — m — 1. Matilda II
d. 1151                    King of England      d. 1118
                           r. 1100 - 1135

2. Geoffrey Plantagenet — m — Empress Matilda — m — 1. Heinrich V
Count of Anjou                 d. 1167              Roman Emperor
d. 1151                                             d. 1125

                    Henry II
                    Henry 'FitzEmpress'
                    King of England
                    r. 1154 - 1189
```

On 30 September 1139, the Empress Matilda, the only legitimate daughter of King Henry I, sailed into the port of Arundel in West Sussex. She was accompanied by her loyal half-brother Robert, Earl of Gloucester and an army of 140 Angevin knights. Like her grandfather William the Conqueror before her, she had come to win a kingdom. The result would be fourteen years of civil war, known as the Anarchy, during which the Anglo-Saxon Chronicle lamented that 'Christ slept, and his saints'.[1]

Birth and Early Life

Matilda, better known as the Empress Matilda, the daughter of King Henry I and Queen Matilda II, was born at Sutton Courtenay on 7 February 1102.[2] After leaving the nursery, she and her younger brother William Aetheling spent the next few years under the care of Archbishop Anselm but destiny soon came calling as it did to all aristocratic girls. In 1109, King Henry I received ambassadors from Heinrich V, the Roman Emperor, who sought the seven-year-old's hand in marriage. Heinrich had been on the German throne since 1106 but he had not yet been crowned emperor by Pope Paschal II, with whom he was embroiled in a bitter argument over the thorny subject of church investitures – essentially who had the right, king or church, to fill vacant church offices. Heinrich had determined on raising an army to march to Rome and force the pope to crown him but he needed money to do so and he knew that King Henry was rich. Henry was delighted at the match and he agreed to a substantial dowry of 10,000 silver marks (the same that William Rufus had paid Duke Robert for Normandy), which he raised by levying a tax of 3 shillings per hide of land in England.[3]

In February 1110 the eight-year-old Matilda said a tearful goodbye to her family and was conducted across the sea to begin her new life. She was betrothed to her husband, seventeen years her senior, at Utrecht on 29 March. On 25 July, she was crowned Queen of the Romans at Mainz. The ceremony was officiated by Frederick, Archbishop of Cologne, and Bruno, Archbishop of Trier, the latter reverently holding the girl in his arms while she was consecrated. Archbishop Bruno was afterwards appointed her tutor and tasked with teaching Matilda the German language and how to behave 'according to the habits of the German people' until she was considered of age to marry.[4] In the meantime, Heinrich launched an expedition to Rome and he succeeded in capturing Pope Paschal and forced him to crown him as emperor. In 1112, Pope Paschal responded by excommunicating Heinrich, but an emperor, once anointed by God, could not be divested of office.

Matilda married Heinrich at Worms in January 1114 when she was just shy of twelve. Her education was now considered complete and she joined her husband's side and took up her official duties. These included acting as a mediator between the emperor and his subjects, and running the kingdom in his absence. Matilda was too young to produce an heir in 1114 – but she would fail to produce any children during the time of their marriage.

In 1118 the sixteen-year-old Matilda was entrusted with the regency of Italy while Heinrich went to quell a rebellion in Germany. She was present at the Concordat of Worms, in September 1122, when the difficulties between pope and emperor were finally reconciled. Then, all of a sudden, Matilda's fate was changed forever when Emperor Heinrich died of cancer on 23 May 1125, aged just forty. She soon received a summons from her father, Henry I, to return to court. A new chapter was about to begin.

Heiress Presumptive

The premature death of William Aetheling in 1120 caused a succession crisis in England. Henry had failed to produce a spare male heir and it looked as if William Clito, the only other legitimate grandson of the Conqueror in the direct male line, would succeed his uncle. Henry had fathered many illegitimate children but illegitimacy was by now considered a bar to the succession.

The nearest legitimate male heirs of the Conqueror after William Clito were the four sons of Henry's sister Adela, Countess of Blois, who had married the disgraced crusader Stephen, Count of Blois. Their eldest son, William, was considered indolent and he was passed over in the succession of the county of Blois in favour of the next son, Theobald. The third son,

Stephen, was sent to be educated in England and became a firm favourite of King Henry, who made him Count of Mortain and married him to Matilda, the heiress of Boulogne. Henry, the youngest of the four, was inducted into the church. It is possible that King Henry considered his favourite nephew, Stephen, as a potential successor but he would prefer to leave the throne to a son of his own and his kneejerk reaction was to remarry. Queen Matilda had died in 1118 and Henry decided to marry Adeliza, the young daughter of Godfrey, Duke of Brabant and Louvain in the hope of procuring an heir. Unfortunately, Henry was now in his fifties and the once virile king would fail to produce the desired heir.

It was thus welcome news when Henry received word of Emperor Heinrich's death in 1125, and he summoned his widowed daughter to his side. It was with a heavy heart that Matilda left her adopted home. She had spent most of her life there, was German in her habits and had received vast estates as part of her marriage portion. She was also popular; several princes of Lorraine and Lombardy travelled with her to England to ask Henry for her hand in marriage, but Henry had a different fate in store for his daughter. At his Christmas court at Windsor in 1126 he took the extraordinary step of having the barons and prelates swear an oath that if he were to die without a male heir then they would unconditionally accept Matilda as their sovereign. Female rule was unknown in England at the time, but Henry was recognising it as a valid alternative if there were to be a failure in the direct male line.[5]

Matilda's uncle, King David I of Scotland, was the first layman to take the oath, after which her cousin Stephen of Blois and her eldest illegitimate brother Robert, Earl of Gloucester jostled with one another to have the honour of being the next. In one of those delicious ironies of history, it was Stephen who won. The barons and prelates named just one condition for accepting Matilda – that Henry would not marry her to anyone out of the country without their consent. This was of particular concern as under the rules of common law any husband of Matilda's would inherit her title and possessions and rule as king.[6] If Matilda married a foreign prince the country could possibly become a mere possession of a foreign power.

Events, however, conspired to force Henry's hand. On 2 March 1127, Charles, Count of Flanders was murdered while attending Mass at the church of St Donatian in Bruges. Charles left no children and King Louis VI secured the countship for William Clito as a descendant of the counts of Flanders through his grandmother, Matilda of Flanders. This threat drove Henry once again to seek the friendship of Fulk of Anjou and, in direct contravention to the promise he made to the nobles, he offered Matilda's hand in marriage to Fulk's eldest son and heir, the fifteen-year-old Geoffrey of Anjou. Matilda was not pleased by her father's choice of husband. After having been married to an emperor she deemed a lowly count beneath her station. She protested at first but had little choice but to accept her father's wishes and on 17 June 1128 she and Geoffrey were married at Le Mans. Soon after, Fulk of Anjou left to become King of Jerusalem and Geoffrey stepped into his shoes as Count of Anjou and Matilda as countess. Matilda, however, continued to refer to herself by the superior title of empress.

The following month Henry received some good news. William Clito had been killed while laying siege to the castle of Aalst in Flanders. Henry could finally breathe a sigh of relief. With the greatest threat to the succession extinguished, his enemies bowed to the inevitable and made peace. Now his barons had little choice but to accept his daughter as queen – or so he thought. On 13 July 1129, Henry returned triumphantly to England but once again the rug was pulled from under his feet. He was informed that Geoffrey had repudiated Matilda and that she had returned to Rouen accompanied by a few attendants. The haughty empress had treated her young husband with contempt and he had responded by banishing her. Matilda remained in Rouen for a year until Henry brought her back to England in 1131.

Soon after, messengers arrived from Count Geoffrey requesting that Matilda be reconciled to him. Matilda returned and this time things proved more amicable between them. Their reconciliation was given form in March 1133 when Matilda gave birth to a son and heir, Henry FitzEmpress, the future King Henry II, at Le Mans. The delighted King Henry had the barons retake the oath to Matilda and swear that if she were to die they would recognise baby Henry as his successor in her place.

That year, Henry travelled to Normandy for the final time. Matilda joined him at Rouen where she gave birth to her second son, Geoffrey, in May 1134. The birth was troubled and Matilda nearly died. The pious lady dished out her vast treasure to religious houses and the poor in expectation of death, not even sparing the silken couch upon which she lay. She gave most liberally to the monastery of Bec, where, she informed her father, she wished to be buried. Henry refused her request, stating that she was to be buried in Notre-Dame Cathedral at Rouen alongside her Viking ancestors Duke Rollo and William Longsword. Matilda was adamant. Her spirit could know no joy, she said, if her request was denied. Henry was won over and he granted her wish, but Matilda fortuitously recovered.

Henry's last year was darkened by a dispute between himself and Geoffrey, reportedly at Matilda's connivance. Geoffrey demanded to be given control of some castles in Normandy that the king had promised as her dowry, but the stubborn king refused. In retaliation, Geoffrey besieged and burnt the town of Beaumont. The exasperated Matilda left her father and returned to Anjou, never to see him again. Later that year, Henry made a hunting trip in the forest of Lyons where he fell gravely ill after eating too many lampreys. As he lay dying, Henry was surrounded by much of the nobility, including Earl Robert of Gloucester, and he once again confirmed the succession on Matilda before dying on 1 December 1135, aged sixty-seven.

King Stephen

Matilda and Geoffrey were still in Anjou at the time of Henry's death. Matilda was once again pregnant, and instead of travelling to England the couple focused their efforts on Normandy and took possession of the southern border castles of Argentan, Exmes, Domfront, Ambrières, Gorron and Colmemont.

Then, in a shocking twist, Matilda's cousin Stephen of Blois, Count of Mortain, crossed from Boulogne to England in a bid to seize the crown. He was elected king by the citizens of London, who claimed the right to elect the next king on the death of the old one. It was imperative that they elected a new king as soon as possible, they asserted, as when the old king died his authority died with him and the kingdom fell prey to all kinds of lawlessness. This period of potential strife between the death of the old king and the anointing of the next one was known as the 'interregnum'. After being elected, Stephen headed to Winchester where he secured the royal treasury as well as the crucial support of his younger brother, Henry of Blois, Bishop of Winchester. William of Corbeil, Archbishop of Canterbury refused to crown Stephen, reminding him that they had all sworn the oath to accept Matilda as sovereign. Stephen's partisans countered that Henry had forced them to take the oath against their will and that he had broken his promise by marrying Matilda to the hated Count of Anjou without their consent. Hugh Bigod even claimed that Henry had disinherited Matilda on his deathbed in favour of Stephen. The archbishop was swayed by their arguments and crowned Stephen on 22 December.

Matilda and Geoffrey were taken by surprise by Stephen's usurpation. They continued to focus their efforts on Normandy and in late September 1136 Geoffrey penetrated the duchy as far as Le Sap, but he was injured by a dart in the foot from a crossbow while laying siege to the castle. Matilda, having only just recovered from giving birth to her third son, William, two months before, arrived with reinforcements, but Geoffrey was forced to call off the siege and he, Matilda and the Angevins fled back home. In March the following year Stephen arrived in Normandy and in May he was recognised as duke by King Louis VI for which his eldest son, Eustace, paid homage. That same month Geoffrey returned to Normandy with 400 men-at-arms but he was dealt with by Stephen who, in return for two years of peace, agreed to pay him an annual pension of 2,000 silver marks.

Matilda's cause in England was also looking desperate, but in 1138 her half-brother Robert, Earl of Gloucester came out in support of her. Robert had initially paid homage to Stephen, but, cognizant of the oath he had made to Matilda, he had secretly awaited an opportunity to espouse her cause. Unsurprisingly, Stephen eyed Robert with suspicion and during his visit to Normandy in 1137 had attempted to have the earl captured and thrown in prison. Fortunately for him, Robert was forewarned of the king's machinations and absented himself from court. Stephen was forced to admit his fault and swore an oath to never make such an attempt again. Robert remained in Normandy when Stephen returned to England and the following year (1138) he sent messengers to him, renouncing his homage and fealty via a *diffidatio*. As a result, Robert's partisans in western England, where his estates lay, rose in rebellion while King David of Scotland raided into Northumberland, ostensibly in the empress's name. Stephen managed to quell the west while an army under the command of Thurstan, Archbishop of York defeated King David at the Battle of the Standard on 22 August.

Matilda began to make an open bid for the throne in April 1139. During the second Lateran Council, held at Rome, Bishop Ulger of Angers argued her case in the presence of Pope Innocent II. She was the legitimate heir to England and Normandy, he reasoned, both by hereditary right and also by the oath the barons and prelates had sworn. Stephen's partisans, led by Arnulf, Archdeacon of Séez, responded by reviving the old story that Matilda was illegitimate because Queen Matilda II had been consecrated a nun before she married King Henry. Pope Innocent put an end to the argument and recognised Stephen as king. Matilda had little choice but to pursue her inheritance at the point of a sword.

The Anarchy

On 30 September 1139, Matilda arrived at the port of Arundel accompanied by Earl Robert and 140 Angevin knights. She was welcomed into Arundel Castle by her mother-in-law, Queen Dowager Adeliza of Louvain, the second wife of King Henry, who had since married the Earl of Arundel. Earl Robert, meanwhile, headed for Bristol to rally their partisans. Robert had not been gone long when King Stephen suddenly appeared before Arundel at the head of a large army. Stephen's brother Henry, Bishop of Winchester, advised Stephen to grant Matilda a safe conduct from the castle and allow her to reunite with her brother. Then, he reasoned, Stephen could take them both in one fell swoop. Stephen agreed and Matilda was allowed to walk free. She was conducted by Bishop Henry and Waleran, Count of Meulan, to an agreed boundary where she was reunited with Earl Robert and conveyed to Bristol Castle. She spent the next two months at the castle, where many came to pay homage. She began to act as queen, 'exercising the prerogatives of the crown of England at her pleasure'.[7] From there she was taken to Gloucester Castle by Miles, Sheriff of Gloucester, one of King Henry I's loyal 'new men' who owed their advancement to her father. Miles became one of her chief advisers and, according to the author of the *Gesta Stephani*, 'always behaved to her like a father in deed and counsel'.[8]

Matilda's arrival was the catalyst for civil war. The country was divided into those who supported her, those who supported Stephen and those who looked for the greatest advantage to themselves. Matilda's sphere of influence was centred on the West Country and the lands of Earl Robert. Castles were besieged and taken on either side but no decisive blow was delivered. On 2 February 1141, Matilda's fortunes changed when Stephen was taken captive at the First Battle of Lincoln. Stephen was brought before Matilda at Gloucester and then confined in Bristol Castle. Many of the king's supporters turned their allegiance to Matilda, while those who continued to support the king were taken prisoner or driven into exile. All but the men of Kent – where Stephen's queen, Matilda of Boulogne, was present – were reported to have supported her. The path to the throne was open. But Matilda would prove the source of her own undoing.

Lady of the English

Matilda was advised to seek the friendship of Henry, Bishop of Winchester, who, as acting papal legate, held great influence in the country. Bishop Henry may have naturally been expected to support his brother Stephen, but he had grown disillusioned with Stephen's treatment of the church, particularly the arrest and forfeiture of Roger, Bishop of Salisbury, and his nephew Alexander, Bishop of Lincoln, in 1139. On 2 March Matilda and Bishop Henry met on a plain on the outskirts of Winchester, where Matilda swore that if Bishop Henry and the church would accept her as queen and remain faithful to her she would make Henry her chief advisor and all would be done at his nod in both church and state. Henry agreed to the terms on the condition that Matilda did not break her promise.

The following day Matilda was led into Winchester in a grand procession, accompanied by many of the great prelates. She was given the crown of England and the small amount of her father's treasure that remained in the treasury. With the throne in her grip, Matilda spent the Easter festivities at Oxford.

After Easter, Bishop Henry convened a church council at Winchester to discuss the problems of the kingdom and how best to restore peace. He recommended that they elect Matilda as queen, it being the church's prerogative 'to elect the sovereign, and also to crown him'.[9] This being agreed, the Londoners were invited to attend the council and have their say. They duly arrived the following day, but instead of supporting Matilda they demanded Stephen's release. Henry did his best to shoot them down but a clerk named Christian rose to his feet and read aloud a letter from Queen Matilda of Boulogne imploring them to restore her husband to the kingdom. The dispirited Londoners left, saying that they would relay the council's decision to their fellow townsmen and support it 'as far as they were able'.[10] Two months later, the Londoners had been placated and Matilda, escorted by King David of Scotland, entered the city in triumph to take up residence at Westminster Palace.

Empress Matilda

Unfortunately, Matilda's sudden victory brought out the worst parts of her personality. According to the *Gesta Stephani* she became haughty, arrogant, stern and proud. Instead of reconciling herself to her enemies she drove them away with threats and taunts while she seized the lands of others and bestowed them on her own followers. Even her greatest supporters, King David, Earl Robert and Bishop Henry, were not spared her scorn. When they came to ask her a favour, on bended knee, she would not deign to rise to meet them as was custom and would often not entertain their entreaties, dismissing them with an arrogant reply. She would not even listen to their counsel as a monarch was expected to but made her own decisions. It must be remembered that the author of the *Gesta* is pro-King Stephen and likely exaggerates her faults, but it is clear from other chronicles that Matilda rode in guns blazing. William of Newburgh states that her successes made her 'elevated in mind and haughty in speech'.[11] Perhaps as a woman in a man's world, Matilda thought that she needed to show an iron will to earn the respect of the nobility. If so, it was a policy that backfired.

Matilda made a fatal error in alienating the Londoners. When she summoned the wealthiest townsmen to her presence and demanded that they pay her a tax, the Londoners protested that they had little money left following the recent upheavals and asked, quite reasonably, if they could pay the tax at a later date once peace had been restored and their wealth increased. Matilda flew into a fury, 'losing every semblance of feminine gentleness'.[12] She would not accede to the Londoners' wishes as they had supported Stephen and provided him with money in his cause against her. The Londoners returned home to deliberate among themselves, promising to give her an answer.

Queen Matilda of Boulogne, meanwhile, sent messengers to Matilda, begging her to bestow the counties of Boulogne and Mortain on her and Stephen's eldest son, Eustace. Matilda refused outright and the queen responded by rallying her supporters in Kent and began to harry the outskirts of London. The Londoners, fearing the tyrannical will of the empress, decided to throw their lot in with the ex-queen. Bells rang out in the city and the Londoners flew to arms and headed for Westminster Palace. Matilda was about to sit down to a banquet when she was warned of the developments in the city and she and her supporters quickly mounted horses and fled in terror, leaving their possessions behind to be ransacked minutes later by the angry mob. Matilda, Earl Robert, King David and Bishop Henry managed to reach the safety of Oxford.

A few days later, Matilda made her second disastrous error – she lost the support of Bishop Henry. The bishop had also requested that Eustace be granted Boulogne and Mortain but he, too, was rebuffed. He repaired in indignation to Winchester and refused to attend Matilda's court when summoned. Consequently, he met Queen Matilda of Boulogne at Guildford where she solicited him to aid her in securing Stephen's release. The bishop, 'being wrought upon by her tears and concessions', agreed and he began to air complaints against the empress, stating that she wished to seize him and that she had not observed the terms they had agreed at Winchester.[13]

Matilda resolved on putting Bishop Henry in chains. Amassing an army, she made haste to Winchester and succeeded in gaining entrance to the castle, whereupon she summoned the bishop to meet her at once. Bishop Henry fled to his fortified residence of Wolvesey Castle and called upon those he knew to be loyal to the king to come to his aid. Queen Matilda answered the summons – along with, we are told, the majority of the earls, showing just how unpopular Matilda's rule had become.

Matilda still had several supporters whom she summoned, including the dependable Miles of Gloucester, now Earl of Hereford; her half-brother Reinald, Earl of Cornwall; Baldwin de Redvers; William de Mohun, Earl of Dorset; and Roger, Earl of Warwick. The empress laid siege to Wolvesey Castle but the tables were turned when Queen Matilda arrived outside of the city walls and laid siege to the empress's army within.

Earl Robert soon perceived that victory would go to the enemy and he decided it was best to make a hasty retreat. He placed the empress in the vanguard of the army so that she would be amongst the first to leave the city and stand a better chance of escape. Robert himself tarried at the rear of the army so 'that the retreat might not resemble a flight'.[14] Bursting through the gates of the city, the army moved as one body. The queen's army attacked them from all sides, breaking up the formation and sending it into confusion.

Matilda and a few of her supporters made it safely to the castle of Luggershall but, fearing capture, she once again took to horse, in 'male fashion' (it was deemed improper for a woman to ride with her legs astride a horse) and reached Devizes.[15] The effects of the siege and subsequent flight took their toll on her and she 'was placed, already nearly half-dead, upon a hearse, and being bound with cords like a corpse, and borne upon horses, was carried, ignominiously enough, to the city of Gloucester'.[16]

The rout at Winchester proved disastrous and signified the end of Matilda's chances of becoming queen. Earl Robert had been captured fleeing Winchester and Matilda had little option but to exchange him for King Stephen. With Stephen's release the war was renewed.

Escape From Oxford

With Robert once again at her side, Matilda held a conference at Devizes in 1142 with her adherents where it was agreed that their next move should be to enlist the help of her husband, Geoffrey, Count of Anjou. Geoffrey had remained on the continent during Matilda's absence and had continued to make inroads on Normandy. He had fared much better than his wife, capturing a large number of castles.

Earl Robert was dispatched to speak to Geoffrey, but the count had little interest in England. He strung Robert along with empty promises but eventually agreed to send the nine-year-old Henry FitzEmpress to England in the hopes that his presence would rejuvenate Matilda's cause.

Matilda, meanwhile, removed to Oxford. Then, on 26 September, Stephen suddenly appeared and laid siege to the castle. He surrounded the perimeter with guards to watch the entrances by day and night to ensure that no one escaped.

Matilda summoned her partisans to her side but they failed to appear. Later, when they learned of her plight, they assembled at Wallingford in the hopes that they might meet the king in a pitched battle, but they were unwilling to risk attacking him at the heavily fortified fortress of Oxford. Earl Robert, hearing of Matilda's predicament, immediately returned to England, landing at Wareham in company with the young Henry FitzEmpress and fewer than 400 horsemen, and laid siege to Wareham Castle in an unsuccessful bid to draw Stephen away from the city.

The siege of Oxford lasted some three months before Matilda and the besieged began to run out of supplies. Driven to desperate measures, she formed a daring plan of escape. It was now winter and the countryside was painted white with snow. One night, Matilda, clad entirely in white so that she blended in with the snow and attended by four guards similarly attired, stole out of the castle through a postern gate. She passed unnoticed by the guards that Stephen had stationed around the castle and crossed the frozen Thames. On reaching Abingdon, she took to horse and galloped to the safety of Wallingford. The following morning, on discovering that Matilda had escaped, Stephen accepted the surrender of the castle. For the third time in her eventful life, Matilda had made a miraculous escape when all appeared lost.

Greatest in Motherhood

Following her escape from Oxford, Matilda features sporadically in the chronicles. The war continued but thoughts now turned to her eldest son, Henry FitzEmpress. The death in 1147 of Earl Robert, the lifeblood of her schemes, caused her to accept the inevitable and the following year she retired to Normandy. Geoffrey of Anjou had by now conquered the duchy where Matilda would remain until her death. Geoffrey died in 1151 and Matilda never married again. In 1153 Henry FitzEmpress was able to have himself recognized as Stephen's heir in the Treaty of Wallingford, bringing the war to a close. Stephen died the following year and Matilda witnessed her son ascend the throne as King Henry II.

Matilda would wield authority in Normandy and acted as regent during her son's absences. She was involved as a mediator in Henry's argument with

Thomas Becket, Archbishop of Canterbury and she even tried to prevent her son from appointing Chancellor Becket to the archbishopric in the first place, perhaps seeing the inherent dangers, but she was overruled. She spent much of her time as a religious benefactor, founding monasteries, including that of Valece, which she had sworn to build if she escaped the siege of Oxford.

In 1161 she was hit by another illness and once again directed her treasure to the poor and to monasteries but, as in 1134, she recovered. She died on 10 September 1167, aged sixty-five, daughter, mother and grandmother to kings of England but never queen herself. She was buried before the high altar at abbey church of Bec, the location she had decreed all the way back in 1134, against Henry I's wishes. The ravages of time would see her remains disturbed: a fire engulfed the abbey in 1282, destroying Matilda's tomb, but fortunately her remains, wrapped in ox hide, survived. They were reburied in a new tomb when the abbey was restored, but this was desecrated by English soldiers in 1421. The abbey church was pulled down in 1841 and Matilda's remains were discovered five years later. In a twist of irony, she was reinterred with her ancestors at Rouen Cathedral as her father had originally commanded.[17] The epitaph on Matilda's original tomb read: 'Here lies Henry's daughter, wife, and mother; great by birth – greater by marriage – but greatest by motherhood.' This is an unfair verdict on a woman who defied the conventions of her time.[18]

England was not yet ready for the rule of a woman and the country would not have its first queen regnant until the sixteenth century.

4

Eustace, Count of Boulogne

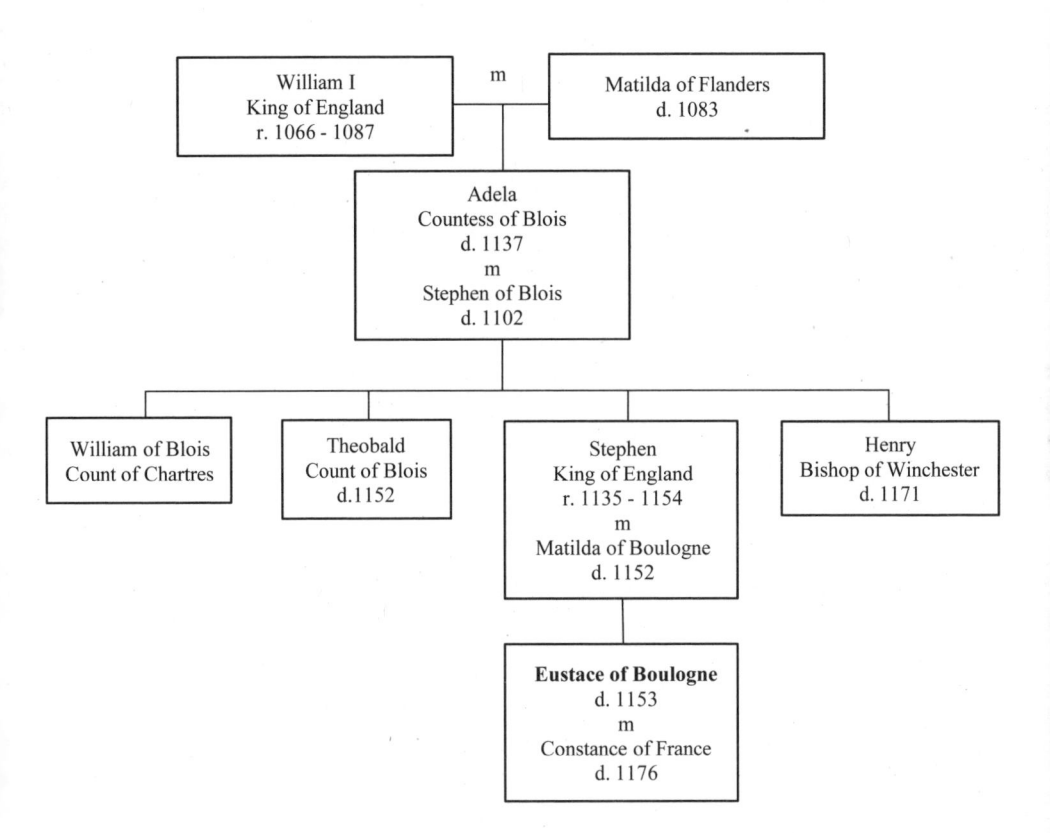

```
                William I                  m      Matilda of Flanders
              King of England                          d. 1083
              r. 1066 - 1087

                         Adela
                    Countess of Blois
                        d. 1137
                          m
                    Stephen of Blois
                        d. 1102

William of Blois   Theobald      Stephen         Henry
Count of Chartres  Count of Blois King of England Bishop of Winchester
                   d.1152        r. 1135 - 1154  d. 1171
                                    m
                                 Matilda of Boulogne
                                    d. 1152

                              Eustace of Boulogne
                                   d. 1153
                                     m
                              Constance of France
                                   d. 1176
```

In April 1152, King Stephen summoned Theobald, Archbishop of Canterbury and the other bishops to London where he made the unprecedented demand that they crown his eldest son, Eustace, as joint king of England. The crowning of a son during his father's lifetime was a French custom that had never been performed in post-Conquest England and was employed as a means of ensuring the undisputed succession of the next heir. Stephen's usurpation of the throne had highlighted the precariousness of an oath, but if Eustace was already a crowned and anointed monarch when Stephen died the barons would have little choice but to accept him as king. Archbishop Theobald bravely informed Stephen that he had been forbidden from crowning Eustace by Pope Eugenius III as Stephen had 'seized the kingdom contrary to the oath'.[1] A wrathful Stephen had Archbishop Theobald and the other bishops cast into prison in order to browbeat them into submission, but Theobald managed to escape to the continent. Once the king's temper had abated he released the other bishops. The only way Eustace was going to come to the throne was by defeating his rival, Henry FitzEmpress, in battle.

Birth and Early Life

Eustace, Count of Boulogne was the eldest surviving son and heir of King Stephen and Queen Matilda of Boulogne. He was born around 1129/30 and he was named in honour of his maternal grandfather, Eustace III of Boulogne.[2]

Like Robert, Duke of Normandy, Eustace was not destined from birth to one day wear the English crown. His father, King Stephen's highest title was that of count and few could have foreseen that he would one day wear the diadem of England. He was not the eldest son of Adela, Countess of Blois, a daughter of William the Conqueror and her husband Stephen, Count of Blois, but the third. He did, however, have the good fortune to be sent by his mother to the court of his uncle King Henry I, where his affability and easygoing nature had won him many friends. He fast became a favourite of the king, who heaped lands and titles on him, including the Honours of Eye and Lancaster in England and the county of Mortain in Normandy.

In 1125 Henry arranged the advantageous marriage between Stephen and Matilda of Boulogne, the heiress of Count Eustace III of Boulogne and his countess, Mary of Scotland. Mary was the younger sister of Henry's queen, Matilda, and a daughter of King Malcolm III of Scotland and Queen Margaret, meaning that Eustace also had the blood of both William the Conqueror and the Wessex kings coursing through his veins and could be seen as fulfilling the green tree prophecy in his own right. Shortly after the wedding, Eustace III retired to a monastery and Matilda came into her inheritance. The county of Boulogne came with a parcel of lands in England known as the Honour of Boulogne, centred on London, and made Stephen the greatest landowner in the country. Eustace, as eldest son, could look forward to one day inheriting his father and mother's vast lands and estates. Then, in 1135, his fortunes changed when Stephen unexpectedly became King of England and Duke of Normandy.

Heir to the Throne

Eustace now went from being the relatively unimportant son of a count to heir apparent to both England and Normandy. His first recorded public act was to perform homage to Louis VI for Normandy in May 1137, when King Stephen paid his only visit to the duchy that year. Then, in 1139, Eustace's inheritance was put in jeopardy when Empress Matilda landed in England to claim the throne. Eustace was too young to play a part in the war that would decide his future but as heir apparent he was still a valuable asset to be exploited.

Eustace, Count of Boulogne

Stephen was too preoccupied with events in England to deal personally with Normandy. He hoped to use Eustace as a bargaining tool to gain the assistance of Louis VII, the new King of France, against Geoffrey of Anjou. In February 1140, Eustace travelled to France with Queen Matilda and a number of English magnates to marry the French king's sister, Constance. It was hoped that the resultant alliance would cause Louis to assist Stephen with the war in Normandy but in reality it was Stephen's money that interested Louis. Stephen had procured the marriage by means of the treasure that he had seized from the wealthy Bishop Roger of Salisbury when he had arrested him at the Oxford Council the previous year.

On their return to England, the new bride was to witness the chaos of England first hand. She was residing with Queen Matilda at the Tower of London, then under the command of the traitorous Geoffrey de Mandeville, Earl of Essex. When Queen Matilda went to depart with her daughter-in-law the unscrupulous Geoffrey seized hold of Constance and refused to let her go. She remained in the Tower until Stephen succeeded in having her released sometime later. There is little record of Constance and Eustace's relationship but that which we have does not paint it in a positive light. The Anglo-Saxon Chronicle states that Constance was a '[g]ood woman ... but she had little bliss with him [Eustace]'.[3] They would have no children and after Eustace's death she retired to the continent and married Raymond V, Count of Toulouse.

Then, in 1141, Eustace's entire future looked uncertain when King Stephen was captured at the First Battle of Lincoln and Empress Matilda was set to be queen. Queen Matilda, after failing to secure her husband's release, determined on securing the countships of Boulogne and Mortain for Eustace and she sent envoys to the empress to make the request. As we have seen, the haughty empress refused. The chronicler William of Malmesbury suggests that she may have already promised them to others.[4] Queen Matilda fought back; the empress was forced from London and she was eventually defeated at Winchester. Eustace played a role in the complex exchange of prisoners that followed the capture of Robert, Earl of Gloucester, which underlined the mutual distrust that existed between both parties. When Stephen was released from Bristol Castle, Eustace and Queen Matilda remained behind as sureties for Earl Robert's release. Stephen hastened to Winchester and Earl Robert was liberated, leaving behind his son, William, in his stead. Robert travelled on to Bristol and Eustace and the queen were released. Finally, when Eustace and Queen Matilda reached Winchester, William was set free and the war returned to a state of stalemate with neither side making any headway to bring the war to a definitive close. Stephen was nearly captured again at the disastrous Battle of Wilton (1143) but in 1145 he achieved a great victory when he captured the newly erected castle of Faringdon in Berkshire, an event that is said to have turned the tide of the war. His enemies were demoralised and some of them, including Ranulf II, Earl of Chester and Philip, a son of Robert, Earl of Gloucester, sued for peace.

From 1147, the seventeen- or eighteen-year-old Eustace began to take an active part in the war. That year he was knighted by his father 'with great state' in the presence of their supporters.[5] No description of the ceremony exists, although it likely followed a similar precedent to that of Geoffrey of Anjou when he was knighted by Henry I, of which we do have a description. Eustace would have first had a bath 'as custom demands of a young man about to become a knight'.[6] Afterwards, he would have been wrapped in linen and dressed in a sumptuous ceremonial robe with silken shoes. Eustace would have exited a secret chamber into the general assembly where he would have been fitted with a cuirass (armour that covers the torso) and had gold spurs placed upon his feet and a shield hung from his neck. A helmet, 'resplendent with many precious stones', was then placed upon his head.[7] A spear was brought over to him and finally a sword from the royal treasury. Now decked in the attire of a knight, he would have climbed onto a horse for all to admire. Thus knighted, Eustace would have been granted lands in England and provided with a household, although it is not certain that he was created Count of Boulogne at this time, as is often believed.[8]

According to the *Gesta Stephani*, Eustace had developed into a courtly young man, noted as sharing his father's gentleness, affability and liberality, although he could be stern when the situation required it. He was a skilled warrior who 'gained the highest honours of fame and glory at the very outset of his career as a knight'.[9] The Anglo-Saxon Chronicle paints a more damning picture, however. To its writers he was 'an evil man ... [who] did more evil than good; he robbed the lands, and levied heavy guilds upon them'.[10] Henry of Huntingdon acknowledges Eustace's martial prowess but says that he was a persecutor of the church.[11]

Eustace's first recorded action in the war is against Ranulf, Earl of Chester. Ranulf, who had reportedly conquered a third of England, had made peace with the king following the fall of Faringdon, but in August 1146 he had been arrested on Stephen's orders for refusing to hand over the royal castles he had seized during the war. Ranulf handed over the castles and was released, but he soon revolted against the king. He began to harry Stephen's men, taking their castles and building others, and the king spent the next year in war against him. Eustace was placed at the head of a body of troops and sent against Ranulf. Unfortunately there is little record of Eustace's actions, but the *Gesta* tells us that he met and bested Earl Ranulf and others several times in battle and that these seasoned veterans greatly admired his military ability.[12]

Henry FitzEmpress

That same year (1147) a new and more dangerous threat emerged. Henry FitzEmpress, the fourteen-year-old heir of Empress Matilda, landed at Wareham in Dorset. He boasted that he had come at the head of an army of thousands to claim his inheritance. It was soon discovered that the hot-headed young prince had only a small army of mercenaries acting on the mere promise of pay. Attacks on the castles of Cricklade and Purton proved unsuccessful, and with the prospect of payment dimming by the day, Henry's mercenaries began to desert him. He immediately sent a request for money to the empress, who informed him that she had none, and then to his uncle Earl Robert, who bluntly refused to help. Henry audaciously sent word to King Stephen, begging for his assistance. Stephen, desperate to remove Henry from the kingdom, sent him some money and the boy returned to Normandy. Although Henry's first attempt at winning the throne had been but a youthful folly it was clear that a new and dangerous threat was entering the arena. Unlike the empress, Henry was male and undoubtedly Henry I's heir. That same year Earl Robert died, and the following year Empress Matilda retired to Normandy.

Henry's next campaign in England took place in 1149 when he travelled to Carlisle and was knighted by his uncle, King David I of Scotland, on 22 May. Henry, King David and Earl Ranulf then rode south with an army and attempted to take York. Stephen left Eustace in charge in London and made a beeline for the northern metropolis. Henry's army disbanded and he made a mad dash for Bristol. Eustace immediately headed for Gloucestershire in the hope of seizing his rival. He learned that Henry was spending the night at Dursley Castle in Gloucestershire and the next morning he placed three groups of knights on the road to ambush him when he emerged. Henry, however, had been tipped off and fled during the night. Eustace spurred his horse after him but failed to catch up with Henry, who reached the safety of Bristol. Eustace laid waste the land around Bristol in an unsuccessful effort to draw Henry out and afterwards took base at Oxford, where he busied himself in attacking the king's enemies at Devizes, Marlborough and Salisbury.

In September, Eustace joined the king for a council at London where it was agreed that their next move would be to lay waste to the area around Devizes, where Henry was then located, in order to starve him into battle. Stephen and Eustace indulged in an orgy of destruction, demolishing houses and churches and burning the crops that had been reaped in the fields, until they received intelligence that Earl Ranulf was laying siege to Lincoln and had almost taken the city. Stephen headed north to deal with Ranulf while Eustace set his sights on attacking Hugh Bigod, who was laying siege to Bedford. Henry used the distraction to leave Devizes and laid waste Devonshire. Eustace pursued him and succeeded on entering the outer bailey of Devizes. He and his men set fire to the houses and butchered the people they came across before laying siege to the castle. Henry rushed back from Devon to help and sent reinforcements ahead of him who managed to drive Eustace away.

In 1150, Henry returned to Normandy to garner further support for another attempt on England. Geoffrey of Anjou handed over the duchy of Normandy to Henry, but King Louis refused to recognise him as duke. In 1151 Louis summoned Eustace, his brother-in-law, to France to wage war on the Angevins. They laid siege to the castle of Arques, near Dieppe, but achieved little else. Louis subsequently fell ill and a temporary peace was settled, transformed into a more permanent one on his recovery. Henry and Geoffrey attended a conference in Paris where Louis accepted Henry's homage and recognised him as Duke of Normandy. It is likely at this time that Henry first saw Eleanor of Aquitaine, the beautiful and unhappy wife of King Louis. As Henry and Geoffrey returned north from this conference, Geoffrey suddenly came down with a fever. At Château-du-Loir, Geoffrey bequeathed the counties of Anjou and Maine on Henry and then passed away on 7 September. Henry proceeded to Le Mans, where he received the homage of the people as Count of Anjou. He was now Duke of Normandy, Count of Maine and Count of Anjou. All that was left was to acquire England and he would be in possession of his full inheritance.

With Henry's fortunes in the ascendant, Stephen launched a desperate bid to crown Eustace, which, as we have seen, ended in failure. The only way that Eustace would succeed his father was if they brought the war to a definitive conclusion in their favour.

Normandy

On the death of Queen Matilda on 3 May 1152, Eustace inherited the county of Boulogne, but the war prevented him from paying his new lands a visit. Another opportunity to fight Henry presented itself when he married Eleanor of Aquitaine, who had recently divorced King Louis. Eleanor was heiress of the great duchy of Aquitaine in south-western France and Louis feared the amalgamation of so many French lands under one person. He held a conference with Eustace; Robert, Count of Perche; Henry, Count of Champagne; and Henry's brother Geoffrey of Anjou, who had been cheated of his hopes of inheriting Anjou. They agreed to wage war on Henry and distribute his possessions between them.

Geoffrey was sent into Anjou while Eustace and the others laid siege to the castle of Neuf-Marchè, near Gournay. On 16 July, Henry, who had been planning an expedition to England, immediately set out to help the garrison at Neuf-Marchè but they surrendered before he reached it. Louis placed the castle in Eustace's hands as a base from which he could lead attacks against Henry.

Louis headed for Pacy but retreated to Meulan when Henry approached. Henry then headed into Anjou and brought Geoffrey to heel. While Henry was busy in Anjou, King Louis made a further attack on Normandy. He burnt part of the town of Tillièrs and made an unsuccessful attempt to lay siege to Nonancourt, but he suddenly came down with a fever and was forced to agree to a truce.

Death

With his enemies on the continent temporarily quietened, Henry continued preparations to invade England. King Stephen, in the meantime, had not been idle. The *Gesta* states that he enjoyed great success and now held much of England under his sway. He laid siege to Wallingford, accompanied by many barons from all over the kingdom.

Henry landed in England in January 1153 with an army of 140 horse and 3,000 foot soldiers. Eustace followed Henry, ready to join his father and protect his inheritance. Henry laid siege to Malmesbury Castle and Stephen and Eustace duly arrived with an army, the sides staring each other down from their respective banks of the Avon. The biting January snow blew into the faces of the royal army and they were unable to grip their weapons, which dripped with water. With the river and weather preventing them from coming to arms, it was agreed that the castle should be destroyed, but the man sent to oversee the demolition of the castle turned coat and placed it in Henry's hands. Disheartened, Stephen and Eustace withdrew to London.

Henry proceeded to attack his enemies, eventually arriving at Wallingford where he laid siege to a fort that Stephen had constructed outside the walls. Stephen, Eustace and their supporters appeared but the armies were once again separated by a river, this time the Thames, which prevented them from engaging in battle. Eustace, Stephen and Henry were eager to come to arms but the barons, wishing to prolong the war, refused to fight and suggested a truce. Stephen and Henry were forced to hold peace talks across the Thames and agreed to a ceasefire. Plans for a more lasting peace settlement were discussed but not confirmed.

Eustace departed in anger, 'because the war, in his opinion, had reached no proper conclusion'.[13] Eustace had been keen on bringing his rival to battle and ending the war once and for all. Battle had not been met and now there were talks of effecting a lasting peace in which Eustace would only be the loser. He gathered a few men and rode into Cambridgeshire where he vented his anger by razing villages in the countryside, hoping to rouse Henry into a confrontation. On 10 August he plundered the lands of the abbey of Bury St Edmunds and a week later, on 17 August, he died. The *Gesta* states that he died of grief but Henry of Huntingdon and Robert of Torigny state that it was due to God's displeasure at his destruction of church lands. He was buried at Faversham Abbey in Kent alongside his mother and where his father would join them a year later. After the dissolution of the monasteries in the sixteenth century, it is said that the remains of Stephen, Eustace and Matilda were dug up from their resting place at Faversham Abbey and thrown into a nearby creek. The bones of Stephen and possibly those of Eustace and Matilda were allegedly gathered and reinterred in a tomb in the Trinity Chapel of the nearby Parish Church of St Mary of Charity, where today a Victorian plaque marks the spot.

The Succession Restored

Eustace's death was the catalyst for a lasting peace that was impossible while he still lived. He was a rash and temperamental figure, brought up in expectation of one day becoming king, and he would not have sat idly by while his rival usurped his place. Although Stephen had another son, William, Earl of Surrey, who was now his heir apparent, he did not resume the war in his name. The king was worn out after years of fighting and he realised that his dynasty would never rest easy while there was a rival for the throne. On 6 November a peace treaty was arranged at Winchester, bringing the war to a close. Stephen recognised Henry as his adoptive son and designated him as his heir while his own children renounced their claim to the throne in exchange for the possessions that Stephen had held before ascending the throne.

Stephen died on 25 October 1154 and Henry, who had previously returned to Normandy, was invited to assume the kingship. Henry and his wife Eleanor crossed over to England and were crowned at Westminster Abbey on 19 December. The green tree prophecy had finally been realised.

5

Henry the Young King

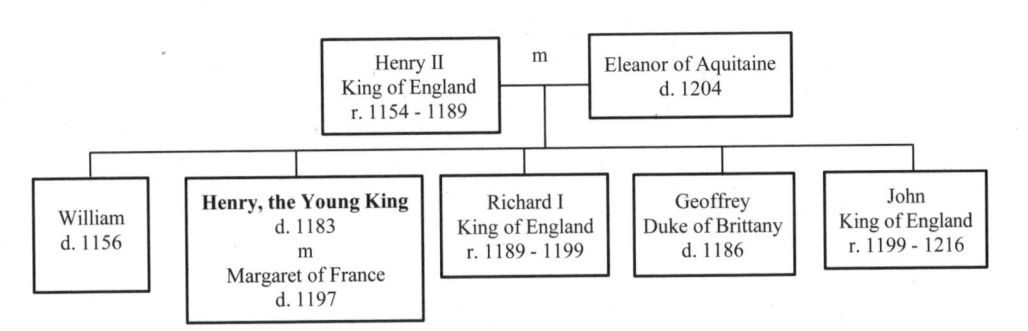

```
                    Henry II         m    Eleanor of Aquitaine
                 King of England          d. 1204
                  r. 1154 - 1189
```

William	**Henry, the Young King**	Richard I	Geoffrey	John
d. 1156	d. 1183	King of England	Duke of Brittany	King of England
	m	r. 1189 - 1199	d. 1186	r. 1199 - 1216
	Margaret of France			
	d. 1197			

In early June 1183, Henry 'the Young King', the eldest surviving son of King Henry II and Eleanor of Aquitaine, lay dying of dysentery at a château in Martel, France. The Young King was an anomaly in the annals of medieval England – he was the only son of a reigning monarch to be crowned during his father's lifetime. The Young King soon discovered that he was king in name only – his jealous father refused to surrender any of his hard-won power or even to delegate any of his responsibilities, with the result that the Young King twice rebelled against him.

Now he was dying, never to grasp the power that he had so longed for. The repentant youth sent word to his father and begged him to come and see him before he died. King Henry yearned to do so, but his companions warned him of the traitorous designs of the rebels who surrounded his son. Instead, Henry sent a ring, said to have once belonged to King Henry I, as a token of his forgiveness. When the ring was presented to the Young King he was overcome with joy and he tenderly kissed it. He would never see his father again.

Birth and Early Life

Henry the Young King was born in London on 28 February 1155. He was not heir apparent from birth; that distinction belonged to his elder brother, William, who had been born on 17 August 1153. William was a sickly child and when Henry had the barons pay homage to him on 10 April 1155 as his heir, he took the precaution of having them pay homage to the Young King as well. It was a shrewd move, as William passed away in 1156 and the Young King became heir apparent in his stead.

As heir, the Young King became a political tool from a young age. King Henry wished to regain some strategic castles situated in the French Vexin, the area of France that bordered Normandy, ceded to Louis back in 1151. With this in mind, he sent his trusted chancellor and friend, Thomas Becket, to Paris in 1158 with the objective of securing the hand of Louis's baby daughter, Margaret, born of his second wife Constance of Castile, for the Young King. Becket was successful in his endeavour and Henry and Louis later held a conference on the border of France and Normandy where they agreed to the marriage and the cession of some of the border castles as Margaret's dowry. As the couple were too young to marry, the castles were placed in the neutral hands of the Knights Templar, to be handed over upon the completion of the marriage. Henry took little Margaret with him and placed her under the care of Robert de Neubourg, Seneschal of Normandy, to be brought up until she was of age to marry.

It was not long before war broke out between the two kings over Angevin expansionism. Henry was lord of a vast swathe of lands known to historians as the Angevin 'Empire', which stretched from the Scottish border to the Pyrenees. He was hereditary King of England, Duke of Normandy and Count of Anjou, and Duke of Aquitaine by right of his wife – *jure uxoris*. This conglomeration of lands made Henry the most powerful ruler in Europe and earned him the jealousy and enmity of his overlord, the much weaker King Louis of France. In 1159 Henry invaded Toulouse, to which he had a claim through Queen Eleanor, and Louis came out in favour of his brother-in-law, Count Raymond V of Toulouse, who had married Eustace of Boulogne's widow, Constance of France. Peace was secured in October 1160 and Henry had the five-year-old Young King perform homage to Louis for Normandy. Shortly after, Louis's queen Constance died in childbirth and two weeks later he married Adela of Blois, a sister of Theobald V, Count of Blois, in the hope of finally procuring a male heir. This marriage provided Louis with a formidable ally on the borders of Normandy, Maine, Anjou and Aquitaine, and Henry reacted by having the Young King marry Margaret at Neubourg on 5 November in order to secure his possession of the border fortresses. A furious Louis swiftly called on the aid of his new brothers-in-law and waged war upon Henry. In September 1162, an uneasy peace was settled between them, which was to endure for the next five years.

Thomas Becket

In 1162, the seven-year-old Young King was taken from the nursery and placed in the household of Chancellor Becket to receive his education. It was a mark of the honour and esteem that Henry bore Becket that he entrusted him with the care of his most precious asset – his son and heir. Many other nobles in England and the neighbouring kingdoms sent their sons to be brought up by the chancellor 'in honourable nurture and doctrine'.[1] The Young King shared his schooling with other nobles his own age, and he was provided with his own masters and servants as befitted his rank. The fact that he was a king's son did not see him singled out for special treatment; he was still disciplined the same as everyone else, 'baring his back to the scourge'.[2]

When Theobald, Archbishop of Canterbury died, Henry decided to appoint Becket as the next archbishop in the belief that he himself would then exercise control over both lay and ecclesiastical affairs. The Young King attended the election of the next archbishop at Westminster Abbey in May 1162. Becket had the clergy and barons take an oath of fealty to the Young King and he was afterwards elected archbishop. The archbishop-elect was then presented to the Young King who, acting as his father's representative, assented to their selection. On Sunday 3 June, the Young King presided over Becket's consecration at Canterbury Cathedral.

Becket did not prove to be the puppet that Henry had envisioned. He surprised all by the sudden devotion that he showed in his new office, a change that contemporaries credited to the hand of God. Thomas immediately gave up his post as chancellor, threw himself into his role of archbishop with gusto and became a zealous defender of church liberties. In 1163, Henry and Becket clashed over the question of whose role it was to punish criminal clerks, the church or lay courts. Henry indignantly removed the Young King from Becket's household and placed the archbishop on trial in October 1164. Becket fled to Flanders and he remained on the continent for the next six years, doing all he could to annoy the king.

After five years of uneasy peace, Louis and Henry once again went to war in 1167 and 1168. On 6 January 1169, Henry and Louis held a peace conference at Montmirail where Henry announced his intention of dividing the Angevin Empire between his sons after his death. The Young King, as heir apparent, would receive England, Normandy and Anjou. His other sons would receive acquisitions – Richard, his second son, would receive Aquitaine and his third son, Geoffrey, Brittany. Henry had invaded Brittany in 1166 and forced its count, Conan IV, to marry his only daughter, Constance, to Geoffrey. Shortly after, Henry had Conan resign in Geoffrey's favour. John, the youngest of Henry's sons, was still only a baby and he was not provided with an inheritance, gaining him the nickname of John 'Lackland'.

The Young King paid homage for Anjou and Brittany and Louis granted him the office of Steward of France, a hereditary post of the counts of Anjou. On 2 February 1170, he performed his new office by waiting on the table of King Louis in Paris.

The Young King

The Young King would unwittingly become the catalyst for the shocking death of his former mentor, Thomas Becket. In 1170, Henry decided to renew the policy of King Stephen and have the fifteen-year-old Young King crowned as a joint monarch. After the troubles of his own childhood, Henry feared that if he were to die early his children's claims to succeed him might be disregarded. Becket was incensed. Crowning a king was the prerogative of the archbishopric of Canterbury and he regarded the king's act as a violation of his rights. He obtained letters from Pope Alexander III forbidding Roger, Archbishop of York and the other bishops from anointing the Young King and sent them to England. His demands fell on deaf ears and on 14 June the Young King was crowned at Westminster Abbey by Archbishop Roger. The following day William 'the Lion', King of Scotland, his brother David, Earl of Huntingdon and the earls and barons of England paid homage to the Young King and swore fealty to him above all others, saving that to which they owed the king.

The Young King's crowning also offended King Louis who, furious that his daughter Margaret had not been crowned alongside the Young King, invaded Normandy. Henry quickly travelled overseas and on 22 July held a conference at Frèteval with Louis and Becket. He placated Louis by agreeing to re-crown the Young King the following year alongside Margaret, while he and Becket were finally reconciled. Becket, however, was still determined to protect the freedoms of the church and the rights of the archbishopric of Canterbury. He obtained letters from the pope granting him permission to suspend Archbishop Roger and those who had assisted at the Young King's coronation, which he sent into England before returning himself on 1 December. The Young King was displeased at the actions of his former guardian and he refused to see Becket when he paid him a visit at Woodstock. Archbishop Roger and the other disgruntled bishops, meanwhile, travelled to Normandy to make complaint to King Henry who was holding his Christmas court at Bures. The vexed king then uttered the infamous words, 'Will no one rid me of this turbulent priest?' Four knights took his words to heart and secretly crossed over to England. They confronted Becket at Canterbury Cathedral on 29 December and murdered him before the altar, spilling his brains across the stone floor.

The news of Becket's murder shocked all of western Christendom and blame naturally fell upon the king. Henry was distraught and occupied himself with a campaign in Ireland. The Young King's reaction is not recorded, but Becket's murder was listed among the causes of his later rebellion, suggesting that he blamed his father for the death of his former governor.

At Christmas 1171, the sixteen-year-old Young King held his first court in Normandy. He was adamant that it would be a magnificent affair, and it was well attended. The chronicler Robert of Torigny tells us that William de St John, Lieutenant of Normandy, and William FitzHamo, Seneschal of Brittany, meeting in one of the great halls, forbade anyone from entering unless they were named William. When all the non-Williams had been turned out there ended up being a total of 117 Williams in the hall alone, ignoring the others so named who dined with the Young King in another hall.[3]

King Henry returned from Ireland on 17 April 1172 and on 21 May he and the Young King met with the papal legates at Avranches in Normandy. There, Henry was absolved of his role in Becket's death. Henry also made peace with Louis and, as promised, the Young King and Margaret were dispatched to England and consecrated king and queen at Winchester on 27 August by Rotrou, Archbishop of Rouen, Giles, Bishop of Évreux and Roger, Bishop of Worcester.

The Young King's Rebellion

The Young King had developed into a handsome, courteous and open-handed seventeen-year-old. He was also impatient and seethed at the fact that even though he was a crowned and anointed monarch, his father had not granted him any real power or responsibility. The chronicler William of Newburgh notes that 'he was impatient to obtain, with the oath and name, the reality of the oath and name, and, at least, to reign jointly with his father'.[4] Those around him fuelled the fires by whispering in his ear that Henry's reign had ceased the moment he had been crowned. King Louis's voice was added to the chorus and when the Young King and Margaret paid a visit to the French court that November the French king induced him to request either England or Normandy from his father. The Young King duly confronted his father but, like William the Conqueror before him, Henry refused to surrender any of his power. The Young King did not immediately break out into open rebellion but awaited a suitable pretext for doing so. The opportunity presented itself the following year when both kings travelled to Montferrat in Auvergne to speak with Humbert, Count of Maurienne regarding a marriage treaty between Henry's youngest son, John, and Humbert's daughter, Alice. As part of the agreement, Henry agreed to grant John the castles of Chinon, Mirebeau and Loudon. This infuriated the Young King as the castles formed part of his inheritance, and he stole off at night and fled to the court of King Louis. Along the way he was knighted by his tutor, the famous knight William Marshal.

The Young King, acting on Louis's advice, recruited allies by foolishly pledging land and money that was not his to give. By these means he enlisted the help of Philip d'Alsace, Count of Flanders, Philip's brother Matthew, Count of Boulogne and Theobald V, Count of Blois. He enticed King William of Scotland with the promise of possession of all of Northumberland down to the Tyne, and William's brother David with the earldom of Huntingdon and Cambridgeshire. Many other nobles, including the veteran Hugh Bigod, Earl of Norfolk, Hugh, Earl of Chester and Robert, Earl of Leicester turned against Henry and joined the Young King's cause. The rebellion took a more ominous turn when the feisty Queen Eleanor, perhaps on account of her husband's infidelity, came out in support of her son and sent his younger brothers Richard and Geoffrey to join him in Paris. Eleanor later attempted to join her sons, stealing away dressed as a man, but was caught and imprisoned on Henry's orders. She would spend the next sixteen years of her life under house arrest until she was finally released at the beginning of the reign of her favourite son, King Richard I.

The Young King played a leading role in the ensuing hostilities. He captured and destroyed the castle of Gournay and afterwards joined Count Philip in laying siege to Driencourt in Normandy. Here he suffered his first setback when Count Matthew was wounded near his knee by an arrow and later died of his injury, causing Count Philip to withdraw from Normandy and return home. The Young King then joined Louis at the siege of Verneuil, but they were forced to retreat at the approach of King Henry at the head of a larger army.

King Henry secured a great victory when he took the castle of Dol in Brittany, which brought Louis and the Young King to the negotiating table. On 25 September they met near Gisors and Henry offered the Young King the choice of half of the revenues of England along with four castles in the kingdom or half of the revenues of Normandy along with three castles in the duchy, one in Maine and one in Touraine. The wily Louis was not ready to cease hostilities and he convinced the Young King to refuse the offer.

Soon after, Robert, Earl of Leicester landed in Kent with a Flemish army but he was defeated near Bury St Edmunds and sent in chains to Henry in Normandy. The war resumed the following year (1174). A double-pronged attack was planned for June. The Young King and Count Philip would invade England while Louis would simultaneously enter Normandy and lay siege to Rouen, but the plans were scuppered when the Young King and Count Philip were prevented from crossing the Channel by contrary winds. Meanwhile, King William of Scotland invaded the north of England and laid siege to Carlisle Castle.

Things were beginning to look bleak for King Henry. On 8 July, he landed at Southampton. Instead of commencing war on his enemies he headed to Canterbury, entered dressed in the woollen gown of a pilgrim, and prayed at Becket's tomb. After, in the presence of Gilbert Foliot, Bishop of London, he professed his innocence in his old friend's death but admitted that the crime had been perpetrated on his behalf. He asked the bishops for absolution and then entered the monks' chapterhouse where he was whipped by them in an act of penance. He then spent the entire night praying at Becket's tomb and the following day he travelled to London. There he was visited by a messenger who brought him the news that King William had been captured near Alnwick Castle. This good fortune had occurred on 13 July, the day after Henry's penitence, and was seen as a sign of God's forgiveness. He received King William at Northampton while the other rebels made peace. 'Thus then, within the space of three weeks, was the whole of England restored to tranquillity,' the chronicler Roger of Howden states.[5]

King Louis recalled the Young King and Count Philip and they joined him in laying siege to Rouen on 22 July. King Henry, flushed by his success, returned to Normandy on 8 August and marched to Rouen's relief. Three days later he entered the city in view of the Young King's army and that night he sent Welsh soldiers into the forest to intercept the enemy supply convoys. The Welsh were so successful that Louis and the Young King were forced to abandon the siege after three days for want of provisions.

On 30 September Louis, the Young King, Richard and Geoffrey held a conference with King Henry between Tours and Amboise where they settled peace. Henry forgave the Young King and granted him two castles in Normandy as well as an annual revenue of 15,000 pounds. He made the Young King and his brothers swear that they would 'never demand of our lord the king ... anything whatever beyond the gifts above-written and agreed upon'.[6] The penitent Young King then offered to perform homage to his father but Henry would not abide it, respecting his dignity as an anointed king.

A Tourney Champion

The following year (1175), king and son publicly demonstrated their reconciliation by eating at the same table and sleeping in the same room. Inwardly, things were not quite so civil. Henry kept his son close, with the effect that the Young King began to feel stifled by his controlling presence. He planned to go on a pilgrimage to the shrine of St James at Santiago de Compostela in Spain but his plans were shelved when his brother Richard requested his help against the rebellious barons of Aquitaine. He joined Richard at Poitiers and together they laid siege to Châteauneuf. They succeeded in taking the castle but afterwards the Young King, 'listening to bad advice', went to Poitou where he was joined somewhat ominously by some of his father's enemies.[7]

During this time the Young King began entering tournaments in France and Normandy, alongside his mentor William Marshal and the knights of his household. These tournaments were not like the jousts of later times but were essentially large-scale melees where teams of knights battled one another for fame, glory and money. The idea was to capture your opponent by knocking him from his horse and then ransoming him or taking his horses and equipment. Participants were mostly landless young men enticed by the opportunity to demonstrate their prowess and accrue wealth, but tournaments also had a practical purpose as they acted as a training ground for new knights. '[T]he science of war,' notes Roger of Howden, 'if not practised beforehand, cannot be gained when it becomes necessary.'[8] These tournaments were not without danger. Knights could be injured or trampled to death by their horses, as had happened to the Young King's brother Geoffrey of Brittany in 1186.

The Young King saw the tournament as a way of occupying his time and of keeping him from mischief, while also bringing him fame and glory. For the first year and a half the Young King's retinue was often humiliated, but their fortunes improved when they borrowed a tactic from Philip, Count of Flanders. They would hold back and wait until everybody was tired and then enter the fray, carrying all before them. The Young King achieved great fame for his exploits. This was largely due to the presence of the formidable knight William Marshal, who acted as his bodyguard and who would often come to his rescue. In their first tournament the Marshal had displeased the Young King when he had left him in the press of his enemies in order to attack another band of knights. The Young King afterwards reproached him and the Marshal promised never to do so again. He was true to his word. 'No man dared stretch out his hand towards him [the Young King] … because of the mighty blows dealt by the Marshal,' the Marshal's biographer states.[9] The Young King became a great sponsor of the tournament and many knights sought his patronage. He is reported to have had over 200 knights with him, paying them a wage of 20 shillings a day. As he had little money himself, his father often footed the bill or he took out loans that he could not afford to repay.

France

On 1 November 1179, the Young King attended the coronation of King Louis's fourteen-year-old son and heir, Philip Augustus, and he had the honour of carrying the crown in the procession to Rheims Cathedral. One figure was absent from the event – King Louis VII had recently suffered a stroke and had lost control of the right side of his body. With the king out of action, the young and impressionable Philip came under the malign influence of Count Philip of Flanders, who sought to become the new power behind the throne. He fomented conflict between the king and his mother, Queen Adela, and she was forced to seek shelter with her brothers at Blois. She solicited the help of the Young King, who crossed over to England in early 1180 to confer with his father. On 28 June, the two Henrys mediated peace between Philip and his mother at a conference on the border of Normandy and France. On 18 September, King Louis died in Paris and was buried at Barbeau Abbey.

King Henry returned to England on 28 July 1181. He left the Young King in charge of Normandy, tasking him with protecting the King of France in case of further hostilities. It was a fortuitous move, for in December Count Philip of Flanders formed a coalition against King Philip. The count invaded Noyon and it fell to the Young King and his brothers Richard and Geoffrey to come to the French king's aid. The three men ravaged the lands of one of the rebels, Count Stephen of Sancerre, and forced him to submit himself to Philip. Then they marched northwards to deal with the Count of Flanders, who immediately retreated inside Crèpy Castle at the sight of them. In March 1182, King Henry came to Normandy and he and the Young King once again settled peace between King Philip and the Count of Flanders.

By now the Young King had once again become disaffected with his position and he demanded Normandy from the king. Henry refused and the Young King and Queen Margaret repaired to the court of King Philip. Father and son were reconciled by the end of the year and the Young King swore not to act against his father in return for 100 pounds of Angevin money a day for his expenses and ten for his queen.

Rebellion and Death

Henry and his sons celebrated Christmas 1182 at Caen, where King Henry demanded that Richard and Geoffrey perform homage to the Young King for their lands. Geoffrey did so willingly but Richard refused, stating that he held Aquitaine as a vassal of the King of France, not his brother. Richard was eventually persuaded to change his mind and when he offered to perform the homage it was the Young King's turn to refuse. Then, on 1 January 1183, the Young King, acting 'of his own accord, and no one forcing him thereto', placed his hands on the Holy Gospels and swore obedience to his father before announcing that he had entered into a league with the disconcerted barons of Aquitaine who had once again risen in rebellion against Richard.[10] His reason for doing so, he attested, was the fact that Richard had fortified a castle at Clairvaux on the borders of Anjou which formed part of the Young King's inheritance. In reality, the Young King had long borne a jealousy of his powerful and independent brother and he was glad of an excuse to take Aquitaine from him.

In order to stave off conflict, King Henry ordered Richard to relinquish the castle and he had his sons swear to keep the peace between them. A conference was arranged to take place between the brothers and the rebellious barons of Aquitaine at Mirabel. Henry sent Duke Geoffrey to summon the Aquitanians but Geoffrey, 'that son of perdition', opted to join them instead and took up residence in the castle of Limoges.[11] On hearing this, Richard withdrew to his lands and began to fortify his castles.

The Young King persuaded his father to let him travel to Limoges and mediate peace. This was agreed but the Young King, in a pre-planned move, joined the rebels instead. On 1 March, King Henry and Richard arrived outside the walls of the city with a small retinue but they were greeted by a flurry of arrows from the inhabitants, some of which pierced the king's armour, and they were compelled to retreat to the nearby castle of Aixe. King Henry laid siege to Limoges in revenge and forced entry into the town. A conference was held between the king and his sons outside the castle, but it was brought to an end when the garrison loosed arrows at the king, one of which would have dealt him a mortal wound had the horse not reared its head at the vital moment and taken the blow meant for him. Pointedly, the Young King did nothing to punish the culprit.

Incredibly, the Young King still had the king's complete trust and he acted as an intermediary between Henry and the rebels. This, according to Roger of Howden, was nothing but a ploy to give Geoffrey time to slip out of the castle with his army of mercenaries and harry the king's lands. When the Young King heard of Geoffrey's actions he professed his innocence to his father and gave him his armour and horse in an act of submission, but a few days later he once again renewed his oath to the rebels. On his return to Henry he admitted that, as he sympathised with the rebels, he could not punish them as they deserved. He made a show of departing for Le Dorat but was recalled by Henry, and on his return he entered the priory of Saint-Martial where he took an oath on the relics of the saint to go on crusade. Henry attempted to persuade his son to give up this vow, fearing he had not sworn through any religious feeling, but the Young King professed that it was done in remission of the sin of rebelling against his father and begged for his permission, which was tearfully granted.

The Young King asked his father to send Maurice de Crouy and some barons to discuss peace with the rebels. However, when Maurice and the barons were talking with the Young King some of their followers were killed. The Young King once again did nothing to punish the rebels. Soon he began to run low on money with which to pay his mercenaries. Fearing that they would defect to his father, he seized the treasures of the priory of Saint-Martial and then launched an expedition into Angoulême and harried Richard's lands. Meanwhile, the people of Maine and Anjou began to desert King Henry's army and he was forced to raise the siege after Easter. After Henry's departure, the Young King returned to Limoges but found that his actions at the abbey had turned the people against him and they refused him entrance in to the town. Still in need of money, he raided south, sacrilegiously stripping abbeys of their treasures, but on reaching the village of Martel he suddenly fell sick with dysentery. When he realised that he was going to die he sent word to his father and asked him to come and see him, but the king, on the advice of his barons, refused, fearing treachery from the Young King's supporters. Henry sent a ring owned by Henry I as a token of his forgiveness which the Young King reverently kissed, bringing him peace of mind.

As the end drew near, the Young King made his confession and was absolved of his sins. Then, in an act of penance, he had a noose tried around his neck and he was dragged from his bed and then placed on a bed covered in ashes. Two large stones were placed under his head and feet and on 11 June, the feast of St Barnabas, he died. Henry was devastated at his son's death. Although the Young King had been ungrateful and rebellious, it is clear that Henry genuinely loved him. Once the Young King was dead the rebellion fizzled out and peace returned to Aquitaine.

The Young King had ordered that his body be buried at Rouen among the monuments of his Norman ancestors, and it was transported in procession by Richard, Archbishop of Canterbury and other ecclesiasts. Along the way they placed the body in the Church of St Julian at Le Mans for the night, and in the morning the Bishop of Mans and the common people secretly buried it within the church. The people of Rouen ordered that the body be returned to them or else they threatened to seize it by force. King Henry stepped in and the Young King's body was exhumed and reinterred at Rouen in accordance with his wishes.

The debacle over the Young King's body demonstrates his popularity with the people; after his death miracles were reported to have happened at his tomb. William of Newburgh states that this was thought to be proof that he was just in his wars against his father, or perhaps that his final acts of repentance had pleased God. One of the lasting effects of the Young King's death was that no other king of England ever crowned an heir during their lifetime.

6
Arthur, Duke of Brittany

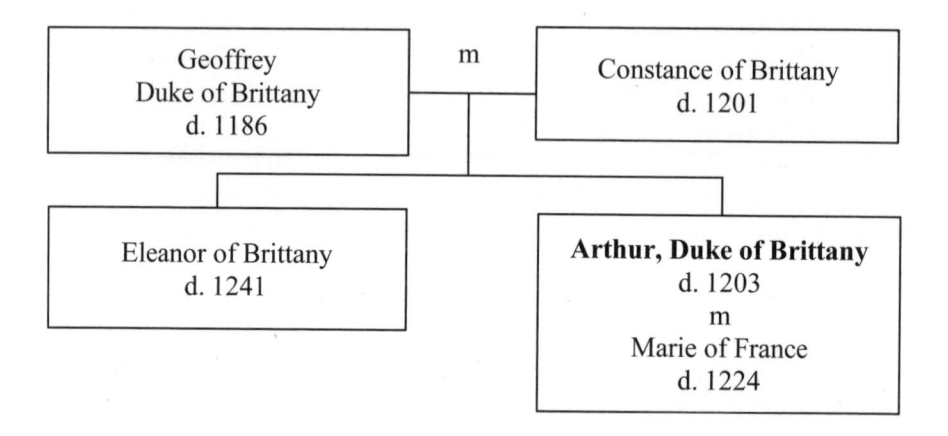

```
┌─────────────────────┐      m    ┌─────────────────────┐
│     Geoffrey        │───────────│ Constance of Brittany│
│  Duke of Brittany   │           │       d. 1201        │
│       d. 1186       │           │                      │
└─────────────────────┘           └─────────────────────┘
            │
    ┌───────┴────────┐
┌───────────────────┐   ┌─────────────────────┐
│ Eleanor of Brittany│   │ Arthur, Duke of Brittany │
│     d. 1241        │   │        d. 1203           │
│                    │   │          m               │
│                    │   │     Marie of France      │
│                    │   │        d. 1224           │
└───────────────────┘   └─────────────────────┘
```

William Marshal was about to retire to bed on the night of 10 April 1199 when he received notice of the death of King Richard I. Dressing hurriedly, he immediately went to see Hubert Walter, Archbishop of Canterbury, to whom he disclosed the sad news. Conversation quickly turned to the question of who was to be Richard's successor to the Angevin Empire. Richard had left no legitimate heirs and the only surviving direct descendants of King Henry II in the male line were his sole grandson, Arthur, son of Geoffrey, Duke of Brittany, and his youngest son, John. Richard had designated John as his successor on his deathbed; but John had a dangerous rival in the form of Arthur.

Henry II's plans for the succession had done much to strengthen the notion of male primogeniture. He had recognised his eldest son, the Young King, as his heir, had him crowned to ensure his succession and on the Young King's death he had made Richard, his second son, heir instead of his two younger brothers. But it was not yet clear who had the better claim – the son of an elder deceased brother, known as the 'representative' as he represented the claim of his deceased father, or a younger son, known as the 'cadet'. In the common law the answer was clear – Arthur had the better claim – but the throne did not devolve entirely on the same principles as land. It was, for instance, acknowledged that the kingdom could not be divided between heiresses – the practice that applied to the transmission of land.

Hubert Walter was of the opinion that Arthur had the better right but Marshal disagreed, warning him that 'Arthur has treacherous advisors about him and he is unapproachable and overbearing. If we call him to our side, he will seek to do us harm and damage, for he does not like those in our realm.'[1] They should, he suggested, choose John, 'since the son is indisputably closer in the line of inheritance than the nephew is, and it is right that that should be made clear'.[2] The archbishop reluctantly agreed – but warned Marshal that he would one day regret his decision.

Birth and Early Life

Arthur, Duke of Brittany was the posthumous son and heir of Geoffrey, Duke of Brittany and his wife, Constance of Brittany. He was born on Easter Sunday, 29 March 1187, seven months after his father's premature death.[3]

Geoffrey, Duke of Brittany was the fourth but third surviving son of King Henry II. King Henry had secured him the hand of Constance, the heiress of Conan IV, Duke of Brittany and Earl of Richmond, in 1166. Soon after Conan had relinquished the dukedom in favour of his daughter and King Henry had taken up the reins of power until 1181 when Geoffrey, then of age, married Constance and ruled the duchy in her stead. Their first child, a daughter named Eleanor, was born three years later in 1184.

Following the Young King's death in 1183, Richard, Duke of Aquitaine, the next senior male, became heir apparent to England, Normandy and Anjou. Geoffrey retained Brittany while John was made Lord of Ireland. The capricious Geoffrey, however, aspired to inherit Anjou and in 1186 he demanded it from his father. Henry shot down his son's hopes and Geoffrey, like the Young King before him, fled to the court of the King of France. Philip Augustus was always eager to meddle in Angevin affairs and he made Geoffrey Seneschal of France and agreed to help him wrestle Anjou from the king. Before they had an opportunity of maturing their plans, however, Geoffrey died. Various causes of death are supplied by the chroniclers. Gerald of Wales states that Geoffrey died of a fever while Roger of Howden suggests he was trampled to death after falling from his horse in a tournament.[4]

Geoffrey left behind him his young daughter, Eleanor, and a pregnant widow. On 29 March 1187, Constance gave birth to a healthy son. King Henry decreed that the child should be named after himself but Constance and the Bretons, who resented Angevin overlordship in the duchy, defiantly named him Arthur after the fabled once and future king. Once she had recovered from giving birth, Constance took up the reins of government in Brittany and raised Arthur with an eye to one day inheriting the duchy.

King Henry continued to meddle in Breton affairs. On 3 February 1189 he forced Constance to marry Ranulf de Blondeville, 6th Earl of Chester, grandson of the rebellious Ranulf II of King Stephen's day. Constance resented the match, looking down upon the union with a mere earl after having being married to a king's son, and the couple lived mostly apart. She actively pursued a divorce, which she would finally acquire by 1199, the year in which she married her third and final husband, Guy of Thouars.

Heir to the Throne

While Arthur grew up in Brittany, events in the Angevin Empire propelled him ever closer to the throne. King Henry II died on 6 July 1189 and was succeeded by Duke Richard of Aquitaine as Richard I, marking the first time a king had been succeeded by his next in blood since before the Conquest. In 1190 Richard embarked on the Third Crusade along with Philip Augustus in an attempt to win back Jerusalem from the Muslim Saladin. His first port of call was the island of Sicily, where he butted heads with King Tancred who had usurped the Sicilian throne on the death of the previous king, William II. King William had been married to Richard's sister, Joan, and Tancred had placed the widow in captivity in Palermo and denied her the payment of her marriage portion. Richard demanded that she be released and granted her marriage portion, and when this ultimatum failed he took the town of Messina by force. This brought Tancred to the bargaining table and the two kings came to a compromise in the Treaty of Messina in October.

In the treaty, Richard proposed that Arthur, 'the excellent duke of Brittany', marry an unnamed daughter of King Tancred.[5] Furthermore, Richard designated Arthur as his heir, declaring that 'if we shall chance to die without issue, [Arthur will be] our heir'.[6] His designation could be seen as a triumph for the representative principle but Richard no doubt considered it a temporary measure to prevent his younger brother, the duplicitous John, from seizing the English throne in his absence. Plans were already afoot for a marriage between Richard and Berengaria, the daughter of Sancho, King of Navarre, which he no doubt hoped would one day lead to the birth of an heir and negate the question of his successor. Early in 1191, Queen Dowager Eleanor of Aquitaine, released from captivity on Richard's accession, came to meet her son at Messina. She brought Berengaria with her and the two married at Cyprus on 12 May.

Richard arrived in the Holy Land in June 1191 and joined Philip Augustus in besieging the city of Acre, which capitulated on 12 July. Later that month, on 31 July, Philip returned home citing illness. In fact, he was secretly planning on exploiting Richard's absence to invade his lands. Richard, meanwhile, continued towards Jerusalem. He defeated Saladin at Arsuf on 7 September but decided against taking the Holy City itself. The following year (1192) he signed a peace treaty with Saladin. On his return home he was shipwrecked and captured near Venice by Leopold, Duke of Austria, who handed him over to the Holy Roman Emperor, Henry VI. Philip Augustus wasted no time in taking advantage of this good fortune and offered to help John conquer the Angevin lands.

Before Richard departed for the Third Crusade he had pacified John's ambitions by granting him the county of Mortain in Normandy and arranging his marriage to Isabella, the wealthy heiress of the earldom of Gloucester, but he failed to give John any role in the government of the kingdom. This he left under the justiciarship of the ambitious and lowborn chancellor, William Longchamp.

The kingdom was not large enough for two such big personalities, and John and Longchamp soon came to blows. Richard had notified Longchamp that he had made Arthur his heir and that if he were to die on crusade then the kingdom was to be held for Arthur until he came of age. Longchamp, with an eye to securing his own position in such an eventuality, solicited the aid of King Malcolm IV of Scotland. When John became aware of Longchamp's machinations he began secretly to bring others to his side. Then, in September 1191, Longchamp made the mistake of ordering the arrest of John's illegitimate brother, Geoffrey, Archbishop of York, when Geoffrey, who had been banned from entering England for a period of three years, arrived to take up office. He was pulled from the altar of the Priory of St Martin, Dover, in a scene reminiscent of the murder of Becket. John channelled the resultant outrage to lead an army against Longchamp, who was forced to flee the country. John, however, was disappointed in his hopes to wield power – Richard appointed Walter de Coutances as justiciar instead.

This was the state of affairs when John received the invitation from King Philip. He eagerly crossed over to France where he paid homage to the king and agreed to hand over the French Vexin if he were successful and also to marry Alice, the king's sister. John returned to England and fortified his castles while Philip entered Normandy at the head of an army. Philip failed to take Rouen and agreed to cease hostilities for a large sum of money and possession of four castles.

In the interim, Richard managed to come to terms with Emperor Henry. He agreed to pay a colossal ransom of 100,000 silver marks, after which he would be set at liberty. When Philip heard of this he sent warning to John that 'the devil was now let loose'.[7] John ignominiously retired from England and took shelter with Philip in France. On 4 February 1194, Richard was released and after restoring order in England he travelled to Normandy where a frightened John prostrated himself before him. Richard forgave his brother but seized his lands. John would serve his brother faithfully for the rest of the reign and in 1195 he was restored to some of his possessions.

Richard then went to war with King Philip in order to win back the lands he had lost during his captivity. The war was brought to an end by a treaty in 1196, allowing Richard to turn his attention to the matter of Brittany. Ever since the death of Henry II, Brittany had enjoyed an independence from its Angevin overlords and Richard was determined to bring it back under control. In 1196 he requested the wardship of Arthur, still his heir, until he came of age, but the Bretons refused to hand him over. Richard ordered Constance to attend a conference at Normandy but she was seized on the border of Normandy by her husband, Earl Ranulf, and confined in his castle at St Jacques de Beuvron. The Bretons responded by raiding into the borders of Normandy and Richard replied in kind, forcing them to escort Arthur to the court of Philip Augustus and beg for his assistance. Philip heartily agreed and he once again commenced war in Normandy.

Arthur remained in the safety of Paris for the next two years, during which time he was brought up alongside Philip's son Louis, the future Louis VIII.[8] The Bretons, meanwhile, finding themselves no match for Richard, were forced to surrender and return to their former allegiance. Sometime afterwards, Constance was freed and she resumed control of Brittany. In 1198, Arthur left Philip's court and he returned to Brittany where he paid homage to Richard and agreed not to support the French king.

In 1199, Richard was mortally wounded by a crossbow bolt while laying siege to the castle of Chalus, near Limoges. The wound turned gangrenous and Richard, realising that his time was short, arranged the succession. He had no legitimate children by his queen, Berengaria, and with no clear successor he opted to designate John as his heir and ordered all those present to pay fealty to him. This done, Richard died on 6 April and was buried beside his father at Fontevrault Abbey.

A Disputed Succession

Richard left behind him a disputed succession. He had designated John as heir to the Angevin Empire but John had a formidable rival in the form of Arthur. As we have seen, it was not yet clear in England who had the better hereditary right, the representative or cadet, and Richard had confused matters further by having declared Arthur to be his heir in the Treaty of Messina. But the Angevin Empire was much more than just England, and each of its dominions had its own developing rules of succession and opinion as to who should rule over it. This meant that John was not guaranteed the whole, and the rivalry between him and Arthur had the potential to destroy the integrity of the Angevin Empire.

John, ironically, was paying Arthur a friendly visit at the Breton court when news arrived of Richard's death. John managed to slip away in the confusion and in emulation of Henry I and King Stephen he headed straight for Chinon in Touraine, where he received the all-important Angevin treasury. Arthur and Constance, meanwhile, entered Anjou at the head of a Breton army and peacefully took possession of its capital city of Angers. On Easter Sunday (18 April), the barons of Anjou, Maine and Touraine chose Arthur as Richard's heir. The barons were of the opinion that 'the son of

Arthur, Duke of Brittany

the elder brother should succeed to what was due to him as his patrimony, namely, the inheritance which Geoffrey, earl [Duke] of Brittany, the father of Arthur, would have had if he had survived Richard, king of England, his brother'.[9] Arthur had thus secured the allegiance of a large part of the Angevin Empire, but Aquitaine remained loyal to Queen Eleanor and she came out in support of John.

If Arthur was going to inherit the Angevin Empire, he needed to capture his rival. An opportunity presented itself on the night of Easter Monday when Arthur received word that John was staying at nearby Le Mans with a small following. Arthur immediately dispatched a band of knights to seize him, but John, having been forewarned, managed to flee before daybreak. When the soldiers arrived in the morning they found nothing but John's baggage and horses, which he had left behind in his haste.

Shortly after, Philip Augustus arrived at Le Mans and threw his support behind Arthur, who, along with his mother, Constance, performed homage and swore fealty to the French king for Anjou, Touraine and Maine. John, in the meantime, had reached the safety of Rouen and on April 25 he was girt with the sword of the dukedom of Normandy at Rouen Cathedral. From there he sent William Marshal and Hubert Walter, Archbishop of Canterbury, over to England to secure his accession there. Arthur's claim was taken seriously in England but it is unlikely that he would have ever been elected king. He was still a minor and an unknown quantity in England while John, although he had proved himself untrustworthy, was an adult and well known. The English barons, however, used the existence of a rival claimant to wrangle some concessions out of John. On 25 May John landed at Shoreham and two days later he was crowned King of England at Westminster Abbey by Archbishop Hubert Walter. Although primogeniture had made great strides under Henry II, it is evident that the elective principle remained a contender in determining the succession. According to the chronicler Matthew Paris, Archbishop Hubert Walter declared that the throne was elective at John's coronation and that they had elected him king.[10]

With England secure, John returned to Normandy to make good his claim to the rest of the empire. On 18 August he and Philip held a peace conference where Philip demanded that John confer Poitou, Anjou, Maine and Touraine on Arthur. Unsurprisingly, John refused to give away any of his inheritance and the conference broke up without resolution. In September, Philip renewed hostilities in Arthur's name. He invaded Normandy and took Conches, near Évreux, but made a costly mistake when he razed the castle of Ballon in Maine in October. William des Roches, Arthur's Seneschal of Anjou and the leader of his army, protested to Philip that he had destroyed Ballon without Arthur's permission. Philip remarked that he would do as he wished without regard to Arthur, and that same night the disgruntled des Roches secretly met with John at Bourg-la-Reine where he agreed to hand over Arthur and Constance. As promised, he took Arthur and Constance to see John at Le Mans and peace was settled between uncle and nephew. It was a boon for John, who had seemingly won the succession dispute, but in what would be a recurring trait he quickly squandered his advantage. Arthur was warned that John intended to throw him in prison and the following night he, Constance and his companions quietly abandoned the city and took shelter at Angers before returning to Philip's side.

After this, Peter de Capua, the legate of the Apostolic See, worked to mend relations between John and Philip, and they agreed to peace in the Treaty of Le Goulet in May 1199. Philip recognised John's rights to the Angevin Empire while John promised to pay Philip 30,000 silver marks and cede to him some territory, including Évreux and the French Vexin. John agreed to recognise Arthur as Duke of Brittany and not to deprive him of the duchy without the lawful judgement of his court. Later, at Vernon, Arthur performed homage to John for Brittany, 'with the sanction and advice of the king of France'.[11]

The treaty of Le Goulet was a disaster for Arthur – of all the Angevin lands he held nothing but Brittany, which he held of his enemy and which John could one day confiscate from him. Tensions ran high and Arthur opted not to enter John's court but remained with Philip as he 'feared treachery on the part of king John'.[12] He spent the next few years in Brittany where he continued his education. Constance died in 1201 and Arthur succeeded her as Duke of Brittany. Constance had been a formidable and determined woman who had fought hard for her son's rights and Arthur no doubt felt her loss keenly on both a personal and a political level.

As it happened, Arthur did not have to wait long for John to once again squander his advantage and renew the war. John decided to divorce his wife of eleven years, Isabelle of Gloucester, and take a new bride. King Philip had suggested another Isabella, the daughter of Audemar, Count of Angoulême, as a potential bride during the negotiations for the Treaty of Le Goulet, but there was one issue – Isabella had previously been betrothed to Hugh de Lusignan, Count of La Marche, who hoped to one day inherit Angoulême in her right. The marriage had not yet taken place as the twelve-year-old Isabella was a minor and had been placed under the Lusignans' wardship until she came of age. The Count of Angoulême, preferring a royal match to that of a mere count, snatched Isabella from the Lusignans and on 26 August 1200 she married John in a ceremony at Angoulême officiated by Helias, Archbishop of Bordeaux. The newlyweds returned to England in October and they were solemnly crowned at Westminster.

The marriage, in the words of the chronicler Roger of Wendover, was 'very injurious to the king as well as the kingdom of England'.[13] Hugh de Lusignan smarted at the king for having stolen his bride and he broke out in rebellion. John crossed over to France in order to deal with the Lusignans but on his arrival he discovered that Philip had stepped in and mediated peace. John, in a foolish move, summoned the Lusignans to his court to stand trial by battle. The Lusignans refused and they appealed to Philip as John's overlord of Aquitaine, who ordered John to make peace with them. On 25 March 1202, John and Philip met at Le Goulet and Philip demanded that John attend his court in Paris to answer for his recent behaviour and be judged by his peers. John reluctantly agreed and a date of 28 April was assigned for the trial. John, however, had no intention of attending the trial and he knew that his absence would result in a return to war. He needed to seize Arthur before the boy could once more be used as a weapon against him. On 27 March 1202 he summoned Arthur to his court to perform homage again:

> The King, &c. to his beloved nephew Arthur, &c. We command and *summon* you to be with us at Argentan, in the octaves of Easter, to do unto us that which ye owe unto your liege lord, and we will gladly do unto you that which we owe unto our dear nephew and our liegeman. Witnessed ourself at Andely, on the 27th day of March.[14]

Arthur ignored John's request and travelled to King Philip's court. John played right into Philip's hands by failing to appear for his trial. It was judged in his absence that he should lose all of his lands in France. Philip immediately raised an army and invaded Normandy in company with Arthur. Arthur was now sixteen years old and Philip knighted him at Gournay. He invested him with all the Angevin lands except Normandy, which he intended to seize for himself, and betrothed him to his young daughter, Marie. Philip then sent Arthur into Poitou, along with Hugh and Geoffrey de Lusignan and an army of 200 soldiers, to subject it to the boy's rule.

Arthur ordered reinforcements from Brittany and Berry to meet him at Tours but while he awaited their arrival he received word that his paternal grandmother, the aged Queen Eleanor of Aquitaine, was resident at the castle of Mirebeau with only a small garrison. Without waiting for the reinforcements, Arthur and the Lusignans made an impetuous dash for Mirebeau. They forced entry into the town and laid siege to the castle. Queen Eleanor took refuge in a stone tower against which Arthur's forces could make no headway. Eleanor quickly dispatched a messenger to John to come and help her. He was on his way to Chinon when the messengers found him and he immediately spun his horse around, travelling furiously by day and night, and 'accomplished the long distance quicker than is to be believed'.[15] On John's arrival the rebel army exited the town in battle array and met John's larger force. They were soon routed and fled back towards the castle. John's army was hot on their heels and they forced entry into the town. Another battle took place within the castle walls, in which Hugh and Geoffrey de Lusignan and the other rebels were captured and placed in chains. Most fortuitously for John, Arthur was amongst those taken prisoner. He finally had his rival in his clutches.

Disappearance

John was jubilant, having taking all his enemies in one fell swoop. As soon as King Philip learned of Arthur's fate, he withdrew from Normandy and returned to Paris. John placed all the prisoners in carts, 'a new and unusual mode of conveyance', and had some sent to England and others to Normandy to be holed up within their castles.[16] The triumphant John then marched to the castle of Falaise where he had Arthur confined under the watchful eye of his trusted chamberlain, Hubert de Burgh.

The nobles and people of Brittany were horrified at Arthur's capture and feared for his life. On 24 August, John was met by Furmie, a servant of Arthur's, who requested a safe-conduct for some of the nobles of Brittany to come and speak with him. John granted their request but offered an ominous threat: 'We command you, however, that ye do naught whereby evil may befall our nephew Arthur.'[17] There is no record of the conference but it evidently achieved little, as Arthur remained in custody.

John was now to destroy his advantage again, this time making the fateful mistake of alienating William des Roches. Des Roches requested that Arthur be placed into his custody but the king refused. Des Roches left John's court indignantly and, combining forces with the disgruntled Bretons and some nobles of Anjou and Maine, broke out in rebellion and seized the castle of Angers on 29 October.

The king's counsellors, meanwhile, warned John that he would never know peace while Arthur still lived. They suggested that he have the boy blinded and castrated, thus making him unfit to rule and thereby forcing the rebels to submit. John agreed and sent three servants to Falaise to carry out the deed. Two of them refused to do it and fled from the court, but the third proceeded to Falaise and announced the sentence to de Burgh. As the man went to Arthur's cell to carry out his orders the duke cried out to his guards, who took pity on him and seized the assailant and threw him out. Hubert de Burgh believed that John had ordered the sentence in a fit of rage and that when he calmed down he would regret it. As such, he kept Arthur unharmed but let it be noised abroad that the act had been carried out and that Arthur had died as a result of his injuries. This enraged the Bretons, who continued their rebellion with a new fervour until Hubert de Burgh was forced to admit his ruse. This quietened the Bretons somewhat and even pleased John.

One day, John came to see Arthur at Falaise. He demanded that Arthur withdraw from his allegiance to Philip and transfer that allegiance to himself as his lord and uncle. Arthur refused and obstinately demanded that John hand over England and all the territories that King Richard had possessed at the time of his death. If he did not, Arthur warned, he would never enjoy peace. John was perturbed by his words and had Arthur sent to Rouen Castle to be confined in a new tower that had been erected there, under the keeping

Arthur, Duke of Brittany

of Robert de Vieuxpont. '[S]hortly afterwards,' states the chronicler Roger of Wendover, 'the said Arthur suddenly disappeared.'[18]

Arthur's fate is unknown, although it is certain that he died. Whether this was by natural causes or sinister means can never be known, but the chroniclers of the time all believed that he had been murdered. Historians tend to favour the account of the chronicle of Margam Abbey in Glamorgan, which states that John murdered Arthur with his own hands in a drunken rage on 3 April 1203 and afterwards cast the body, weighted down by a rock, into the Seine. The body was later brought up in a fishing net and on being recognised was buried secretly at the church of Notre-Dame-des-Près, near Rouen.[19] This version is given some credence as William de Braose, who was certainly present at John's court at the time of Arthur's disappearance, was a patron of the abbey and may have revealed Arthur's fate to the monks. De Braose later fell from favour and his wife, Matilda de Braose, and his son were imprisoned and cruelly starved to death for saying that John had murdered Arthur.

However, historian Stephen Church suggests the less sensational idea that Arthur was put to death by an anonymous executioner with the sanction of John and his most trusted counsellors.[20] This was not an emotional reaction by the king, as per the Margam account, but what Church calls a 'coolly calculated political act'.[21] Arthur was in league with the king's enemies and was thus a threat to the integrity of the Angevin Empire that had to be extinguished.

Whatever his fate, Arthur's disappearance would prove John's undoing. Philip used it as an excuse to deprive John of his lands. He demanded that John hand over Arthur, and when John proved unable to do so, he invaded Normandy. On 24 June 1204 Rouen was taken and Normandy – which had been joined with England since the Norman Conquest – was lost. Philip then turned his attention to Aquitaine. Eleanor of Aquitaine had died in 1204 and the barons of Poitou paid homage to Philip while John nearly lost Gascony, too. Anjou, Maine and Touraine accepted Philip as their overlord. The Angevin Empire was no more.

John's subsequent attempts to reconquer Normandy failed and in 1215 he was forced to sign Magna Carta by the disgruntled and rebellious English barons. The wily John had Magna Carta annulled by the pope, which resulted in the First Barons' War, during which some of the English barons invited Louis, the son of Philip Augustus and the future Louis VIII, to take the throne.

John had two sons by Queen Isabella – Henry of Winchester, born in 1207, and Richard of Cornwall, born in 1209. John had previously had the barons pay homage to Henry as his heir, and when he died in 1216 in the midst of the war, his supporters, led by the loyal William Marshal, crowned the nine-year-old Henry as King Henry III at Gloucester Cathedral. Louis was eventually defeated and before leaving the kingdom he renounced his claim to the throne, bringing the war to a close.

The Succession

The death of King John would have a lasting impact on the rules of succession as it further strengthened the notion of primogeniture. As we have seen, in the aftermath of his death the barons appointed John's eldest son, Henry III, to be his successor. As accords with the rules of primogeniture, this was to the prejudice of John's younger son, Richard of Cornwall. Henry, however, was not the superior claimant – after Arthur's death that distinction belonged to Arthur's sister, Eleanor of Brittany. Poor Eleanor had been captured at Mirebeau along with her brother and John had subsequently had her imprisoned in England to prevent her becoming a new rival for the throne. Eleanor was, of course, hampered by her sex – she was female and it was unlikely that anyone at this time would seriously consider her claim. She would remain in prison for the rest of her life, dying in 1241 during the reign of Henry III. The succession now continued anew in the line of King John and from the succession of Henry III it was the king's eldest son who succeeded him, if he had one. Remarkably, with the accession of Henry III the throne passed from father to eldest son a total of four times. Henry was succeeded by his eldest son, Edward I, in 1272; Edward I by his eldest son, Edward II, in 1307; while Edward II, although the first monarch to be deposed since the Conquest, was succeeded by his eldest son, Edward III, in 1327.

By April 1290, the finer points of primogeniture, such as the ability of females to inherit or the representative question, had been worked out. That month, Edward I created an entail of the throne in which he delineated the order of succession of his children. Edward decreed that his only surviving son, the not-quite-six-year-old Edward of Caernarfon and future Edward II, was his heir apparent. If Edward of Caernarfon were to die, he was to be succeeded by his own sons in order of seniority; if he had no sons, it would be his daughters in order of seniority. This was at odds with common law inheritance, which decreed that if a testator left only daughters then the inheritance would be divided between them. If Edward of Caernarfon died without any children, he would be succeeded by the king's eldest daughter, Eleanora, or her heirs, male and female. If Eleanora died without heirs, she was to be succeeded by her younger sister, Joanna of Acre, and her heirs and so on. Edward was thus stating that females could inherit the throne in order of seniority in the event that there were no direct male descendants and that a representative took precedence over a cadet, whether the heir is male or female.[22]

There were other important developments regarding the succession during this period. In 1254 Henry III had the Lord Edward, the future Edward I, created Earl of Chester, a title that now came to be inherited by the king's eldest son and heir. In 1282 Edward I conquered Wales and in 1301 he bestowed it on his son and heir, Edward of Caernarfon, with the title of Prince of Wales. The title has been borne by the heir apparent ever since, with some exceptions. Prince Edward, when he became king, did not grant the title to his heir, Edward III, but Edward III would grant it to his eldest son, Edward of Woodstock, the Black Prince. The heir is not Prince of Wales from birth but is created so by the monarch, and it has become custom to grant the title to the eldest son and heir along with the dukedom of Chester. As a female could never be an heir apparent they were never granted the title Princess of Wales, which was instead assigned to the wife of the prince.

Edward I's reign also saw the end of the troublesome interregnum, the lawless time between the death of the old king and the crowning of the next. Edward I was on crusade at the time of Henry III's death but his right to the throne was never contested and his reign was considered to have begun the day after his father's death. In the event, Edward did not return to England until 1274. The conflict known as the Second Barons' War, which raged during the reign of Henry III, also saw the beginnings of Parliament, which would over time begin to exert an influence over the succession, culminating in the Glorious Revolution and the birth of constitutional monarchy at the end of the seventeenth century.

The wider terms of Edward I's entail did not come into play. Edward I died in 1307 and was succeeded by Edward of Caernarfon as Edward II. In 1327, after an inglorious reign, the unfortunate Edward II was deposed by his wife, Queen Isabella, the 'She-wolf of France', and her lover, Roger Mortimer, 1st Earl of March, who placed Edward and Isabella's eldest son, the fourteen-year-old Edward III, on the throne in his stead.

7

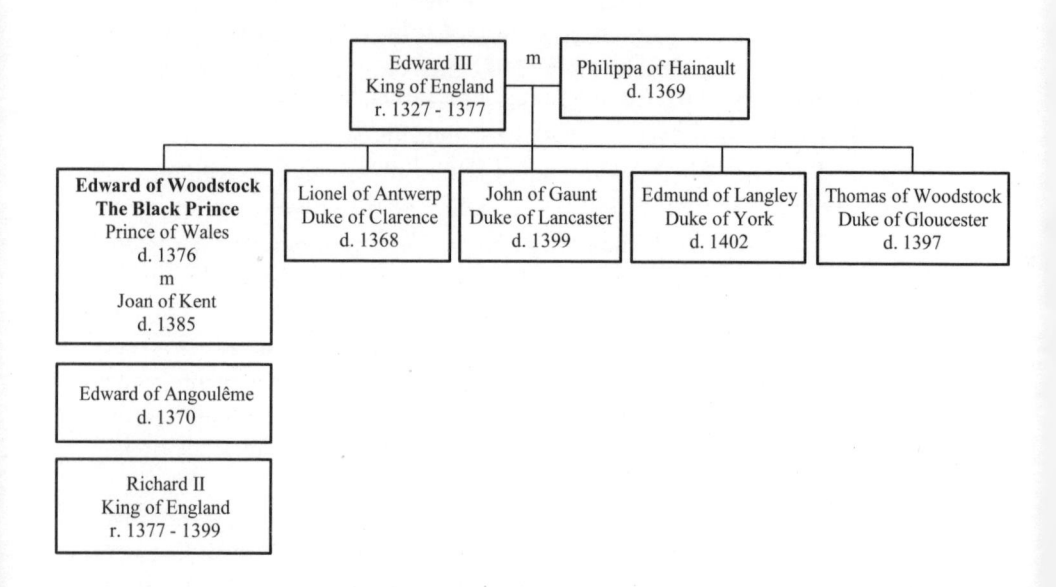

Edward of Woodstock, the Black Prince

```
                    Edward III      m    Philippa of Hainault
                  King of England            d. 1369
                   r. 1327 - 1377
```

- **Edward of Woodstock, The Black Prince**, Prince of Wales, d. 1376, m Joan of Kent d. 1385
- Lionel of Antwerp, Duke of Clarence, d. 1368
- John of Gaunt, Duke of Lancaster, d. 1399
- Edmund of Langley, Duke of York, d. 1402
- Thomas of Woodstock, Duke of Gloucester, d. 1397

- Edward of Angoulême d. 1370
- Richard II, King of England, r. 1377 - 1399

Edward of Woodstock, Prince of Wales, better known to posterity as the Black Prince, was in the thick of battle, parrying blows and dealing them back in kind. He was only sixteen years old and this, the Battle of Crécy, was his first pitched battle. He knew that his father, King Edward III, would be watching him intently and expecting great feats of arms. The enemy, however, was relentless – when those in the front line were killed, wounded or exhausted they were replaced by fresher men and the Black Prince and his companions were in danger of being overwhelmed. Still, it was with some reluctance that the prince and other generals sent Sir Thomas of Norwich to the king to beg him to come to his son's aid.

'Is my son dead or hurt or on the earth felled?' the king enquired.[1] Sir Thomas replied that he was not but that he was hard pressed by his enemies. '[R]eturn to him, and to them that sent you hither, and say to them that they send no more to me for any adventure that falleth, as long as my son is alive,' the king retorted, 'and also say to them that they suffer him this day to win his spurs; for if God be pleased, I will this journey be his and the honour thereof, and to them that be about him.'[2]

The messenger returned and told the prince of his father's words. Instead of discouraging the young prince and his comrades, the reply emboldened them to greater endeavours. 'They fought better than ever and must have performed great feats of arms,' states the chronicler Jean Froissart, 'for they remained in possession of the ground with honour.'[3]

Birth and Early Life

Edward of Woodstock, the eldest son and heir of King Edward III and his queen, Philippa of Hainault, was born on 15 June 1330 at the palace of Woodstock in Oxfordshire. He was baptised by Henry Burghersh, Archbishop of Lincoln and named Edward in honour of his father. 'Edward' was an Anglo-Saxon name but it had been brought back into use by King Henry III, who revered the former Anglo-Saxon king and saint, Edward the Confessor.

Edward's birth acted as a catalyst for his seventeen-year-old father to finally take the reins of power for himself. Edward III had been King of England for the past three years following the deposition of his father, Edward II, but he was king in name and not in deed. The country was run by his mother, Queen Isabella, and her grasping lover, Roger Mortimer, the self-created Earl of March. Mortimer and Isabella used their power to enrich themselves with land and money, signed an unpopular peace treaty with Scotland, probably had Edward II murdered and had Edward's uncle Edmund, Earl of Kent executed for conspiring to free the former king. One day, in October 1330, Edward and his supporters entered Nottingham Castle via a secret passage. The young king surprised Isabella and Mortimer in their bedchamber and had Mortimer arrested. He was tried by Parliament, found guilty of treason and hanged at Tyburn on 29 November. Isabella was permitted to retire to her estates, where she died in 1358.

Baby Edward, meanwhile, was brought up in his mother's household. He is noted as having a nurse by the name of Joan de Oxenford and a rocker called Matilda de Plumton, both of whom the king rewarded with annual pensions in 1336.[4] When Edward left the nursery he was placed under the tutelage of Dr Walter Burley, an Oxford scholar and astrologer who also served as Queen Philippa's almoner.[5] He was the first heir apparent to be granted the traditional titles of Prince of Wales, Earl of Chester and Duke of Cornwall, which have been borne ever since by the heir apparent. He was created Earl of Chester in 1333, Duke of Cornwall in 1337 (the first time that a dukedom had been created in England) and Prince of Wales in 1343.

Edward grew up in a country at war. His father rekindled the conflict with Scotland that had been instigated by his grandfather Edward I, 'the Hammer of the Scots', and disastrously lost by Edward II at Bannockburn. Edward III took advantage of a dispute over the occupancy of the Scottish throne by supporting the claim of Edward Balliol and defeated the Scottish army at Halidon Hill on 19 July 1333. The young King David II, son of King Robert the Bruce, was forced to take shelter in France and sought the aid of King Philip VI. France and Scotland had entered into the 'Auld Alliance' against

England during the time of Edward I and David now renewed it, straining relations between England and France.

Prince Edward was alerted to the dangers of war in 1335 when rumours circulated of an imminent French invasion of England. Edward III, fearing for his son's safety, sent an order to the Black Prince's steward, William de Sancto Omero, and his treasurer, Master John de Burnham, to escort the five-year-old prince to Nottingham Castle: 'On account of news which has reached the king touching him and the state of his realm, he wishes the earl to be brought to some safe place, to stay there until further order.'[6] The invasion failed to materialise but it must have been a frightening experience for the young prince when he was uprooted and rushed into hiding.

The eight-year-old Edward was left as regent or Keeper of the Realm while his father went to wage war with France in July 1338.[7] The previous year, King Philip VI had confiscated Gascony, the last remnant of the Angevin Empire. Edward's regency was only a nominal role as the real work was carried out by a regency council that included John Stratford, Archbishop of Canterbury. It was the job of the council to raise funds for the war effort and in July 1338 Edward presided over a parliament at Northampton where a grant of wool was made by the people to aid the king.

Edward III's first campaign proved an expensive failure, but in 1340 he staked a claim to the throne of France that would spark off the Hundred Years War and would not be relinquished by successive monarchs until the reign of George III. Edward's claim came by right of his mother, Queen Isabella, who was the elder sister of King Charles IV of France. Charles IV, the last of Isabella's brothers, had died in 1328 without an heir, causing a succession crisis. Isabella had pressed Edward's claim at the time but Charles had previously enacted the Salic law, an ancient rule which prevented females from inheriting the throne or transmuting their claim to their children. As such, Philip of Valois, the eldest male cousin of Charles IV, succeeded as King Philip VI, ushering in the Valois dynasty.

Edward would lead a further two campaigns in France during which he left the Black Prince as Keeper of the Realm. At the end of the third campaign in 1343, Edward signed a three-year peace treaty with Philip. He spent the ensuing time planning a new campaign in France which he launched in 1346. This time, the Black Prince would not be left to look after the kingdom in his absence. The prince was now sixteen years old and Edward considered him old enough to join the war and earn his spurs on the battlefield.

Crécy

King Edward had initially planned an expedition to Gascony but contrary winds drove the fleet back to Portsmouth. Sir Godfrey Harcourt, a French exile who had found refuge at the English court, recommended that the king launch an attack on Normandy instead, which was left virtually undefended as most of the French knights were at the siege of Aiguillon. Edward agreed and, meeting with favourable winds, he and the Black Prince landed unopposed at the port of St-Vaast-la-Hogue in the Cotentin on 12 July. There, on the crest of a hill, Edward knighted the prince on the eve of his first campaign. The prince in return bestowed the honour on many other young knights.

King Edward's tactic was to launch a *chevauchée*, a devastating raid across enemy territory, in order to draw Philip into battle. The prince, although untested in battle, was given the honour of commanding the vanguard of the army which would lead the way through the hostile lands. He was accompanied by more experienced soldiers, including Thomas Beauchamp, Earl of Warwick, who had been made marshal of the army, and William de Bohun, Earl of Northampton.

On 26 July, the English came before Caen, the final resting place of William the Conqueror, which was defended by Grand Constable of France Raoul, Count of Eu, the chamberlain Tancarville and some knights, men-at-arms and citizens. When the English approached, the French lost their nerve and retreated across a bridge located in the middle of the city, which they held against the enemy. The English archers showered the French with arrows from the banks while the men-at-arms attacked the fortifications at the bridge. The English broke through and proceeded to pillage the city, capturing 100 knights as well as Tancarville and the Count of Eu. A knight of the Black Prince's retinue seized Tancarville, 'so that he is my lord's prisoner'.[8]

After resting a few days, the army headed towards Rouen where King Philip was positioned with an army. The French king ordered the bridge near Rouen to be destroyed to prevent their crossing and the English were forced to march along the left side of the bank to find a passage across the Seine. On 14 August they arrived at Poissy, near Paris, where they stopped to fix a bridge and then marched south towards the Somme. At Airaines, King Edward dispatched men to find a crossing over the river Somme who discovered that all the bridges had been destroyed. Philip, meanwhile, had arrived at nearby Amiens and hoped to force Edward's army into a corner between the Somme and the Seine. Realising the precariousness of their position, the English headed towards Abbeville where Edward had been notified of the existence of a ford at Blanchetaque. They found the ford barred by an army on the opposite side, led by Gondomar du Fay, but they soon defeated them and crossed over. The French army, meanwhile, turned to Abbeville to cross the bridge there.

Edward and the Black Prince arrived near the town of Crécy in Ponthieu aware that battle was inevitable. They quickly found a favourable spot on a hillside and took up position. Edward arranged the army into three battles. The prince was given command of the van but was once again supported by the more experienced Earl of Warwick, while the Earl of Northampton was given command of the rear and the king the main.

On the morning of the battle the prince joined his father in hearing mass and taking Holy Communion. Afterwards, the army was ordered to arm and take up position on the battlefield. There is some debate over the army's deployment. The historian W. M. Ormrod suggests that the king and his battle were stood to the rear of the army while the vanguard, led by the prince, and rearguard formed up in front, flanked by two triangular wings of archers.[9] The English were all on foot and their horses and carts were penned in behind them.

Philip ordered his own battle lines and approached from Abbeville. The front ranks of the army were taken up by Genoese crossbowmen, followed by cavalry. Four scouts recommended that the king rest his troops and launch an attack the following day, but the impetuous army was eager for battle and they pressed on against the king's wishes until they came in sight of the enemy. Philip did his best to arrange his troops and then ordered the Genoese crossbowmen to begin the battle.

The trumpets blared and the Genoese crossbowmen entered the fray, shooting their bolts at the English. The prince, from his position in the front line, watched as the bolts flew towards them but fell short of their mark. The English archers replied in kind, felling many of the crossbowmen amid a shower of arrows 'so thick that it seemed snow'.[10] The crossbowmen turned to flee but many were crushed to death when the French cavalry, led by the Count of Alençon and Count of Flanders, decided to charge the enemy without regard for the Genoese in front. The cavalry fared little better. The few that were not hit by the archers' arrows and reached the van found the prince and his men waiting.

The prince fought manfully. He 'pierced horses and laid low their riders, shook helmets and broke off lances, and skilfully avoided blows aimed at himself'.[11] The prince and the front line did not give in and they repeatedly took the onslaught of the enemy, who led fifteen different charges over the course of the battle. The prince remained at his station and became so wearied that he was eventually forced to fight kneeling down until he was saved by his standard bearer. At one point came the famous moment when the prince and other lords sent word to the king to bring help. According to Froissart, the king refused, only offering to interfere if the prince were dead, and bade him to earn his spurs. The chronicler Geoffrey le Baker, however, offers the more plausible story that the king sent the Bishop of Durham with twenty knights to his son's aid. On arriving at the front of the army they discovered the prince and the rest of his men leaning on their swords to catch their breath, the enemy having temporarily retreated.[12] The battle continued until dusk when the French finally fled the field, including King Philip, who had been hit in the face with an arrow. Counted among the dead was the blind king John of Bohemia, whose badge of an ostrich feather and motto *'ich dien'* (I serve) was afterwards appropriated by the prince in his honour. This still constitutes the badge of the Prince of Wales today.

The Battle of Crécy was a huge victory for the English. As well as the King of Bohemia, there lay dead on the field the King of Mallorca, the Duke of Lorraine and the counts of Alençon, Flanders and Blois as well as around 1,542 knights and squires. Much was made of the prince's conduct by contemporaries. The chronicler Henry Knighton calls him the 'boldest of knights in battle', while the admiring Geoffrey le Baker writes that '[h]e gave an example to all his men of the right way to fight'.[13] Knighton also suggests that it was the prince who felled the kings of Bohemia and Mallorca. There is no doubt much eulogising in the chroniclers' account of the prince's actions but he was undoubtedly a brave and skilled warrior, fighting tirelessly in the front ranks of the army at the tender age of sixteen. The prince would take the lessons he learned from this battle and apply them with brilliant effect at the battles of Poitiers and Nájera, which would cement his legendary reputation.

The next morning another French battle appeared and the English vanguard, possibly including the prince, was sent out and defeated them. The victorious King Edward's next move was to lay siege to the town of Calais. Located on the French coast directly opposite Dover, Calais would provide the English with a base for future campaigns. The siege began on 4 September and lasted nearly a whole year. In 1347, Philip arrived with an army to relieve it but, fearing a repeat of the humiliation of Crécy, he left the town to its own defences. On 3 August 1347 the town surrendered. It would remain an English possession until its loss in 1558 during the reign of Queen Mary I. Shortly after, Pope Clement VI succeeded in mediating peace between the two monarchs and a treaty was ratified on 28 September to last until 11 June 1348. The following month, King Edward and the prince returned to England.

The Order of the Garter and The Black Death

The prince and his father returned home as heroes. '[I]t seemed to the English people that the sun broke forth after a long cloudy season, by reason both of the great plenty of all things, and remembrance of the late glorious victories.'[14] It was at this time that King Edward founded the Order of the Garter, of which the prince was a founding member. The date of the order's creation is unknown, although it is usually stated to have been founded in 1348. A chapel for the order was constructed at Windsor Castle where a feast was to be held every year on 23 April, St George's Day, in a nod to the order's patron saint. The order adopted a garter as its symbol and a myth would later surround this device. It was said that the Black Prince's future wife, Joan of Kent, then Countess of Salisbury, was dancing with the king at a ball when her garter dropped down her leg on to the floor. The gallant Edward III picked up the garter and affixed it to his own leg, declaring *Honi soit qui mal y pense*, or 'Shame to him who thinks evil', which would become the order's motto.

While the king and prince celebrated their glorious victory at Crécy and Calais with feasts, dances and jousts, the country was devastated by the Black Death, which killed up to half the population. Counted among its casualties was the prince's sister, Joan, who had been on her way to marry Pedro, the heir apparent to the kingdom of Castile in Spain, a figure who would later play a decisive role in the prince's life.

Battles of Calais and Winchelsea (1350)

The prince's next expedition was to accompany his father in foiling a French plot to seize Calais. Calais had been left under the command of Aimeric Pavia, a Lombard mercenary captain of dubious loyalty. Pavia was approached by a French knight, Geoffrey de Charny, who offered him 20,000 crowns if he would surrender the castle and town of Calais to him on the morning of 1 January 1350. Aimeric agreed but he soon developed cold feet and sent a letter to King Edward informing him of the plot. Edward ordered Pavia to continue with the scheme and at the end of December he secretly crossed over the sea along with the prince, Roger Mortimer, 2nd Earl of March and a force of 300 men-at-arms and 600 archers. On the night of 31 December the prince and king concealed themselves within the castle while Geoffrey de Charny, oblivious to their presence, arrived outside the town. He dispatched men to deliver the money to Pavia and take possession of the castle. Pavia admitted the men into the castle and led them to the keep. Upon opening the door the French were surprised by the king, the prince and 200 men-at-arms waiting inside. The French immediately surrendered and were imprisoned.

Geoffrey de Charny, oblivious to Pavia's double-crossing, was waiting for his men to return when the king, prince and others suddenly emerged from the Boulogne gate on horseback. Geoffrey had little choice but to fight. The English carried the victory, and Geoffrey and his men were made prisoners.

That summer, the prince joined his father in a naval engagement against Castile, then allies of the French. Castilian sailors had captured and sunk ten merchant ships transporting wine from Bordeaux to England and killed all those they found on board. When the king heard this he amassed a fleet at Sandwich to deal with them. The prince had command of his own ship and he was accompanied by his third surviving brother, the ten-year-old John of Gaunt, Earl of Richmond, on his first military outing.

The Spanish, who had taken port at Sluys in Flanders, were warned of the English fleet that waited to intercept them but instead of turning back they chose to hire mercenaries to bolster their numbers and then set out, undeterred, towards Calais. The English fleet calmly awaited their arrival off the coast of Winchelsea, listening to minstrels and relaxing, when at about four in the afternoon the lookouts spotted the much larger Spanish ships bearing down on them.

The English ships took up formation and battle commenced. Naval battles in medieval times were not like those of the eighteenth century where ships blasted each other with cannon. Knights would endeavour to board enemy ships by using grappling hooks and then fight hand to hand while archers swept the decks with arrows. During the battle, the prince's ship was grappled by a much larger Spanish vessel. The Spanish ship's extra height gave its sailors the advantage of being able to unleash their crossbow bolts down upon the prince's crew and to throw deadly missiles to make holes in the ship. The prince's ship suffered much damage and was quickly taking on water. The sailors got to work, endeavouring to empty the ship of water before it sank. When all looked lost, Henry Grosmont, Duke of Lancaster came to the rescue. Grappling his ship to the other side of the Spanish vessel, he boarded it and captured its men. The prince, John of Gaunt and the surviving crew managed to climb aboard the Spanish ship just as their own disappeared beneath the waves.

The battle continued until nightfall and the English were victorious, capturing seventeen ships. They rested the night and hoped to continue the battle in the morning, but as they slept the remaining twenty-seven Spanish ships limped away.

Raid into France

King Philip VI died in August 1350 and was succeeded by his eldest son, King John II. The truce with France that had been agreed in 1347 had been continuously extended while both sides attempted to come to a more lasting settlement, but by June 1355 negotiations had failed and Edward determined once again to invade France.

That same year, King Edward had been visited by the Gascon Jean de Grailly, Captal de Buch, who requested that the prince be sent to Gascony to lead the Gascons. At a parliament at Westminster it was agreed that the prince would head an expedition into the territory, accompanied by the earls of Warwick, Suffolk, Salisbury and Oxford, along with 1,000 men-at-arms, 2,000 archers and many Welsh. On 10 July the prince was appointed king's lieutenant in Gascony, giving him power to make treaties, and on 4 August he was given the right to receive homage from the Gascons in the king's name.

The prince sailed from Plymouth on 9 September and he landed at Bordeaux where he was joyfully received by the Gascons. At a council meeting the Gascon nobles complained of the ravages of Jean, Count of Armagnac, the French king's lieutenant of Languedoc, who had been attacking the king's supporters in the duchy. It was agreed that they would lead a *chevauchée* across the count's lands to force him into battle. The expedition began on 5 October and the army marched through friendly territory until they reached the town of Arouille on 11 October, where they unfurled their banners and separated into three battles. The vanguard, consisting of 3,000 men-at-arms, was placed under the command of the Earl of Warwick; the main, under the command of the prince, had 7,000 men; while the rear, under the Earl of Suffolk, had 4,000. The campaign lasted eight weeks, during which time the prince took castles, burnt towns and laid waste the countryside all around. The frightened population fled in their wake, leaving monasteries and towns abandoned and their belongings at the mercy of the ravaging army. Eventually, the prince arrived outside the city of Toulouse where the Count of Armagnac was stationed with a large army. The prince halted for two days to see if the count would fight, but when the latter made no move he resumed the march, taking towns and castles and amassing great riches. At Narbonne the prince met the first show of resistance when the townsmen attacked them, but they were soon overcome.

The prince later received word that Armagnac had left Toulouse and was on their trail. He decided to turn back and give battle but before he could reach the enemy, Armagnac retreated to Toulouse. Realising that the French would not give battle, the prince returned laden with riches to Bordeaux, where he spent the winter.

Although the prince had failed to bring his enemies into battle, his first campaign as a general was a huge success. John Wingfield reported in a newsletter that 'since this war began against the king of France, there was never such loss nor such destruction as hath been in this raid'.[15] The lands and towns which they destroyed were said to be responsible for providing the King of France with more money and resources to perpetuate the war than half of the kingdom of France.

Poitiers

On 6 July the following year, the prince set out on a second campaign with the intention of marching north through France to reach Brittany, where he would join forces with Henry Grosmont, Duke of Lancaster. The prince passed through the Agenais, Limousin, Auvergne and Berry, burning towns and ravaging the countryside as he went. The chronicler Geoffrey le Baker paints the prince as the consummate commander, sending out scouts, planning the route of the march and seeing to the moving of the camp. He had the camp guarded at night and would ride between the van, main and rear camps to ensure that they were not exposed to danger through lack of order.[16]

When he reached Vierzon, the prince learned from his scouts that King John was at Orléans amassing an army. Undeterred, the prince laid siege to and took the town of Romorantin. King John, meanwhile, moved along the Loire to Blois. The prince attempted to cross the Loire to join forces with the Duke of Lancaster, whose campfires he could see in the distance, but he was prevented from doing so by the swollen river and the fact that the French king had destroyed the bridges. Instead, he travelled east along the river until he came near to Tours, John pursuing him all the time, and the two armies eventually met near Poitiers.

The prince took position on the slope of a hill in front of which ran a large hedge. The only entrance to the hill was through an opening in the hedge, so the French would have to use it to reach them. The prince placed the Earl of Warwick in charge of the vanguard, the Earl of Salisbury in charge of the rear while he himself took command of the main. He lined the back of the hedge with archers, ready to rain down arrows upon the approaching army. The French army vastly outnumbered the English, who had 4,000 men-at-arms, 1,000 soldiers and 2,000 archers against 8,000 French men-at-arms. Among the French force was a band of 200 Scots captained by the veteran knight Sir William Douglas. He had fought many battles against the English and was well acquainted with their battle tactics. He advised John to deploy his troops on foot and the French king acquiesced, leaving 500 cavalry who were to be used to crush the archers underfoot.

The French had arranged their forces in three horizontal lines with two wings of cavalry in front of the first line. These wings were captained by Jean de Clermont and Arnoul d'Audrehem, the marshals of France. It was their aim to push through the hedge and destroy the prince's archers. The first line, captained by the Dauphin Charles, would then advance, followed by the second line of the Duke of Orléans and the last by King John himself.

At the beginning of the battle the cavalry under Clermont and Audrehem galloped towards the English but the archers let loose their arrows and the cavalry was soon routed; Clermont was killed and Audrehem taken prisoner. The division under the dauphin then marched up the slope and fought hand to hand with the English, but they were soon overcome and also fled the field in panic, falling upon the Duke of Orléans' division, which also took flight. The English army did not pursue them as this would mean giving up their tactical position, instead awaiting the arrival of King John, who then moved with his standard bearers onto the field. The prince ordered his standard bearer to advance and his troops, who had been kept in reserve, moved against the French. The prince, 'with a roar ... was upon the Frenchmen. Hewing them down with his sharp sword, he cut through their spears, repelled their blows ... and taught the enemy how furious is the desperation in the breast of a man clothed for battle.'[17]

The prince, meanwhile, had sent a separate division under the Captal de Buch, along with sixty men and 100 archers, to come around the back of the French. Fearing they had been surrounded, the French fled in panic, but King John remained on the field. The prince made for John's position, the king's standard bearers were killed and the king was forced to surrender and taken captive.

The prince's first battle in the role of general had been a resounding success, changing the tide of the war.

The Treaty of Brétigny

The gallant prince treated his royal prisoner with all the honour his royal dignity and the rules of chivalry dictated. On the evening after the battle, he entertained and fed the king and other captured nobles in his lodgings, serving at the tables himself. He was courteous in victory, applauding King John for his prowess on the battlefield. The following day, the army began the long journey, laden down with all the booty they had won, towards Bordeaux. When they arrived they were given a hero's welcome by the citizens and the clergy. The prince spent the winter there in celebration, sending his valet, Geoffrey Hamelyn, to England to present the king with John's helmet and coat of mail.[18]

The following spring the prince assembled a fleet to convey him and his royal prisoner into England. The prince made a truce on 23 March 1357 with the regency council that had been set up in the wake of John's capture to last until Easter 1359. The prince and King John arrived at Plymouth on 5 May and travelled to London where King Edward had put on a sumptuous welcome. King John progressed through the city to Westminster on a white horse while the prince humbly accompanied him on a smaller black horse. King John was kept in comfortable confinement at the Savoy and then at Windsor. He was treated well, being permitted to go hunting and hawking in the forests around Windsor, was often entertained by King Edward and Queen Philippa and was granted the liberty to converse with other captives.

In May 1359 the conditions for the king's release were hammered out between King John, King Edward, the prince and the Duke of Lancaster. John agreed to pay 1,000,000 marks and cede all of Aquitaine, Anjou, Normandy and Calais (in essence the entire Angevin Empire), in return for which King Edward would renounce his claim to the French throne. The proposal was sent into France but John's eldest son, the Dauphin Charles, acting as regent in his father's absence, refused to accede to such harsh terms. King Edward responded by launching another campaign in France, with the intention of having himself crowned King of France at Rheims, the traditional venue for French coronations. He was accompanied once again by the prince and three of his other sons, Lionel of Antwerp, John of Gaunt and Edmund of Langley. They laid siege to Rheims over Christmas, but it was successfully defended by John of Craon, Archbishop of Rheims, with many knights and squires. On 11 January 1360, Edward decided to lift the siege and, with the prince and Duke of Lancaster, headed into Burgundy where he forced Philip, Duke of Burgundy to sign a three-year truce and pay 200,000 florins.

The English then headed towards Paris where the dauphin was stationed. After the dauphin failed to materialise, after five days they headed for Beauce, from where Edward intended to head to Brittany in order to resupply and make a fresh attack on Paris. The dauphin and regency council, meanwhile, decided to sue for peace and sent envoys to discuss terms. Edward was against peace, but the Duke of Lancaster advised him to take it. A violent hailstorm erupted and, taking it as a sign from God, Edward finally acquiesced. On 8 May at the village of Brétigny, near Chartres, they came to an agreement. Edward was to give up his claim to the throne of France as well as to Normandy, Anjou and Maine, while he would be given full sovereignty over Aquitaine (restored to its original extent), Ponthieu and Calais, meaning he would no longer hold them as a vassal of the French king. King John was to be returned and King Edward was to be given a ransom of 3,000,000 gold ecus, to be paid over six years. After the first payment, King John would be released and then hostages given in lieu of payment of the rest. The prince and dauphin, as eldest sons of their respective fathers, were made to swear to uphold the truce. On their return to London, the king, prince and others celebrated with King John, after which they took him to Dover and on 8 July the prince escorted him across the sea to Calais. Shortly after, King Edward travelled to Calais where he and John ratified the treaty on 24 October.

The first instalment of 600,000 florins was duly paid and hostages, including the king's son the Duke of Anjou, were handed over. The prince and Duke of Lancaster conducted King John to Saint-Omer where he entertained them for three days and then took his leave, following which the prince returned to England.

Prince of Aquitaine

On 10 October 1361, the prince, now aged thirty-one, married the great beauty Joan, Countess of Kent, at Windsor. Joan, better known to posterity as 'the Fair Maid of Kent', was the daughter of Edmund, Earl of Kent, the half-brother of King Edward II who had been executed on the orders of Roger Mortimer, 1st Earl of March, in 1330. She and the prince were therefore both descended from Edward I and were cousins. The chronicler Jean Froissart opines that the marriage was made for reasons of love. This is likely so as the marriage brought with it no great political advantages as would the usual marriage of the heir apparent to a foreign bride. After Joan's father's death she had been brought up in the household of Queen Philippa, where she had no doubt caught the prince's eye. In 1347, she had married William Montagu, Earl of Salisbury, but, somewhat scandalously, a knight named Sir Thomas Holland later claimed that he had previously married Joan in a clandestine ceremony when she was fifteen or sixteen and that they had consummated the marriage.[19] The case was brought before the pope, who found in favour of Holland, and Joan's marriage to Montagu was declared void by a papal bull dated 13 November 1349. Joan would bear Holland four children before his death on 28 December 1360. Once Holland was dead, the prince spotted his opportunity and pounced; he found Joan to be receptive to his advances. As the two were related, a papal dispensation had to be sought and was soon granted. Although Joan was two years older than the prince, she had proven herself fertile and it was therefore likely that she would soon give birth to an heir to the throne.

After the marriage, the king decided to send the prince and princess into Aquitaine to rule the newly restored principality and Edward was created Prince of Aquitaine on 19 July 1362. He was granted near-sovereign powers and was allowed to receive the homage of the barons and confirm privileges, although King Edward still retained the sovereignty. The prince agreed to pay his father an ounce of gold every year in recognition of his subordinate status.

In February 1363, the prince and Joan travelled to Aquitaine and set up a sumptuous court at Bordeaux where they became known for their extravagant lifestyle. The Chandos Herald tells us that 'since Christ was born no-one ever lived in such state and honour'.[20] He asserts that there were daily more than eighty knights at the prince's table and that he often held jousts and feasts at Bordeaux and Angoulême. He was liberal to his friends and began to reward them with offices but, we are assured, he also took pains to reward some of the natives as well so as not to show favouritism. On 27 January 1365, Joan bore the couple's first child at Angoulême, a son and heir named Edward.

Nájera

In the summer of 1366, Pedro I, King of Castile arrived at the prince's court. Pedro is known to historians by the epithet of 'the Cruel' as his reign saw a spate of assassinations with a casualty list including some of his half-brothers, his stepmother and possibly his own wife, Blanche of Bourbon, the sister-in-law of King Charles V of France. As a result, Pedro had recently been driven out of his kingdom and replaced by his half-brother, Henry of Trastamara. He came to court to seek the prince's help in regaining the throne.

Some of the prince's council advised against helping Pedro as they saw his downfall as God's punishment for a wicked rule. The chivalrous prince, however, felt duty bound to help. Edward III and Pedro had previously formed an alliance which they were obliged to honour. More importantly, Castile was now an ally of France and its proximity to Gascony could prove problematic. By helping Pedro, the prince hoped to restore a pro-English monarch to the Castilian throne. At the urging of the Gascon nobles, he sent messengers to Edward III who commanded the prince to help their ally.

Pedro made many promises in order to garner the prince's support, including making the prince's son, Edward of Angoulême, King of Galicia and paying the wages of the prince's army once he regained his throne. However, the exiled Pedro had no money and the prince foolishly agreed to loan him some in good faith. He melted down some of his plate to raise funds and was also sent money from England. Alliances were made with King Charles II of Navarre, a petty kingdom wedged between France and Spain, whose lands they would have to pass through to enter Castile.

While preparations were being made for the expedition, Joan gave birth to a second son, Richard of Bordeaux, the future Richard II, on 6 January 1367. A few days later the prince travelled to Dax where his numbers were swelled by the arrival of his brother John of Gaunt, who had brought with him an English army. Gaunt had now become Duke of Lancaster in right of his wife, Blanche, the daughter of Henry Grosmont, Duke of Lancaster, following the latter's death by plague in 1361. The prince placed the van under Gaunt, the rear under King James of Majorca and the main under himself, Pedro and King Charles of Navarre. The combined forces made their way through the Pyrenees by way of the valley of Roncesvalles, which was made treacherous by the winter snow. By 20 February they had mustered at Pamplona on the Spanish side of the Pyrenees. From there they made their way through the straits and passages of Arruazu until they came to the town of Salvatierra. Here, the prince received word that Henry of Trastamara was advancing at the head of an army towards the town of Vittoria. Anxious for battle, the prince made haste to Vittoria and took up position. That night, King Henry's brother Don Tello made a surprise raid on the prince's camp. The commotion woke John of Gaunt, who quickly drew as many men as possible to his banner on a hillside. He was joined by the prince and they succeeded in driving off the assailants.

The following day, the prince travelled south to Viana where the army refreshed itself. Two days later they crossed the Ebro at Logroño and camped in the surrounding orchard and olive groves while King Henry arrived outside of Navarrete and set up camp. When the prince heard of this he sent the king a letter outlining his reasons for entering the kingdom and stated that he wished to reconcile the two brothers if possible. Henry spoke with his counsel and they agreed that battle should be met.

The prince rode out the next morning in battle array and halted two leagues from Henry's army, the prince's men spending the night sleeping in their armour in readiness. The following day the prince resumed the march and on reaching the crest of a hill saw the enemy positioned on the plain below. The English army dismounted and the prince prayed to God to grant him the victory. The army was separated into three battles. John of Gaunt had the vanguard, the prince the main and the King of Majorca, mounted, had the rear. In King Henry's army the van was commanded by the Frenchman Bertrand de Gueselin while Henry had the main, which was placed further back and flanked by two divisions of cavalry on either side.

The cavalry on the left was commanded by Don Tello and that on the right by the Conde de Denia.

The battle opened with the English archers letting loose a volley of arrows while the Spanish crossbowmen shot back in kind. The van under Gaunt charged the line of Bertrand de Gueselin and came to blows.

The prince, meanwhile, led an attack on Don Tello's wing, but before they had landed a single blow Don Tello and his mounted knights fled from the field. They were soon followed by the other wing under de Denia. The prince's division then turned on de Gueselin's van in order to help his brother. King Henry, in a desperate attempt to change the narrative of the battle, attempted three times to come to the van's aid but was eventually forced to take flight. The Spanish began to flee and they were pursued by the victorious army, with only the enemy vanguard remaining on the field under de Gueselin. The van was soon routed and de Gueselin himself captured. The prince had secured his second victory as a general and Pedro was restored to his throne. It would turn out to be a hollow victory for the prince, who would soon learn the fickle nature of his ally.

After the battle, the prince and Pedro travelled west to Burgos where the prince remained for a month in celebration. When the time came to leave, he reminded Pedro of his oath to pay the wages of his men. Pedro had no intention of doing so and slyly promised to pay the prince if he and the army retired to Valladolid. Seeing little choice, the prince did as asked. While they waited in vain for the money, the army was devastated by an outbreak of disease that killed many. Unfortunately, the prince himself also fell ill, possibly of dysentery. He sent men to see Pedro but the wily king held up his hands and confessed that he could not raise the money. The prince, realising that he had been duped, limped back across the Pyrenees with the remainder of the army and returned to Bordeaux. The expedition was an unmitigated disaster. The prince was left heavily in debt and, more disastrously, he would never recover from his illness. His days of leading armies and fighting were nearly over.

Limoges

The prince had to find the wages promised to his army. His solution was to order a *fouage* or hearth tax to be raised over a period of five years, at a cost of 1 livre per fire. Most of the Gascon nobles accepted the tax but some of them, including the counts of Armagnac and Albret, who were opposed to English rule, said that they were free of such exactions as they were under French overlordship. This, of course, was not true, as all of Aquitaine had been united and ceded to Edward III in the Treaty of Brétigny. The nobles agreed to go away and deliberate among themselves and return their answer by an assigned date. They took the opportunity to appeal to the new French king, Charles V, to intervene. On 25 January 1369, Charles summoned the prince to appear at court in Paris to answer his nobles' complaints. The furious prince retorted that he would come to court but at the head of an army of 60,000 men. The messengers who had brought the summons were at first granted permission to return to France but the prince changed his mind and had them thrown in prison. On hearing this, the Gascons rebelled and launched an attack on the prince's Seneschal of Rouergue, Thomas Wake.

When the prince failed to turn up on the allotted day, King Charles sent a lowly valet to Westminster who announced King Charles's defiance of the Treaty of Brétigny. On 3 June, King Edward resumed the title of King of France and declared war. In spring 1370 Charles V sent two armies into Aquitaine, one headed by Louis, Duke of Anjou and another by John, Duke of Berry, which raided into the Limousin. The Duke of Berry laid siege to Limoges, which capitulated on 21 September at the instigation of the Bishop of Limoges, John le Cros. The bishop's defection stung the prince as he had been a close friend and was godfather to Edward of Angoulême.

The prince was determined to punish the people of Limoges and duly set off at the head of an army, but he was so ill that he could not ride a horse and had to be carried in a litter. The army found that the city was too well fortified to be taken by force, so the prince employed miners to undermine the walls. When the enemy realised what the prince was doing they began to mine from the other side in a bid to stop the English, but their endeavours failed. A month passed and then all was ready. The miners set fire to the mine, causing one of the walls to collapse and form a bridge over the dyke. The Englishmen swarmed into the city, captured the gates and admitted the rest of the army. The resultant sacking of Limoges, in which 3,000 people were reported to have been killed, has blotted the prince's reputation ever since. The army slew not only the malefactors but innocent civilians, including women and children, without mercy in an orgy of destruction. 'It was great pity to see the men, women, and children, that kneeled down on their knees before the Prince for mercy; but he was so enflamed with ire that he took no heed to them, so that none was heard, but all put to death as they were met withal, and such as were nothing culpable,' the chronicler Froissart states.[21] Bishop John was pulled from his palace and brought before the furious prince who admonished him but spared his life.

There is some doubt today over whether the prince really allowed such a wholesale killing. Froissart, who usually sings the prince's praises, is the only source to report the slaughter and he is contradicted by Aquitanian chronicles that put the number of casualties at a more modest 300, roughly the size of the French garrison.[22]

Once the looting had ceased, the city was torched and the prince travelled to Cognac where he disbanded his forces. He returned to Bordeaux where he learned of the tragic death of his eldest son, the seven-year-old Edward of Angoulême. The prince's illness was by now getting worse, and his physicians advised him to return to England to recover his health. He left Aquitaine in the charge of John of Gaunt and he, Princess Joan and the young Richard of Bordeaux returned to England the following year.

Final Years

The last six years of the prince's life saw him debilitated by his illness. He watched on hopelessly as Aquitaine was lost to the French piece by piece. Several campaigns were launched to help the duchy but King Charles refused to be drawn into battle and the English armies could do little but ravage the land. In August 1372, King Edward attempted to lead an army in person and he was joined by the prince, but contrary winds meant that the expedition never reached its intended destination. By 1374, the French possessions had been whittled down to just Bordeaux and Bayonne in Gascony, and Calais. On 27 June 1375, a year-long truce was arranged between England and France by the pope.

Edward III was now growing old and senile. Queen Philippa had died in 1369 and the king was controlled by his mistress, Alice Perrers. Normally it would have fallen to the prince as heir apparent to act as regent for the king, but he was prevented from doing so by his own ill health. The king's second-eldest son, Lionel of Antwerp, Duke of Clarence, had died in 1368 and it fell to John of Gaunt, the next male in line, to take the reins of government. Gaunt's rule was unpopular and at the 'Good Parliament' of April 1376 the Commons demanded the removal of some of King Edward's closest advisers, the banishment of Alice Perrers and the appointment of a group of trustworthy nobles and prelates to assist the king.

Gaunt had become an object of suspicion for the Commons and they believed that he had designs on the throne. The death of the prince and the king would create a similar situation to that of 1199. The prince's remaining son, Richard of Bordeaux, was only nine years old while his uncle John of Gaunt was an adult in his mid-thirties. While it was generally accepted by now that a representative (i.e. Richard) took precedence over a cadet (i.e. Gaunt), rules could be broken. As we shall see in the next chapter, Gaunt may have indeed have been aiming for the throne and the prince was sufficiently alarmed to make Gaunt and the king swear to recognise Richard of Bordeaux's rights. The king later had Richard declared heir in Parliament.

The prince was by now nearing the end of his days. The sickness that had plagued him on and off for the past seven years was finally winning. He was confined to his bed at Westminster Palace where, on 7 June 1376, he drew up his will. On the following day, Sunday 8 June, he died. The day of his death happened to be the Feast of the Trinity, which he is said to have celebrated every year. He was buried in Canterbury Cathedral on 5 October in the Lady Chapel near the shrine of St Thomas Becket. The people mourned the loss and even King Charles V is said to have held obsequies for him at the Sainte Chapelle in Paris, admiring the prince's martial ability. Edward III died the following year, to be succeeded by Richard of Bordeaux as King Richard II.

For such a famous individual, the prince himself remains an elusive figure. His story was embellished in the telling and a chivalric legend grew around him during his life and after his death, making it difficult to unpick fact from fiction. To contemporaries he was 'the chief flower of chivalry of all the world'.[23] He epitomised the chivalric ideal, embodying everything a great knight was supposed to be: noble, loyal, generous, brave and courteous in victory. Today his glorious reputation is tarnished by the sack of Limoges but, as we have seen, there is reason to doubt its veracity. To the English population, who had suffered years of defeat and humiliation in war during Edward II's reign, he was a hero who for a time shone bright, one whom the chronicler Knighton regards 'as one deserving to be remembered amongst kings'.[24]

8

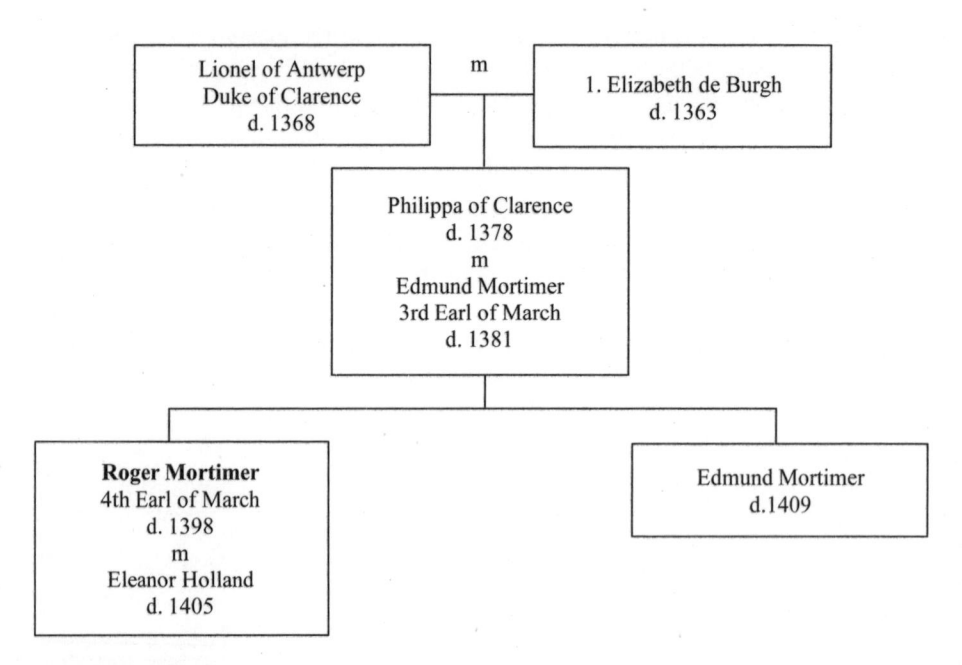

Roger Mortimer, 4th Earl of March

```
Lionel of Antwerp          m        1. Elizabeth de Burgh
Duke of Clarence                           d. 1363
    d. 1368

            Philippa of Clarence
                 d. 1378
                   m
            Edmund Mortimer
            3rd Earl of March
                 d. 1381

Roger Mortimer                      Edmund Mortimer
4th Earl of March                       d. 1409
    d. 1398
      m
 Eleanor Holland
    d. 1405
```

In late January 1398, Roger Mortimer, 4th Earl of March arrived at Shrewsbury in order to attend Parliament. He was greeted by a crowd of 20,000 people, each donning a hood coloured in his livery of red and white. They hoped that Roger, as heir presumptive to the throne, had come to deliver them from the evil exactions of the tyrannical king, Richard II. Roger was sympathetic to the people but he was in no position to defy the king. Richard had recently done away with many of his enemies at court in the 'Revenge' Parliament and he was seeking a reason to destroy Roger and seize his possessions. Roger would have to tread carefully if he wanted to return to his lands in Ireland alive.

Birth and Early Life

Roger Mortimer, 4th Earl of March, was the eldest son of Edmund Mortimer, 3rd Earl of March and his wife, Philippa of Clarence. His claim to the throne derived from his mother, Philippa, the only child and heiress of Edward III's second surviving son, Lionel of Antwerp, Duke of Clarence and his first wife, Elizabeth de Burgh.

Roger Mortimer, 4th Earl of March

On his father's side, Roger was heir to the vast estates of the Mortimer family. The Mortimers were a powerful and influential family of Welsh Marcher lords who reached their zenith during the reigns of Edward II and III. Roger Mortimer, 1st Earl of March (d. 1330) was central to the plot to overthrow Edward II, after which he ruled the country for three years at Queen Isabella's side (see above, chapter 7). He had himself created Earl of March (of Wales) during the Salisbury Parliament of 1328. After Roger's execution in 1330, his lands were attainted and the earldom of March became extinct. Roger's grandson, another Roger (d. 1360), was able to restore the family's fortunes by fighting in the Hundred Years War. He was knighted by the Black Prince and fought at the Battle of Crécy in 1346 and also took part in the rescue of Calais in 1350. In 1354, Edward III revoked the attainder against the 1st Earl and Roger became the 2nd Earl of March. He died of an illness on 26 February 1360, contracted while fighting in Burgundy. Roger had married Philippa, a daughter of William de Montacute, and their eldest son, Edmund, became 3rd Earl of March.

Edmund was only eight years old at the time of his father's death and he became a ward of the crown. The wardship of an heir was one of the feudal prerogatives enjoyed by the king when one of his tenants-in-chief died and left a minor as heir. This granted him control of the tenant's lands, allowing him to accrue the rents and profits of it for himself, as well as giving him the right to arrange or sell the heir's marriage. In May 1368, Edmund married Philippa of Clarence, only daughter of Duke Lionel, when he was sixteen and she was twelve. The marriage provided Edmund with the earldom of Ulster in Ireland as well as the Clare estates in England, which Philippa inherited from her mother. More importantly, when Duke Lionel died that same year Philippa became third in line to the throne after the Black Prince and Richard of Bordeaux according to the rules of primogeniture.

The couple's first child was a daughter, Elizabeth, who was born in 1371. Roger, their second child and heir, was born on 11 April 1374 at Usk in Monmouthshire.[1] He was baptised on 17 April by William, Bishop of Hereford and confirmed by Roger, Bishop of Llandaff, who stood as his godparent along with Thomas Horton, Abbot of Gloucester and the Prioress of Usk.[2]

No details survive of Roger's early childhood. He was joined by a second sister, Philippa, in 1375 and a brother, Edmund, in 1376. Sadly, Roger's mother died when Roger was not quite four years old. Philippa had been predeceased by the Black Prince and Edward III, making Roger heir presumptive of the new king, Richard II. In May 1380, Roger and his siblings travelled to Ireland in company with their father who had been appointed King's Lieutenant for a term of three years. It was an office that Edmund only enjoyed for a short time as he died at Cork on 27 December 1381 after contracting pneumonia while crossing a river, leaving Roger and his brother and sisters as orphans.[3]

Orphan

Roger was seven years old when his father died, and this meant that his possessions reverted to the crown until he came of age at twenty-one. The king did not receive all of the Mortimer lands. Edmund had had the foresight to grant his lands in Shropshire and the March to friends and associates with the permission of Edward III.[4] Those lands that the king did acquire were bolstered by those of Roger's grandmother, Philippa de Montacute, who passed away shortly after her son.

Once Edmund had died the vultures circled, demanding parts of the Mortimer inheritance from King Richard. Richard was still an impressionable boy and he immediately granted their requests and sent word to the chancellor, Sir Richard Scrope, to confirm the charters. Scrope refused to do so as Richard had inherited Edward III's massive debts and needed all the money he could get to pay them back. The men duly complained to the king and he had Scrope removed from office.[5] The king's council saw wisdom in Scrope's thinking, however, and in November 1382 it was ordained that the money accrued from the lordships, manors and lands of the Mortimer inheritance was to be allocated to allay the costs of the royal household.[6] However, in September 1383, the king and council gave custody of the Mortimer lands to Richard, Earl of Arundel, Thomas de Beauchamp, Earl of Warwick, Henry de Percy, Earl of Northumberland and John, Lord Nevill, for a yearly rent of £4,000.[7]

In January 1382 the seven-year-old Roger, who had been appointed Lieutenant of Ireland, was sent into the country. As he was too young to run affairs himself, it was down to his uncle Thomas Mortimer to oversee things as his deputy. On 29 March Roger was ordered to summon a parliament in the king's name, but as he was ill he did not attend the subsequent parliament in Dublin.[8] By the following July a new lieutenant, Peter de Courtenay, was appointed in his place for a period of ten years and Roger returned to England.

In December 1383 King Richard granted custody of Roger to Richard, Earl of Arundel, but in August 1384 he transferred Roger's custody and marriage rights to his half-brother Thomas Holland, Earl of Kent, for the sum of 6,000 marks.[9] Roger was later married to Holland's daughter, Eleanor, who would produce two sons, Edmund, 5th Earl of March and another Roger, as well as two daughters, Anne and Eleanor.

Heir Presumptive

Richard II would never have any children, and the identity of his heir presumptive during his reign is confused and hotly debated between historians. Edward III had a total of five sons who survived to adulthood:

Edward, the Black Prince; Lionel, Duke of Clarence; John of Gaunt, Duke of Lancaster; Edmund of Langley, Duke of York; and Thomas of Woodstock, Duke of Gloucester. By the beginning of Richard's reign both the Black Prince and Lionel were dead, but the latter was represented by his eldest grandson, Roger Mortimer. Gaunt, by his first marriage, had a son and heir, Henry of Bolingbroke, while Edmund of Langley had at this time one son, Edward, Earl of Rutland.

By the rules of primogeniture and the exemplar of Edward I's entail, Roger was Richard's heir presumptive and also what is known as the king's 'heir general' as he was descended through the female line. There is evidence that contemporaries believed Roger to be Richard's heir. The Westminster Chronicle reports that 'if (as God forbid) the king were to die childless it would be upon one of these brothers [Roger and Edmund] that the crown of England would devolve by hereditary right'.[10] However, the existence of an entail, dating from the end of the reign of Edward III, suggests that Edward III had in fact entailed the throne in the male line or in 'tail male'. The Black Prince's illness and death had caused great concern about the succession in 1376. There were fears that John of Gaunt would attempt to seize the throne from the Black Prince's son, Richard of Bordeaux, like King John before him.

In October that year, Edward III devised an entail in which he not only designated Richard as his heir but also outlined the wider order of succession in the event that Richard should die without an heir. Unlike Edward I's entail, he decreed that Richard would be succeeded by the next senior male in the direct male line, with reversion to heirs general.[11] This, of course, meant that Roger, descended from Edward III's second son but via a female, was passed over in favour of the king's next senior surviving direct male heir and would only succeed on the death of the king's sons and their sons. According to Edward III's entail, then, Richard's heir presumptive was in fact John of Gaunt, Edward III's third surviving son. This invites an intriguing possibility: after Gaunt's death in 1399, his eldest son, Henry Bolingbroke, would overthrow King Richard and usurp the throne as King Henry IV, marking the beginning of the Lancastrian dynasty. Did Henry IV succeed as he was in fact Richard's heir male?

Unfortunately, the entail is problematic. It only exists as a partly burned fifteenth-century copy, was not mentioned in any chronicles or other records, stood in direct contravention of Edward III's claim to the French throne and most inexplicably of all, was seemingly not used by Henry Bolingbroke to justify his usurpation of the throne.[12] As we shall see, Bolingbroke would seemingly base his hereditary claim on inheritance through the female line. The confusion surrounding the entail has led to speculation on whether or not the document was genuine or legal. W. M. Ormrod suggests the likely theory that the document was genuine but that it had been made at the devise of Gaunt, who at the time had ascendancy over the seriously ill Edward III.

There is no evidence, he suggests, that crown and polity even felt bound by the entail and there were questions as to whether the king had the right to make such a provision in the first place.[13] David J. Seipp, on the other hand, suggests that the entail was fake. The king could not, he suggests, change the succession rules from primogeniture to tail male as to do so would require the king to surrender the kingdom up to a feudal superior and have it regranted under the new succession pattern, something that a king, who had no feudal superior, was unable to do.[14] Whatever the reality of the entail, Edward recovered and it was seemingly suppressed or ignored, perhaps because it caused uneasiness by simply ignoring Philippa and her sons' claim without any form of consultation or consent, or perhaps as it was simply not legal for the king to do so.[15]

Richard II did not feel bound to the terms of the entail. In a parliament held at Westminster in 1385, he is said to have 'had it publicly proclaimed that the earl of March was the next heir to the crown of England after himself'.[16] Richard was eighteen at the time and he had been married to his queen, Anne of Bohemia, since 1382 but she had yet to produce an heir. Like Edward III's entail, there is also controversy among historians as to whether Richard really made this announcement. It is only mentioned in one chronicle, the *Continuatio Eulogii*, a source not known for its accuracy, which has led some historians to doubt its authenticity.[17] To confuse matters further, the capricious Richard seems to have later preferred the claims of his uncles. Roger was not given any precedence over Edward III's surviving sons in the witness list of charters, something that signified the seniority of the individuals in relation to the throne, when he appears on the lists from 1394, and Richard may have subsequently considered Gaunt and later his uncle Edmund, Duke of York to be his heir, although there is no evidence of them being officially declared as such.[18] What right Richard had in doing so is unclear, although he would prove to be a proud and tyrannical king who likely considered himself able to dictate the succession as he wished.

A Troubled Reign

Richard II's reign was to prove tumultuous. Richard was surrounded by a group of young favourites, including Michael de la Pole and Robert de Vere, Earl of Oxford, who became his closest advisers and on whom he heaped lands and titles. Pole was created chancellor in 1383 and Duke of Suffolk in 1385 while de Vere was made Marquess of Ireland (a title unheard of in England) in 1385 and then Duke of Ireland in 1386, the first person to be created a duke outside of the royal family.

This blatant favouritism rankled with the rest of the nobility, as did the king and his favourites' policy towards the Hundred Years War. Suffolk advocated peace with France and Scotland while much of the nobility, led by Richard's uncle Thomas of Woodstock, Duke of Gloucester, the fifth and youngest son of Edward III, were for continuing it. In the Wonderful Parliament of 1386 the Commons demanded the removal of Suffolk as chancellor. Suffolk was arrested and Thomas Arundel, Bishop of Ely was set up as chancellor in his place. A body of eleven nobles known as the Lords Appellant was then appointed to reform the government and run it in the king's name. The proud and haughty Richard was unwilling to have the royal prerogative undermined and on 26 August the following year he convened a council of judges at Nottingham Castle who declared that it was illegal for the king to be forced to appoint a council against his will and for the Commons to impeach members of his council. Richard summoned Gloucester and Arundel to London where he intended to seize them, but the earls were forewarned and took to arms. Amongst the earl's supporters were John of Gaunt's son and heir, Henry Bolingbroke, and Roger Mortimer's uncle, Thomas. They confronted the royal army, headed by de Vere, at Radcot Bridge on 19 December. De Vere fled before the battle began and travelled overseas where he remained for the rest of his life, dying in a hunting accident in Louvain in 1395. The victorious Lords Appellant marched on London and Richard agreed to remove the 'traitors' who surrounded him. On 3 February 1388, the 'Merciless' Parliament began where many of Richard's favourites were condemned to death or exiled. Michael de la Pole was not amongst those judged as he had fled to France where he died in 1389. The country was then run by the appellants. On 3 May 1389, however, Richard summoned a council meeting where, now twenty-two, he declared himself of age to rule. He dismissed chancellor Arundel, Gloucester and Warwick from the council and introduced men of his own choosing.[19]

Lieutenant of Ireland

In 1392, the eighteen-year-old Roger Mortimer was once again appointed Lieutenant of Ireland, although he did not take up his position for a further two years. In February 1394 he was granted full livery of his lands, 'notwithstanding that he is not of full age ... the king having received his homage and retained him to stay with him for life'.[20] His castles and mansions had been well maintained during his minority, his farms were abounding in cattle and he had a treasury of 20,000 marks.[21]

Now he was fast approaching manhood, Roger became a person of interest to the king's enemies. Froissart, a source not known for accuracy, tells us that Thomas, Duke of Gloucester plotted to dethrone Richard and place Roger on the throne. He duly arranged a meeting with Roger where he disclosed his plans. Roger was perturbed by the idea and made his excuses, saying he would consider it. The plot was heard of no more, as he went to Ireland on 1 October 1394 in company with the king and never saw Gloucester again.

The English position in Ireland had been in a state of decline for many years. The wars with France and Scotland had meant that Ireland had been neglected and the native Irish chiefs were reconquering lost land. Due to a string of minorities, the Mortimer position in Ulster had been usurped by the O'Neill clan and Roger intended to restore his rights. The army landed at Waterford on 2 October and then moved against Art MacMurrough, King of Leinster. Roger brought with him 100 men-at-arms, eight knights, 200 archers on horseback and 400 on foot. The Irish were overawed by Richard's forces and would not be brought to battle, relying on guerrilla tactics to annoy the English. Eventually, several of the Irish chieftains were forced to submit themselves and the king kept some of them in his company to ensure good behaviour. One of the chieftains who submitted was none other than Niall Mor, the head of the O'Neills, who recognised Roger as Earl of Ulster. King Richard remained in Ireland until 1 May 1395 when he returned to England, leaving Roger in charge.

In October 1396, Richard settled a peace with France that would last twenty-eight years. To cement it, he married Isabella, the eight-year-old daughter of King Charles VI, his previous wife, Queen Anne, having died two years before. Anne had never had any children and with Isabella still a child herself, it was unlikely that any would be coming soon. There was still a chance that Roger might one day become king.

The Crouchback Legend

At a parliament held in 1396, John of Gaunt, Duke of Lancaster is reported to have asked King Richard to recognise his eldest son, Henry Bolingbroke, as heir apparent to the throne. Gaunt did not attempt to have Bolingbroke's right to the throne recognised by his descent from Edward III, as per the entail, but his son's right by his descent from Henry III through the female line by Bolingbroke's mother, Blanche of Lancaster.

Henry III had two sons, Edward I and Edmund 'Crouchback', Earl of Lancaster. Gaunt claimed that Edmund was in fact the elder of Henry III's sons but had been passed over in the succession in favour of Edward I due to a spinal deformity. It had been agreed, he stated, that Edward would be succeeded by Edmund's heirs, although this agreement was subsequently ignored. Blanche, who had died in 1368, was a descendant of Edmund and thus Bolingbroke was in fact rightful King of England. Roger, who had presumably returned to England for the Parliament, is said to have protested this, pointing out that Edmund was the second son and that he in fact had no spinal deformity. Roger was correct in both assertions. Edward I was certainly the eldest son and Edmund's nickname of 'Crouchback' did not refer to a deformity but to the cross that Edmund had worn on his back during the Ninth Crusade. Before a full-blown argument erupted, Richard put an immediate end to the matter.

As with Richard's purported designation of Roger as his heir, this story is only found in the *Continuatio Eulogii* and its authenticity is likewise questioned, particularly as it was bold of Gaunt to raise a matter which, if true, gave Bolingbroke a superior claim to the throne than Richard. The so-called 'Crouchback legend', which also features in another chronicle by Adam of Usk, was undoubtedly real and Bolingbroke would later use it to justify his seizure of the throne in 1399.

Death

The following year (1397), King Richard finally decided to have his revenge on the Lords Appellant. He suddenly had Arundel, Gloucester and Warwick arrested and then summoned the 'Revenge' Parliament at Westminster to put them on trial for treason. Arundel was found guilty and beheaded, Gloucester was sent to Calais where he was put to death by being smothered with a pillow, and Warwick was attainted of his lands and sent to perpetual imprisonment on the Isle of Man. Another figure convicted of treason was Roger's uncle Thomas Mortimer. Thomas was not present at the parliament and he was summoned to stand trial within six months. Knowing his fate should he attend, Thomas fled to Scotland and then on to Ireland where he claimed the protection of Roger.

On 28 January 1398, Parliament resumed at Shrewsbury and Richard summoned Roger to appear and answer for his harbouring of Thomas. When Roger arrived at Shrewsbury he was greeted joyously by the aforementioned crowd of 20,000 dressed in hoods of his livery, 'hoping through him for deliverance from the grievous evil of such a king'.[22] The people's hopes were dashed – Roger was politic and, knowing that the king and others sought any excuse to destroy him and distribute his lands between them, he toed the line and told Richard that his recent actions 'were pleasing to him, although in very truth they displeased him much'.[23]

According to the chronicler Adam of Usk, inimical to Richard, the king distrusted Roger and sought to kill him with his own hands. Roger must have acquitted himself well, for the tyrannical Richard allowed him to return to Ireland, but he was tailed by his brother-in-law Thomas Holland, Earl of Surrey, who had subsequently been appointed lieutenant with orders to capture his predecessor. However, Holland discovered on his arrival that the twenty-four-year-old Roger was already dead. On 20 July Roger had been riding near Kells in Kilkenny, dressed in Irish attire. '[T]oo bold in his warlike valour', he had travelled in front of his troops when he was ambushed by supporters of the O'Briens who did not recognise him in his Irish attire and he was slain.[24] He was taken back to England for burial at Wigmore Abbey alongside his mother and father, leaving his six-year-old son, Edmund, as his heir.

9

Edmund Mortimer, 5th Earl of March

```
                    Roger Mortimer   m   Eleanor Holland
                    4th Earl of March     d. 1405
                       d. 1398
```

Edmund Mortimer	Roger Mortimer	Anne Mortimer	Eleanor Mortimer
5th Earl of March		d. 1411	
d. 1425			
m			
Anne Stafford			

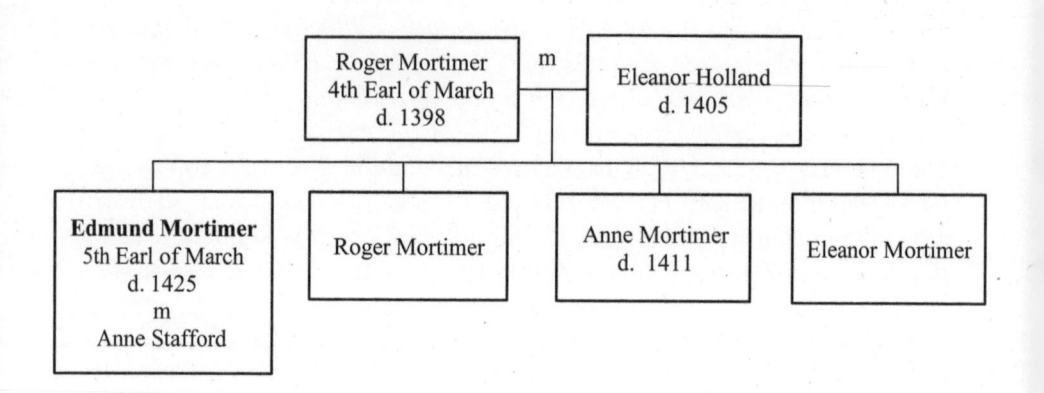

In the spring and summer of 1415, King Henry V mustered his forces at Portsmouth for what would be the famous Agincourt campaign. As Henry waited at Portchester Castle for preparations to be completed he was delivered some troubling news by his cousin Edmund Mortimer, 5th Earl of March. Edmund revealed that a plot was afoot to murder the king before he embarked for France and set up Edmund as king instead. The conspirators included the king's cousin and Edmund's brother-in-law, Richard of Conisburgh, Earl of Cambridge, Thomas Grey of Heton and Henry, Lord Scrope of Masham, who were said to have been persuaded by French bribes to prevent the expedition from happening. They had brought Edmund into the plot and he had sworn not to disclose it to anyone, but his nerves had gotten the better of him and he divulged all to the king.

That same day, the king summoned the unsuspecting conspirators to a council at the castle where they were immediately arrested and put on trial. They were found guilty and on 5 August Cambridge, Grey and Lord Scrope were beheaded at Southampton. Two days later, Edmund was pardoned for his role in the conspiracy and he accompanied the king on the expedition to France where he would serve faithfully.

Birth and Early Life

Edmund Mortimer, 5th Earl of March, was the eldest son and heir of Roger Mortimer, 4th Earl of March and his wife, Eleanor Holland. He was born at New Forest on St Leonard's Day, 6 November 1391, and was aged six at the

Edmund Mortimer, 5th Earl of March

time of his father's death in 1398. The Mortimer heir was once again a minor and he and his brother Roger (born in 1393) were placed under the wardship of King Richard while their sisters, Anne and Eleanor, were left under the care of their mother. Edmund, as eldest son, now inherited the Mortimer claim to the throne. But in 1399 Henry Bolingbroke, the eldest son of John of Gaunt, usurped the throne. In September 1398 Bolingbroke had been unfairly exiled from the country for ten years by King Richard, who had long borne a grudge against him for his role in the Merciless Parliament. Bolingbroke had found refuge at the court of the King of France. The broken-hearted John of Gaunt died in February the following year and Richard foolishly extended Bolingbroke's exile into one of perpetuity and seized the duchy of Lancaster. Shortly after, Richard set off for Ireland to quell a rebellion and in his absence Bolingbroke invaded England in order to reclaim his inheritance. Bolingbroke landed at Ravenspur in Yorkshire on 2 July with no more than fifteen knights, but his numbers were soon swelled to 6,000 by those who had become dissatisfied with Richard's arbitrary rule, including Henry Percy, Earl of Northumberland, his son Henry 'Hotspur' and Ralph Neville, Earl of Westmorland.

Richard, on learning of events in England, landed at Milford Haven in Wales in order to raise a force to meet Bolingbroke in battle. Richard soon realised that Bolingbroke enjoyed popular support and he disbanded his force and fled to Conwy Castle. There he was met by Northumberland and Thomas Arundel, Archbishop of Canterbury, and escorted to Flint Castle to treat with Bolingbroke before he was imprisoned at Chester Castle and then the Tower of London.

Bolingbroke, flushed with success, now resolved on seizing the throne for himself and employed a panel of doctors and bishops to look into the legality of Richard's deposition and of his own accession. They found a precedent for Richard's deposition in the *Liber sextus Decretalium*, in a chapter which documented the deposition of Emperor Frederick II in 1245 for similar crimes. According to the chronicler Adam of Usk, who was present at the deliberations, the matter of the Crouchback legend was also discussed; if proved true, it would mean that Bolingbroke was the rightful king. Chronicles were searched but, unsurprisingly, no evidence could be found to substantiate the claims.

On 29 September Richard agreed to abdicate the throne. According to the *Record and Progress*, the official account of Richard's deposition, Richard presented Henry with his signet ring, thereby designating him his heir.[1] During Parliament the following day Richard's deposition was read aloud and agreed, after which Bolingbroke stood up and laid claim to the throne:

> In the name of the Father, Son, and Holy Ghost; I, Henry of Lancaster challenge this Realm of England, and the Crown with all its members and appurtenances, inasmuch as I am descended by right line of the blood

coming from the good lord King Henry the third, and through that right that God of his grace has sent me, with the help of my kin and my friends, to recover it; which realm was on the point of being undone by default of governance and the undoing of the good laws.[2]

Bolingbroke's claim is interesting as it invoked some of the different criteria that had previously governed royal succession. First and foremost, he cites a hereditary claim based upon descent from Henry III. The claim is unspecific – what was the right line of blood from Henry III? Some historians have taken this to mean that he was claiming the throne as the direct male descendant of Henry III. This begs the question – why refer to Henry III when he was also the direct male heir of the more recent Edward III and Richard II? If Edward III had indeed entailed the throne in the male line, why not refer to this instead? If Bolingbroke was referring to his double descent from Henry III, through both his mother and father, this did not strengthen his claim either. It is likely, therefore, that Bolingbroke was in fact referring to the Crouchback legend. Realising, however, that this left him open to challenge, he shored up his position by adding right of conquest – God had sent him as the rightful heir to recover the crown. Finally, he presented the ring Richard had given him, suggesting he was also the king's designated successor. Whatever Bolingbroke's actual claim was, his seizure of the throne was already a fait accompli. He had no doubt canvassed support beforehand, and when those gathered were asked if they accepted him as king they all answered yes. The hereditary right of Edmund, who was just seven years old and thus unable to push his own claim, was quietly passed over. It would not be forgotten.

On Monday 13 October 1399, Bolingbroke was crowned as King Henry IV, the first king of the Lancastrian dynasty. After his coronation, Henry had his eldest son, Henry of Monmouth, the future Henry V, created Prince of Wales and recognised as his heir.

Plots and Intrigues

The superior hereditary claim of Edmund and his brother Roger constituted a real threat to Henry IV's fledgling dynasty as the boys could become the focus of plots against the king by those who were dissatisfied by his rule or who believed that he had wrongly seized the throne. To protect against this, Henry had the two boys placed under close guard at Windsor Castle. He treated them well and on 20 November he allocated an annual pension of 300 marks from the Clare estates to provide for their maintenance and equipment.[3]

It was not long before the first plot was hatched against Henry. The Epiphany Plot was a plan to murder Henry and his sons at Windsor amid preparations for a tournament to be held on Epiphany Day (6 January

1400) and restore King Richard. Henry was forewarned of the plot and the conspirators, fleeing towards Cheshire, were killed by a mob. This sealed King Richard's fate and he died, probably from starvation, on 14 February. In the summer Henry headed north to face the Scots and learned of the revolt of the Welshman Owain Glyndwr. Glyndwr was a wealthy Welsh gentleman who was descended from the old princes of Wales. He was involved in a dispute with Sir Reginald Grey of Ruthin over lands that the latter had seized from him. Having found no satisfaction from the English courts, Glyndwr had declared himself Prince of Wales in September and raided into Ruthin's lands. King Henry invaded Wales in return, but Glyndwr took refuge in the mountains of Snowdonia and could not be brought to battle. The following year, Glyndwr, in league with the northern Welsh, attacked the English in those parts. The king moved against him but Glyndwr once again took to Snowdonia, although not before seizing the arms, horses and tents of the Prince of Wales.

In April 1402, Glyndwr managed to capture Sir Reginald. Then in June he raided into the Mortimer lands of Maelienydd where, on 22 June, he met Edmund's uncle Sir Edmund Mortimer in battle at Pilleth in Radnorshire. In the heat of the battle, the men of Maelienydd turned against Mortimer with the result that the English were heavily defeated and Mortimer taken captive. Rumours reached the king that Sir Edmund was in connivance with Glyndwr and that he had been willingly 'captured'. Henry, believing the reports to be true, refused to pay his ransom or allow Henry Hotspur, the son of the Earl of Northumberland and also Mortimer's brother-in-law, to do so. Sir Edmund was left with little choice but to form an alliance with Glyndwr, and in November he married one of his daughters. The following month he issued a letter to the people of Radnor announcing that he had joined in league with Glyndwr and that they would release King Richard, who was rumoured to still be alive, from his captivity or, if Richard was indeed dead, 'that my honoured nephew, who is the right heir to the said crown, shall be King of England'.[4]

Things took a more threatening turn in 1403 when Glyndwr and Mortimer were joined by the Duke of Northumberland and his sons Henry 'Hotspur' and Thomas Percy, Earl of Worcester. The Percy family had been pivotal in Henry IV's usurpation and they had been handsomely rewarded as a result, but relations had since soured. Northumberland and Hotspur had defeated a Scottish force at the Battle of Homildon Hill (14 September 1402) but the king would not let them ransom their prisoners and ordered that they be handed over to himself, while Henry's refusal to ransom Mortimer added fuel to the fire.

Hotspur raised an army in Cheshire and attempted to link up with Glyndwr in Wales but he was intercepted by the king and Henry, Prince of Wales, at Shrewsbury on Saturday 21 July. During the battle Prince Henry received a permanent disfigurement when an arrow became lodged in his face but the royal army carried the victory. Hotspur was killed during the action and Thomas Percy was executed after the battle.

Glyndwr's rebellion continued and in 1405 he formed a tripartite agreement with Sir Edmund Mortimer and the Earl of Northumberland, who had been pardoned by Henry IV after the Battle of Shrewsbury but still seethed at the death of his sons, to divide the realm between them. Mortimer would be given southern England, Northumberland would have the north and Glyndwr an enlarged Wales. In February 1405 they plotted to abduct the young Edmund and Roger Mortimer from Windsor and spirit them away to Wales. The plot was made in conjunction with Constance, Lady Despenser, the daughter of Edward III's fourth surviving son, Edmund of Langley, Duke of York. Lady Despenser's husband, Thomas, Lord Despenser, had been executed by the king for his role in the Epiphany Rising and she was motivated by thoughts of revenge. Lady Despenser was resident at Windsor Castle over the Christmas of 1404/5 when she had the keys to castle copied by a blacksmith. On the morning of 15 February 1405 the door to Edmund and Roger's chamber was opened and they were snuck out of the castle by one Richard Milton. Lady Despenser joined the fugitives and they made a beeline for her castle at Cardiff. The boys were soon discovered missing and a search was conducted. They were discovered, along with Lady Despenser, in a wood near Cheltenham and returned to Windsor. Lady Despenser was thrown into confinement and brought before the council at Westminster where she accused her brother, Edward, Earl of Rutland, 2nd Duke of York, of masterminding the plot. She claimed that the abduction of the boys had been part of a larger conspiracy by York to kill the king at Eltham during the Christmas festivities by scaling the walls of the castle.

The Duke of York professed his innocence but Lady Despenser offered to pick a champion to face trial by combat and stated that she would willingly be burnt to death if her champion was defeated. York threw down his glove and accepted the duel but he was imprisoned at Pevensey instead and his estates seized. Both Lady Despenser and York were later released and granted back their lands, the latter dying at the Battle of Agincourt.[5] Richard Milton was pardoned on 8 February 1406, but the blacksmith fared less well, first having his hand chopped off and then his head. As a result of the plot, King Henry decided it was best to keep the boys under closer confinement and they were placed under the wardship of Sir John Pelham, who was granted 500 silver marks from the lordship of Clare for their maintenance.[6]

King Henry's troubles were not yet over. The Earl of Northumberland raised his forces and he was aided by Richard Scrope, Archbishop of York, who assembled an army at York. The king sent the Earl of Westmorland to York and by cunning he managed to capture Scrope, who was later executed, and Northumberland was forced to flee to Scotland.

Perhaps due to the rising support of the Mortimer claim, Henry IV decided to entail the throne in the male line in 1406. He had previously created an entail of the throne in 1404 in which recognised that females could succeed in their own right, but unlike previous entails, he had this confirmed by Parliament. Then, in June 1406, he had a new entail created in tail male. This was done by a charter, sealed with the great seal and the seals of the Lords and Speaker of the Commons. Historian Mortimer Levine suggests that this use of a sealed charter shows that a normal parliamentary enactment was not deemed appropriate to enact tail male for the first time.[7] However, six months later Parliament repealed the entail as being too restrictive and it returned to the 1404 settlement, once again strengthening the Mortimer claim. That same year (1406), Glyndwr's rebellion began to falter and the English were on the front foot. In 1408 Northumberland once again tried to raise rebellion in the north but he was killed at the Battle of Braham Moor, while Sir Edmund Mortimer was killed during the siege and capture of Harlech Castle in 1409. With Wales quietened and Mortimer dead, the king granted Edmund and Roger's wardship to Prince Henry, who received 500 silver marks for their maintenance.[8] At some point Roger died, but Edmund continued in his cousin's household until the death of King Henry IV.

France

The death of Henry IV on 20 March 1413 left his eldest son and heir, Henry of Monmouth, Prince of Wales, as King of England. One of Henry V's first acts was to release Edmund from his captivity and he was knighted before the new king's coronation, which took place on Passion Sunday, 9 April 1413.

Edmund was now twenty-one years old and he petitioned Parliament for full livery of his lands. This was granted on 9 June and Edmund duly performed homage to the new king. Although King Henry showed great leniency towards his cousin, he ensured his good behaviour by undertaking a recognisance of 10,000 silver marks on the condition that 'he shall be of good behaviour toward the king and people, so that no hurt or harm happen to any of them by him, or by his abetment, incitement or procurement'.[9] Edmund fell foul of the recognisance in 1415 when he married Anne Stafford, the daughter of Edmund, Earl of Stafford and granddaughter of Edward III's youngest son, Thomas of Woodstock, Duke of Gloucester, without first securing the king's permission. He was made to pay the 10,000 marks specified as well as a further 2,000, leaving him heavily indebted to the king. Regardless, Edmund appears not to have borne King Henry any ill will. He proved himself a loyal subject to the king who had always treated him kindly and he appears not to have harboured any aspirations to the throne, even though others goaded him to pursue his claim. There is some suggestion in the chronicles that Edmund was considered a simpleton, and it may be that

Henry did not perceive him to be a threat. Edmund's loyalty, however, was called into question on the eve of the Agincourt campaign.

At his accession, the new king was intent on rekindling the war with France which was then preoccupied with civil war. King Charles VI, who had ascended the throne in 1380, suffered from bouts of insanity (he sometimes thought he was made of glass) and the regency of the country was disputed between the king's nephew Charles, Duke of Orléans and his cousin John 'the Fearless', Duke of Burgundy.

Henry summoned an army and fleet to muster at Southampton which was set to embark for Normandy on 24 June 1415. At some point Edmund was approached by his brother-in-law, Richard of Conisburgh, Earl of Cambridge (married to Edmund's sister Anne), Henry, Lord Scrope and Thomas Grey. Cambridge was the second son of Edmund Langley, Duke of York and brother of the current duke, Edward and Lady Despenser. They told him that if he took an oath not to reveal their plan they would kill the king and set him up as king in his place. According to the chronicler Thomas of Walsingham, Edmund 'shuddered with horror when he heard this, but on that occasion did not dare to oppose them or to say anything'.[10] He later divulged the plot to the king, who summoned the conspirators to Portchester Castle under the guise of a council, where he had them arrested, tried and executed.

Henry V was convinced of Edmund's innocence. The 'Southampton Plot' provided the perfect opportunity to destroy his rival but Henry instead opted to pardon Edmund on 7 August. Edmund accompanied the king when he embarked for Normandy on 11 August, landing at Chef-de-Caux (St-Adresse) on 13 August. Henry's first move was to lay siege to the port of Harfleur, which would act as a base for future operations. Edmund joined in the siege but like many others he contracted dysentery from the unsanitary conditions of the camp and he returned to England before the town surrendered on 22 September.

So Edmund did not participate in the glorious Battle of Agincourt, fought on 25 October 1415 against a numerically superior French force. The English army, tired from the long march towards Calais and the effects of dysentery and hunger, defeated a French force twice its size. After this stunning victory, Henry continued to Calais and returned to England on 16 November to a hero's welcome.

Edmund joined in a second expedition to Harfleur in 1416 when a French blockade by land and sea threatened to starve the citizens into surrender. The English fleet was under the command of King Henry's brother John, Duke of Bedford, and on the morning of Saturday 15 August they encountered the enemy at the mouth of the Seine. The battle lasted some six hours and the English carried the victory, capturing three enemy carracks, a hulk and four sloops. The enemy fled towards Honfleur, leaving the victorious English to sail unopposed into Harfleur and convey much needed supplies into the town.

Edmund also took part in the king's second expedition to Normandy in 1417/18 in which he had command of 93 lances and 302 archers. The army landed at Touques on 1 August and captured Caen and Falaise. Henry celebrated the Feast of St George in 1418 at Caen and in the meantime he sent Edmund with an army into the Cotentin. Edmund laid siege to the city of Saint-Lô but found it too strong to take and was forced to return to the king empty-handed. In May, Edmund joined the expedition of the king's brother Humphrey, Duke of Gloucester, into the Cotentin. This time they took Saint-Lô and then proceeded to subjugate the rest of the area before joining the king in laying siege to Rouen. The siege of Rouen had begun in July, but the city did not surrender until 19 January 1419. With the capture of Rouen, Henry was now master of Normandy and in a position to open negotiations with the warring French parties. He was aided in his endeavour by the horror felt at the cold-blooded murder of John, Duke of Burgundy during a parley on the bridge at Montereau, which took place in the presence of King Charles's son and heir, the Dauphin Charles. The result was the Treaty of Troyes, ratified on 21 May 1420, in which Henry V was betrothed to Catherine de Valois, the daughter of Charles VI, and recognised as heir to the kingdom of France. In the meantime he was to act as Regent of France for the mentally incapacitated king. Henry V had realised the dream of Edward III. When King Charles died, he would assume the kingship of France. Edmund was with King Henry and King Charles on 22 July at the siege of Melun, which surrendered on 1 November.

Henry and Catherine were married on 3 June 1420 and in February the following year they returned to England. Edmund accompanied them and had the honour of holding the queen's sceptre at her coronation, celebrated on the 23rd. The Dauphin Charles, meanwhile, smarted at the treaty which disinherited him and continued hostilities. In March, Henry's younger brother Thomas, Duke of Clarence was killed in battle. Thomas had been the childless king's heir presumptive, a distinction which now passed to the Duke of Bedford.

Henry returned to France to seek revenge but he was unable to bring the dauphin to battle. Edmund was with the king at the siege of Meaux, which lasted until 5 May 1422, when the king contracted dysentery and died at Vincennes on 30 August at the age of thirty-five. Henry left behind him an eight-month-old son and heir, Henry VI, born on 6 December 1421.

Death

Henry V's premature death left England in the unenviable position of having an eight-month-old child as king and with it the prospect of a long minority. At his death, Henry V had made his next brother, John, Duke of Bedford, Lieutenant-General of France and his youngest brother, Humphrey, Duke of

Gloucester, Regent of England. In the first parliament of the reign, Gloucester was denied the role of regent and given the less prestigious title of Protector of the Realm of England. In his place a regency council, comprising seventeen members, was established and Edmund, as one of the senior peers of the realm, was appointed as one of its members. His superior hereditary claim to the throne saw him regarded with suspicion, in particular by Gloucester, who thought he might take advantage of the new king's youth to seize the throne.

Suspicions were heightened when, on 14 February 1423, one Sir John Mortimer, Edmund's cousin, who had been sent to the Tower of London in 1421 on suspicion of treason, attempted to escape. The plot had been disclosed to Parliament by one William King who testified that John Mortimer had asked for his aid in escaping the Tower. Once free, Mortimer intended to go to Wales, raise an army, kill the Duke of Gloucester and the other lords and raise Edmund as king. 'The earl of the March was but a dawe,' Mortimer had mockingly said, 'save he was the greatest, noblest, and worthiest blood of this land.'[11] When William countered with the fact that he was the noblest blood save the king, Mortimer retorted, 'The earl of the March should be king, if he had right and truth.'[12] If Edmund did not want to be king, Mortimer reasoned, then he would succeed as the next in line. Mortimer was allowed to escape but he was apprehended on the Tower Wharf and on 22 February he was hung, drawn and quartered at Tyburn. It is likely that, as with previous plots, Edmund did not have any involvement, but his behaviour at the beginning of the parliament may suggest otherwise. On his arrival in London he had brought with him a suspiciously large retinue and proudly kept open house at the Bishop of Salisbury's residence.[13] On 9 May, Parliament, arms no doubt twisted by Gloucester, appointed Edmund as Lieutenant of Ireland for a period of nine years in order to get him out of the way.[14]

Edmund put off taking up his new post until autumn 1424. Six months later, on 18 January 1425, he caught the plague and died at Trim Castle, County Meath.[15] Edmund's marriage to Anne Stafford had been childless and the Mortimer line ended. His possessions reverted to his nephew Richard, Duke of York, the son and heir of his late sister Anne Mortimer, and the traitorous Richard of Conisburgh, Earl of Cambridge, in whom the Mortimer claim now rested. Unlike his uncle, Richard, Duke of York would be willing to fight for the crown.

10

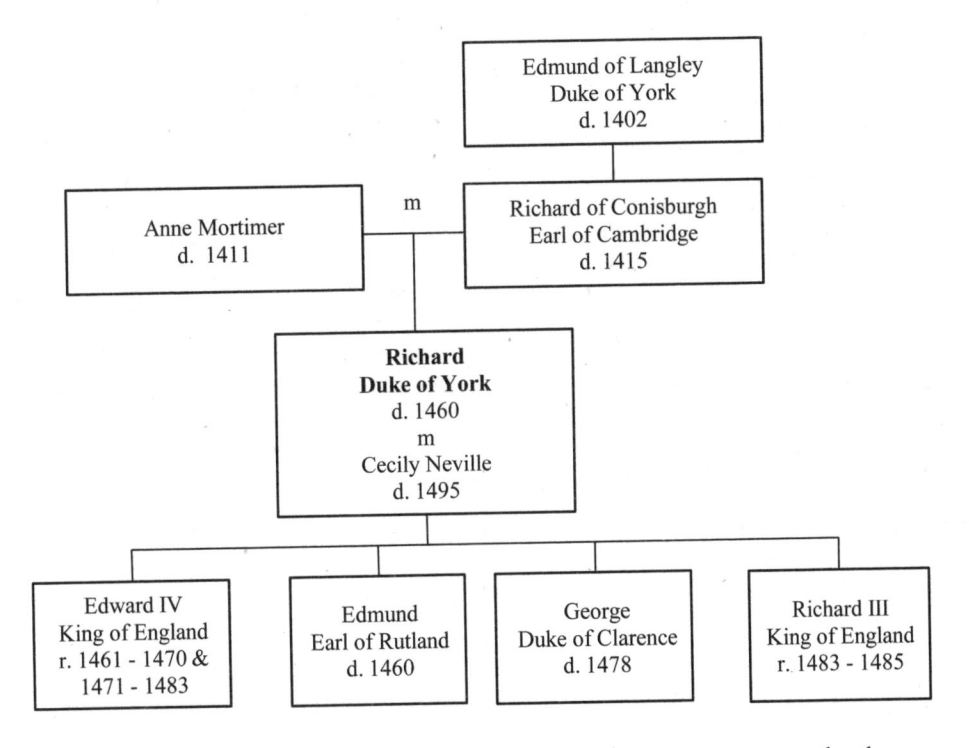

Richard, Duke of York

```
                    ┌─────────────────────┐
                    │  Edmund of Langley  │
                    │    Duke of York     │
                    │      d. 1402        │
                    └─────────────────────┘
                              │
┌──────────────────┐   m   ┌─────────────────────┐
│  Anne Mortimer   │───────│ Richard of Conisburgh│
│    d. 1411       │       │  Earl of Cambridge  │
│                  │       │      d. 1415        │
└──────────────────┘       └─────────────────────┘
                    │
            ┌───────────────┐
            │   Richard     │
            │ Duke of York  │
            │   d. 1460     │
            │      m        │
            │ Cecily Neville│
            │   d. 1495     │
            └───────────────┘
```

Edward IV	Edmund	George	Richard III
King of England	Earl of Rutland	Duke of Clarence	King of England
r. 1461 - 1470 &	d. 1460	d. 1478	r. 1483 - 1485
1471 - 1483			

The spectators gathered about Micklegate Bar in York, staring up at the three severed heads impaled upon poles above them. One of the heads was of a young man, just seventeen years old, while the other two heads belonged to middle-aged men. One of the older men had a paper crown derisively surmounted upon his head. He was Richard, Duke of York, the progenitor of the House of York and heir apparent to the English throne.

Birth and Early Life

Richard, Duke of York, the only son and heir of Richard of Conisburgh, Earl of Cambridge and Anne Mortimer, was born on 22 September 1411.[1] He was descended from Edward III through both his mother and his father. Cambridge was the second son of Edmund of Langley, Duke of York, Edward III's fourth surviving son, but Richard's claim to the throne derived from his descent from Edward III's second surviving son, Lionel of Antwerp, Duke of Clarence, through Clarence's granddaughter Anne Mortimer. Anne Mortimer died from complications shortly after Richard's birth and the subsequent execution of the Earl of Cambridge on 5 August 1415 rendered him an orphan. Richard did not receive his father's earldom, which had been attainted, but the death of his childless uncle Edward, 2nd Duke of York at the Battle of Agincourt over two months later left him as heir to the dukedom of York.

Henry V placed York under the wardship of Sir Robert Waterton, a staunch Lancastrian, who paid the sum of £100 a year for the privilege.[2] He would remain under Waterton's care until 1423 when his wardship was sold to Ralph Neville, Earl of Westmorland, for 3,000 silver marks.[3] The Nevilles were a powerful and numerous northern family affiliated with many of the great noble lineages by marriage, and they would be York's greatest allies during the Wars of the Roses. Westmorland was also affiliated with the Lancastrians through his marriage to Joan Beaufort, an illegitimate daughter of John of Gaunt by his long-time mistress-cum-wife, Catherine Swynford. Gaunt had married three times. His first wife was Blanche of Lancaster, the mother of Henry IV, who died in 1368. He then married Constance, a daughter of Pedro the Cruel, in a bid to win the throne of Castile. Constance produced one daughter, Catherine, who was later married to the King of Castile following Gaunt's failed invasion of the kingdom. Constance died in 1394 and Gaunt then married Catherine Swynford. He already had four children by her, known by the surname of Beaufort after their place of birth in Montmorency-Beaufort in France. The Beauforts would play an important part in the Wars of the Roses and would eventually succeed to the throne in 1485 in the form of Henry VII. The eldest of the four Beaufort children was John Beaufort, followed by Henry, Thomas and Joan.

The wily Westmorland took the opportunity of marrying York to his daughter, Cecily Neville (b. 1415), known as the Rose of Raby for her great beauty. It was a fortuitous move, for when Edmund Mortimer, 5th Earl of March died in 1425 York became heir to the vast Mortimer estates, making him one of the richest magnates in the land with an annual income of some £5,000.[4] More importantly, York also inherited the Mortimer claim to the throne. The Earl of Westmorland died that same year and York's wardship was transferred to Westmorland's widow, Countess Joan. On 19 May 1426, the fourteen-year-old York was knighted at Leicester by the boy king, Henry VI. Two years later he left the care of the Countess of Westmorland and joined the king's household.

France

The Wars of the Roses, the dynastic struggle between the houses of York and Lancaster that would claim the life of Richard, Duke of York, had its roots in the disastrous end to the Hundred Years War. Charles VI, King of France

Richard, Duke of York

had died two months after Henry V, making the infant Henry VI the new King of France according to the terms of the Treaty of Troyes. The Dauphin Charles, on the other hand, claimed to be the deceased king's rightful heir and so waged war against the English. It fell to Henry V's eldest brother, John, Duke of Bedford, in his capacity as Lieutenant of France, to retain the English position in France and ensure that Henry VI was crowned. He proved more than up to the task and even increased the English possessions in France, including the addition of Maine. He secured the all-important alliance with Philip 'the Good', Duke of Burgundy by marrying the duke's sister Anne, and on 17 August 1424 he defeated the Dauphinists at the Battle of Verneuil, in a feat to rival that of Agincourt.

Then, in 1428, when the French were at a low ebb, Joan of Arc, a seventeen-year-old peasant girl, appeared at the dauphin's court with a miraculous story. She claimed to have had a vision in which God had told her to unite the people of France and drive out the hated English. The Dauphin Charles was convinced and he sent her to Orléans, then under siege by the English, at the head of an army. The English were driven back and then suffered defeat at the Battle of Patay, after which the victorious Joan conducted the dauphin to Rheims Cathedral, the traditional venue for the coronation of French kings, where he was anointed as King Charles VII on 17 July 1429. Bedford advised that the English should counter by crowning Henry VI as King of France, but first he had to be crowned as King of England. On St Leonard's Day, 6 November 1429, York watched as the crown was placed on the boy king's head at Westminster Abbey.

The following year, the eighteen-year-old York was given his first official duty when he acted as Constable of England in the absence of the Duke of Bedford and presided over a duel fought at West Smithfield in London.[5] Later that year, York accompanied King Henry to France for his coronation in Paris and is noted as having taken with him twelve lancers and thirty-six archers.[6] The coronation did not take place until 6 December the following year, when Henry was crowned King of France at Notre-Dame Cathedral. York returned to England with the king and on 12 May 1432, now aged twenty, he was granted full livery of his lands on the condition that he paid the king the sum of 1,000 silver marks over a period of five years.[7] In 1433, he was invested into the Order of the Garter.

The situation in France, meanwhile, went from bad to worse. Joan of Arc had been seized by the Burgundians in 1430 and the following year she was burnt at the stake on the charge of being a witch. Although her earthly remains were gone, her spirit rejuvenated France. Crucially, the English also lost the support of Burgundy. Bedford's wife, Anne of Burgundy, died in 1432 and Bedford quickly took a new wife, Jacquetta of Luxemburg, without consulting Duke Philip. This embittered relations between the two, leading Duke Philip to make peace with King Charles and turn against the English.

Then, on 15 September 1435, Bedford breathed his last.

Lieutenant of France

Bedford's death caused a power vacuum in France, and in January 1436 it was decided by the Regency Council to invest the twenty-four-year-old Duke of York as Lieutenant of France and Normandy. York did not embark for France until June, by which time Paris had been lost to the French. He took with him an army of 8,000 men and was joined by his brother-in-law Richard Neville, Earl of Salisbury, setting up base at Rouen. York's first stint as lieutenant was largely uneventful, although he captured the town and abbey of Fécamp. He is noted to have been an able administrator and dispenser of justice.[8] When his year's term expired he waited to be sent home, but the council asked him to remain in France while they arranged his replacement. Unfortunately, his powers had also expired and he could do nothing but watch as King Charles took the town of Montereau-Fault.[9] After a six-month delay, he was replaced as lieutenant by King Henry's former tutor, Richard Beauchamp, Earl of Warwick. Warwick died in April 1439 and York was once again appointed lieutenant, this time for the duration of five years.

York departed from Portsmouth in June 1441 and immediately upon landing went to the relief of Pontoise, which was being besieged by King Charles. He challenged the king to battle but Charles's counsellors, mindful of the past French defeats at the hands of the English, advised against it. York determined to pass over the River Oise, which ran between the two armies, and bring the king to battle. He had Richard Talbot, Earl of Shrewsbury feign a crossing at the gate at nearby Beaumont-sur-Oise to draw the attention of the French army while another force crossed the Oise in leather boats near the abbey and succeeded in erecting a bridge of cords and ropes across it. The English crossed and chased the French into the town, capturing many. Charles retreated to Poissy, leaving behind his treasure. York stalked after him but Charles refused to be brought to battle, so York and Talbot returned to Rouen. Once they were gone, King Charles re-emerged and once again laid siege to Pontoise, which surrendered three days later. The following year Richard led a campaign into Anjou and Maine while Talbot took Dieppe and Edmund Beaufort, 2nd Duke of Somerset invaded Brittany. It was during his second lieutenancy that Duchess Cecily gave birth to York's eldest son, Edward of Rouen, the future King Edward IV of England, on 28 April 1442.

In England, meanwhile, the death of Bedford had seen the council splintered into two factions over the war in France. One party, led by Cardinal Henry Beaufort, the second of Gaunt's Beaufort children, was for making peace with France while the other, led by Humphrey, Duke of Gloucester, was for continuing the war. Unluckily for England (arguably), Henry VI had come into his majority in 1437 and he proved strikingly dissimilar to his warlike father. Simple, gentle and pious, he was easily controlled by those around him who used their influence to enrich themselves at his and the realm's expense. As the chronicler Edward Hall notes, 'he was governed of them whom he should have ruled, and bridled of such, whom he sharply should have spurred'.[10] His natural inclinations aligned with the peace party, who by 1444 had settled upon a marriage between the king and the fifteen-year-old Margaret of Anjou, daughter of René, Duke of Anjou and niece of the Queen of France, in order to facilitate peace. René was in name King of Naples and Jerusalem but in reality only Duke of Anjou. Furthermore, he was poor and Margaret did not provide a dowry. William de la Pole, Earl of Suffolk, the grandson of Richard II's hated chancellor and a protégé of Cardinal Beaufort, journeyed to France in order to discuss the marriage at a conference at Tours. René demanded that Maine and Anjou be restored to the king as a dowry and Suffolk, on the king's secret orders, assented and agreed to a two-year truce. Suffolk stood as a proxy for the king and married Margaret at Nancy in March 1445. York met the new queen at Pontoise on 18 March and conducted her to Harfleur for her journey to England, little sensing the great animosity that would soon engulf them. Margaret married Henry on 22 April and was crowned queen at Westminster Abbey on 30 May.

When news of the cession of Maine and Anjou was made known, it played right into the hands of Duke Humphrey and the war party. In a parliament held at Bury St Edmunds in February 1447, Duke Humphrey was arrested on charges of treason. By 23 February he was dead, likely of a stroke although rumours abounded that he had been killed at the urging of Suffolk and the queen. Whatever the case, it was obvious that the peace party wished to silence their greatest critic. Six weeks later, Cardinal Beaufort passed away. The king was now dominated by Suffolk, Queen Margaret and Edmund Beaufort, 2nd Duke of Somerset, the nephew of Cardinal Beaufort.

York had returned to England in 1445 and he now stepped into Duke Humphrey's shoes as head of the war party. With the death of the king's uncles, York was now the childless King Henry's heir presumptive, but he had a rival in the form of Edmund Beaufort, Duke of Somerset, who could claim to be nearest in blood to the king. The Beauforts had been legitimated by Richard II but they had subsequently been barred from the throne by Henry IV. The Beaufort claim was still a threat, as their impediment to the throne could simply be overturned or ignored, while it is remains unclear if the king had the power to impose such a limitation in the first place.. This rivalry came to the fore when York was once again appointed Lieutenant of France but Somerset, eyeing the great riches and honour he could accrue from such a position, convinced the king to grant it to him instead. York simmered with anger and swore revenge, beginning the great rivalry that would lead them both to their ruin. York was appointed Lieutenant of Ireland for a period of ten years in order to keep him out of sight.[11] York dragged his feet but he eventually took up his post in June 1449.

Somerset did not possess York's military and administrative capabilities, and Normandy was lost during his lieutenancy. In March 1449, Somerset allowed some English soldiers to raid the town of Fougères in Brittany in blatant contempt of the Treaty of Tours. King Charles used this as an excuse to resume hostilities and by 12 August he had retaken Normandy.

The country was aghast at the loss of Normandy. The blame fell on the shoulders of those around the king, particularly Suffolk, who was impeached by the Commons in Parliament. Henry unwillingly banished him from the kingdom for a period of five years, but as Suffolk crossed the Channel on 2 May 1450 his ship was intercepted by *The Nicholas of the Tower*. He was taken aboard the *Nicholas* and beheaded, probably after some kind of mock trial. His head, impaled upon a spike, was deposited on the beach at Dover.

Worse was to come. In June the commons of Kent arose and assembled on Blackheath, outside of London. They were led by Jack Cade, a Kentishman who used the alias of John Mortimer and claimed kinship with the Duke of York. The rebels marched on London, calling for the heads of the traitors that surrounded the king. Among the rebels' demands was that the king 'take about his noble person his true blood of his royal realm, that is to say, the high and mighty prince the Duke of York, exiled from our sovereign lord's person by the noising of the false traitor the Duke of Suffolk and his affinity'.[12] Unfortunately this brought York under suspicion. He shared many of the complaints of the rebels. He blamed the loss of Normandy and the poor state of the kingdom on the king's rapacious advisers, particularly Somerset. He also felt that he had a right to be on the king's council as the greatest nobleman in the country and as heir presumptive to the throne, but there is no evidence to suggest that he actually masterminded events. York had thus far proven a loyal supporter of the crown and it was only later, as things grew worse, that his thoughts turned to taking the throne for himself.

On 3 July the rebels took London Bridge and entered the city. The following day they executed Lord High Treasurer Sir James Fiennes and William Crowmere, Sheriff of Kent. On the evening of the third day the Londoners rose against the rebels and a battle raged on London Bridge until eight the following morning. Later that day, John Kemp, Archbishop of Canterbury offered the rebels a general pardon and most of them, including Cade, accepted it and returned home. Cade, however, had a bounty on his head. He was later caught in a garden in Sussex and killed, his head displayed upon London Bridge.

Reformer

In September, York suddenly returned from Ireland in a bid to defend his name against accusations that he was behind the rebellion. King Henry and his household were said to have been 'afraid right sore' of his coming and they sent soldiers to arrest him on arrival.[13] York managed to land in Wales unopposed and, raising an army of 4,000 retainers from his lands in the Welsh Marches, moved on Westminster. He forced his way into the palace and presented the king with a bill in which he protested his innocence in the recent rebellion and professed, 'I have been, and ever will be, your true liegeman and servant.'[14] Henry accepted his protestations and responded that 'for the easing of your heart in all such matters, we declare, repute and admit you as our true and faithful subject, and as our faithful cousin'.[15]

York was not done. He had come to answer the calls of the Kentish rebels and reform the government. In a second bill, he pressed for the traitors around the king to be removed from office. Henry agreed to create a 'sad and substantial Council' in which York would be but a member.[16] The resultant parliament convened on 6 November, and during its proceedings Somerset was arrested and sent to the Tower of London. He was soon released and Henry, in a demonstration of his faith in the man, created him Captain of Calais.

On the resumption of Parliament in January 1451, the Commons called for the removal of the king's evil counsellors. The king assented in part, but the disgraced Somerset remained at his side. Parliament was brought to an abrupt halt in May when Thomas Young of Bristol petitioned that York be recognised as Henry's heir presumptive. It is not clear if York was behind the petition, but if he was this does not suggest that he was as yet plotting to take the throne. He may simply have wanted his position as heir presumptive to be recognised against that of the Duke of Somerset. The king and lords refused to do so, Parliament was dissolved and Young was dispatched to the Tower of London.

Tensions continued to mount in England while in France King Charles invaded Gascony. York spent Christmas stalking around Ludlow Castle, fearing that Somerset, who 'laboureth continually about the king's highness for my undoing', was poisoning the king's mind against him.[17] On 9 January 1452 he sent a letter to the king in which he once again protested his allegiance and offered to swear it upon the Holy Gospels. By February he had resolved on forcibly removing Somerset from the king's side. York marched on London at the head of an army of 20,000 men in a bid to win the support of the Londoners. Henry and Somerset, meanwhile, raised their own considerable force and moved to intercept him, but York managed to reach London, where he found the gates firmly closed against him. Undeterred, York crossed Kingston Bridge and entered Kent in the hope of rallying the rebellious Kentishmen to his side, setting up camp at Brent Heath near Dartford.

Henry and Somerset encamped on Blackheath and Henry dispatched William Wainflete, Bishop of Winchester and others to mediate peace. York protested that he had not come to harm the king but to remove Somerset and other 'evilly deposed persons' from his side.[18] Henry agreed to imprison Somerset and place him on trial on the condition that York first disbanded his army. Foolishly, York did as commanded, but on triumphantly entering Henry's tent he found Somerset stood at the king's side. York was arrested and made to walk ungirt through London to his own house where he was temporarily confined. He was soon released but not before he was compelled to swear a humiliating oath at St Paul's Cathedral to never again rebel against the king. On 7 April, Henry issued a general pardon to all those who applied to the chancery. York was among those who took it.

In 1453, Gascony, which had been a part of the possessions of the kings of England since the time of Henry II, was lost for good, leaving Calais as the only remaining English possession in France. When King Henry heard the news he suffered his first mental collapse at Clarendon, rendering him unable to speak or even move without assistance. He was incapacitated for eighteen months, in which time he appeared oblivious to the fact that Queen Margaret had given birth to a son and heir, Prince Edward, on 13 October 1453. Just like that, York was no longer heir presumptive. His chances of one day becoming king seemed remote.

When it became evident that Henry would not soon recover, York, as the next senior member of the royal family, was appointed Protector and Defender of the Realm and chief councillor. His appointment was to last until the king recovered or his newborn son, Edward, came of age. York's position was strengthened by the appointment of his brother-in-law, the Earl of Salisbury, as chancellor. On 28 July, York was appointed Captain of Calais and also king's lieutenant in the Marches.[19] The hated Somerset, meanwhile, was cast into the Tower.

Then, on Christmas Day 1454, the king suddenly returned to his senses and York was forced to surrender the office of Protectorate. The duke had governed the country skilfully during his tenure and was reported to have 'resigned his office much honoured and much loved'.[20] King Henry released Somerset on 7 February 1455, once again made him Captain of Calais and restored him as his chief councillor. Salisbury was relieved of the chancellorship, replaced by Thomas Bourchier, Archbishop of Canterbury. The 'evil councillors' once again surrounded the king and York was cast aside to languish in political obscurity. This was made apparent when he was not summoned to attend the Leicester Parliament in May 1455, called with the objective of protecting the king against his enemies. The insinuation was clear for all to see – York and his adherents were enemies of the crown.

St Albans

York and Salisbury took counsel at Sandal Castle in Wakefield where it was agreed that they had no choice but to remove Somerset once and for all. In the middle of May, they raised their armies and marched south, joining forces with Salisbury's son Richard Neville, Earl of Warwick, known to posterity as Warwick the Kingmaker. At Ware, York penned a letter to Henry explaining why they had raised an army, but this was intercepted by Somerset and never reached the king. That same day, King Henry and Somerset set off from Westminster with an army.

By the next morning, Henry's army was encamped at St Albans. The force was about 2,000 strong and included the dukes of Buckingham and Somerset, the earls of Pembroke, Northumberland, Devon and Stafford as well as Thomas, Lord Clifford. At seven o'clock that morning, York arrived outside the city and set up camp on Key Field. The first part of the day was taken up by abortive negotiations in a bid to prevent battle. York demanded custody of Somerset but the wily Somerset whispered in the king's ear that York had come for the crown, and the king would not hand him over. The Wars of the Roses had begun.

Sometime between eleven and twelve o'clock, York, Salisbury and Warwick assaulted the town in three different locations. Warwick managed to fight his way through some gardens on the east side and gained entry. Battle erupted within the town and York and Salisbury were able to break through and win the day. Somerset, Northumberland and Clifford were killed during the action while King Henry himself received an arrow wound to the neck. After the battle, York, Salisbury and Warwick found the king hiding in the house of a tanner. Prostrating themselves before him, they pledged their allegiance and reassured him that they had never intended to hurt him. The king was said to be 'greatly cheered' by their admission, likely fearing that the Yorkists had meant to kill him.[21] He accepted their protestations and asked them to command their men to stop pillaging the city, which they did. The first battle of the Wars of the Roses thus drew to a bloody close.

With Somerset finally dead, the Yorkists were in the ascendant. The following day they accompanied the king into London, York riding on the king's right and Salisbury on his left, while Warwick carried the sword of state before him. The king was treated with all signs of honour, but it was clear who now called the shots. Warwick was made Captain of Calais and Salisbury was reinstated as chancellor. At a parliament held at Westminster in July, York and the others were pardoned for their actions at St Albans while the blame was placed squarely upon the shoulders of the deceased Somerset and other members of the king's household.

Unfortunately, Henry fell sick again in October. When Parliament convened the following month, York opened proceedings as the king's lieutenant. He was appointed Protector again on 19 November, although he first made a show of turning down the office. He would continue in this role until 25 February 1456 when the king, having once again recovered his wits, dismissed him.

Ludford Bridge

With the death of Somerset, the feisty Queen Margaret now came to prominence. It was said that 'almost all the affairs of the realm were conducted according to the Queen's will, by fair means or foul, as was said by divers people'.[22] Margaret regarded York as a threat to her son's future and was determined to destroy him. She gathered the sons of those killed at St Albans who thirsted for vengeance, including Somerset's son Henry Beaufort, 3rd Duke of Somerset and John Clifford, the son of the fallen Thomas, Lord Clifford.

Margaret brought Henry into the Midlands, an area of strong Lancastrian affinity as opposed to the Yorkist London, and arranged a council meeting at Coventry in which many of the Yorkists were dismissed from office. York attended the council and was reported to have been in good favour with the king but he was 'not in great concert with the ... Queen'.[23] Animosity grew between the parties over the next year and in January 1458 King Henry decided to play the part of conciliator, summoning the two factions to Westminster. York arrived in London with his household on 26 January and stayed at Baynard's Castle. Over the next few weeks discussions were held and a compromise reached. York, Salisbury and Warwick agreed to pay compensation to Eleanor, Duchess Dowager of Somerset, Henry, Duke of Somerset and Lord John Clifford as well as £45 a year to St Albans Abbey for Masses to be said for those slain in the battle. The council culminated in the farcical 'Love Day', a solemn procession through London to St Paul's, organised by the deluded king. Henry triumphantly led proceedings, followed by York and Queen Margaret who walked hand in hand. There followed the Earl of Salisbury with Somerset, Warwick and Exeter and others, each pair linking arms in a symbol of reconciliation. Although each person played their part in honour of the king, tensions must have boiled beneath the surface.

Unsurprisingly, the 'Love Day' was an abject failure. The following year hostilities were recommenced when Warwick was attacked in London by members of the king's household after attending a council meeting and barely managed to reach the safety of his barge. Queen Margaret ordered Warwick's arrest but Warwick made his way safely to Yorkshire where he bemoaned his plight to York and Salisbury. As a result, the Yorkists were indicted for treason on 24 June 1459. York, Salisbury and Warwick resolved on fighting and began to raise their forces. Queen Margaret had been preparing for war for some time. In September, the Queen dispatched Lord Audley to arrest Salisbury as he rode to join York at Ludlow. When they met the two sides clashed in the Battle of Blore Heath on 23 September, with the Yorkists victorious and Audley counted among the dead. Salisbury reached Ludlow and he and York marched to Worcester where they were joined by Warwick. King Henry offered York and Warwick a pardon if they submitted themselves, but he did not offer one to Salisbury. York declined and the three men retreated to Ludlow.

Shortly after, Henry and Margaret summoned an army and then marched on Ludlow. York prepared to fight but one of his captains, Sir Andrew Trollope, defected to Henry's camp in the night and the heavily outnumbered Yorkists decided to flee. York and his second son Edmund, Earl of Rutland, headed for Wales where they took ship for Ireland while Salisbury, York's eldest son Edward, Earl of March and Warwick went to Calais. York's wife, Cecily, Duchess of York, and their two youngest sons, George and Richard, the future Richard III, were left alone in Ludlow at the mercy of the royal army, which ravaged the town. Cecily and her two boys were placed under the guard of her sister Anne, Duchess of Buckingham. In November, York and his affinity were attainted of their lands during the Coventry Parliament.

Heir to the Throne

In March 1460, Warwick travelled to Ireland where he took council with York and planned their next move. On 26 June Warwick, Salisbury and March landed at Sandwich and headed for London, which opened its gates to them. Leaving Salisbury in charge, Warwick and March made for Northampton where they fought the king's forces on 10 July. It was a resounding victory for the Yorkists. Buckingham, Shrewsbury and Lord Egremonde were killed while the king himself was taken with all due reverence to London. Word of the victory was sent to York and on 8 September he landed at Redbank near Chester and headed for London. His retinue was dressed in his livery of white and blue, embroidered with his badge of a fetterlock.[24] He met Duchess Cecily along the way and they rode together to Abingdon where the duke ordered trumpeters and clarioners to bring him to London. Ominously, York had them carry banners displaying the royal arms while a sword was borne before him as if he were a king. York arrived at Westminster on 10 October where Parliament convened. In an act which shocked contemporaries, York entered the House of Lords and placed his hand upon the cushion on the king's throne, thereby announcing his claim to it. Silence descended, only to be broken when an incredulous Archbishop Bourchier approached him and asked if he wished to see the king. 'I do not bethink me that I know of any within the realm for whom it were not more fitting that he should come to me and see me than for me to attend on him and visit him,' York retorted.[25] Bourchier hurried to notify the king while York broke into the king's apartments and took up residence.

It is not clear when York's ambitions changed from reform to ruling in his own right. He had proven himself a loyal servant to the Lancastrian dynasty and his wish for reform appears to have been genuine. It may have been the fear of destruction at the hands of the king's party which motivated him to change his objective. On the other hand, it could have been at the back of his mind all along and he simply felt that now was the time to act.

The people began to murmur against York's presumptuousness. Even Warwick was displeased at his actions and expressed disapproval. On 16 October, York formally made his claim to the throne, stressing his descent from Lionel, Duke of Clarence over Henry's from John of Gaunt. The judges refused to give an opinion on such a weighty matter and said that it was for the king and lords to decide. After reviewing the evidence, it was ceded that York did in fact have the superior claim and on 25 October a compromise was arrived at in the Act of Accord. York was made the king's heir, disinheriting the king's son, Edward of Lancaster, and receiving the titles of Prince of Wales, Duke of Cornwall and Earl of Chester, as well as an annual pension of 10,000 marks. The lords swore allegiance to him and York in turn swore allegiance to the king. The Yorkists had seemingly won the war – but fate had a different plan for York.

Wakefield

The feisty Queen Margaret was not going to sit idly by while her son was disinherited. After the Battle of Northampton she had fled to Harlech Castle in Wales with young Edward. She then headed to Scotland where she secured an army from the king, thereafter summoning Somerset and the Lancastrian affinity to meet her at Hull. She soon commanded a force of 15,000 men. York, his second son Edmund, Earl of Rutland, the Earl of Salisbury and others headed for York on 9 December with 6,000 men to deal with Margaret, but with Christmas fast approaching a temporary truce was arranged between both sides so that they could enjoy the festivities. The Yorkists celebrated Christmas at Sandal Castle in Wakefield but on 30 December the Lancastrians suddenly appeared outside the castle and challenged York to battle. Many of the duke's men were absent at the time, foraging for supplies, and his numbers were greatly reduced. For unknown reasons, but perhaps out of pride, York bravely accepted the challenge. It would prove a costly mistake.

York, Salisbury and Edmund left the castle and bore down the hill towards the Lancastrian army, but they were routed by the force led by Lord Clifford and the Earl of Wiltshire. Within half an hour the battle was over. York was likely killed during the melee, although the Whethamsted Chronicler, as quoted by Holinshed, states that he was taken captive and afterwards made to stand on a molehill wearing a crown of thorns. His captors, according to this story, took the knee in mock deference and stated, 'Hail king without rule, hail King without heritage, hail duke and prince without people or possessions.'[26] He was then beheaded. Salisbury was taken captive and beheaded at Pontefract while York's son, the seventeen-year-old Edmund of Rutland, was killed during the battle by a vengeful Lord Clifford as he fled across Wakefield Bridge in a bid to reach the safety of the town.

Clifford caused York's head to be severed from his body, mounted on a pole and topped with a paper crown. After being presented to the queen, York's head was placed upon Micklegate Bar in York along with those of Edmund and Salisbury, a warning to all who rebelled against the king.

York and Edmund's heads would later be removed when York's eldest son, Edward, Earl of March, won the throne at the Battle of Towton in March 1461. He would be buried humbly at the House of the Mendicant Friars in Pontefract, but in July 1476, when Edward IV had consolidated his rule, he decided to honour his father and brother with a more fitting burial. He had their bones removed to Fotheringhay Church in Northamptonshire, where they remain to this day.

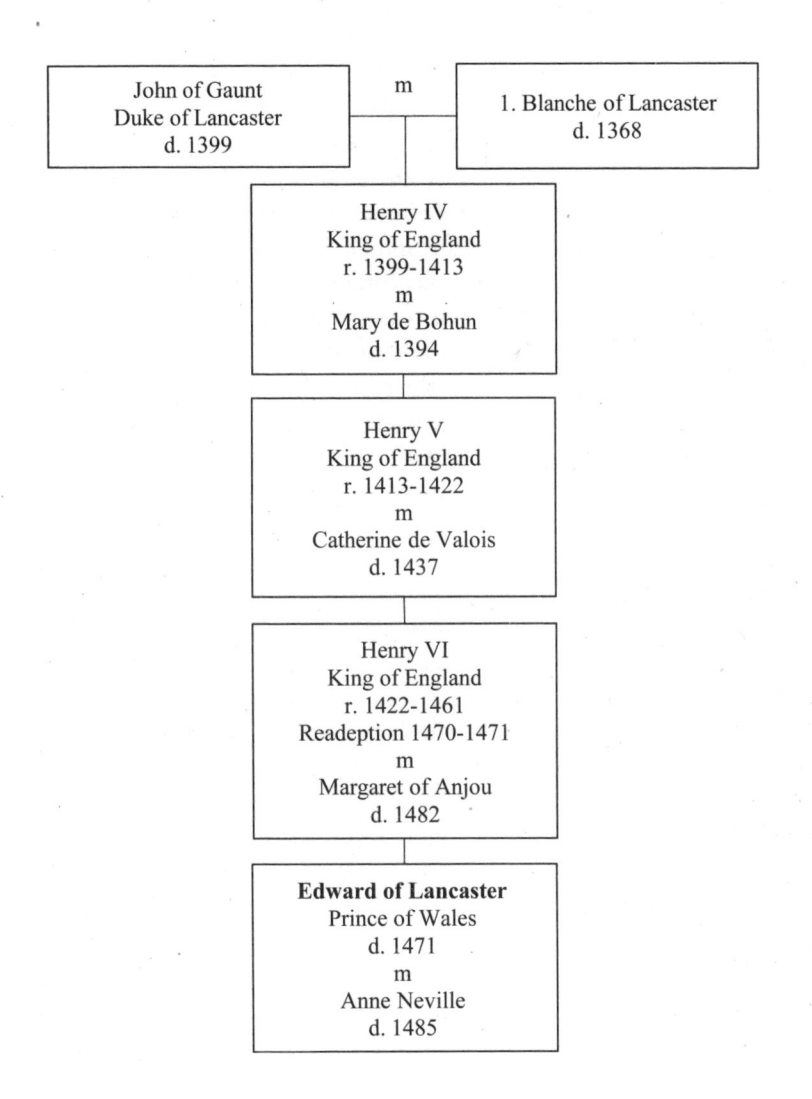

11

Edward of Lancaster

```
┌─────────────────────┐     ┌─────────────────────────┐
│   John of Gaunt     │  m  │  1. Blanche of Lancaster│
│  Duke of Lancaster  │─────│         d. 1368         │
│      d. 1399        │     │                         │
└─────────────────────┘     └─────────────────────────┘
```

Henry IV
King of England
r. 1399-1413
m
Mary de Bohun
d. 1394

Henry V
King of England
r. 1413-1422
m
Catherine de Valois
d. 1437

Henry VI
King of England
r. 1422-1461
Readeption 1470-1471
m
Margaret of Anjou
d. 1482

Edward of Lancaster
Prince of Wales
d. 1471
m
Anne Neville
d. 1485

On the floor of the quire of Tewkesbury Abbey in Gloucestershire, a plaque records the final resting place of Edward of Lancaster, Prince of Wales, the only son and heir of Henry VI and Margaret of Anjou. Positioned directly above it, on the abbey's vaulted ceiling, is a large sun in splendour, the badge of the Yorkist king Edward IV, an eternal reminder that the prince had been vanquished by his enemy and denied his birthright.

Birth and Early Life

Queen Margaret of Anjou, wife of King Henry VI, gave birth to a 'fair prince' at Westminster Palace on St Edward's Day, 13 October 1453.[1] The prince's birth occurred at a troubled time in England. Two months before, King Henry VI had suffered his first mental collapse at Clarendon and was completely oblivious to the fact that he was now the father of a healthy male heir. To make matters worse, he could not acknowledge the child as his own and thereby legitimate him.[2] The queen's enemies spread rumours that the child was not Henry's at all but in fact the offspring of Margaret's favourite, Edmund Beaufort, 2nd Duke of Somerset.

The boy was christened at Westminster Abbey by William Wainflete, Bishop of Winchester and named Edward in honour of Henry's favourite saint, Edward the Confessor. Cardinal John Kemp, Archbishop of Canterbury and Edmund Beaufort, Duke of Somerset stood as the boy's godfathers and Anne, Duchess of Buckingham as his godmother.

In early January 1454, the Duke of Buckingham presented the three-month-old Edward to his father at Windsor in the hope that the king would acknowledge him, but Henry continued to stare vacantly into space. A frustrated Margaret snatched the infant from Buckingham and made her own attempt to elicit a response from her husband. Hopes were raised when the king glanced at the baby but were dashed just as quickly when he immediately cast his eyes blankly back to the floor.

When it became evident that the king would not soon recover, Margaret took the initiative. She was determined to protect her son's inheritance at all costs and she feared what would happen if Richard, Duke of York was to take power. A contemporary describes Queen Margaret as 'a great and strong laboured woman, for she spareth no pain to sue her things to an intent and conclusion to her power'.[3] Her attempts to gain the regency for herself were unsuccessful and in March the hated York was installed as Protector instead. Margaret had little choice but to stand by while the Yorkists assumed control and her power and influence were diminished. Margaret's fears were assuaged somewhat when Parliament had the baby Edward created Prince of Wales in a ceremony at Windsor on 9 June, confirming his position as heir apparent.

Fortunately, Henry was restored to his faculties at the end of the year. When Margaret once again presented the child, the king was overjoyed. He asked the child's name and when Margaret told him he 'held up his hands and thanked God thereof'.[4] York was ousted from power and Margaret and Somerset, who had been released from prison, once again assumed control over the feeble monarch.

Margaret's fears were heightened after the Battle of St Albans when Somerset was killed and the king led to London as a prisoner. Henry fell ill again in late 1455 and York was once again made Protector, but this was

Edward of Lancaster

brought to a close in February 1456 when the king recovered. Henry's illness was less severe this time and he was able to declare Edward to be Prince of Wales, Earl of Chester and Duke of Cornwall.

Shortly after, Margaret and Edward removed to Tutbury in Staffordshire in order to canvas support in the pro-Lancastrian Midlands. In June, she and Edward travelled into the prince's earldom of Chester in a bid to win the affections of the knights and squires there. The two-year-old Edward played his part, presenting the knights with his badge of a silver swan.

Margaret, not trusting pro-Yorkist London, brought the king into the Midlands. The year 1458 saw Henry's unsuccessful attempts at reconciling the parties and the next year, war resumed. After the king marched on Ludlow, the Yorkists fled overseas and they were attainted in the Coventry Parliament. Then, in 1460, the Earl of Warwick and Edward, Earl of March returned to England and defeated the Lancastrians at the Battle of Northampton. Margaret and Edward were at Coventry at the time, awaiting the outcome of the battle. When they received news of the Lancastrian defeat they fled towards Wales. As they passed the castle of Malpas in Cheshire they were confronted by a former servant of the prince who robbed them of their goods 'and put her [Margaret] so in doubt of her life and son's life also'.[5] After this terrifying experience, Margaret and Edward were guided to the safety of Harlech Castle by a fourteen-year-old boy. Harlech was owned by King Henry's half-brother Jasper Tudor, Earl of Pembroke. Jasper was related to Henry through his mother, Queen Catherine, who had scandalously married the Welshman Owen Tudor after the death of Henry V.

Margaret and Edward were given gifts by Jasper and recuperated at the castle. Margaret soon learned of the Act of Accord which disinherited her son. The Yorkists attempted to entice her and the prince back to London, sending members of King Henry's household who presented her with a token. Before the Battle of Northampton, King Henry had warned the queen not to return to him unless he presented her with a particular token that only they knew. The king had likely revealed the identity of the token but the household officers, loyal to the Lancastrian cause, warned Margaret to take no heed. Margaret and Edward left Harlech and travelled north into Scotland to secure Scottish help against York. King James II of Scotland had recently been killed when a cannon had exploded near him while laying siege to Roxburgh Castle and he had been succeeded by his eight-year-old son, James III. As James was a minor, his mother, Mary of Gueldres, acted as regent. Margaret and Edward found the young king and queen dowager at Lincluden Abbey, where the two exiles were entertained and discussed plans to invade England in Henry's name. A treaty was concluded at Dumfries in which the desperate Margaret agreed to the high price of handing over Berwick-upon-Tweed, while Edward was to marry one of the Scottish king's sisters. Margaret and Edward, now at the head of a Scottish army, met the Lancastrian affinity at Hull and moving south clashed with York at the Battle of Wakefield on 30 December and killed him.

St Albans and Towton

With York dead, all that remained was for the Lancastrians to take back the king's person, reinstate loyal Lancastrian officers to the government and overturn the Act of Accord. But it would not be that simple. A new and able Yorkist claimant now entered the ring. Edward of Rouen, Earl of March, York's eldest surviving son, was heir apparent to the throne according to both hereditary right and the Act of Accord. The eighteen-year-old March was still young and untested in battle but he would prove himself an excellent soldier, never losing a battle. March had been collecting forces in the Welsh Marches in anticipation of joining his father at Wakefield when he received the devastating news about his father, uncle and brother. March decided to confront the Lancastrian army before it reached London but found himself tailed by a force commanded by Jasper Tudor, Jasper's father Owen and James Butler, Earl of Wiltshire. March swung his army around and met the Lancastrian force at Mortimer's Cross, between Wigmore and Leominster in Shropshire, on 3 February. The Yorkists carried the victory, slaying some 3,000 men. Jasper Tudor and the Earl of Wiltshire managed to escape but Owen Tudor was captured, taken to Hereford and summarily beheaded at the Market Cross.

Margaret and Edward, meanwhile, proceeded south with the northern army, 'robbing all the country and people as they came, and spoiling abbeys and houses of religion and churches'.[6] The continuator of Gregory's Chronicle notes that all the men wore the livery of the prince, 'a blend of crimson and black with ostrich feathers'.[7] By 17 February they had reached the outskirts of St Albans, where they found Warwick and the king encamped with an army on Barnet Heath and went on the attack. Although Prince Edward did not participate in the battle, it was his first taste of a military engagement. The Yorkists suffered defeat and Warwick and the other lords fled, abandoning King Henry. Once the battle was over, Edward came to his father's tent and the grateful king dubbed him a knight. The prince wore 'a pair of brigantiers covered with purple velvet ibete [burnished] with goldsmith's work'.[8] Edward then proceeded to knight many others, including Sir Andrew Trollope who had defected from the Yorkists at Ludlow.

The following day, Edward was given his first taste of kingly authority when he presided over the trial of Lord Bonneville and Sir Thomas Kyriel, who had been placed in charge of the king's person during the battle. They had made ready to flee when the battle was lost, but the well-meaning King Henry had given them his word that they would be treated with honour. Edward, however, declared them guilty. He was present when they were later beheaded at St Albans.

The victorious Lancastrian army swept towards London but the citizens, fearing the depredations of the northern army, refused to open the city gates. Margaret soon learned that March and Warwick were approaching with an army and she had little choice but to retreat north to York.

March and Warwick reached London on 26 February and were welcomed into the city with great joy. There, on 4 March, Henry was deposed by a council for his 'imbecility and insufficiency'.[9] By joining with Margaret and Edward, King Henry was perceived as having broken the terms of the Act of Accord and thus lost his throne. March was elected as King Edward IV, although this was a popular acclamation rather than election in the general sense.[10] The new king could not rest on his laurels. As long as Margaret, the king and Prince Edward were still present with a large army in the north his position was not safe. He duly headed north and met the Lancastrian army on Palm Sunday, 29 March, at Towton near Tadcaster, where a bloody and brutal battle took place in the snow. The Yorkists had the victory but the cost was dear. It was reported that 28,000 perished, making it the bloodiest battle ever fought on English soil. The casualties on the Lancastrian side included Sir Andrew Trollope and the earl of Northumberland while the earls of Devonshire and Wiltshire were beheaded in the aftermath.

Margaret, Edward and Henry were at York awaiting the outcome of the battle when Henry Beaufort, 3rd Duke of Somerset, Henry Holland, Duke of Exeter and others delivered the unhappy news. They fled to the safety of Scotland in order to regroup and plot their next move. England officially had a new dynasty on the throne and Edward of Lancaster's chances of one day becoming king looked slim.

The day after Towton, Edward IV entered York and solemnly removed the heads of his father, younger brother and uncle from Micklegate Bar. After tarrying a few days, he left the north under the watchful eye of Warwick and proceeded to London where he was crowned King Edward IV on 28 June, claiming the throne by both hereditary right and conquest. At King Edward's first parliament in November the Lancastrian kings were declared usurpers and the queen, Edward and the king were attainted of their possessions.

Failing Hopes

In order to gain support or at least sanctuary in Scotland, Margaret was once again forced to cede Berwick to the Scots. The Lancastrians were not well treated in Scotland and Margaret would later complain that she, Henry and Edward once spent five days with nothing to eat but one herring between them.

Realising that Scotland would be of little help, Margaret sent Somerset, Robert Whittingham and Robert, Lord Hungerford to France in July 1461 to visit her uncle Charles VII and request his assistance. Charles had passed away and his successor, his son Louis XI, the so-called 'spider king', was not inclined to help her. Hungerford and Whittingham penned a letter to Margaret from Dieppe informing her of Charles's death and warned her not to venture to France with the prince until they had spoken with Louis. Margaret, however, decided to take matters into her own hands and with Edward at her side crossed over to Brittany on 2 April 1462. She met Louis at Chinon and agreed to hand over Calais in return for 20,000 livres and a small army of 800 men.

On 25 October, Margaret and the prince landed in Northumberland with their French force and proceeded to take Alnwick Castle. On hearing of the queen and prince's arrival, King Edward went north with an army. Margaret, the prince and the army quickly retreated to their ships and attempted to return to France, but they met with bad weather and were forced to take a fishing boat to the safety of Berwick. It was a wise move, as Margaret's ship sank, taking with it all her treasure. The French soldiers fared worse. While Margaret and the prince limped into Berwick, some 400 of them were shipwrecked on Holy Island and arrested.

In March 1463, Margaret, Edward and the king invaded Northumberland but retreated to Berwick when they heard that Warwick was approaching with an army. The queen now made the momentous decision to take Edward to the safety of France. She left her husband in Scotland and took ship to Sluys in Burgundy, where she landed in August. Neither she nor Edward would see Henry again. Philip the Good, Duke of Burgundy was a Yorkist but he treated the exiles well, giving Margaret money and escorting her to see her father, Duke René, at Bar in Lorraine. She and the prince took up residence in the town of Mighel-en-Barrois where they would spend the next seven years. Their court became a refuge for the exiled Lancastrians. Thoughts now turned to the prince's education and Sir John Fortescue, the former Lord Chief Justice, was made the prince's tutor.

As he grew, Edward proved to be more in the mould of his fiery mother than his docile father, bringing great hope to the disheartened Lancastrians. When he was thirteen he was said to talk of nothing but cutting off heads and waging war – an indication, perhaps, of the kind of king that he would have one day become.

In England the Lancastrian position went from bad to worse. On 15 May 1464, Somerset fought against a Yorkist army commanded by John Neville, Lord Montagu, one of Warwick's brothers, at the Battle of Hexham. The Yorkists won and Somerset was executed the following day. The following year, Henry VI was captured while at dinner at Waddington Hall and brought 'on horseback, and his leg bound to the stirrup' to the Tower.[11] Margaret did not give up, and in 1465 began to lobby King Louis for help. By May 1467 Louis had invited her and Edward to reside at his court, where a ray of hope came from an unlikely source.

Warwick, the Kingmaker

Richard Neville, Earl of Warwick and Salisbury was the most powerful and wealthy nobleman in England. He and the Nevilles had been largely responsible for Edward IV's accession to the throne and he naturally expected to be the king's chief counsellor. As time wore on, however, he found his sway

Edward of Lancaster

with the young king decreasing as Edward matured and began to take the initiative.

The first sign of Warwick's waning influence over the king occurred on 1 November 1464 when Edward announced that he had secretly married one of his subjects, Elizabeth Woodville. Warwick was 'greatly displeased with the King' as he had been pursuing a match between Edward and a sister of the king of France in a bid to prevent the French from giving aid to the exiled Lancastrians.[12] Elizabeth brought no great dowry or political advantages with her. She was a widower and the lowly daughter of a squire, Sir Richard Woodville, Lord Rivers, and Jacquetta of Luxembourg, Duchess Dowager of Bedford. To make matters worse, Edward began to bestow honours on the queen's large extended family. Her father was created Earl Rivers, her brother Anthony Woodville was made Lord Scales and her sisters were married into great noble families. The Nevilles' loss of favour was made apparent when Warwick's brother George Neville, Bishop of Exeter, was dismissed from the chancellorship and replaced by Robert Stillington, Bishop of Bath.

In 1467 Warwick was sent over to France to treat for peace with Louis XI. Edward, meanwhile, was intent on rekindling the Hundred Years War and pursued an alliance with the Duke of Burgundy to this end. He proposed the marriage of his sister Margaret of York to Philip of Burgundy's son Charles, Count of Charolais. The marriage was confirmed, and when Warwick returned with some French ambassadors he realised he had been duped.

In a bid to reassert his power, Warwick brought Edward's younger brother and heir presumptive, George, Duke of Clarence, under his wing and plotted to place him on the throne. He had Clarence secretly marry his eldest daughter, Isabelle Neville, at Calais and afterwards he and Clarence invaded England. They captured Edward at Coventry and imprisoned him at York. Earl Rivers was put to death and for a few weeks the country was under Warwick's control. Eventually, Edward managed to escape and was restored to power, forgiving Warwick and Clarence in the process.

In March 1469, Warwick and Clarence incited Richard Welles, Lord Willoughby and his son Robert, Lord Welles to raise a rebellion in Lincolnshire in Henry VI's name. The rebellion was quashed by Edward and Warwick and Clarence fled to Southampton, took ship and headed to the court of the King of France. It was the piece of good fortune that the Lancastrians needed. King Louis set about reconciling Margaret and Warwick and launching a joint venture to restore Henry VI to the throne. At first, Margaret was averse to forgiving her erstwhile enemy but on 23 July they were reconciled at Angers when the earl knelt before her in all humility and begged her forgiveness. Margaret left him snivelling on his knees for a quarter of an hour and then pardoned him. Days later, a treaty of marriage between Prince Edward and Warwick's youngest daughter, Anne Neville, was agreed, and it was decided that Edward should be deposed and King Henry restored to the throne. Prince Edward would remain his heir but if the prince were to die without issue then George, Duke of Clarence would become king. Margaret still distrusted Warwick and would not send her beloved son into England until she was sure it was safe to do so.

Tewkesbury

Prince Edward and the young Anne Neville were duly married in July 1470. In August, Warwick and Clarence departed for England. They landed at Dartmouth, surprising King Edward, who was busy putting down some rebellions in the North. Edward and his youngest brother, Richard, Duke of Gloucester, were forced to flee abroad to the court of the Duke of Burgundy while the triumphant Warwick marched on London and had Henry VI released from the Tower. The feeble king was ceremonially recrowned on 13 October at St Paul's in a period known as the 'Readeption'. In the parliament held that November, Edward IV was declared a traitor and attainted of his possessions. The succession was entailed in the line of Henry VI and Prince Edward was declared his heir. If both Henry and Edward were to die without issue then George, Duke of Clarence, now demoted from his position as heir presumptive, would become king, followed by his issue.[13]

The exiled Lancastrians were called over from France and reclaimed their lands and titles while Warwick was restored to his place as chief counsellor. Margaret and Edward received word from the king, imploring them to return, but contrary weather prevented them from making the crossing.

King Edward, meanwhile, was preparing to retake the throne. He was given money and ships by the Duke of Burgundy and on 11 March 1471 he set sail for England with a force 2,000 strong. After failing to land in Norfolk he arrived amid a storm at Ravenspur in Yorkshire, the same spot where Henry IV had landed in his bid to reclaim his inheritance nearly seventy-two years before. Edward, like Bolingbroke, claimed that he had come to be restored to his rights as Duke of York and he was able to march south peacefully while his numbers were swelled at Nottingham and Leicester. Warwick and Clarence, who had raised an army in Warwickshire, fled at the ex-king's approach and took refuge in Coventry. Edward attempted to goad Warwick into battle, but the earl would not budge from behind Coventry's stout walls. Travelling to nearby Warwick, Edward abandoned his pretence and announced his intention to reclaim the throne.

The Lancastrian cause was then hit by the loss of George, Duke of Clarence, who returned to his brother's side. According to the *Arrival of Edward IV*, Clarence was always distrusted by the Lancastrian affinity and he feared that they planned to destroy him.[14] He attempted to reconcile Edward and Warwick but the Kingmaker remained obdurate. Eventually, Edward decided to move towards London. He gained entry to the city on 11 April and George Neville, Archbishop of York, who had been left in charge of King Henry, switched his

Edward of Lancaster

allegiance and handed over the king. Later that day, Edward was reunited with Queen Elizabeth who had taken sanctuary at Westminster and for the first time he saw his son and heir, Edward, the future Edward V, who had been born during his absence. King Edward already had three daughters but the birth of a male heir would help secure his hold on the throne.

Warwick left Coventry, hoping to take Edward by surprise while he celebrated the Easter festivities. Edward, though, was aware of Warwick's plan and, taking King Henry with him, set up camp in a field outside of Barnet, 10 miles from London. That night Warwick bombarded Edward's men with cannon fire but the gunners aim was hindered by the darkness and the shots flew over Edward's camp. Battle was met the following morning, on 14 April, shrouded in an impenetrable morning mist. The conditions caused much confusion in the Lancastrian ranks. At one point Warwick's men mistook the Earl of Oxford's livery of a star with streams for King Edward's sun and splendour and fell upon them. Crying treason, the earl and his 800 men fled the field. Warwick, attempting to flee, was caught and killed. Edward returned triumphant to London and the next day had Warwick's naked body exhibited at St Paul's to quash rumours that the earl still lived.

Fatefully, on the same day that Edward crushed Warwick at Barnet, Margaret and Prince Edward left Honfleur and landed at Weymouth in Dorset. They moved to nearby Cerne Abbey where they were met by Edmund Beaufort, 4th Duke of Somerset, the younger brother of the deceased Henry Beaufort, 3rd Duke of Somerset, his brother John Beaufort and Thomas Courtenay, Earl of Devon. There, Margaret was delivered the devastating news of Warwick's defeat. Somerset and the others nonetheless remained confident that they could raise a considerable force, particularly in the West Country where the Lancastrians were popular, and defeat Edward. It was decided that they would head for Wales where they could join forces with Jasper Tudor before coming to battle. To reach Wales they would have to cross the Severn at Gloucester, Tewkesbury or Worcester. At Exeter they rallied the people of Devon and Cornwall to the prince's standard and on 19 April they arrived at Bath, where they were soon notified that King Edward was approaching with an army.

King Edward had still been at London when he received news of Margaret's landing. He summoned a fresh army to muster at Windsor, where he celebrated the Feast of St George. His spies informed him of the Lancastrians' plan to rendezvous with the Welsh force and he decided to intercept them before they could cross the Severn and increase their numbers.

Undeterred, the Lancastrians headed to Gloucester but found themselves denied entry by the Yorkist Sir Richard Beauchamp, governor of the castle. Margaret threatened to besiege the town, but with King Edward so close it proved an empty threat. The only option was to march to Tewkesbury where there was another Severn crossing. The army marched the 26 miles in blistering heat and reached Tewkesbury at 4 p.m., tired, thirsty and hungry. King Edward was hot on their trail, no more than 6 miles distant and it was agreed that they had little choice but to find a favourable position to the south of the town, close to the abbey, and give battle. That evening, King Edward set up camp 3 miles from them and the following day, Saturday 4 May, battle was met.

The Lancastrian army was divided up into the usual three battles. The untested Prince Edward was given command of the main under the watchful eye of the veteran warrior John, Lord Wenlock. Somerset had command of the van and the Earl of Devon the rear. On the Yorkist side, King Edward had the main, his brother Richard, Duke of Gloucester the van and William, Lord Hastings the rear. The Lancastrians were in a well-fortified position, protected by 'evil lanes, and deep dykes, so many hedges, trees, and bushes, that it was right hard to approach them near, and come to hands'.[15] The battle began with the customary cannon fire exchange, while Gloucester's archers launched arrows at the Lancastrians who replied in kind. However, the Lancastrians came off worse as they 'had not so great plenty [arrows and cannon] as had the king'.[16] Somerset, in a pre-planned move, stealthily left the field by a secret path that he had scouted out earlier and came over a hill on Edward's flank. He had expected the support of Lord Wenlock but, frustratingly, the baron remained still. King Edward and Gloucester quickly forced Somerset back up the hill. Meanwhile, a body of 200 spears that Edward had placed further away to watch for such a surprise attack now entered the battle and Somerset's men were routed and fled. An angry Somerset returned to the field and, in sight of the horrified prince, confronted Wenlock, 'called him traitor, [and] with his axe he struck the brains out of his head'.[17]

King Edward then turned his attention to the centre of the Lancastrian force, where the prince was positioned. It was soon routed and the prince, John Beaufort and the Earl of Devon were killed. Prince Edward's fate is revealed in differing accounts by the chroniclers. Warkworth's Chronicle states that he died on the field, calling on his cousin George, Duke of Clarence to help him. *The Arrival of Edward IV*, a pro-Yorkist piece of propaganda, states that the prince was taken while fleeing towards the town and killed. The chronicler Robert Fabyan states that he was taken alive and after the battle was brought before King Edward. Edward demanded to know why his cousin had dared enter *his* kingdom and, not liking the prince's response, slapped him across the face with the back of his gauntlet, after which some men around the king dispatched him in cold blood.[18]

The Tudor chronicler Edward Hall gives a similar but more detailed account. He states that the prince was taken by Sir Richard Croft, 'a wise and a valiant knight'.[19] At the end of the battle King Edward had declared that whoever brought him the prince would be richly rewarded and promised that the prince would come to no harm. Trusting the king's words,

Croft handed over the prince, 'a goodly feminine & a well featured young gentleman', to the king who demanded to know why he had entered his kingdom with banners displayed.[20] The prince, 'being bold of stomach & of a good courage', responded that he had come to recover his father's kingdom and inheritance.[21] Edward slapped him with the back of his gauntlet and then Gloucester, Clarence, Thomas, Marquis of Dorset and Lord Hastings murdered him. It is most likely that the prince was killed during the melee and rout of the main battle and did not have the opportunity to talk to his cousin, the king. In a letter the Duke of Clarence wrote to Henry Vernon, he states that the prince was 'slain in plain battle'.[22] The prince was later buried in the choir of Tewkesbury Abbey.

Following the battle, Somerset claimed sanctuary in Tewkesbury Abbey but he was forcibly removed, tried by Gloucester in his role as Constable of England and sentenced to death. Somerset was beheaded in the centre of the town, and with that the direct male line of the Beauforts, the illegitimate descendants of John of Gaunt, became extinct. On 7 May, as Edward left Tewkesbury, he received word that Queen Margaret had been found at 'a poor religious place' where she had taken refuge before the battle.[23] On 11 May she was brought, with the prince's widow Anne Neville, to the king at Coventry and afterwards conveyed with the king to London. She would remain a prisoner until 1475 when King Louis paid her ransom of 50,000 crowns and she returned to France. She died there seven years later, in 1482.

On 21 May, King Edward returned to London. The death of the prince had sealed the deposed Henry VI's fate. Two days later he died mysteriously in the Tower, 'of pure displeasure, and melancholy'.[24] The truth was not nearly as romantic as the author of the *Arrival* would have us believe. It is evident that Edward IV had Henry killed, but how he died and by whose hand is unknown. The Crowland Chronicler's comment that Edward's youngest brother, Richard, Duke of Gloucester, was present at the Tower has led many to believe that he carried out the act but this has no foundation. The author is merely stating that Richard was present, not that he was Henry's murderer.

The deaths of Prince Edward and Henry VI brought an end to the second phase of the Wars of the Roses. King Edward would reign peacefully for twelve years. But when he died in 1483, the wars would begin anew – and dramatically extinguish the House of York.

12

Edward V

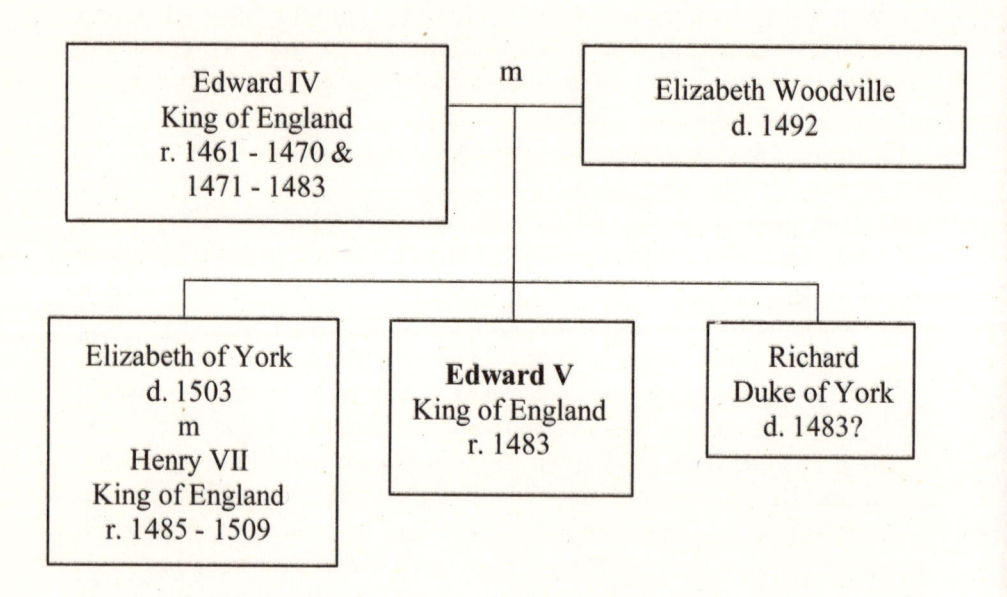

```
┌─────────────────────┐         ┌─────────────────────┐
│     Edward IV       │    m    │  Elizabeth Woodville│
│   King of England   │─────────│       d. 1492       │
│   r. 1461 - 1470 &  │         │                     │
│     1471 - 1483     │         └─────────────────────┘
└─────────────────────┘
           │
   ┌───────┼───────────────────────┐
┌──┴──────────┐  ┌──────────────┐  ┌──┴──────────┐
│Elizabeth of │  │   Edward V   │  │   Richard   │
│    York     │  │King of England│ │Duke of York │
│   d. 1503   │  │   r. 1483    │  │   d. 1483?  │
│      m      │  └──────────────┘  └─────────────┘
│  Henry VII  │
│King of England│
│ r. 1485-1509│
└─────────────┘
```

In the summer of 1483, twelve-year-old King Edward V, the eldest son and heir of King Edward IV and Elizabeth Woodville, entered the Tower of London to prepare for his upcoming coronation on 22 June. He was later joined by his younger brother, the nine-year-old Richard, Duke of York, and no doubt eagerly anticipated the pomp and celebrations to come. It was not to be. In a surprise twist, Edward and Richard were suddenly declared illegitimate and their uncle Richard, Duke of Gloucester was crowned as King Richard III in Edward's place. Soon after, the two boys disappeared under mysterious circumstances, never to be seen again.

Birth and Early Life

King Edward V, the eldest son and heir of King Edward IV and Queen Elizabeth Woodville, was born on 2 November 1470.[1] He was the fourth child but first son born to the couple, their three preceding children being daughters. King Edward's eldest child, Elizabeth of York, the future queen of Henry VII, had been born in 1466, followed by Mary in 1467 and Cecily in 1469.

Edward V

Elizabeth did not give birth to Edward in the comfort of a royal palace but rather in the sanctuary at Westminster Abbey. The previous month, Edward IV had fled to the continent when the Earl of Warwick and George, Duke of Clarence had invaded England and placed Henry VI back on the throne during the Readeption. On 1 October, a heavily pregnant Elizabeth, accompanied by her mother, Jacquetta, Duchess Dowager of Bedford, her three daughters and Elizabeth, Lady Scrope, had stolen out of the Tower and sought sanctuary at the abbey. Just over a month later, Elizabeth gave birth to a son and heir. The boy was baptised, 'with small pomp like a poor man's child', and named Edward in honour of his absent father.[2] His godfathers were Thomas Milling, Abbot of Westminster and John Eastney, Prior of Westminster, while Lady Scrope stood as his godmother.[3]

Warwick seems to have respected the laws of sanctuary and he left Elizabeth and her family in peace. When King Edward made his triumphant return and entered London on 11 April 1471 he wasted no time in going to Westminster, where he met his newborn son for the first time 'to his heart's singular comfort and gladness'.[4] The birth of a male heir after a reign of nearly ten years was regarded as God's blessing over the new dynasty. That night, the young prince left the safety of Westminster for the first time and was taken by his parents to Baynard's Castle. On the afternoon of 13 April, King Edward rode out to battle Warwick at Barnet, not knowing if he would see his son again. Edward was victorious and less than a month later he had secured his son's future by the deaths of both Edward of Lancaster and Henry VI. The legitimate Lancastrian line was extinct and the Yorkists were now undisputed kings of England.

The first ten years of Edward V's life was thus largely a time of peace and tranquillity. The prince was provided with his own household, which included a chancellor (his godfather Thomas, Abbot of Westminster), a steward (Richard Fenys of Dacre) and chamberlain (Thomas Vaughn). The usual honours afforded the heir apparent soon followed. On 26 June 1471 he was created Prince of Wales and Earl of Chester and on 17 July he was created Duke of Cornwall. On 3 July he was declared to be the king's heir and those present, including Richard, Duke of Gloucester, took an oath to crown him if he should survive his father.[5] Five days later, King Edward appointed a council, including Queen Elizabeth, George, Duke of Clarence, Richard, Duke of Gloucester and the queen's brother Anthony, Earl Rivers, to administer his lands 'until he shall be of the age of 14 years'.[6]

Like all royal children, Edward was at first placed in the nursery and it is recorded that a lady named Elizabeth Darcy oversaw it. In 1473, the king decided to send the three-year-old Edward to reside at Ludlow Castle on the border of Wales where he was to act as a royal presence in the lawless principality. He was nominally to head the Council of the Welsh Marches, whose role it was to administer Wales in his name. The prince's uncle Anthony, Earl Rivers, was appointed governor of the prince and John Alcock, Bishop of Rochester was appointed tutor, so that he 'may be brought up in virtue and cunning'.[7] Alcock was also made president of the Council of the Marches.

On 27 September 1473, King Edward produced a set of statutes and ordinances for the education and running of the prince's household. They offer us an invaluable insight into the daily life of the prince and show the care and diligence that the king applied to his upbringing. Edward was to be woken up 'at a convenient hour, according to his age' and while he prepared himself for the day ahead his chaplains were to say matins in his presence.[8] He was then led to his chapel where he celebrated Mass. After breakfast, he was to be 'occupied in such virtuous learning as his age shall now suffice to receive', until dinner.[9] The prince's curriculum included 'grammar, music, and other cunning and exercises of humanity'.[10] At dinner time, 10 a.m. or 11 a.m. on fasting days, he was to be 'honourably served' by servants who bore the king's livery and read stories that 'behoveth to a Prince to understand'.[11] The prince would then celebrate evensong in his chapel, have his supper at 4 p.m. and he was then allowed to play until 8 p.m., when he would go to his chamber, 'joyous and merry towards his bed'.[12]

As well as his practical education, the prince was given some political responsibilities to prepare him for his future role as king. In 1475 he acted as keeper of the Realm and king's lieutenant while King Edward embarked upon an abortive invasion of France. Before he left, the king knighted Edward and his brother Richard, Duke of York, born on 18 April 1473 at Westminster.

The Succession

One event which would have profound implications for the succession was the attainder and execution of Edward IV's second brother, George, Duke of Clarence, in 1478. Clarence had married Isabel Neville, the eldest daughter of the Earl of Warwick, by whom he had two children who survived infancy, Margaret and Edward. Isabella died in 1476 and the following year the distraught Clarence, suspecting she was killed by a poisoner, had illegally put to death one of his servants. The following year the king, who had never truly forgiven Clarence for his past rebellions, scuppered his plans to marry Mary, heiress of Burgundy, souring relations between them. Things reached a crisis point when the king had Thomas Burdet, one of Clarence's household, arrested and executed for practising witchcraft. Clarence, sure of the man's innocence, strode defiantly into the council chamber at Westminster and had the condemned man's last words read aloud. The king was furious and had Clarence thrown into the Tower. In January 1478 Clarence was put on trial on a range of charges, including inciting the people to rise against the king, plotting the king and his family's destruction and spreading rumours that the king was illegitimate and that Clarence was therefore rightful King of England. He was found guilty, attainted and executed, possibly by being drowned in a butt of Malmsey wine. Clarence's attainder passed on to his

Edward V

children, thereby nullifying their claim to the throne and making Richard, Duke of Gloucester hereditary heir after King Edward's children.

Young Edward would later be joined by six more siblings: Margaret, born in 1472; Richard, Duke of York, born the following year; and then Anne, George (who died young), Catherine and Bridget. Therefore the prospect of a smooth succession seemed sure when King Edward died on 9 April 1483, aged just forty, possibly of an apoplexy or from a chill caught while fishing. King Edward's premature death left England in the unenviable position of once again having a minor on the throne, with Prince Edward just twelve years old. On his deathbed, King Edward appointed Richard, Duke of Gloucester to act as Protector during his son's minority. The stage was set for the wars to begin anew.

Kingship

Unlike the majority of other figures in this book, Prince Edward actually succeeded his father as king. However, his reign would prove extremely short and he would never be crowned. At the time of Edward IV's death, the new king was still residing at Ludlow.

Following Edward IV's funeral, the nobles gathered at Westminster to discuss the government of the realm during the new king's minority. Gloucester, who had been appointed Protector, was not present at the deliberations but was at Middleham Castle in Yorkshire. The haughty Woodvilles, who were afraid of losing the power and influence that they had enjoyed under the old king, pressed for a regency council to be formed instead, with Gloucester begrudgingly accepted as its head. Gloucester was notified of the Woodvilles' machinations by Edward IV's chamberlain and former bosom buddy William, Lord Hastings, an inveterate enemy of the Woodvilles, who counselled Gloucester to bring a force and seize control of the new king and impose his rights as Protector. Gloucester wrote letters to the council begging them to honour the dead king's wishes, but his pleas were ignored and the regency council was formed. Young Edward's coronation was scheduled for 4 May and he was summoned to London in preparation.

Edward, now Edward V, set out for London on 24 April in the company of his uncle Earl Rivers, his half-brother Richard Grey (one of the sons from Elizabeth Woodville's previous marriage) and his household. It had been previously agreed that Edward would rendezvous with Gloucester at Northampton in order that they may enter the city together. Gloucester, meanwhile, had left Middleham and met with Henry Stafford, Duke of Buckingham at Northampton. Buckingham was himself a descendant of Edward III through Edward's fifth and youngest son, Thomas of Woodstock. Buckingham hated the Woodvilles and he had been forced by the previous king into marrying one of Queen Elizabeth's sisters, a bride he regarded as being beneath him.

Edward arrived at Stony Stratford on Tuesday 29 April and dispatched Earl Rivers and Richard Grey to meet the two dukes at Northampton. On their arrival, Gloucester treated them kindly and dined with them that evening. The next day, the four of them rode together to see Edward but as they reached the outskirts of Stony Stratford, Gloucester suddenly had Rivers and Grey seized and sent them to be imprisoned in his castles in the north. Then, on reaching Edward's presence, he arrested the king's aged chamberlain, Thomas Vaughan, and other members of his household. Gloucester paid deference to the king and explained that he had arrested Rivers, Grey and Vaughan as they had sought to deny him the role of Protector and that they had plotted to destroy him by laying ambushes for him on the road and at London. Gloucester opined that these evil ministers, who had contributed to Edward IV's vices and death, should be removed and he, who was best suited to the task, be made Protector. The young Edward professed that he had seen no evil in his counsellors and that he trusted in his mother and the peers to see to the good governance of the realm. He had little choice, however, but to surrender himself into Gloucester's care. Gloucester dismissed the rest of Edward's attendants and escorted the young king to London. Before they reached the city, Gloucester's accusations were seemingly proven true when four carts full of weapons, each bearing the Woodville device, were apprehended.

The queen, on receiving word of Gloucester's manoeuvres, attempted to raise a force, but on discovering that the other nobles were unwilling to help she once again sought sanctuary at Westminster along with her daughters and sons Richard, Duke of York and Thomas Grey. On 4 May, the day appointed for the coronation, Edward, Gloucester and Buckingham arrived outside London. They were greeted by the mayor and citizens who escorted them honourably into the city. Edward was dressed in blue velvet while Gloucester and Buckingham wore black as a sign of mourning for the recently deceased king.[13] They had dragged before them the carts full of weapons, a public display of the slipperiness of the Woodvilles. Edward V was placed in the Bishop of London's Palace and Gloucester had the nobles, mayor and aldermen of London pay fealty to him. 'This ... was done by all with the greatest pleasure and delight,' notes the Crowland Chronicler.[14] A council meeting was then convened where it was decided to place the young king in the safety of the Tower of London while preparations were made for the coronation. This was not an insidious move by Gloucester but ordinary practice, as kings at the time would leave in procession from the Tower to Westminster Abbey on the day of their coronation.

Gloucester was made Protector of the Realm, 'with the consent and good-will of all the lords, with power to order and forbid in every matter, just like another king, and according as the necessity of the case should demand'.[15] At the same time the date of the coronation was rescheduled for 22 June.

Gloucester summoned two council meetings to convene on 13 June, one at the Tower and one at Westminster. The Protector was himself present at the Tower when, in a shock move, he suddenly seized Lord Hastings and, using his powers as constable, had him beheaded immediately on charges of treason.

Gloucester also had Thomas, Archbishop of York and John, Bishop of Ely arrested and sent to castles in Wales. Hastings' elation at Gloucester's rise to power was recorded by the Crowland Chronicler, and his alleged offences remain a mystery. Dominic Mancini, an Italian who was present in London during the summer of 1483, notes that these three men had often gathered at each other's houses. Were they plotting against the duke, or was this just a ploy to rid the king of his closest supporters? Mancini paints Hastings as loyal to Gloucester but the Crowland Chronicle mentions that before Gloucester had entered London on 4 May, Hastings had raised his own army in the city. Was this to aid Gloucester, or to oppose him?[16] Polydore Vergil, writing during the reign of Henry VII, states that Hastings had repented of his support for Gloucester and had attempted to raise an army in order to pluck the king from his grasp but that he did not enjoy the backing of the rest of the nobility.[17]

It was decided that Edward's brother Richard, Duke of York, who was currently in sanctuary with the queen, should join his brother at the Tower and take part in the coronation. Gloucester sent armed men to surround Westminster Abbey while Thomas Bourchier, Archbishop of Canterbury, negotiated with the queen. He promised that the boy would be returned to her after the coronation and she, believing the word of a man of God, duly handed him over.

After this, Mancini reports, Edward V and Richard were isolated from their adherents and placed within the inner apartments of the Tower, and 'day by day began to be seen more rarely behind the bars and windows, till at length they ceased to appear altogether'.[18]

Disappearance

On 22 June, the rescheduled date for Edward's coronation, Dr Ralph Shaw delivered a sermon to the people from St Paul's Cross in which he declared that Edward V, Richard, Duke of York and their sisters were illegitimate and therefore unable to ascend the throne. Before Edward IV had married Elizabeth, Shaw explained, he had been precontracted in marriage to one Lady Eleanor Butler (*née* Talbot), the daughter of the Hundred Years War hero John Talbot, Earl of Shrewsbury. Edward had seemingly used the promise of marriage to get the lady into bed, a move he would later repeat on Elizabeth Woodville. Edward of course did marry Elizabeth, but a precontract was binding by law and he hadn't bothered to have it annulled, meaning that his marriage to Elizabeth was bigamous and their children illegitimate. The children of George, Duke of Clarence were already barred from the succession by his attainder and thus the only direct male descendant of Richard, Duke of York who was legitimate was the Duke of Gloucester.

A few days later the case was put before the judges and magistrates of the city at the Guildhall. They found in Gloucester's favour, and the following day he rode to Westminster Hall and took his seat on the marble royal chair. On 6 July, at Westminster, he was crowned King Richard III by Archbishop Bourchier alongside his queen, Anne Neville, the former wife of Edward of Lancaster.

This begs the question: had Richard planned to seize the throne all along, taking steps to eliminate those standing in his way? This is, of course, the prevalent view, most damningly portrayed in William Shakespeare's play, *Richard III*. Richard, in a carefully orchestrated plan, is said to have lain the chess pieces, eradicating threats to his ambitions and getting the two princes in his clutches before making his final move, the story of the pre-contract, and having himself crowned as king. There are, however, those who take a more nuanced approach. Historian David Baldwin suggests that Richard, at least initially, did not seek to take the throne but that he was driven to do so by his fear that the Woodvilles would use their influence with the new king to destroy him, either physically or politically. Richard, he suggests, after much soul searching and having taken the advice of senior nobles, decided his best avenue was to take the crown himself.[19] As we have seen, Richard's fears may have been valid. The Woodvilles certainly attempted to take the protectorship from him and, if we put stock in the weapons discovered near London, were willing to use force. Another possibility is that Richard was taken by surprise by the discovery of the pre-contract and genuinely believed that he was rightful heir. Another factor that gives pause for thought is Richard's previous good character. Unlike the Duke of Clarence, Richard had proven a loyal supporter of Edward IV and a pillar of his regime. He had shared the king's exile in 1470 and had fought at his side at Barnet and Tewkesbury, leading the king to shower him with honours and entrust him with the lieutenancy of the unruly north.

Richard, however, was left with a predicament: what was he to do with the ex-king Edward V and his little brother, still resident in the Tower? Like Arthur of Brittany, the two boys could be used as a weapon against Richard by his enemies and, if Richard were deposed, set up as king. Unfortunately, the danger they posed was soon brought home. After his coronation, the newly crowned King Richard III began a progress around the realm, during which he received the troubling news that there had been an attempted rising in young Edward's favour. The plot was unsuccessful but soon after rumours spread that King Richard had arranged for the two boys to be killed. Their true fate remains unknown to this day, although they were never seen again, alive or dead.

Mancini reports that Edward's doctor, John Argentine, who was the last attendant to see him before his disappearance, said his charge had 'sought remission of his sins by daily confession and penance, because he believed that death was facing him'.[20] Was this the fear of being murdered, or had the boy fallen ill? According to the Great Chronicle of London, the boys were last seen 'shooting [archery] and playing in the garden of the Tower at sundry times'.[21] Mancini reports the rumours of their demise but admits that he has been unable to ascertain if and how they had died.

By the time Henry VIII sat on the throne, the mystery had apparently been solved. Sir Thomas More, Henry VIII's chancellor, recorded in his work

Edward V

The History of King Richard The Third that Richard, while on progress, had ordered Sir Robert Brackenbury, Constable of the Tower, to have the boys put to death. Brackenbury refused to do so and Richard instead entrusted Sir James Tyrell, his Master of the Henchmen, to procure the keys to the Tower and carry out the act. Tyrell appointed one of the prince's guards, Miles Forest and his horsekeeper, John Dighton, to carry out the deed. At midnight the following night, Forest and Dighton crept into the boys' chamber and smothered them with their pillows. Their bodies were afterwards buried at the foot of some stairs in the Tower, but Richard later ordered them to be removed to a more honourable spot. The reburial was carried out by a chaplain of Sir Robert Brackenbury and the location conveniently went with him to the grave. More attributes the story to the confession of Sir James Tyrell before his execution in 1502 on unrelated charges of treason. There are problems with the story, however. No official record or publication was ever made of Tyrell's confession, which is strange considering it could only strengthen the Tudors' precarious hold on the throne. Strangely enough, although More notes that Miles Forest died of natural causes, he ventures that Dighton was still a free man at the time of his writing even though he was a known regicide and child-killer.[22]

Various alternative theories have been offered to explain the boys' fate. They could have died of natural causes or been shipped abroad by Richard into the safety of the Low Countries. During the reign of Henry VII, a pretender appeared claiming to be the grown-up Richard, Duke of York. Blame for their possible murder has also been attributed to Buckingham, who had his own claim to the throne and, as we shall see, later rebelled against Richard. Another possible culprit is Henry VII, who, after defeating Richard III at the Battle of Bosworth, had Edward IV's children legitimated so that he could marry his eldest daughter, Elizabeth of York. In doing so he was giving Edward V and Richard, Duke of York a better claim to the throne than his own. Based on the evidence available, it is entirely plausible that Henry VII ordered their deaths. The generally held view – hotly disputed – is that Richard was responsible. Richard had both the motive and the means. As the failed rebellion proved, the boys would be a threat to him so long as they lived.

This was seemingly confirmed during the reign of Charles II, when the skeletons of two children were discovered under some stairs in the Tower of London during construction work on the White Tower. This discovery tallied partly with More's account of the princes' murder and burial. The remains were assumed to belong to the two princes and were placed in an urn in Westminster Abbey that can still be seen today. In the 1930s the bones were examined and declared to be those of Edward and Richard, but the conclusions drawn have been questioned and there are calls to have them examined again with modern technology.[23] Interestingly, Thomas More's account of the murder, if we are to take it as the truth, states that the bodies were buried *before* the stairs rather than under them. More also states that they were later removed, suggesting that these bones could not possibly be those of the princes. The mystery continues.

13

Edward of Middleham

```
    Richard III         m         Anne Neville
  King of England                    d. 1485
   r. 1483 - 1485

            Edward of Middleham
              Prince of Wales
                 d. 1484
```

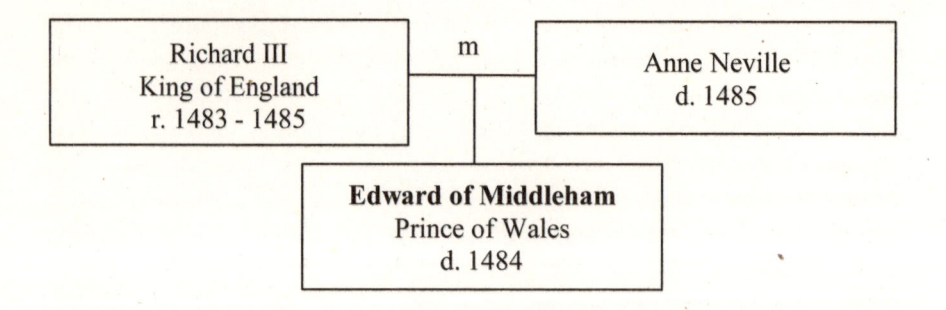

Edward of Middleham, Prince of Wales was the only child and heir of King Richard III and his queen, Anne Neville. He was born in 1476 at his father's palatial residence of Middleham Castle in Wensleydale, Yorkshire and was baptised Edward in honour of his uncle King Edward IV.[1]

Richard had married Anne Neville, the youngest daughter of Warwick the Kingmaker and widow of Edward of Lancaster, in 1472. Warwick's death at the Battle of Barnet in 1471 had left his two daughters, Isabel and Anne, as wealthy heiresses. Common law stipulated that when a testator died leaving only daughters, their property would be divided between them. George, Duke of Clarence had already married Isabel and Richard wished to marry Anne in order to take his own share of the prize. Unsurprisingly, Clarence did not want to relinquish any of his wife's property and he had Anne disguised as a kitchen maid and concealed in a house in London. Richard, not to be outdone, soon discovered her whereabouts and managed to steal her away to the sanctuary of St Martin's Church. This caused a heated argument to erupt between the two brothers that was eventually brought before the king and council, which pronounced that Richard would marry Anne and that the brothers were to share the inheritance between them. Among the castles awarded to Richard was that of Middleham, where Richard himself had spent many years of his childhood as a ward of Warwick the Kingmaker.

Details of Edward of Middleham's short life are unsurprisingly sparse. He likely spent the first seven years of his life with his mother at Middleham. He is noted as having a nurse named Isabel Burgh who on 28 June 1485 is recorded in the patent rolls as having received an annuity of twenty silver marks from the issues of Middleham.[2] At the time of his birth, Edward could look forward to one day inheriting his parents' lands and titles, but once Edward IV had his own brood of children he had little hope of ever wearing the crown. He did, however, profit from the death of George, Duke of Clarence when on 15 February 1478 he gained his disgraced uncle's title of Earl of Salisbury.[3]

Heir Apparent

Edward next comes into prominence after Richard's accession in 1483. Edward now went from being an unimportant son of a duke to heir apparent to the throne. He was not present at Richard and Anne's coronation on 6 July but remained at Middleham. The reason for his absence is unknown but his short life has led historians to believe that he was a sickly child. On 19 July, Richard appointed Edward, 'the king's firstborn son', as Lieutenant of Ireland, the title his Mortimer forebears had enjoyed, for a period of three years.[4] After the coronation, Richard and Anne went on a royal progress of the kingdom. Young Edward joined his parents' procession at Pontefract sometime in late August, where they remained a few days.[5] From Pontefract they travelled on to York where they received a sumptuous welcome and many feasts and pageants were held in the new king's honour. Queen Anne is said to have followed behind her husband in the progress, holding Edward by the hand, 'crowned also with so great honour, joy, and congratulation of the inhabitants'.[6]

The highlight of the visit occurred on Monday 8 September, when Richard dubbed Edward as Prince of Wales.[7] Edward was invested 'as the custom is by the girding on of the sword, the handing over and setting of the garland on his head, and of the gold ring on his finger, and of the gold staff in his hand'.[8] Richard continued to Lincoln while Edward and his mother returned to Middleham. It was at Lincoln that Richard learnt that a rebellion was afoot, headed by his erstwhile ally the Duke of Buckingham. Buckingham's reason for rebelling against Richard is unknown but it may be that Buckingham, as a descendant of Edward III himself, had his own designs on the crown. A more troubling threat came from Margaret Beaufort, now the senior member of the Beaufort family. Margaret was the granddaughter of John Beaufort, the eldest of John of Gaunt's Beaufort children, and in 1455 she had married Edmund Tudor, Earl of Richmond, eldest son of Owen Tudor and Henry V's queen, Catherine of Valois. Edmund Tudor died in January 1457 and Margaret, then fourteen years old, had afterwards given birth to his son, Henry Tudor, Earl of Richmond, the future King Henry VII. Henry Tudor thus had Lancastrian blood and, after the deaths of Edward of Lancaster and Henry VI, could claim to be heir male to the House of Lancaster. Margaret Beaufort had a superior hereditary claim according to primogeniture but, although female succession was in theory accepted, she did not push her own right, instead focussing her efforts on her son. Henry's claim was dubious, however, as the Beauforts, though legitimated by Richard II, had been barred from the throne during the reign of Henry IV.

After the Battle of Tewkesbury, Henry's uncle Jasper Tudor had whisked the young Henry Tudor away to Brittany. His claim to the throne, no matter how flimsy, made him a person of interest to Edward IV who attempted to lure him back to England with promises of marrying his eldest daughter, Elizabeth of York. Later, when people believed that the Princes in the Tower were dead, their thoughts turned to Henry across the Channel. The objective of Buckingham's rebellion was to place Henry on the throne and boost his claim by marrying him to Elizabeth of York.

Buckingham's rebellion was a failure. The duke was at his manor of Brecknock in Wales and intended to cross the Severn into England and join up with the other rebels. Richard's supporters destroyed the bridges over the Severn while the river, which had been swollen by heavy rains, prevented Buckingham and his army from crossing. Buckingham's adherents deserted him and he was forced to take shelter in Shropshire where he was soon captured. He was brought before Richard at Salisbury and afterwards beheaded. Henry Tudor made it to Plymouth but was informed of Buckingham's fate and quickly turned back, heading to Brittany to fight another day. After quelling the rebellion, Richard spent Christmas in London in 'pompous celebration'.[9]

Richard opened his first and only parliament in January 1484 when his title to the throne was confirmed in the statute known as *Titulus Regius*. One day, in February, Richard called together the majority of the lords of the realm and the knights and esquires of his household and met them 'in a certain lower room, near the passage which leads to the queen's apartments' where he had them take an oath that they would accept his son Edward as king if anything were to happen to him.[10] After Parliament had closed, Richard convinced Elizabeth Woodville and her daughters to leave sanctuary and come to his court.

Death

So far Richard's reign had proven a success. He had managed to have himself crowned, had seen off his opponent's attempts to replace him with the hated Henry Tudor and had an heir waiting in the wings to carry on his dynasty. Then, just like that, everything changed. Prince Edward died suddenly at Middleham after a short illness, aged just seven or eight, on 9 April 1484. His parents were residing at Nottingham Castle when they were given the devastating news. '[Y]ou might have seen his father and mother in a state almost bordering on madness, by reason of their sudden grief,' records the Crowland Continuator, who was no fan of the king.[11]

It is not recorded where Edward was buried, although a tomb in St Helen's Church in Sheriff Hutton has traditionally been said to contain the prince. Edward's death was a turning point in Richard's reign. He had no other legitimate children to whom he could leave the throne, and misfortune heaped upon misfortune until he was killed fighting against Henry Tudor at the Battle of Bosworth.

14

John de la Pole, Earl of Lincoln

```
┌─────────────────┐
│    Richard      │
│  Duke of York   │
│    d. 1460      │
│       m         │
│  Cecily Neville │
│    d. 1495      │
└─────────────────┘
         │
    ┌────┴──────────────────────────┐
┌───────────────────┐         ┌──────────────────────┐
│ Elizabeth         │    m    │  John de la Pole,    │
│ Plantagenet       │─────────│  2nd Duke of Suffolk │
│ d. 1503/4         │         │  d. 1492             │
└───────────────────┘         └──────────────────────┘
         │
  ┌──────┼──────────────────┐
┌───────────────┐  ┌───────────────┐  ┌───────────────┐
│ John de la Pole│  │    Edmund    │  │   Richard     │
│ Earl of Lincoln│  │ Earl of Suffolk│  │ 'The White Rose'│
│   d. 1487     │  │   d. 1513    │  │   d. 1525     │
└───────────────┘  └───────────────┘  └───────────────┘
```

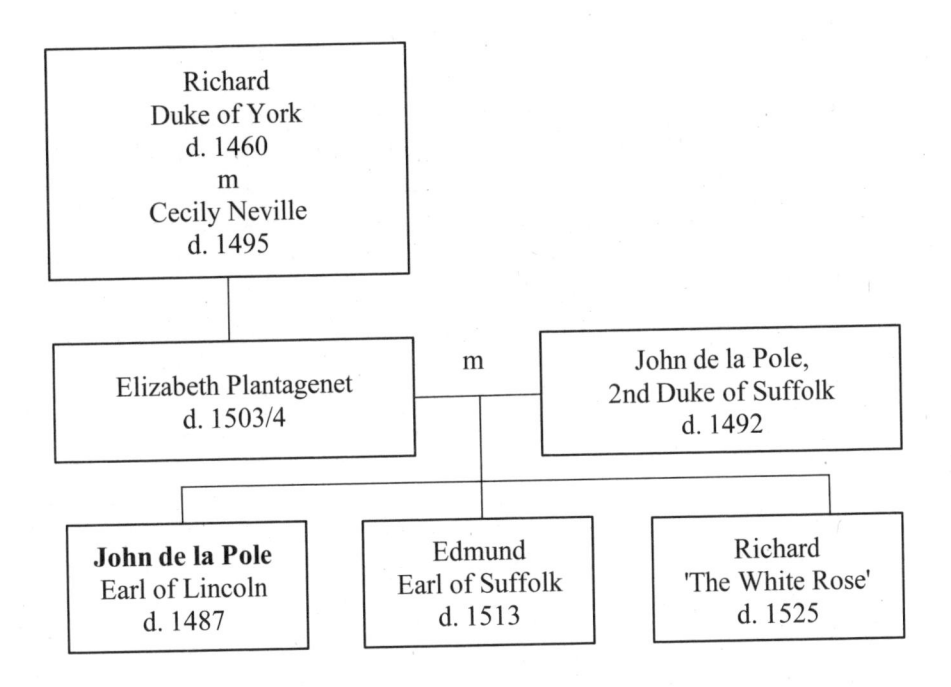

On 4 June 1487, John de la Pole, Earl of Lincoln, landed at Furness Fells in modern Cumbria at the head of an army of Irish and German mercenaries. He had come to overthrow King Henry VII, the first Tudor king, and place his cousin Edward, Earl of Warwick, the son of George, Duke of Clarence, on the throne. But all was not as it seemed. The ten-year-old boy who accompanied Lincoln and who purported to be the Earl of Warwick was a fake. The real earl was languishing in the Tower of London. Undeterred, Lincoln marched on to meet his fate at the Battle of Stoke, the final battle of the Wars of the Roses.

Birth and Early Life

John de la Pole, Earl of Lincoln, was the eldest son and heir of John de la Pole, 2nd Duke of Suffolk and his wife, Elizabeth Plantagenet, the second surviving sister of Edward IV and Richard III. As the senior grandson of

Richard, Duke of York, Lincoln had a claim to the throne that potentially saw him designated as Richard III's heir presumptive after the premature death of Edward of Middleham.

Lincoln's date of birth is unrecorded but he is thought to have been born about 1464.[1] His paternal grandfather was William de la Pole, Duke of Suffolk, the detested chamberlain of King Henry VI who had been exiled and beheaded at sea in 1450. Suffolk, however, was never attainted of treason and his lands passed to Lincoln's father, John, who was then only seven. Lincoln was thus at birth heir to the Suffolk inheritance. Few details survive of his early years. He may have been educated in his parents' household or sent into the household of another great nobleman or that of his uncle, the king.

On 13 March 1467, Edward IV created the three-year-old John as Earl of Lincoln and granted him an annuity of £20 from the issues of its estates.[2] On 18 April 1475 he was made a knight of the Bath alongside Edward, Prince of Wales (Edward V) and his brother Richard, Duke of York. Lincoln was present at the reburial of his grandfather Richard, Duke of York and his uncle Edmund, Earl of Rutland at Fotheringhay on 29 July 1476,[3] as well as attending the wedding of his cousin Richard, Duke of York to Anne Mowbray in 1478.

Lincoln acted as chief mourner at the funeral of his uncle Edward IV, held at Westminster Abbey on 16 April 1483.[4] He walked in procession behind the coffin with the other members of the laity as it was borne into Westminster Abbey for the funeral service. Two days later, at the service at Windsor Chapel, Lincoln offered a Mass penny and then joined in the ceremonial laying of cloth over the body. The amount of cloth a person laid depended upon their proximity to the deceased. Lincoln offered four pieces of cloth of gold to the body 'because he was the king's nephew and son and heir of the duke of Suffolk'.[5]

At some point Lincoln married Margaret, the daughter of Thomas FitzAlan, Earl of Arundel and Margaret Woodville, one of the sisters of Elizabeth Woodville.[6] In the tumultuous events that followed Edward IV's death, the nineteen-year-old Lincoln backed the claim of his uncle Richard, Duke of Gloucester. He carried the orb at Richard's coronation on 6 July 1483 and supported his uncle during Buckingham's rebellion, for which he was amply rewarded 'for his good service against the rebels'.[7]

Richard's Heir?

After Edward of Middleham's death, Lincoln was the next senior male member of the Yorkist dynasty. Edward IV's children had been declared illegitimate while Edward, Earl of Warwick and his sister Margaret, the children of George, Duke of Clarence, had been attainted along with their father. This was confirmed in the statute *Titulus Regius*, which stated that 'George, Duke

John de la Pole, Earl of Lincoln

of Clarence, brother to King Edward [was] convicted and attainted of high treason, by reason whereof all [his] issue ... was and is disabled and debarred of all right and claim ... they might have ... to the crown and royal dignity of this realm'.[8] King Richard had no legitimate heir and he could not afford to reverse the attainder in favour of the Earl of Warwick as it would invite a claim superior to his own. The other option was to designate his loyal and eldest nephew, the Earl of Lincoln. Lincoln was not the next in blood according to the rules of primogeniture. Of the eight daughters of Richard, Duke of York, only three had reached adulthood. The eldest of these, Anne Plantagenet (d. 1476), had married Sir Thomas St Leger and had a daughter named Anne who could claim to be heir presumptive, but she was young and female. With the prospect that Henry Tudor may one day invade, the pragmatic choice would be Lincoln, who was male and already an adult and could thus lead an army.

It is a matter of dispute whether Richard ever named Lincoln as his heir or even if he had the right to do so. The only source to say he did is the historian John Rous, who tells us that Richard had at first designated the Earl of Warwick as his heir apparent but that Warwick was later 'placed in custody and the Earl of Lincoln was preferred to him'.[9] It seems unlikely that Richard would ever recognise Warwick as his heir due to the reasons noted above, and this throws the rest of Rous's statement into doubt. As historian Matthew Lewis points out, Rous states that Richard named Warwick and then Lincoln as heir *apparent*, not heir presumptive, making the unlikely inference that Richard had given up on the idea of fathering another legitimate child of his own. In fact, we know that he hadn't.[10] Richard's grant of offices may be evidence that even if he did not designate Lincoln as his successor, he at least regarded him as such. He made Lincoln Lieutenant of Ireland on 21 August 1484 and President of the Council of the North to fill the void left behind by the death of Edward of Middleham. He was certainly the best possible candidate and would ensure that the Yorkists remained on the throne in the event of Richard's death without an heir of his body.

After the failure of Buckingham's rebellion, King Richard celebrated the Christmas of 1484 in great splendour at the palace of Westminster. Lincoln was likely present, as well as his cousin Elizabeth of York, who was seen dancing with Queen Anne. Rumours soon began to spread that the king intended to murder or divorce Anne and marry Elizabeth to prevent her from marrying Henry Tudor and to reconcile him with the Yorkists who had been alienated by his accession. It is unlikely that Richard intended to marry his niece as he was busy arranging a marriage for himself with Joanna of Portugal at the time.

During the festivities, Richard received word that Henry Tudor planned to invade England the following summer and he began preparing to meet him. Soon after, Queen Anne fell sick and died. Richard's enemies spread rumours that he had poisoned her so that he could marry Elizabeth, and he was forced to deny having done so in front of the mayor and citizens of London.

Richard spent the rest of the year readying for battle with Henry Tudor. On 7 August 1485, Henry landed at Milford Haven in Wales. On the 22nd, he met Richard near Market Bosworth in Leicestershire. It is likely that Lincoln was present at the ensuing Battle of Bosworth, although his participation is not recorded anywhere. During the battle, Richard was betrayed by the traitorous Stanley brothers and killed fighting in the press of his enemies, making him the second and last English king to die on the battlefield. With Richard dead, the victorious Henry Tudor was handed Richard's crown. The Plantagenet dynasty, which had reigned over England for a period of 331 years, was at an end.

Survivor

The day after the battle, Henry Tudor sent a circular letter announcing the death of Richard III and listing all those who had died in the battle. On it we find the name John, 'late Earl of Lincoln'.[11] Lincoln was not actually dead but he was presumed to be so in the confusion following the battle. Francis, Viscount Lovell, the loyal chamberlain of Richard III, is also listed among the dead when in reality he had escaped the battle and took sanctuary at a church in Colchester, vowing to fight another day.

Ever the pragmatist, Lincoln made his peace with Henry shortly after the battle. It is likely that his recognition of Henry was a temporary measure and that he secretly awaited a favourable opportunity to pursue his own claim. As the eldest male member of the Yorkist dynasty, Henry naturally eyed him with suspicion, but he did not attaint him of his lands.

One of Henry's first moves was to send Sir Robert Willoughby to Sheriff Hutton in order to gain custody of the ten-year-old Edward, Earl of Warwick. Although Warwick had been attainted along with his father, he now formed a beacon of hope for the Yorkists and Henry wanted him safely locked away before he could become a source of opposition to his rule. Warwick was duly handed over to Willoughby and he was deposited in the Tower of London.

Lincoln was present at Henry's coronation at Westminster Abbey on 30 October and then at his first parliament, which opened on 7 November. Henry ingeniously had his reign dated from 21 August, the day before Bosworth, making Richard III and all who fought for him at Bosworth guilty of treason. Henry, who intended to shore up his tenuous claim to the throne by marrying Elizabeth of York, had *Titulus Regius* repealed, thereby legitimating Edward IV's surviving daughters. Once the parliament had concluded, he married Elizabeth on 18 January 1486, uniting the warring houses of York and Lancaster.

In March 1186 Henry went on a royal progress around the country, particularly to show himself off in the Ricardian heartlands of the north. Henry had been warned by Sir Hugh Conway that Francis, Viscount

Lovell and the Staffords, who had also sought sanctuary in Colchester after Bosworth, planned to mount an insurrection. Henry did not believe the story but took Lincoln with him on his progress as a precaution.

Henry and Lincoln spent the Easter festivities at Lincoln and were there when news came that Francis, Viscount Lovell and the Staffords had indeed left the sanctuary at Colchester. On the way to York Henry learnt that Lovell was in the vicinity with an army while the Staffords were raising rebellion in Worcestershire. Henry sent Jasper Tudor, now Duke of Bedford, against Lovell and offered a general pardon to any who desisted. The rebels quickly melted away and Lovell took ship and fled to the Low Countries.

With disaster averted, the royal entourage continued its journey. Lincoln is noted as being present at a feast at the Bishop's Palace in York and he accompanied Henry to Worcester Cathedral where he once again attended a feast.[12] On 11 May, Lincoln was one of those appointed to hold a session of oyer and terminer in Hereford, Worcester and Warwick against the rebels.[13] On 5 July, Lincoln was once again appointed among the lords to hold a session of oyer and terminer in the city and suburbs of London, 'to enquire of treasons, felonies and conspiracies ... and to hear and determine the same'.[14]

On 20 September, Elizabeth of York gave birth to Henry's first son and heir, Prince Arthur, at Winchester. Lincoln was present at Arthur's christening and had the honour of walking beside his aunt Cecily Plantagenet, the youngest of Richard, Duke of York's daughters, who carried the infant in her arms during the procession to Westminster Abbey. After Elizabeth's churching, Lincoln accompanied the king to Greenwich where they celebrated All Saints' Day. Lincoln had thus far proven a loyal and trusted servant to the new regime, but soon an opportunity for rebellion reared its head.

Rebel

Sometime between late 1486 and early 1487, a mysterious ten-year-old boy and a priest arrived at Dublin in Ireland. The priest, one Richard Simonds of Oxford, claimed that the boy was none other than George, Duke of Clarence's son Edward, Earl of Warwick. He claimed to have helped the boy escape from the Tower and brought him to Ireland, where the Yorkists were well loved, in order to raise an army and gain his rightful inheritance.

The boy known as 'Warwick' began to receive popular support. Thomas Geraldine, Earl of Kildare and Deputy of Ireland, lodged him at Dublin Castle and took up his cause with gusto. He set about convincing the rest of the Irish nobility to join him and sent messengers to Yorkist allies in England rallying them to the cause. Other messengers were also dispatched to the court of Margaret, Duchess Dowager of Burgundy, the sister of Edward IV and Richard III, and she joined the plot.

The boy's true identity has remained a mystery ever since. According to the official Tudor version of events, his real name was Lambert Simnel and, rather than being of royal birth, he was the son of an Oxford joiner and a pupil of Richard Simonds. The priest, it was said, dreamt of attaining a high ecclesiastical office and had at first decided to play upon the popular dissent and rumours that pervaded throughout England that one of the Princes in the Tower still lived. He educated Simnel in 'princely behaviour, civil manner & fruitful literature' and instilled in him a knowledge of his royal lineage so that he 'might the rather give credit to his deceitful pretence & false coloured invention'.[15] When rumours began to stir that Edward, Earl of Warwick had broken out of prison, Simonds changed the boy's alias to that of the Earl of Warwick. Lambert Simnel was near in age to Warwick and was said to have been of a similar stature. It no doubt helped that Warwick had not been seen in Ireland for many years.

Henry VII soon received word of this new threat and in early February 1487 he summoned a Great Council at Sheen. Lincoln attended the meeting, which suggests that Henry did not believe him to be involved. It was decided at the council to offer a general pardon to the rebels and also to parade the real Earl of Warwick through London to St Paul's to prove that the boy in Ireland was an impostor.

Lincoln now decided to play his hand. Soon after the meeting he threw off his Tudor mantle and went to visit one Sir Thomas Broughton. It was agreed that Lincoln would go to Flanders to see his aunt Margaret, Duchess Dowager of Burgundy, raise an army and join in the Irish expedition. It is not evident when Lincoln first became involved in the conspiracy. According to Bernard André, a blind poet from Henry VII's court, Margaret of Burgundy had sent letters to Lincoln at some point informing him of the plot and summoned him to her court.[16]

When Lincoln arrived at Margaret's court he met the exiled Francis Lovell, who had arrived a few days previously. It was agreed that they would raise an army and join forces with the Irish in leading an invasion of England. Margaret and Lincoln knew that the boy was a fake – Lincoln had likely seen the real Warwick many times at the Tower – so their ultimate intentions are open to speculation. According to the chronicler Edward Hall, they planned to set the real Earl of Warwick free and have him crowned King of England.[17] The author of the Chronicle of Calais, however, states that Margaret intended to put Lincoln on the throne.[18]

Margaret succeeded in raising an army of 2,000 German mercenaries, headed by Martin Schwartz, 'a noble man in Germany, and in martial feats very expert'.[19] Lincoln, Lovell and the army landed at Dublin on 5 May and Lincoln's Yorkist blood saw him take charge of the plot. On 24 May Simnel was solemnly crowned as King Edward VI at Christ Church Cathedral, where Lincoln and the others paid him homage. Then, accompanied by a large Irish force commanded by Kildare, they sailed for England and landed at Furness

John de la Pole, Earl of Lincoln

Fells in Lancashire (now Cumbria) on 4 June. Their forces were swelled by those of Sir Thomas Broughton and his brother John, as well as other Yorkists supporters, bringing their strength to 8,000. By 6 June Lincoln and the army had marched east to the town of Masham, from where he dispatched a letter to the Mayor of York under the regnal name Edward VI, requesting shelter and supplies for the army. From Masham, Lincoln proceeded to York in the hope of raising more men. Lincoln proved an able general and kept discipline among the unruly Irish soldiers, forbidding any ravaging of the land so that they might win hearts and minds. He was to be disappointed, however, as few men joined them. Undeterred, Lincoln instead made for Newark-upon-Trent hoping to attract more to the cause and then chance all in battle. Henry VII himself had done such a thing nearly two years before at Bosworth and had been victorious.

Henry, meanwhile, had not been idle. Having summoned an army, he moved off and met Lincoln's forces at the Battle of Stoke on 16 June. There are few descriptions of the battle. We know neither the deployment of the rebel army nor Lincoln's position in it, although it is likely that he took command of the main. The vanguard of the king's army, commanded by John de Vere, Earl of Oxford, was the first on the scene and they encountered the rebels around 9 a.m. and bore the brunt of the combat, the middle and rear seemingly languishing somewhere behind. The German mercenaries were a good match for the Englishmen but the Irish, although brave and valiant, were easily slaughtered as they were dressed 'after the manner of their country almost naked, without harness or armour'.[20]

Sometime during the battle, Lincoln was killed. Henry was not best pleased as he had hoped to interrogate the earl to uncover his fellow conspirators among the nobility. Lincoln was supposedly killed by some of the king's soldiers in order to hide their own treachery against the king.

The surviving rebels fled the field and were pursued by the victors. Thomas Broughton and Schwartz were counted among the dead while Francis, Lord Lovell escaped, never to be seen again. Lincoln's remains were buried on the field of battle in an unmarked grave. It is reported that 4,000 of the rebel army perished. Simnel, the false king, was spared due to his youth and innocence. He was soon employed in the king's kitchen as a turnspit and later promoted to the office of king's falconer.

At a parliament held on 9 November, Lincoln was attainted of all his lands and the earldom of Lincoln became extinct. But he had three younger brothers, and they now inherited his claim to the throne. Edmund de la Pole, his next brother, succeeded to the greatly diminished Suffolk inheritance in 1492 after their father's death. He became disillusioned with Henry VII and in 1501 fled to the court of Maximilian, King of the Romans, alongside his brother Richard de la Pole. Maximilian pledged to help him take the throne, but in 1502 he signed a treaty with Henry VII in which he agreed not to harbour any English rebels. Edmund eventually ended up a captive of Maximilian's son Philip of Burgundy. In 1506 Philip was forced by a storm to shelter in England while on his way to claim the throne of Castile. Philip signed a treaty with Henry and agreed to hand over Edmund. Henry promised not to kill Edmund and when he was shipped over had him thrown in the Tower. Edmund's brother Richard de la Pole, known as the 'White Rose', remained on the continent and joined the French court in 1512 as a pretender to the English crown.

On hearing this, Henry VIII, Henry VII's son and successor, had Edmund beheaded in 1513 while Richard, now the senior Yorkist claimant, was killed at the Battle of Pavia in 1525. Their final surviving brother, William, a captive in the Tower, died in 1538, bringing to an end the de la Pole claim to the throne.

15

Arthur Tudor, Prince of Wales

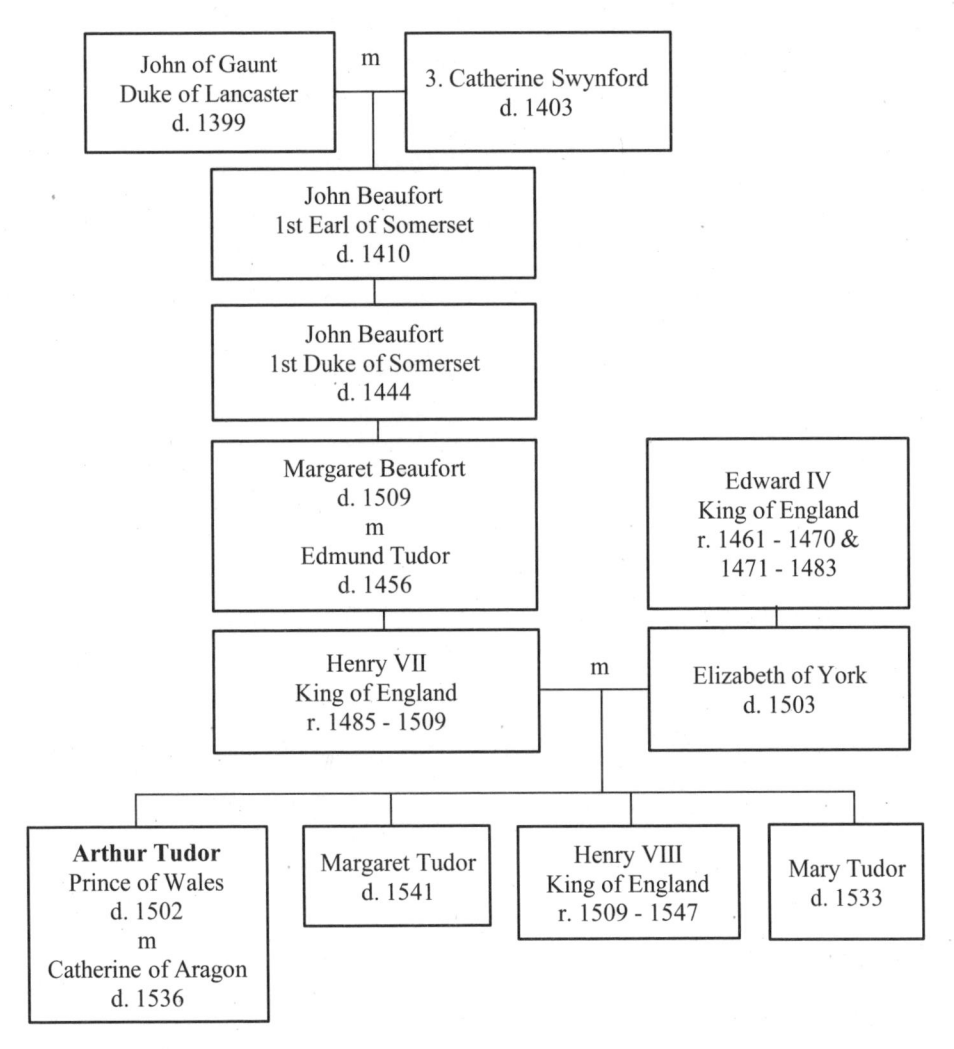

```
John of Gaunt — m — 3. Catherine Swynford
Duke of Lancaster         d. 1403
d. 1399

John Beaufort
1st Earl of Somerset
d. 1410

John Beaufort
1st Duke of Somerset
d. 1444

Margaret Beaufort          Edward IV
d. 1509                    King of England
m                          r. 1461 - 1470 &
Edmund Tudor               1471 - 1483
d. 1456

Henry VII — m — Elizabeth of York
King of England            d. 1503
r. 1485 - 1509

Arthur Tudor    Margaret Tudor    Henry VIII         Mary Tudor
Prince of Wales  d. 1541          King of England    d. 1533
d. 1502                           r. 1509 - 1547
m
Catherine of Aragon
d. 1536
```

Cecily of York held the infant tightly against the cold, as much for herself as for the child. It was a chilly October morning and the air felt pregnant with rain. Before her she could see the line of the procession snaking through the ancient city of Winchester to the cathedral.

The baby was wrapped snugly in a mantle of crimson cloth of gold, its edges trimmed with white ermine and its long train supported by the Lady Marquis of Dorset and Sir John Cheney. Flanking Cecily on one side was her half-brother Thomas Grey, Marquis of Dorset and on the other her cousin

John de la Pole, Earl of Lincoln. A canopy was held in place above them – the past week had seen incessant rain which, thankfully, seemed to be holding off. Today was the day of the christening of Arthur Tudor, the son and heir of King Henry VII and Elizabeth of York.

All had gathered inside the cathedral, but the ceremony was delayed due to the tardy John de Vere, Earl of Oxford, who was to stand as the boy's godfather. The ceremony had been postponed once before on Oxford's account, but King Henry would not stand for it again. After a wait of three hours he ordered that the ceremony commence. The earls of Derby and Maltravers stood as the child's godfathers while Elizabeth Woodville, his grandmother, was godmother. As the baby was submerged in the font, the Earl of Oxford casually strode in. The boy was carried to his traverse, chrisomed and clothed, after which Elizabeth Woodville conveyed him to the high altar. While the evening service was being celebrated, Oxford, still permitted a role in the event, scooped the infant up in his right arm while the Bishop of Exeter confirmed him and the Bishop of Salisbury put a linen cloth about his neck, after which presents were given at the high altar. Once the christening had been performed, the boy was returned to Winchester Castle where he received the blessing of his proud parents.[1]

Birth and Early Life

After winning his decisive victory at Bosworth Field, King Henry VII had married Elizabeth of York, the eldest daughter and heiress of King Edward IV. The marriage was conceived as a symbolic way of uniting the two warring factions of York and Lancaster, as well as boosting Henry's somewhat dubious claim to the throne. Their child would thus embody the blood of both York and Lancaster and be the rightful heir to the throne. '[T]he lines of Lancaster & York ... were now brought into one knot and connexed together, of whose two bodies one heir might succeed,' the chronicler Edward Hall states, 'which after their time should peaceably rule and enjoy the whole monarchy and realm of England.'[2]

Elizabeth was soon pregnant, and she gave birth to a son and heir at Winchester Castle on St Eustace's Day, 20 September 1486.[3] The baby was born a month prematurely but this did not seem to adversely affect him. He was named Arthur after the legendary King Arthur, one of the ancient British kings from whom Henry claimed descent in his Welsh ancestry to bolster his claim to the throne. Arthur would one day be King Arthur and his reign would mark the glorious return of the once and future king. Even Henry's choice of birthplace was symbolic. Winchester Castle, complete with its Arthurian round table, was believed to have been the location of Camelot. Unfortunately, the round table did not have so illustrious a heritage – it in fact dated from the time of King Edward I and can still be seen at the castle today.

The birth of a future king was a joyous occasion for both rulers and realm, promising better days ahead after years of civil war. Bonfires were lit in the streets and messengers dispatched around the country to proclaim the happy news to the 'rejoicing of every true Englishman'.[4]

Arthur was baptised at Winchester Cathedral on Sunday 1 October, the ceremony having been postponed due to the weather and the Earl of Oxford not being able to attend. Shortly after his baptism, Arthur was placed in the royal nursery at Farnham in Sussex, under the care of the same nurses who had attended upon the young Edward V.[5] In charge of the nursery once again was Lady Elizabeth Darcy, listed as the 'lady mistress to our dearest son the prince'.[6] Henry allocated 1,000 silver marks to meet Arthur's expenses, drawn from some of the lands of the late Henry Stafford, Duke of Buckingham.[7]

As time went on, Arthur was joined by siblings. A sister, Margaret Tudor, the grandmother of Mary, Queen of Scots, was born in 1489. There followed Henry, Duke of York, the future King Henry VIII, in 1491; Elizabeth, born in 1492, who died young; Mary, who would be the grandmother of the ill-fated Lady Jane Grey; and Edmund, who was born in 1499 but died the following year. Their final child was a daughter, Catherine, who died along with her mother during birth in 1503.

Prince of Wales

Arthur was Duke of Cornwall from birth and on 29 November 1489 the three-year-old was created Prince of Wales, Earl of Chester and a knight of the Bath in a ceremony at Westminster Palace. An account of the ceremony still survives.

On the morning of 26 November, Arthur had entered the king's barge at the Palace of Sheen, which had been 'royally prepared' for the occasion, and he sailed in procession down the Thames towards Westminster.[8] He landed by Westminster Bridge and was conducted into Westminster Hall, flanked by the crafts of London who formed a guard of honour from the bridge into the hall. Once inside he met his father in the Great Chamber of the Brick Tower. Two days later he attended upon the king at dinner, bearing the towel to dry the king's hands. Later that night he took his customary bath in the king's closet.

The following morning Arthur heard Mass and was then conducted from St Stephen's Chapel towards the vicar's lodgings where he was mounted on his horse. The prince led the other Knights of the Bath into Westminster Hall, the Earl of Essex carrying the prince's sword and spurs. They dismounted from their horses at the court of King's Bench and then proceeded on foot into White Hall where they were met by the king. The Marquis of Berkeley and the Earl of Arundel led little Arthur up to the king while Oxford took the sword and spurs from Essex and offered the king the right spur. At the king's command Berkeley fastened the right spur to Arthur's right foot while

Arundel fastened the left. The king then girded on his sword and dubbed him a knight. This was just the first stage of the ceremony and Arthur was then led into the king's closet where he was dressed in his robes of estate to be created Prince of Wales. Berkeley led him to the king, now located in the Parliament Chamber. The earls of Arundel and Derby brought in his cape, coronet, golden sceptre and ring while the Earl of Shrewsbury carried his sword, the pommel held upwards. After the ceremony had been performed, Arthur spent the rest of the day seated under his cloth of estate. Along with the earls and the newly created knights of the Bath he even ate his dinner in the hall, to the accompaniment of minstrels.[9] One wonders how all this was possible in an age before Calpol.

Education

At the age of four or five, Prince Arthur left the nursery at Farnham and began his formal education. Henry VII had learnt from Edward IV's error in appointing a nobleman to act as governor or master of his son. It was the Woodville influence with the boy king, Edward V, that had alienated Richard III and which led to Edward V being declared illegitimate and possibly put to death. Henry would not make the same mistake. He did away with the office of governor entirely. However, he still appointed a nobleman, his kinsman Sir Richard Pole, to act as Arthur's chamberlain.

The Renaissance had seen the revival of classical learning. The study of Greek and Latin classical authors had originated in Italy and had soon spread north of the Alps. Arthur was provided with a first-rate humanist education. At first, he had an unnamed tutor who instructed him in the basics of grammar, which he quickly mastered, and afterwards he was taught the 'finer points' by John Rede, a former head of Winchester School.[10] From 1496 to 1501 he was taught by Bernard André, a blind French humanist and poet laureate of Henry's court. André has left us a highly embellished account of Arthur's education in his *Life of Henry VII*. He notes that Arthur demonstrated an aptitude for learning from an early age and that by the time of his death he had 'committed partly to memory or at least had turned the pages of or read on his own' many works of the classical canon.[11] It is often stated that Arthur was taught afterwards by Thomas Linacre, a Greek scholar, but historian Aysha Pollnitz suggests that this is in fact a mistake. Linacre attempted to enter Arthur's service, she states, but his hopes were dashed by the jealous André who turned Henry VII against him.[12] Arthur's education was considered complete by the time of his marriage to Catherine of Aragon in 1501.

Henry VII took inspiration from Edward V's upbringing by sending Arthur into Ludlow to nominally govern Wales and Chester. His appointment had a symbolic quality. As the future Arthur II he ruled over the ancient Britons like his legendary namesake before him. It is not known for certain when Arthur took up residence at Ludlow. It is often stated by historians that he did so after his marriage in 1501, but it is more likely that he did so in 1493 when he was seven.[13]

Marriage

King Henry VII wished to have his fledgling dynasty recognised as an equal by the old ruling houses of Europe, and he intended to achieve this by marrying Prince Arthur into one of them. He decided to seek the friendship of King Ferdinand II of Aragon and Queen Isabella of Castile, the Spanish monarchs who had married in 1469 and united their respective kingdoms.

In 1488, Henry sent an embassy to propose a treaty of peace and alliance between the two powers which would be cemented by the marriage of Arthur to their youngest daughter, Catherine. The Spanish monarchs were receptive to Henry's advances. Ferdinand's father had lost the counties of Roussillon and Cerdagne to Louis XI of France in 1462 and he wished to get them back. Ferdinand and Isabella were too preoccupied with their war against Moorish Granada to make an attempt themselves, but they thought Henry might do it for them. At the time France was making war on Henry's old ally Duke Francis II of Brittany, who had given him shelter during his exile. The Spanish monarchs hoped to convince Henry to declare war against France and win back the two counties in the process. This placed Henry in a predicament, as France had also supported him during his exile and in his invasion of 1485, and the two powers were on friendly terms.

Ferdinand and Isabella sent their own ambassadors to London in April to discuss terms, during which the ambassadors were shown the baby Arthur. 'On our arrival,' one ambassador marvelled, 'we discovered such excellent qualities in the Prince as are quite incredible.'[14] After some haggling over the size of the dowry, the Treaty of Medina del Campo was agreed on 27 March 1489. Arthur and Catherine were to marry as soon as they came of age and Catherine's dowry was fixed at 200,000 gold scudos, half to be paid on her arrival and the rest over a period of two years. She would, in return, receive a third of the revenues of the duchy of Cornwall and principality of Wales and Chester.

As part of the treaty of alliance, Henry agreed to wage war on France. Duke Francis died on 9 September 1488, leaving a daughter, Anne of Brittany, as his heir. Henry and Ferdinand sent troops to aid Anne but by 1491 their intervention in Brittany had failed. Louis's successor, King Charles VIII of France, married Anne and Brittany was absorbed into France. Henry retaliated by invading France in October 1492, during which time he left the six-year-old Arthur to nominally act as regent. Arthur's tenure was short as Henry, like Edward IV before him, signed a peace treaty, the

Treaty of Étaples, in which he was granted a pension by the French king, and returned home. In January 1493 the disappointed Ferdinand and Isabella made their own peace with France in the Treaty of Barcelona by which they received back Roussillon and Cerdagne and agreed not to marry any of their children to those of the King of England. The Treaty of Medina del Campo was null and void, and Henry's hopes of a Spanish alliance were for the time scuppered.

King Henry had more pressing concerns, however. He was troubled by another Yorkist pretender who this time claimed to be Richard, Duke of York, the younger of the two Princes in the Tower. His real name, according to his later confession, was Perkin Warbeck and he was a native of Tournai in Flanders. Warbeck, who had an uncanny resemblance to members of the House of York, had been spotted by Yorkists while visiting Cork in Ireland and he was pressed to assume the identity of Edward IV's second son. When word spread of this new pretender, he was summoned to France by Charles VIII in 1491. As part of the terms of the Treaty of Étaples, Warbeck left France and found shelter with Margaret of Burgundy, the troublesome sister of Edward IV, who recognised him as her nephew. Then, in 1494, Warbeck travelled to Austria where he received the backing of Maximilian, King of the Romans.

Plans for the marriage between Arthur and Catherine were given a fresh impetus in 1495 when Charles VIII invaded and seized the kingdom of Naples. Ferdinand and Isabella formed the Holy League, which included Pope Alexander VI and Maximilian of Austria, now Holy Roman Emperor, against France. Ferdinand and Isabella hoped to lure Henry into the league by once again raising the prospect of a marriage between Arthur and Catherine. A new treaty was agreed on 1 October 1496, which stipulated that the marriage would take place when Arthur reached the age of fourteen. On 1 January 1497, the Spanish ambassador was empowered to perform the marriage by proxy. In August 1497, Arthur and Catherine were married by proxy at Woodstock, with Doctor de Puebla, the resident Spanish ambassador, representing Catherine. The pair were betrothed for a second time on 19 May 1499 at Tickenhill Manor in Bewdley, and de Puebla once again stood as a proxy for the princess. During the ceremony, Arthur, now aged thirteen, took the right hand of de Puebla in his while Sir Richard Pole, the prince's chamberlain, cupped both their hands in his. Arthur then declared that he accepted Catherine as his lawful and undoubted wife and Puebla did the same for the absent princess.

Throughout the negotiations, the spectre of Perkin Warbeck remained at large. After a failed attempt at landing in England in 1495 he was invited to the court of King James IV of Scotland who promised him support and married him to Lady Catherine Gordon, a daughter of the Earl of Huntly. In September 1496, James and Warbeck attempted to invade Northumberland and trigger a rebellion but they found the people unwilling to support them.

Above: 1. Thirteenth-century effigy of Robert II, Duke of Normandy, from his tomb at Gloucester Cathedral. (With permission from the Chapter of Gloucester Cathedral)

Right: 2. The sinking of the *White Ship* as depicted in a fourteenth-century manuscript. (© British Library Board (Royal 20 A II, f. 6v))

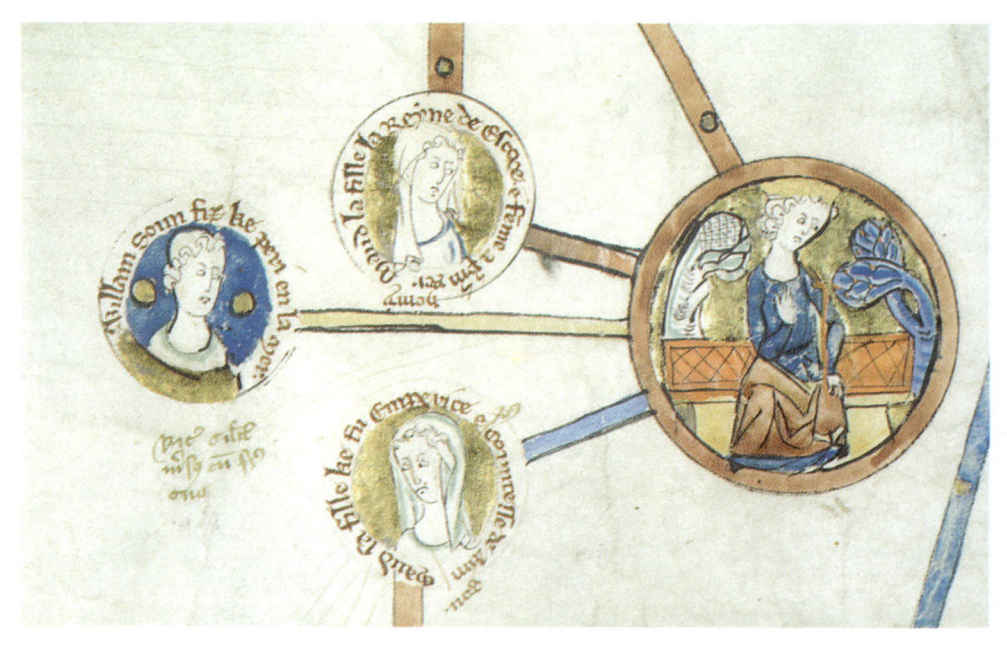

3. Depiction of William Aetheling (far left), Empress Matilda (bottom) and their parents, King Henry I and Matilda II. (© British Library Board (Royal 14 B V, Membrane 5))

Above left: 4. Legend has it that after the dissolution of the monasteries the remains of King Stephen and possibly those of Matilda of Boulogne and Eustace of Boulogne were reinterred in this tomb at the Parish Church of St Mary of Charity, Faversham. (Author's collection)

Above right: 5. Effigy of Edward of Woodstock, the Black Prince, from his tomb at Canterbury Cathedral. (Reproduced courtesy of the Chapter of Canterbury)

Above left: 6. The badge of the Princes of Wales, depicted on the tomb of the Black Prince at Canterbury Cathedral. Legend has it that the prince appropriated the badge of three ostrich feathers from John the Blind, King of Bohemia after the latter's death at the Battle of Crécy. (Reproduced courtesy of the Chapter of Canterbury)

Above right: 7. The Mortimer arms quartered with the Clare/de Burgh coat of arms, badge of Roger, 4th Earl of March and Edmund, 5th Earl of March, from the Trinity Chapel at St John the Baptist, Cirencester. (With kind permission of the Parish Church of St John Baptist, Cirencester)

8. Richard, Duke of York, depicted in a stained-glass window at St Laurence's Church, Ludlow. (With kind permission of St Laurence's Church, Ludlow; image courtesy of Matthew Lewis)

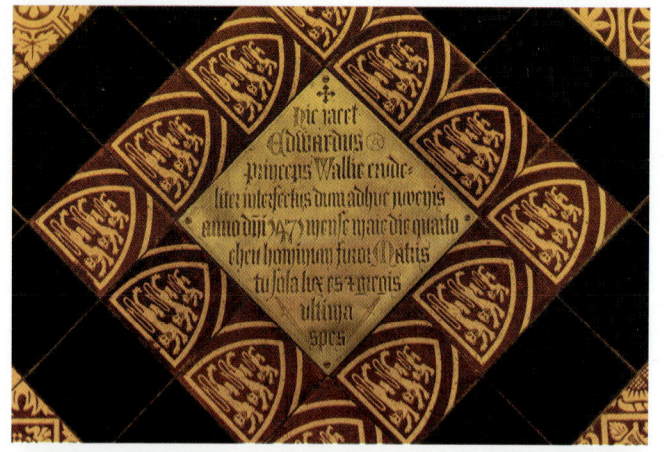

9. Plaque denoting the burial spot of Edward of Lancaster in the quire of Tewkesbury Abbey. (With kind permission of the Vicar and Churchwardens; image courtesy of Matthew Lewis)

10. The Sunne in Splendour, badge of Edward IV, which overlooks the fallen prince below it. (With kind permission of the Vicar and Churchwardens; author's collection)

11. Edward V (left) and Arthur Tudor (right) depicted in a stained-glass window at St Laurence's Church, Ludlow. (With kind permission of St Laurence's Church, Ludlow; image courtesy of Matthew Lewis)

Above: 12. Middleham Castle in Wensleydale, Yorkshire, site of the birth, life and death of Edward of Middleham, son and heir of King Richard III. (Author's collection)

Right: 13. Prince Arthur's Chamber at Ludlow Castle, Shropshire. (Author's collection)

Below right: 14. The Tower of London, site of the disappearance of the Princes in the Tower, the execution and burial of Lady Jane Grey, and the captivity of Lady Catherine Grey. (Author's collection)

15. Possible portrait of Lady Jane Grey, now housed in the National Portrait Gallery. (© National Portrait Gallery, London)

16. Lady Catherine Grey depicted in a miniature portrait with her eldest son, Edward, Lord Beauchamp. (Bridgeman Images)

Above left: 17. Lady Mary Grey. (By kind permission of the Chequers Trust / © Mark Fiennes Archive / Bridgeman Images)

Above right: 18. Mary, Queen of Scots, aged around seventeen, painted during her time in France. (Bridgeman Images)

Above left: 19. Henry Frederick, Prince of Wales. (© Royal Collection / Royal Collection Trust © Her Majesty Queen Elizabeth II, 2022 / Bridgeman Images)

Above right: 20. Princess Sophia, later Duchess of Brunswick-Lüneberg and Electress of Hanover, aged seventeen or eighteen. (© Royal Collection Trust © Her Majesty Queen Elizabeth II, 2022 / Bridgeman Images)

Above left: 21. James Francis Edward Stuart, known as James III, the 'Old Pretender' and 'Chevalier de St George'. (© National Galleries of Scotland / Bridgeman Images)

Above right: 22. Nineteenth-century engraving of Frederick Louis, Prince of Wales. (Author's collection)

Above left: 23. Portrait of Frederick, Prince-Bishop of Osnabrück and later Duke of York and Albany, as a child. (Courtesy of the Walters Art Museum)

Above right: 24. Nineteenth-century cartoon of Frederick, Duke of York and Albany, and Mary Anne Clarke, entitled 'A Bishop and his Clarke or A Peep into Paradise'. (Courtesy of the Lewis Walpole Library, Yale University)

Henry concluded a seven-year truce with King James in September 1497, which would be extended into a Treaty of Perpetual Peace by the marriage of James to Henry's eldest daughter, Margaret, paving the way for the later union of England and Scotland.

After leaving Scotland, Warbeck had travelled to Ireland. After some time there, in September he landed in Cornwall and made an unsuccessful attempt on Exeter. He was defeated and later captured and held at King Henry's court. He attempted to escape in 1498 and Henry had him thrown into the Tower of London. The wily Henry sensed an opportunity of ridding himself of another Yorkist claimant: Edward, Earl of Warwick, the son of George, Duke of Clarence, who had been rotting in the Tower since 1485. An alleged plot between Warbeck and Edward to break out of the Tower was uncovered in 1499 and both were sentenced to death. Warbeck was hanged at Tyburn on 20 November and Edward, Earl of Warwick was beheaded eight days later on Tower Hill. Edward's death, likely on trumped-up charges, was carried out in order to pacify the anxious Ferdinand and Isabella. 'The fame after his death sprung,' notes Hall, 'that Ferdinand king of Spain would never make full conclusion of the matrimony to be had between prince Arthur and the lady Catherine his daughter nor send her into England as long as this earl lived.'[15] This is backed up by a letter from de Puebla, the Spanish ambassador, in which he notified his royal masters that with the death of Edward, Earl of Warwick there was no longer 'a drop of doubtful Royal blood [in England]'.[16]

Arthur, meanwhile, had still not met his betrothed, but the couple now began a correspondence in Latin, talking of their desire to see one another. One of these letters, dated 5 October 1499, still survives:

Most illustrious and most excellent lady, my dearest spouse, I wish you very much health, with my hearty commendation.

I have read the most sweet letters of your highness lately given to me, from which I have easily perceived your most entire love to me. Truly those your letters, traced by your own hand, have so delighted me, and have rendered me so cheerful and jocund, that I fancied I beheld your highness and conversed with and embraced my dearest wife. I cannot tell you what an earnest desire I feel to see your highness, and how vexatious to me is this procrastination about your coming. I owe eternal thanks to your excellence that you so lovingly correspond to this my so ardent love. Let it continue, I entreat, as it has begun; and, like as I cherish your sweet remembrance night and day, so do you preserve my name ever fresh in your breast. And let your coming to me be hastened, that instead of being absent we may be present with each other, and the love conceived between us and the wished-for joys may reap their proper fruit.

Moreover I have done as your illustrious highness enjoined me, that is to say, in commending you to the most serene lord and lady the king and queen my parents, and in declaring your filial regard towards them, which to them was most pleasing to hear, especially from my lips. I also beseech your highness that it may please you to exercise a similar good office for me, and to commend me with hearty good will to my most serene lord and lady your parents; for I greatly value, venerate, and esteem them, even as though they were my own, and wish them all happiness and prosperity.

May your highness be ever fortunate and happy, and be kept safe and joyful, and let me know it often and speedily by your letters, which will be to me most joyous. From our castle of Ludlow, 3d nones (5th) October, A.D. 1499.

Your highness' most loving spouse,
ARTHUR, Prince of Wales, Duke of Cornwall, ETC.
Eldest son of the King.[17]

In September 1500, Arthur reached the age of fourteen. At the request of Ferdinand and Isabella, this milestone was marked with a third betrothal in the chapel at Ludlow Castle on 22 November 1500. After many delays, Catherine finally left Spain on 27 September 1501, accompanied by guards and nobles of her country. After weathering stormy seas, she arrived safely at Plymouth on 2 October 1501. Henry sent his steward, Sir Robert Willoughby, Lord Brooke, to greet the princess and provide her with any necessities she needed. The Duchess of Norfolk and other noblewomen were also dispatched to accompany her to London.

Dissatisfied with the welcome Catherine received, King Henry decided to ride out and greet her himself. On 4 November he set off from Richmond Palace in the company of his nobles. Arthur, meanwhile, had departed from Ludlow to join his father and the two met at East Hampstead the following day. Father and son spent the night in each other's company and on 6 November continued their journey. Along the way they were met by the Prothonotary (a prelate of the Roman Curia with specific duties regarding papal documents) of Spain, who told them that King Ferdinand and Queen Isabella had forbidden them from seeing or communicating with Catherine before the day of the wedding. Henry discussed the matter with his nobles and it was agreed that since Catherine was in his kingdom she was now under his jurisdiction. He left Arthur behind and entered the nearby town of Dogmersfield, where Catherine had arrived a few hours before. The archbishop, bishop and earl who had accompanied Catherine from Spain were taken by surprise at Henry's sudden appearance and they blustered that she was resting in her chamber. An undeterred Henry announced that he would see Catherine even if she was in bed. The bride met Henry in her third chamber and the two conversed. Henry was struck by Catherine's beauty, 'as well as her agreeable and dignified manners'.[18]

After the meeting, the king changed out of his riding clothes and was met by Prince Arthur. This time the prince accompanied his father to the princess's chamber where he finally saw his bride, the girl he had been set to marry since he was just one year old. They were betrothed for a final time, in person. With the ceremony over, Arthur was taken for his supper but afterwards he and the king returned to Catherine's chamber and Catherine ordered her minstrels to play and her ladies to dance. Arthur did not dance with his bride-to-be but with Lady Guildford, 'right pleasantly and honourably'.[19] Arthur and the king departed from Dogmersfield the next day while Catherine continued her steady journey towards London, reaching Kennington on 9 November. She entered London on 12 November via London Bridge and proceeded towards St Paul's Cathedral. She was greeted at the churchyard by the Mayor of London and twenty-four aldermen who presented her with plate and gold. She then entered St Paul's and made an offering at the shrine of St Erkenwald before being led to rest at the Bishop's Palace.

On the morning of 14 November, the feast of St Erkenwald, Prince Arthur was led from his lodgings to the south door of St Paul's. He entered the cathedral, made his devotions and then passed through into a secret room in the adjoining Bishop's Palace where he changed into his wedding clothes of white satin.

Catherine, meanwhile, left the Bishop's Palace and was led in procession to the cathedral by Henry, Duke of York, the future Henry VIII, in his first public appearance. Her train was borne by Cecily of York, the queen's sister, who had also carried baby Arthur to his baptism many years before. They entered the cathedral via the west door and proceeded to the altar where they were greeted by Henry Deane, Archbishop of Canterbury and eighteen other bishops and abbots and members of the king's council. Here, Catherine was presented with sealed letters patent which denoted the lands that were to form her dowry. With this formality out of the way, the couple were married. King Henry and Queen Elizabeth watched proceedings from a private box erected for the purpose. Once the ceremony was over, Arthur took Catherine's hand and they were led to the high altar where they heard Mass. Duke Henry then led Catherine back to the Bishop's Palace where she was treated to a banquet.

Arthur was later conducted to his chambers where the princess was in bed. Once Arthur climbed in beside his wife, the bed and chamber were blessed by some bishops and prelates who then left the newlyweds alone. The question of whether Arthur and Catherine consummated their marriage became one of great importance after Arthur's death when the prospect of her marrying Arthur's younger brother, Prince Henry, arose. Catherine swore that she still remained a virgin, but when Henry later wished to divorce her in the 1530s, a witness, Sir Anthony Willoughby, who had been present at Arthur's bedding ceremony, said that the next morning the prince had jocularly remarked that he had 'been in the midst of Spain'.[20] It is unknown if this was mere bravado on Arthur's part or even if Willoughby's statement was true, but it is likely that the couple had consummated the marriage.

Death

The celebrations continued. On Tuesday 16 November, Arthur, King Henry and many of the nobles and prelates attended a service of thanksgiving at St Paul's. Jousts were held outside Westminster along with masks and pageants, dances, feasts and hunting. Once the celebrations were over, most of the Spanish who had accompanied the princess returned home laden with gifts.

In December the newlyweds travelled to Ludlow where they set up their new court as husband and wife. After all the years of haggling over the marriage their time together proved fleeting. Arthur fell sick and died after a short illness on Saturday 2 April 1502. His cause of his death is unknown, although it is often thought that he died of the sweating sickness, a mysterious disease prevalent in England at the time. The chronicler Hall describes the symptoms: 'For suddenly a deadly & burning sweat invaded their bodies & vexed their blood with a most ardent heat, infested the stomach & the head grievously,' he notes, 'by the tormenting and vexation of which sickness, men were so sore handled & so painfully panged that if they were laid in their bed, being not able to suffer the importunate heat, they cast away the sheets & all the clothes lying on the bed ... All in manner as soon as the sweat took them, or within a short space after, yielded up their ghost.'[21]

The prince's council and his chamberlain, Sir Richard Pole, sent letters to the king and council, then at Greenwich, informing them of the death. The council, not wishing to be the bearers of such devastating news, sent for the king's confessor and tasked him with presenting the king with the letters. The following morning, Tuesday 5 April, the confessor arrived promptly at Henry's chamber door and on entering told the king that his son was dead. In a rare display of emotion, Henry ordered the queen to be brought to his presence so that 'he and his queen would take the painful sorrows together'.[22] Elizabeth consoled her husband, reminding him that they still had another fair prince, Henry, Duke of York, and two daughters. Henry thanked her for her kind words but when the queen entered her own chamber she gave vent to her own violent grief. Her ladies-in-waiting sent for the king and it was now his turn to comfort his consort, saying that 'he for his part would thank God for his son, and would she should do in like wise'.[23]

Arthur's body was embalmed and placed in a wooden coffin in his chamber at Ludlow Castle where it remained, guarded day and night, until 23 April when it was transported, in procession, the short distance to St Laurence's Church. As was custom, neither Catherine nor any members of the royal family were present at the service. Thomas Howard, Earl of Surrey acted as chief mourner and walked behind the hearse, dressed in a black mantle and with a mourning hood on his head. A canopy was borne above the coffin by four individuals who each carried a banner – one of the Trinity, Patible Cross, Our Lady and St George – while ahead of the coffin rode Sir Gruffydd ap

Rhys carrying the prince's banner. On 25 April, St Mark's Day, the procession reached the town of Bewdley. The journey was made difficult by the rain and wind and at times oxen had to be employed to drag the hearse when it became stuck on the muddy roads.

Arthur's coffin was left in the parish church and the following day the procession proceeded towards Worcester, where the prince was to be laid to rest in the cathedral. The weather was much more pleasant and when the cortege reached the cathedral grounds the coffin was removed from the hearse and borne inside. The following day the funeral service took place, amid much weeping.

During the service the Man-of-Arms, Lord Gerald FitzGerald, son of the Earl of Kildare, dressed in the prince's armour and astride his horse with a downturned poleaxe in hand, rode into the cathedral to the middle of the choir. He climbed off the horse and gave it as an offering to the Abbot of Tewkesbury. The coffin, 'with weeping and sore lamentation', was carried to its final resting place at the southern end of the high altar and lowered into the grave.[24] The Bishop of Lincoln, officiating, placed a cross on the coffin and cast holy water and earth on top of it. One by one, the officers of the prince's household broke their staffs of office and cast them into the grave. The service ended with a feast.

Arthur's death saw his younger brother, Henry, Duke of York, become heir apparent to the throne. Princess Catherine had expected to return to Spain after the death of her husband, but King Henry and King Ferdinand had other ideas. Her temporary father-in-law was intent on securing the rest of the marriage portion and it was agreed in a treaty of 1503 that she would marry Prince Henry. This gave rise to the question of whether Arthur and Catherine had ever consummated their marriage. If they had done so then Henry and Catherine were said to be related within the first degree of consanguinity, requiring a papal dispensation for the marriage to go ahead. Catherine protested that she had never consummated the marriage, but her pleas fell upon deaf ears and a papal dispensation was applied for and granted. A few years later, on 21 April 1509, Henry VII died and his son succeeded as King Henry VIII. Within months the new king had married Catherine, with massive repercussions for the country and for the succession.

The Succession

We now enter the period of the English Reformation. Protestantism had been born in Germany in 1517 when Martin Luther, an Augustinian friar and professor of theology, tacked to the door of a church in Wittenberg his *Ninety-Five Theses* in which he criticised the Catholic doctrine of indulgences. Luther sparked off a religious revolution and the development of the printing press saw his ideas seep into England, where they found a ready audience among the educated. The English Reformation did not arise from a call for religious change, however, but from Henry VIII's marital woes. The marriage to Catherine had begun well and a son and heir, Henry, was born to the couple in early 1511. The infant passed away just over a month later and there followed a succession of stillbirths, only interrupted by the birth and survival of a daughter, Mary, the future Mary I, in 1516. As we have seen, female succession was possible in theory in England, but there had not yet been a queen regnant to put that theory to the test.

By 1527 Henry had become sufficiently alarmed by his lack of male issue and was convinced that this was due to God's displeasure at his having married his deceased brother's wife, as condemned in the book of Leviticus. He had an illegitimate son, Henry FitzRoy, in 1519 with his mistress Elizabeth Blount, but FitzRoy's illegitimacy meant that he was unable to succeed to the throne. Catherine was nearing forty and Henry thought it unlikely that she would produce the much-needed heir. Henry's roving eye had now fallen upon Anne Boleyn, one of Catherine's maids of honour, but she refused to become just another of Henry's mistresses. Henry saw a practical answer to both his problems – he would end his marriage to Catherine and wed Anne.

Henry applied to Pope Clement VII for an annulment, but the pope, who had recently fallen under the power of Catherine's nephew Emperor Charles V, was in no position to grant the annulment and offend his captor. There followed years of stalemate during which Henry established the Reformation Parliament (1529), which slowly sapped away the pope's powers in England in an effort to force his hand. Things came to a head in 1532 when Anne Boleyn apparently finally succumbed to Henry's advances and became pregnant. This placed Henry in a predicament: if Anne's child was born while he remained married to Catherine then it would be illegitimate. He therefore married Anne in secret on 25 January 1533. In May, Thomas Cranmer, the newly installed Archbishop of Canterbury, declared Henry's marriage to Catherine to be null and void. When Pope Clement countered by threatening to excommunicate Henry if he did not take Catherine back, the English king defiantly issued the Act of Supremacy (1534), declaring himself the Supreme Head of the Church of England and finalizing the departure of the English church from Rome.

Anne's child, born on 7 September 1533, proved to be yet another daughter – the future Elizabeth I. According to the rules of primogeniture, Henry's eldest daughter, Mary, stood to inherit before Elizabeth. This, of course, was anathema to Henry, who now introduced the first of three Acts of Succession, the first of which finally established that a female could inherit the throne in her own right in the absence of male heirs. It is interesting to note here that Henry felt that he needed the sanction of Parliament to alter the succession, and Parliament would indeed come to exert a greater control over it in the next few centuries. The resultant First Succession Act of 1534 declared Henry's marriage to Catherine to be null and void and

Mary illegitimate. The succession was entailed in any future male heirs King Henry had by Anne or any future wives, and in the default of any male issue the succession was invested in Princess Elizabeth and her heirs. As everyone knows, Anne failed to produce a living male heir and she was beheaded on 19 May 1536 on charges of adultery.

On 30 May Henry married his third wife, Jane Seymour. This required the creation of a second Act of Succession in which both Henry's previous marriages were declared null and void and Elizabeth was deemed illegitimate. The succession was invested as before but with Jane and her children taking the place of Anne. More importantly for the succession, Henry was granted the remarkable power to appoint his successor by letters patent or by his will in the absence of legitimate heirs. This was done, according to the historian Eric Ives, to prevent the next in blood, at that time James V, King of Scotland, son of Henry's eldest sister Margaret, from ascending the throne, but also to allow Henry to appoint his illegitimate son, Henry FitzRoy, or daughters Mary and Elizabeth as his successor if need be.[25] If Henry did wish to appoint Henry FitzRoy as his heir, he was to be disappointed. FitzRoy died later that year.

Queen Jane produced the coveted male heir. Edward VI was born on 12 October 1537. Queen Jane Seymour died twelve days after giving birth and in January 1540 Henry married Anne of Cleves. He divorced her six months later and married his fifth wife, Catherine Howard, who was executed in 1542 on charges of adultery. The following year Henry married his sixth and final wife, Catherine Parr. When Henry went to wage war in France in 1544 he passed the Third Succession Act (1544), in which Mary and Elizabeth were restored to their rightful places in the succession although they remained illegitimate. Then, on 30 December 1546, the dying Henry signed his last will and testament in which he made provision for the succession as per the terms of the Second Succession Act. Princesses Mary and Elizabeth retained their places in the succession but this now came with the condition that they did not marry without the permission of their brother's Privy Council. Henry also made provision for the succession in the event that his children died without heirs. He passed over the line of his eldest sister, Margaret Tudor, now represented by Mary, Queen of Scots, the young daughter of King James V, in favour of the line of his youngest sister, Mary Tudor, of whom Lady Jane Grey was granddaughter.

16

Lady Jane Grey

```
┌─────────────┐    ┌──────────┐    ┌──────────────────┐
│ 1. Louis XII│ m  │Mary Tudor│ m  │ 2. Charles Brandon│
│King of France│───│ d. 1533  │───│1st Duke of Suffolk│
│   d. 1515   │    │          │    │     d. 1545      │
└─────────────┘    └──────────┘    └──────────────────┘
```

| Henry Earl of Lincoln d. 1534 | Lady Frances Brandon d. 1559 m Henry Grey third Marquis of Dorset d. 1554 | Lady Eleanor Brandon d. 1547 |

| **Lady Jane Grey** Queen of England r. 1553 m Guildford Dudley d. 1554 | Lady Catherine Grey d. 1568 | Lady Mary Grey d. 1578 |

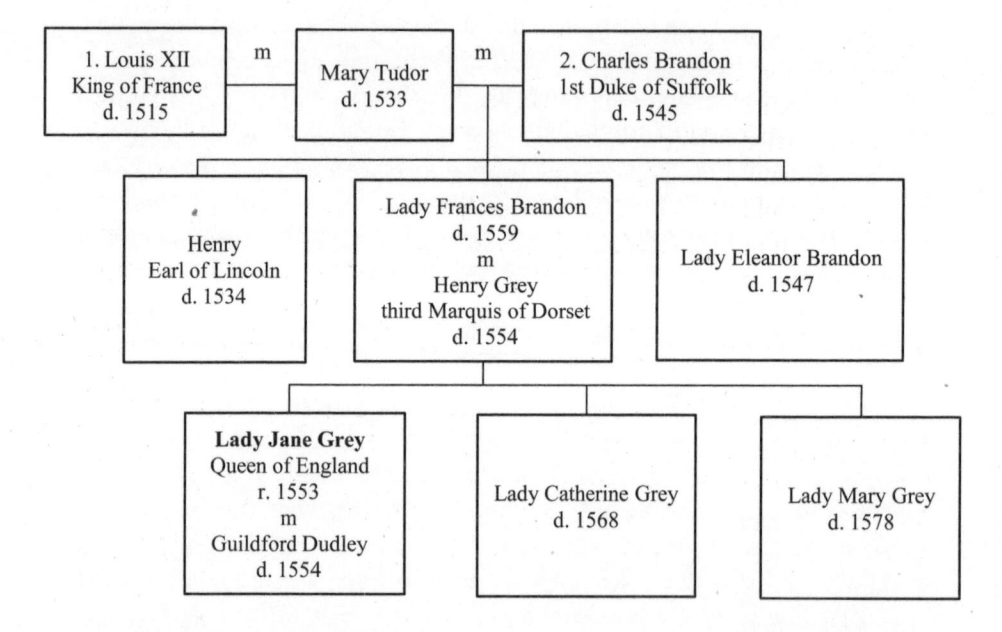

On the night of 9 July 1553, sixteen-year-old Lady Jane Dudley (*née* Grey) arrived at Syon House in Middlesex. She had been summoned to Syon by the order of the Privy Council but found the house empty on her arrival. Members of the council soon arrived, including her father-in-law, John Dudley, Duke of Northumberland. Northumberland, as President of the Council, announced that Jane's cousin King Edward VI had died. Before Jane could process this sad news, Northumberland dropped a further bombshell – Edward had designated her as his heir.

Jane watched in disbelief as the members of the council took to one knee and swore to protect her right with their lives. The shock, exacerbated by an illness she had recently been suffering, caused her to swoon and she fell weeping to the floor, bewailing her unworthiness for such a role and lamenting the king's death. Then, collecting herself, she prayed to God that if 'what was given to me was rightly and lawfully mine, his Divine Majesty would grant me such grace and spirit that I might govern it to his glory and service, and to the advantage of this realm'.[1]

The following day, Jane was conducted to the Tower of London to prepare for her coronation. So began the tragic nine-day reign of Queen Jane, the first queen regnant of England.

Birth and Early Life

Lady Jane Grey was the eldest daughter of Frances Brandon and her husband, Henry Grey, 3rd Marquis of Dorset. She was born sometime during the spring of 1537, possibly at the family seat of Bradgate in Leicestershire, where she was christened Jane in honour of Henry VIII's then wife, Queen Jane Seymour.[2] Jane's claim to the throne derived from her mother, Frances, the eldest daughter of Mary Tudor.

Mary Tudor, the youngest sister of Henry VIII, had married the French king Louis XII in October 1514 but the sickly king had died shortly after. She then married Charles Brandon, Duke of Suffolk, Henry VIII's best friend. The couple would have one son and two daughters: Henry, Earl of Lincoln, their eldest child, was born on 11 March 1516; Lady Frances Brandon was born on 16 July 1517; and Lady Eleanor Brandon, the youngest, was born sometime during 1519. Lady Frances married Henry Grey, a ward of the Duke of Suffolk, in 1533. Henry was a great-grandson of Elizabeth Woodville by her eldest son Thomas Grey, Marquis of Dorset, born from her first marriage to the Lancastrian Sir John Grey.

Few details survive of Lady Jane's early years. We know that she mainly resided at Bradgate with her two sisters, Catherine and Mary, born in 1540 and 1545 respectively. As the Dorsets had no sons, Jane became the lifeblood of their ambitious schemes.[3] They envisaged her one day marrying her royal cousin and becoming queen consort, and they thus provided her with the best humanist education. The Marquis of Dorset was himself highly educated and a great patron of scholars. The chronicler Ralph Holinshed compared him with Gaius Maecenas, the Roman diplomat, counsellor and patron of Virgil.[4] Jane's first tutor was Thomas Harding, her father's chaplain, but from 1545 she was taught by John Aylmer, one of Dorset's patrons and the future Bishop of London, 'a young man singularly well learned both in the Latin and Greek tongue'.[5] Jane proved to be a highly intelligent and precocious child and she is reported to have studied eight languages – Latin, Greek, English, Hebrew, Chaldean, Arabic, French and Italian – although it is unlikely that she attained such a mastery of them all as claimed by her eulogist, Sir Thomas Chaloner.

More importantly, Jane was brought up in the Protestant faith, and this would determine the outcome of her short life. Henry VIII's break with Rome had not, in fact, led England immediately to become a Protestant country. The king had remained conservative in matters of religion but he was surrounded by factions of Catholics and Protestants who vied for influence in determining the theology of the fledgling Church of England. The Protestants held sway at first, leading Henry to dissolve the monasteries and introduce an English translation of the Bible, but in 1539 he issued the Act of Six Articles, which reintroduced much of the Catholic doctrine.

Dorset was himself a keen religious reformer and he had his three daughters brought up as Protestants. Jane was at first instructed in the new religion by Thomas Harding, whom she would later berate for converting to Catholicism during the reign of Queen Mary I, and then by Aylmer, under whom she studied the Scriptures. Jane proved a zealous protestant. After her execution she would become a Protestant martyr, included in John Foxe's *Acts and Monuments*.

A Pawn in the Game

As we have seen, Henry VIII's will bypassed the line of his eldest sister, Margaret Tudor, in favour of that of the youngest, Mary Tudor. Mary had died in 1533 and her only son, Henry, Earl of Lincoln, had died the following year, leaving Lady Frances and Lady Eleanor as her surviving children. Strangely, Henry's will also passed over the claims of Frances and Eleanor themselves in favour of their daughters, making Jane third in line to the throne in 1547. Less than a month later, King Henry died and was succeeded by the nine-year-old King Edward VI. Henry's will established a Privy Council to rule during the king's minority but this soon came to be dominated by Edward Seymour, Earl of Hertford. The young king's maternal uncle, he was soon appointed Lord Protector and Governor of the King's Person. On 17 February he was elevated to the dukedom of Somerset. The duke was a Protestant and his protectorate (1547–1549) would see the further reformation of the English church into a more Protestant shape.

Unfortunately, Somerset's rise brought him into conflict with his ambitious younger brother, Thomas Seymour. Thomas Seymour had been made Lord Admiral and Baron Seymour of Sudeley at the same time that his brother had been created Duke of Somerset, but this did not satisfy his lust for power. As the king's uncle, he believed that he should be made Governor of the King's Person as the offices of governor and protector had previously been held by separate individuals. He soon began to plot against Somerset, buying support from some of the king's servants and attempting to curry favour with the boy king by giving him money.

Due to her proximity to the throne, Lady Jane became an object of interest to Thomas Seymour. Shortly after Henry VIII's death, he had sent John Harington, one of his servants, to Bradgate to request wardship of the girl. Harington remarked that he had often heard Seymour say that Jane was 'as handsome a lady as any in England' and that Seymour would 'see her placed in marriage, much to his (Dorset's) comfort'.[6] Dorset asked about plans for her marriage, to which Harington replied, 'I doubt not but you shall see he will marry her to the king; and fear you not but he will bring it to pass, and then you shall be able to help all the friends you have.'[7] Dorset later paid a visit to Thomas Seymour at Seymour Palace in

London. There they reached an agreement, and Jane took up residence in Seymour's household.

Thomas Seymour's intentions regarding the young Jane are unknown. It may be that he intended to marry her to Edward to gain influence over him or he may have envisaged her as a potential royal bride for himself, although shortly after Jane's arrival he married the queen dowager, Catherine Parr, the last wife of Henry VIII. Jane would spend much of her time in Catherine's household at Hanworth and the queen dowager, an educated woman herself, would nurture her love of learning and her Protestantism. Jane shared her wardship with her fourteen-year-old second cousin, Princess Elizabeth. The princess's presence caused friction between Catherine and Seymour as he made improper advances to young Elizabeth and she was eventually sent away. When Catherine fell pregnant, Jane accompanied her to Sudeley Castle in Gloucestershire where she gave birth to a daughter. Sadly, Queen Catherine died soon after. Jane acted as chief mourner at her funeral, which was held at the castle.

Thomas Seymour hastily wrote to Dorset and requested that Jane be sent home, but once the immediate grief had subsided he regretted his move and he asked that Jane remain with him. The Dorsets, however, did not wish to leave her in Seymour's household now that there was no female presence to 'correct her as a Mistress'.[8] In a letter to Seymour, Dorset explained that he wanted Jane to be placed under the care of her mother so that she could 'most easily be ruled and framed towards virtue'.[9] Jane duly returned to Bradgate, but Seymour was not a man to be denied. Shortly after, he paid the Dorsets a personal visit in London where he once again persuaded them to entrust him with the care of their daughter. Dorset later stated that Seymour was 'so earnest with him in persuasion, that he could not resist him'.[10] Seymour once again promised to marry Jane to Edward – but it was the douceur of £2,000, of which he immediately paid £500, which secured the deal.

Jane returned to Seymour's household, but her second term under his care proved short-lived. Seymour had hatched a daring plan to seize the king and supplant his brother. Jane was present at Seymour Palace when, on 17 January 1549, Seymour was arrested. He was charged with treason and beheaded on Tower Hill on 20 March. Jane once again returned to her family's care at Bradgate.

Bradgate

It was during this time that Roger Ascham, Princess Elizabeth's former tutor, made his famous visit to Bradgate which he recorded in his book *The Schoolmaster*. Ascham was surprised to find Jane in the great hall, her head buried in Plato's *Phaedon* in Greek, which she studied 'with as much delight as some gentlemen would read a merry tale in Bocase', while her parents and other members of the household were out enjoying the hunt.[11] When he asked her why she did not join in the frivolities, Jane announced, 'I wist all their sport in the park is but a shadow to that pleasure that I find in Plato. Alas! good folk, they never felt what true pleasure meant.'[12] The astonished Ascham asked how she had come to know the true meaning of pleasure, which few men had ever experienced. Jane explained that when she was in the presence of her parents she had to act with proper decorum and that if she did not they would taunt and threaten her and at times physically hurt her with 'pinches, nips, and bobs'.[13] She was only happy, she confided, when in the presence of her tutor Aylmer, 'who teacheth me so gently, so pleasantly, with such fair allurements to learning, that I think all the time nothing whilst I am with him'.[14] When her tuition ended she would weep, 'because whatsoever I do else but learning is full of grief, trouble, fear, and whole misliking unto me'.[15]

Jane's treatment at the hands of her parents may seem cruel today but it was common practice at the time and was done with the best intentions. The Dorsets still hoped that Jane would one day marry Edward or make some other advantageous marriage, and they were eager to make her as refined as possible.

Jane's intellect and piety caught the interest of some of the continental religious reformers, including Henry Bullinger, the learned head of the reformed church of Zurich in Switzerland. Jane was put into contact with Bullinger by another of Dorset's patrons, John Ulmer, and a warm correspondence sprang up between the two. Bullinger sent her religious treatises, advised her on educational matters such as the best method of learning the Hebrew language so that she could study the Scriptures, and instructed her in the reformed faith. When Aylmer observed that Jane was taking too much pride in her appearance, he turned to Bullinger to 'instruct my pupil ... as to what embellishment and adornment of person is becoming in a young woman professing godliness'.[16] He suggested that Bullinger may want to use Princess Elizabeth as an example of how to dress accordingly. Bullinger's letter to Jane does not survive but it evidently had the desired effect. When Princess Mary, a devout Catholic, later sent her 'goodly apparel of tinsel cloth of gold and velvet', Jane refused to wear them.[17] She remarked that it was a 'shame to follow my Lady Mary against God's word, and leave my Lady Elizabeth, which followeth God's word'.[18]

A large part of the reformers' interest in Jane arose from the rumours that she would one day marry King Edward and further the Protestant cause. 'Oh! If that event should take place,' Ulmer stated euphorically in a letter to Bullinger, 'how happy would be the union, and how beneficial to the Church!'[19] Unfortunately for the reformers, when Jane eventually did marry, it would not be to the king.

Heir to the Throne

While Jane pursued her studies at Bradgate, changes were happening in the government that would directly affect the outcome of her short life. In 1549 Protector Somerset was overthrown by a group of disgruntled counsellors led by the ambitious John Dudley, Earl of Warwick, a renowned military commander and victor of the Battle of Pinkie (1547). Dudley did not take upon himself the title of Protector but instead settled for that of Lord President of the Council. On 11 October 1551 he was created Duke of Northumberland (a title formerly belonging to the Percy family) and at the same time he won Dorset's support by having King Edward bestow on him the dukedom of Suffolk in right of his wife. Shortly after, ex-Protector Somerset, who had been released from prison earlier in the year, was once again arrested, this time for plotting to murder Northumberland and reclaim the protectorship. He was beheaded in January the following year.

Dorset, now Duke of Suffolk, was constituted as a member of the king's council. As a result, Jane and her sisters were often in London and made appearances at court. Jane was present during the visit of Marie of Guise, queen dowager of Scotland and mother of Mary, Queen of Scots, on her return from France where she had paid her daughter a visit. In the summer of 1552, Jane visited Princess Mary at her manor of Newhall in Essex. One evening, when Jane was walking past Mary's chapel in the company of Lady Anne Wharton, the latter made a low curtsy to the host that was hanging on the altar. Jane, somewhat bemused, asked if she bowed to the Lady Mary. 'No,' the pious lady responded, she curtsied 'to him that made us all'.[20] 'Why,' Jane asked, 'how can he be there, that made us all, and the baker made him?'[21] When word of this blasphemy reached the ears of Princess Mary she is reported to have ever after borne a grudge against Jane.

In early 1553, the fifteen-year-old King Edward VI contracted a cough which steadily grew worse until it became apparent that he might die. According to the provisions of The Third Succession Act (1544) and Henry VIII's will, Princess Mary was next in line to the throne. This was anathema to the Protestant Edward, who feared that she would restore Catholicism, and his fear would lead him to alter the succession and bequeath the throne to Lady Jane in his infamous 'Devise for the Succession'. It is often assumed that the Duke of Northumberland was the mastermind behind the 'Devise'. If Mary were to become queen he would lose his power, his influence and possibly his life, as his government had cruelly persecuted Mary for her Catholic beliefs. Whatever the truth of the matter, Edward was a willing participant. In the spring or summer he drew up the first draft of the 'Devise'. This passed over both Mary's claim and Elizabeth's, and entailed the throne in any male heirs of Frances Brandon, followed by the male heirs of her daughters. Neither Frances nor her daughters had any male heirs at the time but Edward no doubt hoped that some would arrive before he died.

On 21 May, Lady Jane was married to Northumberland's nineteen-year-old son, Lord Guildford Dudley, at Durham Palace. Two other marriages took place at the palace that day. Jane's sister Catherine was married to Henry, Lord Herbert, the son of William Herbert, Earl of Pembroke. Guildford's sister Katherine married Henry Hastings, the Earl of Huntingdon's heir, Later, Edward, realising that a male heir was unlikely to be born in his lifetime, altered the 'Devise' and made Jane his heir. This meant that Northumberland would have a son on the throne and one day a grandchild, securing his and his family's influence. Edward had Letters Patent drawn up on 21 June and confirmed by thirty-three counsellors. Edward Montagu, a lawyer, warned that Parliament should be summoned quickly and the 'disowning of the royal sisters should be effected by Act of Parliament ... because the law of the land would otherwise forbid it'.[22] Their rights to the throne derived from the Third Succession Act and Henry VIII's will rather than hereditary right, and it was only another Act of Parliament that could legally bar them from the throne. A parliament was planned for September, but on the night of 6 July, Edward died.

Jane, meanwhile, was blissfully unaware of the momentous events going on around her. After her marriage to Guildford she had resided at Syon House with her in-laws. Jane Dudley, *née* Guildford, Duchess of Northumberland had promised Jane that after the marriage she would be allowed live with her mother, but when news arrived that the king might die at any moment the duchess forbade her to leave. According to Jane's testimony, the duchess told her to make herself ready to go to the Tower when Edward died as he had made her heir to the kingdom. Jane was confused and perturbed at these words but she did not take them seriously. After a few days she secured leave to go to Chelsea Palace, another of Northumberland's possessions, where she fell ill, later claiming that she had been poisoned. On 9 July, three days after Edward's death, Northumberland's daughter Lady Sidney arrived at the palace to notify Jane that the Privy Council had requested her immediate presence at Syon House. The two girls travelled there by barge that night and, as we have seen, Jane was then given the unwelcome news that she was to be Queen of England.

Jane is often portrayed as an innocent victim of the ruthless ambition of others. She did, indeed, have the crown thrust unwillingly upon her, a fact which is backed up by the letter that she wrote to Queen Mary after her imprisonment in the Tower. We must also bear in mind, however, that Jane was a devout Protestant who would have shared King Edward's concerns about the restoration of Catholicism and may have regarded it as God's will that she was to continue Edward's role as the champion of the true religion.

The Nine Days Queen

The following day Jane was conducted by barge to the Tower of London, there to await her coronation. After disembarking she walked in a grand procession to the Tower, accompanied by her husband Guildford and many lords and ladies. Her mother Frances diligently carried the train of her robes. Baptista Spinola, a Genoese merchant who was present, has left us a description of Jane's appearance. Jane was 'very short and thin ... but prettily shaped and graceful. She has small features and a well-made nose, the mouth flexible and the lips red. The eyebrows are arched and darker than her hair, which is nearly red.'[23] The new queen was greeted by gun salutes as she approached the gates and upon entering the Tower she took up residence in the state apartments.

About seven o'clock that night, three heralds proclaimed the death of Edward VI and the accession of Queen Jane at Cheapside. This announcement was not greeted with the usual enthusiasm among the people but with bemused looks. Few, it is noted, said 'God save her'.[24] They had expected Mary, as the next heir according to the rules of primogeniture, to be queen. One Gilbert Pot defiantly claimed that Mary was the true heir, an outburst which saw him placed in the stocks and his ears cut off.

The next morning the treasurer, Winchester, brought the crown jewels to Jane and insisted that she try on the crown to see how it fit. Jane made her excuses not to and Winchester, noting her dismay, told her to take it without fear and that another one would be made to crown Guildford alongside her. It was then that it dawned on Jane that she had been duped. The Dudleys hoped to make Guildford king and rule in her stead. Jane confronted Guildford, who admitted that he wished to be made king by Act of Parliament, but Jane, showing that she had inherited the fiery Tudor temper, shot down his hopes.[25] She was only willing to make Guildford a duke. The Duchess of Northumberland was furious and forbade Guildford from sleeping with Jane any longer. Jane even had to send the earls of Pembroke and Huntingdon to prevent the disgruntled Guildford from departing for Syon House.

The following day there arrived some unwelcome news: Princess Mary had fled to Framlingham Castle, where she was busy raising an army to fight for her inheritance. On 9 July she had sent an ambassador to Northumberland and the council with a letter demanding that they renounce Jane and declare her to be queen. This was ignored and the Privy Council decided to send Jane's father, Suffolk, at the head of an army to bring Mary to heel, but Jane took fright at the prospect of losing her father. With 'weeping tears', she besought them to send someone else.[26] The council opted to send Northumberland instead. The duke reluctantly agreed but he feared that the council would betray him and Jane in his absence. The next day, when he dined with the members of the council, he took the opportunity to have them swear to uphold the rights of Jane, 'who,' he reminded them, 'by your and our enticement is rather of force placed therein, than by her own seeking and request'.[27]

On 14 July Northumberland departed from London with an army of more than 3,000 men and thirty cannon. As the army passed through Shoreditch, the duke noted ominously to one of his companions that '[t]he people press to see us, but not one sayeth God speed us'.[28]

Jane mostly disappears from view as the events that sealed her fate play out. She once again fell ill and would later claim that she had been poisoned. In Northumberland's absence, many members of the council began to get cold feet. On the night of 16 July, the treasurer, Winchester, managed to sneak out of the Tower to his house. Jane panicked and ordered the gates shut and had the keys taken up to her to prevent anyone else from leaving. Winchester was brought back, ostensibly for having one of the official seals on his person but likely in an effort to stop him joining Mary.

The die was cast for Jane on 18 July when some of the council, including the Earl of Pembroke, secretly convened at Baynard's Castle where they agreed to support Mary and afterwards had her proclaimed queen at Cheapside. The people's reception of the news was markedly different to that of Jane's accession. Countless caps were thrown to the heavens in joy, the bells of the parish churches rang out, while numerous bonfires were lit in the streets and banquets held until ten o'clock that night. The following day, Northumberland, who had reached Bury St Edmunds, heard the news and realised that all was lost. His men began to desert him en masse and his thoughts turned to self-preservation. He retreated to Cambridge, where he proclaimed Mary queen in the marketplace, throwing his hat in the air 'as if in celebration'.[29] Northumberland was likely terrified but he did not attempt to flee. The next day he was arrested by Henry FitzAlan, Earl of Arundel and committed to the Tower.

Jane and Dudley were confined in the Tower, now prisoners. Jane was held in the house of William Partridge while Dudley was placed in the Beauchamp Tower. Suffolk was arrested on 28 July and also incarcerated at the Tower but Duchess Frances, an old friend of Mary, managed to secure his release.

Mary entered London that same day, trailed by Princess Elizabeth and Frances, Duchess of Suffolk, and lodged in the Tower to prepare for her coronation. Northumberland was brought to trial on 18 August and sentenced to execution. Once back in the Tower he renounced Protestantism and became a Catholic. This is usually seen as an attempt to appease Mary and save his life, although in truth Northumberland was likely a Catholic at heart and doing what he believed was necessary to save his eternal soul. It did him little good in this world. On 22 July he was beheaded upon Tower Hill.

Death

Lady Jane remained in the Tower for her rest of her short life. She was treated well and was allowed to retain two of her ladies-in-waiting. On Tuesday 29 August, an individual simply known as the Harleian Chronicler dined with Jane and has left us an account of their meeting. Jane sat at the end of the table and after she had drank to her visitor's health they had conversed on Jane's favourite topic of religion. Jane asked if Mass was now being said in London, to which the chronicler replied that it was in some places. 'It may so be,' Jane mused, 'it is not so strange as the sudden conversion of the late duke [Northumberland]; for who would have thought ... he would have so done?'[30] The chronicler reasoned that he may have done so in hope of a pardon. 'Pardon? ... Woe worth him! He hath brought me and our stock in most miserable calamity and misery by his exceeding ambition,' she flamed.[31] She admitted, though, that she did not believe he had converted out of hope of a pardon. One who was 'odious to all men', who had taken the field against the queen and was hated by the commons, she reasoned, had little hope of a pardon.[32] Jane asked rhetorically if she, who was still young, should forsake her faith for the love of life. 'Nay,' she exclaimed, 'God forbid!'[33]

On 13 November Jane and Guildford Dudley were brought to trial at the Guildhall. They were led from the Tower with an axe borne in front of them, signalling treason. Jane was dressed 'in a black gown of cloth, turned down; the cap lined with fese velvet, and edged about with the same, in a French hood, all black, with a black billiment, a black velvet book hanging before her, and another book in her hand open'.[34] Jane pleaded guilty to the charges and she and Guildford were duly sentenced to death. The carrying out of the sentence was put off by Queen Mary, who was reluctant to have Jane executed and instead left her in the Tower. On 18 November Jane was granted the liberty to walk in the queen's garden while Guildford Dudley was allowed to walk the leads in the Bell Tower.

Jane spent an uneasy Christmas in the Tower but the following year her fate was sealed by the ambition of others. Queen Mary's wish to marry the Catholic prince Philip of Spain met with much opposition in the country. It was feared that England would become a dependency of Spain and would once again fall under the pope's power. Three distinct rebellions rose in the country, one in Devonshire, one in Kent and one in the Midlands.

Unfortunately for Jane, Suffolk decided to join the rebellion. It is not clear what his goal was, although he may have hoped to restore Jane to the throne. He rode from his house in Sheen to Leicester where he denounced the queen's marriage. He found little support in the town and when he rode to Coventry, which he had been informed was sympathetic to his cause, he found its gates barred against him. Queen Mary had sent Francis Hastings, Earl of Huntingdon to raise a force and prevent Suffolk from his designs, and the citizens of Coventry thought it best to support the queen. Suffolk retreated to his manor of Asteley, 5 miles away, where he dispersed his troops. He and his brother John Grey hid in Asteley Park but they were betrayed to the Earl of Huntingdon, who seized them and took them to the Tower. The other rebellions were systematically put down. The most formidable was that of Sir Thomas Wyatt, who plotted to place Princess Elizabeth on the throne, which saw the princess temporarily held prisoner at the Tower.

Suffolk's rebellion determined Jane's fate. Mary had no choice but to put her to death. While she lived she was a threat to Mary's throne and to the stability of the kingdom. Jane's execution was scheduled for 12 February 1554, and she seems to have taken the news in her stride. Letters that she penned from the Tower in her final days allow us to see her state of mind. In one she wrote to her father she told him that she rejoiced in her mishaps and considered herself blessed: 'And thus, good father, I have opened unto you the state wherein I presently stand, my death at hand, although to you perhaps it may seem woeful, yet to me there is nothing that can be more welcome than from this vale of misery to aspire to that heavenly throne of all joy and pleasure, with Christ my saviour.'[35]

On 10 February Queen Mary sent Dr John Feckenham, Abbot of Westminster, to see Jane in an attempt to convert her to Catholicism. Jane and Feckenham sparred over some of the religious controversies, such as transubstantiation, which concerns whether the bread and wine is in fact transformed into the blood of Christ. Jane stood her ground, using her humanist education and rhetorical abilities to argue her points. Realising the futility of trying to convert Jane, Feckenham eventually departed after saying that he felt sorry that the two would never meet in Heaven. Jane responded that they would indeed never meet unless God changed Feckenham's heart.

On the night of 11 February, Jane inscribed a message to her sister, the Lady Catherine, at the end of her copy of her Greek New Testament. In it she states that if Catherine read the Bible and followed its advice it would bring her 'an immortal and everlasting life'.[36] As for herself, Jane asked her sister to rejoice that she was going to die as by losing a mortal life she was going to win an immortal one. She finished by imploring Catherine to put her only trust in God.

Jane also left notes in a small prayerbook to her father in which she told him that although God had taken away two of his children (herself and Guildford Dudley) he had not lost them as they had won eternal life. 'And I, for my part, as I have honoured your grace in this life, will pray for you in another life.'[37]

The morning of her execution, 12 February, Jane turned down Guildford's wish to see her one final time. At ten o'clock she watched from her apartment window as Guildford was led out of the Tower to face his destiny upon Tower Hill. Some beleive she witnessed, a little later, the return of the cart containing her husband's decapitated corpse, which was conveyed into the Tower Chapel.

A scaffold had been erected on the green besides the White Tower where Jane was to be executed. When the time came, she was led to the scaffold by the Lieutenant of the Tower, accompanied by Feckenham and two ladies. She clutched a prayerbook in her hand and prayed fervently until she was mounted upon the scaffold. She betrayed no signs of fear, a chronicler noting that no tears stained her face.

Lady Jane Grey

Once on the scaffold, Jane spoke to the gathered spectators, accepting that her usurpation of the throne had been unlawful but offering that she was innocent of ever aspiring to it. 'I do wash my hands thereof in innocency, before God, and the face of you, good Christian people, this day.'[38] She then asked the crowd to witness that she died a true Christian woman and asked them to pray for her. She turned to Feckenham and asked if she should read the psalm *Miserere mei Deus*, and he said yes.[39] Jane recited the psalm in English and then, standing up, she gave her gloves and handkerchief to her maid and her book to Master Bruges, the lieutenant's brother, and began to remove her gown. The executioner moved to help her but Jane told him to leave her and she instead had her gentlewomen help her undress. One of them handed her a handkerchief with which to cover her eyes. The executioner knelt and asked Jane's forgiveness, which she freely granted, and then he directed her to stand upon the straw. Jane's eyes fell upon the block and she said, 'I pray you dispatch me quickly.'[40]

Kneeling before the block, Jane asked the executioner if he would remove the handkerchief before she lay down, to which he said no. Jane tied the handkerchief about her eyes and then, in a moment of blind panic, felt around for the block. 'What shall I do', she cried, 'Where is it?'[41] One of the people around her guided her to the block and she laid her head across it. Her last words were 'Lord, into thy hands I commend my spirit,' and then the axe fell and she knew no more.[42] So ended the tragic life of Lady Jane Grey, victim of the ambitions of others. She was later laid to rest in the church of St Peter ad Vincula at the Tower of London.

The Duke of Suffolk was arraigned at Westminster on 17 February and given the death sentence. At nine o'clock on 23 February he was taken to Tower Hill and there executed upon the scaffold.

17

Lady Catherine Grey, Countess of Hertford

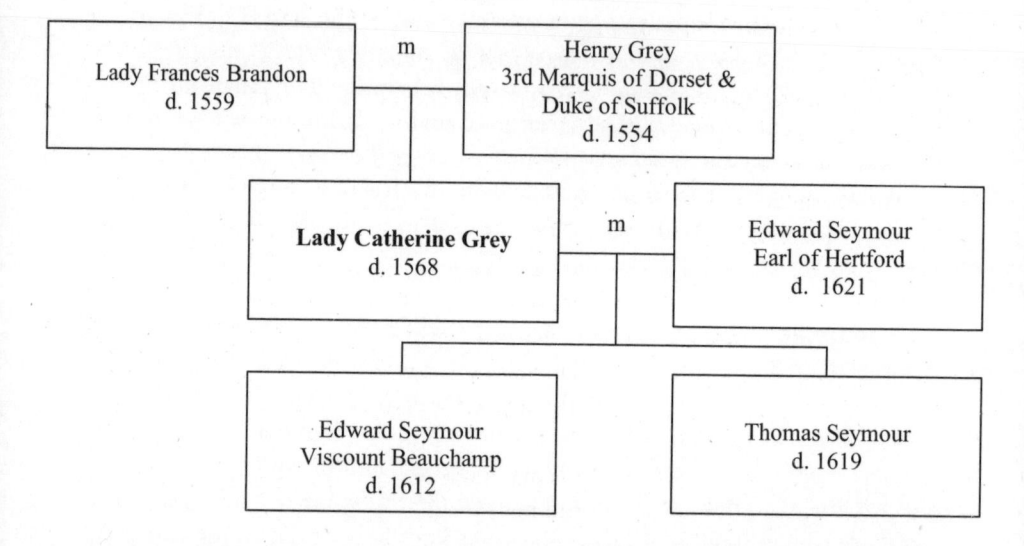

```
Lady Frances Brandon  —m—  Henry Grey
d. 1559                      3rd Marquis of Dorset &
                             Duke of Suffolk
                             d. 1554
              │
    Lady Catherine Grey  —m—  Edward Seymour
    d. 1568                    Earl of Hertford
                               d. 1621
              │
    ┌─────────┴─────────┐
 Edward Seymour      Thomas Seymour
 Viscount Beauchamp    d. 1619
 d. 1612
```

Lady Catherine Grey could conceal her pregnancy no longer. People had begun to notice and it was the talk of the court. It would not be long until it was brought to the attention of Queen Elizabeth I. Then Catherine's secret would be out and she would be at the queen's mercy.

Birth and Early Life

Lady Catherine Grey, the second daughter of Lady Frances Brandon and Henry, Marquis of Dorset and Duke of Suffolk, was born sometime during August 1540 at Dorset Place, Westminster.[1] She spent much of her childhood at Bradgate in Leicestershire where she was educated along with her two sisters, Jane and Mary, by John Aylmer. As a second daughter, the Dorsets did not hold the same lofty ambitions for Catherine as they did for her elder sister, Jane, but she still received a first-rate humanist education. Her intellectual abilities are not recorded but Jane's gift of her Greek Testament to Catherine in 1534 demonstrates that she had attained at least some knowledge of Greek and Latin.[2]

When she was nearly thirteen, Catherine was married to Henry, Lord Herbert, the eldest son of William Herbert, Earl of Pembroke, on the same day that Jane had married Guildford Dudley. Once the marriage had taken place, Catherine was sent to live with her new husband and father-in-law at Baynard's Castle in London.

Catherine was still resident at Baynard's Castle when the tragic events that cost Lady Jane her life played out, and it was there that she received the letter scrawled by her doomed sister within the empty pages of her treasured Greek Testament. Loss followed loss, and on 23 February her father was executed. The Earl of Pembroke, in order to distance himself from Jane's usurpation, secured Lord Herbert's divorce from Catherine and she returned to her mother's care. Catherine was devastated. She had become attached to Lord Herbert; many years later she was reported still to cherish hopes of marrying him again. She was, according to Thomas Fuller, 'seldom seen with dry eyes for some years together, sighing out her sorrowful condition'.[3]

The Duchess of Suffolk, on the other hand, moved on surprisingly quickly from her husband's death. Two weeks after his execution she married Adrian Stokes, Suffolk's twenty-one-year-old Master of the Horse. William Camden notes that the marriage was made to her dishonour as Stokes was but 'a mean gentleman'.[4] He notes, however, that she married him for her own security. By marrying below herself the Duchess of Suffolk hoped to alleviate Queen Mary's fears that she would make any challenges to the throne in her own name or that of her daughters.

The decision paid off. Queen Mary made the duchess one of her ladies of the bedchamber and Catherine and her younger sister Mary were employed as ladies of the privy chamber to the queen. Mary likely wanted to keep her young Grey relations under scrutiny lest they become the subject of Protestant plots, but she nevertheless treated them kindly. She provided them with a pension of £80 a year and they were given precedence over the other ladies of the court sufficient to their royal rank. The Duchess of Suffolk and her two daughters even converted to the Catholic faith and joined the queen in hearing Mass.[5]

Catherine found a friend and confidante in fellow maid Lady Jane Seymour, a daughter of Protector Somerset. Like her Grey namesake, Lady Jane Seymour had been highly educated by her parents with a view to one day marrying King Edward VI. Lady Jane fell ill in the summer of 1558 and Queen Mary sent her to recuperate at the residence of her mother, Anne Stanhope, Dowager Duchess of Somerset, at Hanworth. Catherine was given leave to accompany her friend and it was at Hanworth that Catherine caught the eye of Jane's elder brother, the charming nineteen-year-old Edward Seymour. Edward had been educated alongside Edward VI and he had been created Earl of Hertford in 1547. He had inherited his father's land and titles after Protector Somerset's execution in 1552 but he was shortly after attainted of them by an Act of Parliament, also losing the earldom of Hertford. Catherine and Edward embarked on a whirlwind romance and Edward soon asked her to marry him.

The Duchess of Somerset quickly perceived the intimacy between Catherine and Edward and, awake to the dangers that may arise from such a relationship, warned her son to stay clear of Catherine. Edward obstinately responded that 'young folks meaning well might well accompany together, and that both in that house and also in the court he trusted he might use her company, being not forbidden by the Queen's Highness express commandment'.[6]

The couple's courting days came to an end when Lady Jane recovered and she and Catherine were sent back to court. Queen Mary had by now fallen ill, possibly with influenza, and in expectation of death she named her half-sister, Elizabeth, as her heir.[7] She passed away on the morning of 17 November, and Catherine and Jane attended her funeral at Westminster Abbey on 14 December.

Heiress Presumptive

On 19 January 1559, the twenty-five-year-old Princess Elizabeth was crowned as Queen Elizabeth I. In her first parliament the unmarried queen was petitioned by the Commons to take a husband as soon as possible and procure heirs, but Elizabeth had no intention of marrying. This made the question of her heir presumptive one of vital importance throughout her reign. Henry VIII's statutes and will had caused confusion in the minds of contemporaries as to who had the best claim. By the terms of Henry VIII's will it was Catherine Grey who would inherit after Elizabeth, but according to the rules of primogeniture Mary, Queen of Scots was heir. It was hoped that Queen Elizabeth would clarify the situation by naming her successor, but she refused to do so. 'The people (such is their inconstancy) in a loathing of things present, do look to the rising sun, and leave the setting,' she told an ambassador of Mary, Queen of Scots.[8]

Catherine's proximity to the throne earned her the enmity of the new queen. She and her sister Mary retained their roles as maids of honour but Catherine was demoted from a lady of the privy chamber to a lady of the presence. Catherine bemoaned her plight to a friend, the Count de Feria, the Spanish ambassador at court, revealing that Elizabeth did not want her to succeed if she were to die childless. 'The present Queen,' de Feria told King Philip II of Spain, 'probably bears her no goodwill.'[9] Catherine promised the ambassador not to change her religion and not to marry without first taking his advice. He also notes that Catherine had stopped speaking of Lord Herbert – her heart was now set on another.

A Clandestine Marriage

Catherine was in love with Edward Seymour and she wished to marry him. Seymour had been treated favourably by the new queen and at the beginning of the reign he had been restored to his titles, including the earldom of Hertford. Unfortunately for the couple, an Act passed by Henry VIII in 1536 had forbidden any of the king's children, siblings or siblings' children from marrying without express permission from the monarch. The couple knew that the inimical and perhaps jealous queen was unlikely to do so. They decided instead to seek the help of Catherine's mother in placating the queen, and so it was that in March 1559 Seymour paid a visit to the Duchess of Suffolk's residence at the Charterhouse at Sheen. The duchess was ill and in the last few months of her life. Hertford asked for her permission to marry Catherine and the delighted duchess gladly assented, agreeing to write to the queen and council to gain their permission. Sometime later she summoned Catherine from court and on her arrival told her of the marriage, to which Catherine replied that she was 'very willing to love Hertford'.[10] The duchess then dictated to her husband, Adrian Stokes, a letter to the queen. Unfortunately, the letter never reached its destination and on 21 November Lady Frances passed away, taking with her the couple's best hopes of securing the queen's approval. Catherine and Mary attended her funeral at Westminster Abbey on 5 December, at which Catherine acted as chief mourner.[11]

The new Spanish ambassador, Bishop Quadra, notes in his correspondence of January 1560, that Elizabeth had mysteriously began to call Catherine her daughter, reinstated her as a Lady of the Presence Chamber as she had been under Queen Mary and even spoke of formally adopting her, fuelling Catherine's hopes of being named her successor. Unfortunately for Catherine, Quadra notes that this sudden volte face was done 'in order to keep her quiet.'[12] Elizabeth's secretary William Cecil had recently been informed of an abortive plot by King Philip II of Spain to spirit Catherine out of the country and marry her to his son Don Carlos. Philip feared that his hated enemy, King Henri II of France, intended to invade and conquer England in the name of Mary, Queen of Scots, who had married his son, the Dauphin Francis. To counter this, Philip planned to wed his son to Catherine, 'who is supposed to be the next heir to the realm'.[13] It was hoped that Catherine, said to be 'in the Queen's great displeasure, who could not well abide the sight of her', and not loved by her mother or her uncle, would be a willing accomplice if approached.[14]

The plot involved sending ships into England to wait in the Thames, outwardly for the use of the Spanish ambassador but in reality to spirit Catherine away. Before the plot could be matured, King Henri died in a jousting accident and Philip did not fear his successor, the young and sickly King Francis II, so he abandoned the idea. Catherine was never approached and remained unaware of the plot, and so she was spared arrest. However, Catherine would sow the seeds of her own destruction. One day, in Lady Jane Seymour's apartments at Westminster, Catherine and Hertford vowed to secretly marry the next time the queen travelled abroad and left her and Lady Jane behind. As a token of their engagement, Hertford presented Catherine with a ring with a pointed diamond in it.

Their chance arrived in November or December 1560 when Elizabeth travelled to Eltham Palace in order to go hunting. Catherine and Lady Jane both made excuses not to accompany her – Catherine said she had toothache and had wrapped a bandage around her face – and Elizabeth allowed them to remain at Westminster. An hour after the queen had departed, the two girls crept out of the palace 'by the stairs at the orchard' and went along the foreshore of the Thames, it being low tide, to Hertford's house at Canon Row.[15]

Hertford had sent his servants away for the morning and he met Catherine and Jane in his withdrawing chamber. Lady Jane departed immediately to fetch the priest who was to officiate the ceremony, returning with him fifteen minutes later. Catherine and Hertford would later recall that the priest was a man of 'mean stature, fair complexion, with an auburn beard, and of middle age, and was apparelled with a plain long gown of black cloth'.[16] In their excitement, neither of them thought it wise to learn his name.

The service was carried out in the earl's chamber and the priest married them 'with such words and ceremonies and in that order as it is set forth in the Book of Common Prayer' , suggesting that Catherine had by now returned to being a Protestant.[17] Hertford afterwards placed upon Catherine's finger a ring containing five links of gold. On the links was inscribed in English metre:

As circles five, by art compressed, show but one ring to sight
So trust uniteth faithful minds, with knot of secret might,
Whose force to break (but greedy death) no wight possesseth power,
As time and sequels well shall prove. My ring can so no more.[18]

Once the ceremony was over, Jane paid the priest ten pounds and escorted him from the premises. She returned soon after and then left the couple to consummate the marriage. About two hours after they had arrived, Hertford led them to the waterstairs, the tide having now come in and recovered the foreshore. He kissed his new wife and bade her farewell. Catherine and Jane rowed back to Westminster and returned just in time for lunch at the comptroller's table. Their absence had not been noticed and during the meal Catherine had the satisfaction of wearing beneath her hood a coif, a handkerchief covering the hair, as was custom for all married women.

Over the next few months Catherine and Hertford would meet whenever the opportunity presented itself. Their overfamiliarity at court was noted by some of the ladies, who warned Catherine to be careful, but she denied that there was anything between them. All was well until Catherine suspected that she was pregnant. It was a terrifying moment. If she was indeed pregnant then their secret would be out and they would be at the queen's mercy. Catherine decided to keep the news to herself, until Lady Jane informed her that Hertford was planning to go to France for a time. Catherine confronted Hertford and he denied the rumours, but her fears were confirmed when she later caught sight of his passport. She confided in both Hertford and Lady Jane that she might be pregnant and they reasoned that if it she were indeed pregnant then they had little choice but to 'trust to the Queen's mercy', while Hertford assured Catherine that he would not go to France and leave her to face the queen's wrath alone.[19] Unfortunately, the couple had made one major oversight. The only witnesses to the marriage were Lady Jane and the unnamed priest. Sadly, Lady Jane died in March 1561 and took the identity of the priest with her to the grave, meaning the couple had no way of proving that the marriage had taken place.

Catherine was still not sure that she was pregnant, and Hertford eventually left for France, but her fears were soon confirmed. She was alone, pregnant and unable to share her troubles with anybody. As she neared her due date people at court began to take notice of her swollen stomach and she was forced to reveal all to her friend Elizabeth Talbot, Lady St Loe, the famous Bess of Hardwick, on Saturday 9 August. Bess burst into tears, 'saying that she was very sorry that she had so done [married] without the consent or knowledge of the Queen's Majesty or any other of her friends'.[20] The following night the desperate Catherine tiptoed into the room of Robert Dudley, the queen's favourite and possible lover, and begged him to intercede with the queen. Dudley did so, but the next day a furious Elizabeth had Catherine sent to the Tower. She was hauled before an inquiry and asked about the marriage, while Edward was ordered to return immediately from France. He arrived at Dover in early September where he was arrested and thrown in the Tower. The next day he, too, was put in front of an inquiry, led by Matthew Parker, Archbishop of Canterbury and Edmund Grindal, Bishop of London, where he declared that the pair had married but admitted that the only witnesses to the event were his deceased sister and a priest he could not name. The only evidence that the wedding ever took place was the wedding ring, and he recounted the hidden metre on its five links. Catherine was questioned again. Her story mainly chimed with that of her husband, and she produced the ring which affirmed her husband's claim.

On 24 September, Catherine gave birth to a baby boy in the Tower.[21] According to Henry VIII's will this baby was now third in line to the throne behind Catherine herself. The following day he was christened Edward Seymour in the church of St Peter Ad Vincula, located within the Tower grounds.

On 12 May 1562, sentence was passed at the Bishop of London's Palace that Catherine and Hertford were not married and that their child was therefore illegitimate and unable to ascend the throne. The couple returned to the Tower to await their fate.

The Elizabethan Succession Question

As Catherine whiled away her hours in the Tower, the question of the succession became more urgent. In October 1562 Queen Elizabeth fell dangerously ill with smallpox. There were fears that she was going to die and thoughts turned to the identity of the next heir. The Privy Council discussed the matter but could not reach an agreement. Some favoured Catherine while others preferred the claim of Henry Hastings, Earl of Huntingdon, a descendant of George, Duke of

Clarence. Elizabeth recovered but at the next parliament, held in January 1563, the Commons and Lords petitioned her to marry or appoint an heir. Elizabeth once again refused to do so, proroguing the parliament in anger.

Prisoner

In February 1563, Queen Elizabeth received some news that infuriated her. Catherine had given birth to another son, named Thomas Seymour, on 10 February 1563. Catherine and Hertford had managed to bribe their wardens to leave their doors unlocked with the result that Catherine once again became pregnant. Edward was hauled before the Star Chamber and fined the enormous sum £15,000 (£5,000 for 'seducing a virgin of the royal blood', £5,000 for leaving his prison cell to visit Catherine in her cell and £5,000 for the birth of a second son).[22]

That summer there was an outbreak of plague in London which reportedly took 1,000 lives a week, and Queen Elizabeth ordered that Catherine and Hertford be removed to safer climes. Catherine and her youngest son, Thomas, were sent into the custody of her uncle Lord John Grey, while Hertford and their elder son were sent into the Duchess of Somerset's keeping. Elizabeth commanded that 'neither of them shall depart from the said places without our leave [neither attempt to have any converse together], otherwise than to take the air near to the same'.[23]

Lord John Grey was the youngest surviving brother of Henry Grey, Duke of Suffolk. He had joined his brothers' side in Leicestershire during Wyatt's Rebellion and he was the only one of them not to be executed after it. In Elizabeth's reign he was restored to favour and was granted Pyrgo, a royal estate that had once belonged to the queen dowagers of England, where Catherine now resided. Catherine found in Lord John a caring and compassionate individual who fought for her reconciliation with the queen. He often wrote to Cecil and Robert Dudley and urged them to use their influence with the queen to gain a pardon for his niece. Catherine's loss of favour with the queen caused her much distress and she would eat little and was prone to fits of weeping. On 20 September, Lord John wrote to Cecil, telling him of her anguish. 'I assure you cousin Cecil ... the thought and care she taketh for the want of her Highness' favour, pines her away ... if it come not the sooner, she will not long live thus, she eateth not above six morsels in the meal. If I say unto her, "Good Madame, eat somewhat to comfort yourself," she falls a weeping and goeth up to her chamber; if I ask her what the cause is she uses herself in that sort, she answers me, "Alas uncle, what a life is this, to me, thus to live in the Queen's displeasure; but for my lord, and my children, I would to God I were buried."'[24] In November, Catherine wrote a petition to the queen that Lord John forwarded to Cecil to check and amend. The petition runs as follows:

Lady Catherine Grey, Countess of Hertford

I dare not presume, Most Gracious Sovereign, to crave pardon for my disobedient and rash matching of myself, without your Highness' consent, I only most humbly sue unto your Highness, to continue your merciful nature toward me. I acknowledge myself a most unworthy creature to feel so much of your gracious favour as I have done. My just felt misery and continual grief doth teach me daily, more and more, the greatness of my fault, and your princely pity encreaseth my sorrow, that have so forgotten my duty towards your Majesty. This is my great torment of mind. May it therefore please your excellent Majesty to license me to be a most lowly suitor unto your Highness to extend towards my miserable state your Majesty's further favour and accustomed mercy, which upon my knees in all humble wise I crave, with my daily prayers to God, long continue and preserve your Majesty's reign over us. From Pyrgo the vi of November 1563.[25]

The queen was unmoved. A month later Sir John wrote to Cecil, warning him of Catherine's deteriorating state. She had spent the last four days in bed, and Sir John feared that he would have to call for the queen's physician. Whenever he went to see her he either found her crying or with tell-tale puffy eyes. '[S]he is so fraughted with phlegm by reason of thought, weeping, and sitting still, that many times she is like to be overcome therewith.'[26] Her gentlewomen feared that in the morning they would find her dead.

In April 1564, John Hales, a Chancery official, published a tract entitled *A Declaration of the Crown Imperial of England,* in which he discussed the validity of Henry VIII's will and the merits of the several claimants to the throne. He declared against Mary, Queen of Scots' right and concluded by stating, 'Thus have I declared unto you my judgment touching the right heirs to the crown of England in remainder and reversion; which is, as I take it, presently the Lady Catherine, daughter to the Lady Frances, both by King H. his will, and also by the Common Laws of this realm; and that we be bound both by our oaths and also by our laws so to take her.'[27]

Elizabeth had Hales cast into prison and Lord John, who appears to have had some involvement in the matter, was confined to Pyrgo. Catherine was removed from his dutiful care to Ingatestone where she was placed under the keeping of Sir William Petre. Sadly, Lord John died of gout on 19 November.

Catherine remained in Petre's keeping for eighteen months until she was moved once again, this time to Gosfield Hall under the keeping of the elderly and sick Sir John Wentworth. Wentworth complained to the Privy Council of this unwelcome burden as both he and his wife were ill, but his protestations fell on deaf ears. Catherine spent seventeen months at Gosfield Hall, then was moved once again in October 1567, following Wentworth's death, to her final abode at Cockfield Hall in Yoxford, Suffolk.

Death

Catherine's final keeper was the friendly Sir Owen Hopton. Years of imprisonment and of eating little had by now taken their effect on her health, and shortly after arriving at Cockfield she fell seriously ill. Sir Owen wrote to Cecil and requested that the queen's physician, Dr Symonds, be sent to treat her. Symonds duly attended, but once he left Catherine declined further. Symonds later paid a second visit but announced her to be beyond help.

Catherine, knowing that death awaited her, spent the night of 26 January 1568 in deep prayer. At seven o'clock on the morning of 27 January she summoned Sir Owen to her side. She asked him to deliver her final suit to the queen, that the queen will look after her children and not impute them with her faults. She also requested that the queen release her husband 'to glad his sorrow'.[28] She then requested one of her attendants to fetch a jewellery box from which she removed a ring set with a pointed diamond and asked Sir Owen to deliver it to her husband. 'What say you, madam,' he exclaimed, 'was this your wedding ring?'[29] Catherine shook her head, telling him that it was the ring Hertford had given her when they were betrothed on that distant, happy day. She then removed her wedding ring from the box and handed it to Sir Owen. Finally, she removed a third ring, surmounted by a death's-head along with the motto 'While I live yours', which she gave to Sir Owen.[30] Then, perceiving that her time had come, she cried, 'Welcome Death!' She lifted her eyes and hands towards heaven, beating her hands on her breast and said, 'O Lord! For thy manifold mercies, blot out of thy Book all mine offenses!'[31] She then fell into a fervent prayer. At about nine o'clock, she closed her eyes with her fingers and passed away. Catherine, the second of the three tragic daughters of Lady Frances and Henry, Duke of Suffolk, was just twenty-seven years old.

Catherine was embalmed and then buried at Yoxford Church on 21 February. At Hertford's death in 1621 at the grand age of eighty-two, Catherine was disinterred from Yoxford and reburied alongside her husband at Salisbury Cathedral by their eldest son, Edward Seymour, Lord Beauchamp. Catherine's pleas that Hertford be released were partially successful and in 1571 he was released after an incarceration of nine years. Hertford married a further two times following Catherine's death but both of his wives failed to produce any children. He fought to have his two children by Catherine legitimated and in 1595 he was once again cast into the Tower for six months for bringing the case before the Court of Arches. In 1609, during the reign of Elizabeth's successor, King James I, Hertford and Catherine's marriage was finally proven valid when Hertford managed to identify the elderly priest who had married them. King James recognised the right of Hertford's eldest son, Lord Beauchamp, to inherit the earldom of Hertford, but he would not go so far as to legitimate his and Catherine's sons, thereby nullifying their claim to the throne.

18

Lady Mary Grey

```
┌─────────────────────┐  m  ┌─────────────────────┐
│ Lady Frances Brandon│─────│    Henry Grey       │
│      d. 1559        │     │ 3rd Marquis of Dorset &│
│                     │     │   Duke of Suffolk   │
│                     │     │      d. 1554        │
└─────────────────────┘     └─────────────────────┘
              │
    ┌─────────────────────┐
    │   Lady Mary Grey    │
    │      d. 1578        │
    │        m            │
    │   Thomas Keyes      │
    │      d. 1571        │
    └─────────────────────┘
```

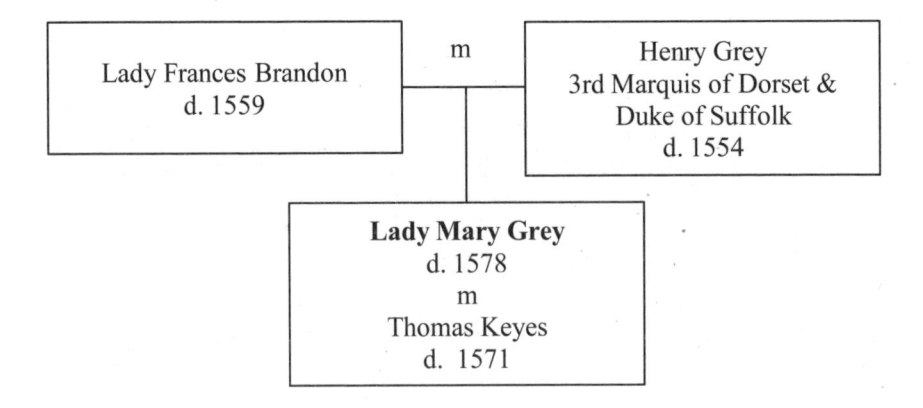

At around nine o'clock on the night of 16 July 1565, Lady Mary Grey, the youngest of the three Grey sisters, briskly made her way to the chamber of Master Thomas Keyes, the sergeant-porter at Whitehall Palace. There, in the presence of a few witnesses, she married Keyes in a clandestine ceremony. When Queen Elizabeth I learnt of the marriage just over a month later, she had Mary and her husband hauled before an inquiry and, like her elder sister Catherine before her, she was cast into prison.

Birth and Early Life

Lady Mary Grey was the third and youngest daughter of Henry Grey, Marquis of Dorset and Duke of Suffolk and Lady Frances Brandon. She was born at Bradgate in 1545 where she was raised alongside her two sisters. There is no record of her intellectual abilities but an inventory of her library made after her death shows that she knew both French and Italian.[1] There is, however, a dearth of classical texts recorded, suggesting that she could not read Latin or Greek, or possibly that she simply did not enjoy them.[2]

When she was just eight years old, Mary was betrothed to her kinsman Arthur, Lord Grey de Wilton. This occurred on the same day that both Jane and Catherine had been married as a part of Northumberland and Edward VI's machinations. The betrothal did not survive the events of July 1553 and Mary was once again free to marry. Her whereabouts during the tragic deaths of Jane and their father are unrecorded, although it is likely that she remained with her mother.

As Mary grew it became evident that she suffered from some form of spinal deformity. She was very short and is often said to have been a dwarf. A Spanish ambassador later described her as 'little, crook-backed and very ugly'.[3] It is possible, as historian Leanda De Lisle suggests, that she suffered from scoliosis, a condition that often runs in families and the same condition that Richard III is now known to have had.[4] On the accession of Queen Mary, she served as a maid of honour along with her sister Catherine, a role which she continued under Queen Elizabeth. She was granted a yearly pension of £80 by both queens, which was given to her by Lady Clinton, and a further £20 a year 'by the hands of one Astell'.[5]

Mary was just fourteen when her mother passed away and sixteen when her sister Catherine was imprisoned for marrying without the queen's permission. Somewhat incredibly, Catherine's treatment by the queen did not prevent Mary from making the same mistake, although she did learn some lessons from her elder sister. Like her mother, the Duchess of Suffolk, Mary chose for her husband someone further down the social ladder in the hope that it would alleviate any fears that she was planning on seizing the throne. Thomas Keyes was a mere gentleman from Kent who served as sergeant-porter and master of the revels at the Palace of Whitehall, a role he had performed under Henry VIII, Edward VI and Queen Mary. It was Keyes's role to furnish the rooms at the palace, to provide cards and dice for playing and to act as an arbitrator when disputes arose during the games.[6] He also manned the Watergate, the main gateway into the palace from the busy river Thames.

Keyes was an unlikely choice of husband. Not only was he socially inferior but he was over twice Mary's age and a widower who already had several children. He was also a giant of a man, standing at 6 foot 6 inches tall – he must have towered over the diminutive Mary. In a letter written to a contemporary shortly after the wedding Secretary Cecil states, 'Here is an unhappy chance and monstrous. The Sergeant Porter, being the biggest gentleman in this court, hath married secretly the Lady Mary Grey; the least of all the court.'[7] An unlikely romance blossomed between the two and Keyes showered her with love tokens, presenting her with two rings and another ring adorned with four rubies and a diamond. He later gave her a chain and a little hanging bottle of mother-of-pearl.[8] The two eventually decided to marry in secret, but they needed to find a day when the queen would be absent from the palace. Their chance came on 16 July 1565 when Queen Elizabeth was due to attend the wedding of Henry Knollys and Margaret Cave at Durham House.

Mary and Keyes were married at nine o'clock that night in the privacy of Keyes's lodgings beside the Watergate. Mary and Thomas had taken heed of Catherine's mistake in not having any witnesses present at the wedding and they invited Keyes's brother Edward, one Martin Cawsley (a student from Cambridge), 'Mr Cheyny's man' and Frances Goldwell (a servant of Lady Howard).[9] Unfortunately, they too did not see fit to record the name of the priest who officiated at the service, later described by Mary as being 'old, fat, and of low stature' and attired in a short gown.[10] They were married by the Protestant rites, the priest having a Book of Common Prayer from which he recited the Prayers of Matrimony. Thomas placed a small ring on his bride's tiny finger before they kissed in front of those present. Once everyone had left, they consummated the marriage.

A Most Woeful Wretch

By 19 August, word of the marriage had reached Queen Elizabeth who immediately had the unlucky couple seized and questioned before the Privy Council. Frances Goldwell was questioned by William Lord Howard but denied that the marriage had taken place. Mary and Keyes were afterwards ordered to be imprisoned in different locations, perhaps in order to prevent the birth of a child. Keyes was sent to Fleet Prison while Mary was placed under house arrest at Chequers in Buckinghamshire, under the care of Sir William Hawtrey. She was allowed one waiting-woman and a groom and was strictly prohibited from holding communication with anyone or from leaving the precincts of Chequers.

Like Catherine before her, Mary wrote several letters to Sir William Cecil in the hope that he would exert his influence with the queen to gain her forgiveness and restore her to favour. In her letters she laments her predicament and calls herself a 'most woeful wretch'.[11] She evidently expected her time in captivity to be of short duration. In a letter written to Cecil on 16 December she states, 'I did trust to have wholly obtained her Majesty's favour before this time; the which, having once obtained, I trust never to have lost again. But now I perceive that I am so unhappy a creature, as I must yet be without that great and long desired jewel; till it please God to put in her Majesty's heart to forgive and pardon me my great and heinous crime.'[12]

While Mary fretted about Chequers, her husband fared much worse. His large bulk was ill suited to the confines of his tiny prison cell at the Fleet. In August 1566, after nearly a year in confinement, he offered to have the marriage declared null and void if he were allowed to return to his native Kent. Grindal, Bishop of London, denied the request but suggested to Cecil that Keyes should be allowed to walk the gardens of the Fleet to take in fresh air and stretch his legs. This small mercy was granted but revoked shortly after when a new and cruel warden took over the prison. The new warden even fed him with some beef which had inadvertently fallen into some poison prepared for a dog that had mange. Keyes was forced to send for a doctor which cost him 6s 8d. He recovered.

After two years, Mary was moved from Chequers into the keeping of her step-grandmother Catherine Willoughby, Duchess of Suffolk. Catherine was the fourth wife of Mary's grandfather Charles Brandon, Duke of Suffolk, whom he had married shortly after the death of Mary Tudor. Hawtrey and Mary, along with her maid and groom, arrived at Catherine's house in the Minories (a street near the Tower of London) late one night when the duchess was about to set out for Greenwich Palace. She was astonished to see that Mary had brought no belongings with which to furnish her chambers. Hawtrey explained that Mary had so little of her own possessions that he had to provide her with his own furniture while she stayed at Chequers. Catherine, who spent most of her time in Lincolnshire and usually borrowed furniture from her friends while she was at London, had no furnishings to lend. She was horrified when she later saw the extent and condition of Mary's belongings when Hawtrey delivered them. There was an old livery feather bed, 'all to torn and full of patches', two old pillows, 'one longer than the other', an old silk quilt and two old hangings.[13] The next day they travelled to Greenwich Palace where Catherine was compelled to write to Cecil and ask the queen for some furniture to fit out one chamber for Mary and her maid, along with some old silver pots with which to fetch drink and two cups, one for wine and one for beer. Mary was ashamed and embarrassed to be seen in such a pitiful condition by her step-grandmother and she refused to eat 'so much as a chicken's leg'.[14] Catherine hoped that a little comfort would soon bring her round.

Mary resided with Catherine for two years. In January 1568 she received news of her sister Catherine's death and of her elevation to the rank of heiress presumptive according to the terms of Henry VIII's will. Catherine had left behind her two sons but, as we have seen, they were declared illegitimate and were thus unable to take the throne. Mary's claim never seems to have been seriously considered and no voices were raised on her behalf in Parliament, perhaps due to her spinal deformity. There is no evidence that Mary had any pretensions of ascending the throne. The tragic fates of her father and two sisters would have made her all too aware of the inherent dangers while her choice of husband surely indicates that she was content to remain a private person, or at least a 'minor royal'.

In June 1569, Mary was moved from Catherine's care to that of Sir Thomas Gresham, a wealthy merchant from London, and resided with him and his wife at Gresham House. Mary was an unwelcome burden on the Greshams and Sir Thomas wrote many times to Cecil and Robert Dudley imploring them to take her off his hands.

Mary would remain in Gresham's keeping for three long years. On 8 September 1571, Mary's physician, Dr Smith, informed Gresham that Keyes had passed away. After three years at Fleet he had been moved to Lewisham, possibly on parole, and then to Sandgate Castle. At Sandgate he had written to Matthew Parker, Archbishop of Canterbury, asking him to

Lady Mary Grey

intercede on his behalf with the queen to see if he could live with Mary as man and wife. Unsurprisingly, this was denied and in early September 1571 he died. Gresham broke the tragic news to Mary, which, he reported to Cecil, she 'grievously taketh'.[15] Once the shock had settled in, her thoughts turned to Keyes's orphaned children. She asked Gresham to write to Cecil and petition the queen to let her look after them. The heartless Gresham was delighted at the prospect of her finally leaving, writing hopefully to Cecil of his trust 'that now I shall be presently dispatched of her, by your good means'.[16] He also enquired if he was to allow her to wear any mourning clothes for her husband, which the queen cruelly forbade. Unfortunately, both Mary and Gresham were to be disappointed.

Keyes's death was a devastating blow to Mary but it offered the possibility that Elizabeth would now free her. She wrote another letter to Cecil, which she defiantly signed 'Mary Keyes'. She must have thought better of inflaming the queen's displeasure, as in the next letter she wrote she returned to using her maiden name.

Gresham now took matters into his own hands. He personally rode for London, where he asked that Mary be removed to the house of her father-in-law, Adrian Stokes. Gresham's personal petition fared no better and Mary continued to live under his roof, spending the winter of 1571/2 at his residence at Mayfield in Sussex. By March 1572, progress had been made. Cecil was sweetened by a bribe from Gresham and Mary was finally freed two months later.

Death

Mary had been more fortunate than Catherine, which suggests that Elizabeth did not consider her a threat. She had her freedom but she had little money to her name and even fewer friends. She wrote to Cecil deploring her poor financial straits – she only had the £80 pension provided by the queen and £20 of her own annual income, which was not enough to pay for her board anywhere.[17] Elizabeth agreed to give her an enlarged income and she moved in with her father-in-law, Adrian Stokes, who had by now taken another wife. She remained with Stokes a short while until she could finally afford her own house at St Botolph without Aldgate in London. Her rehabilitation with the queen continued and she was permitted to attend court and she once again enjoyed the royal favour. She was present at the Christmas festivities held at Hampton Court in 1576 where she is noted as having given the queen a present of '2 pairs of sweet gloves, with four dozen buttons of gold, in every one a seed pearl', for which the queen gave her a silver cup and cover weighing 18 ounces in return.[18]

Mary would not remarry. She died on 20 April 1578, aged just thirty-three, of an unknown illness.[19] Her will is extant, written three days before her passing. In it she bequeathed her prized possessions to her friends, relatives and servants: 'Itm. I give & bequeath unto my very good lady and grandmother the Duchess of Suffolk's grace one pair of hand bracelets of gold with a jacinte stone in each bracelet which bracelets were my lady grace my late mothers or else my jewel of unicorn's horn whichsoever liketh her grace best to take and whichsoever her grace refuseth I give and bequeath the same to my very good lady the lady Susanne Countess of Kent.'[20]

Her servants were not forgotten. She named two ladies, Anne Goldwell and Catherine Duport. To Anne she bequeathed six silver spoons and a silver plate and to Catherine one plate with silver-gilt edge. Her two manservants are named as Robert Saville and Henry Goldwell, possibly the husband of Anne. To William Parfoot, a servant boy, she thoughtfully left money to pay for an apprenticeship.[21]

She left the choice of her burial spot to Queen Elizabeth, who had her interred alongside her mother in the Chapel of St Edmund in Westminster Abbey on 14 May.[22] Mary's life was undoubtedly tragic and short, but unlike her two sisters she was fortunate enough to die in the comfort of her own home, a free woman, of natural causes.

19

Lady Margaret Clifford, Countess of Derby

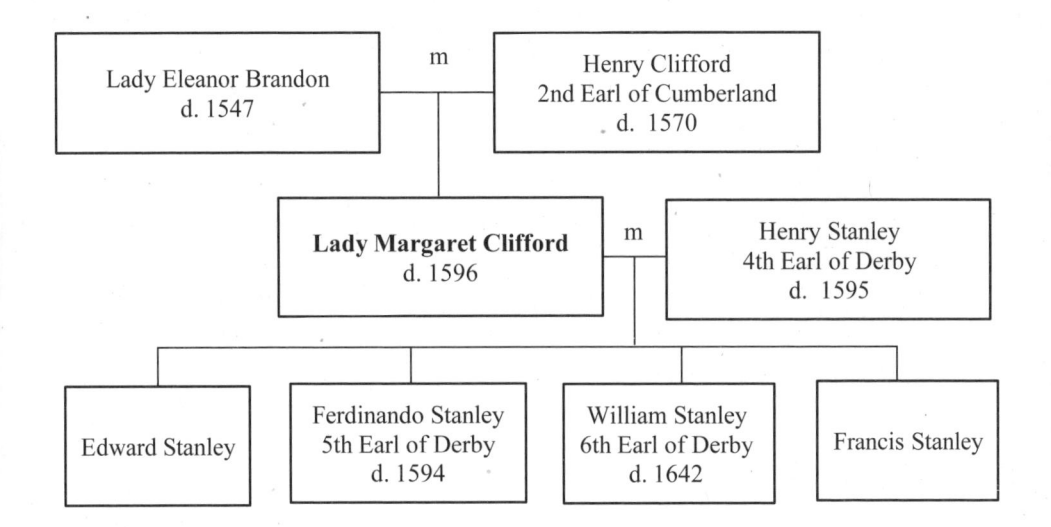

```
Lady Eleanor Brandon —m— Henry Clifford
d. 1547              2nd Earl of Cumberland
                     d. 1570

   Lady Margaret Clifford —m— Henry Stanley
   d. 1596                    4th Earl of Derby
                              d. 1595

Edward Stanley | Ferdinando Stanley | William Stanley | Francis Stanley
               | 5th Earl of Derby  | 6th Earl of Derby |
               | d. 1594            | d. 1642           |
```

In late August 1579, Lady Margaret Clifford, Countess of Derby was placed under house arrest in London. She had been detained for discussing the arrival of Francis of Valois, the brother of King Charles IX of France, who was then in discussions with Queen Elizabeth I over a possible marriage. Three days later, Margaret was charged with the much more serious crime of resorting to witchcraft to determine the date of the queen's death. If Elizabeth were to die, Margaret would be the next monarch according to Henry VIII's will.

Birth and Early Life

Lady Margaret Clifford was the only surviving child of Lady Eleanor Brandon and Henry Clifford, 2nd Earl of Cumberland. She derived her claim to the throne from her mother, Lady Eleanor, who was the second daughter of Mary Tudor and Charles Brandon, Duke of Suffolk. Lady Eleanor had been betrothed to Henry Clifford, the eldest son of the 1st Earl of Cumberland, also Henry, in March 1533 and the wedding had been celebrated two years later in June 1535 at the Church of St Mary Overies, Suffolk Place. It was attended by King Henry VIII, who bore a great affection for Cumberland having been brought up and educated alongside him. After the marriage,

Eleanor went to live with her husband at Cumberland's main seat of Skipton Castle in Yorkshire. Eleanor would give birth to three children. Their first two children were sons, Henry and Charles, while the third was a daughter, Margaret, born in 1540 at her father's castle of Brougham in Westmorland (now Cumbria).[1] Both Henry and Charles died young but their sister thrived, becoming heir presumptive to the earldom of Cumberland.

Lady Margaret was most likely brought up in her mother's household and travelled with her to Brougham Castle following the tragic loss of her sons. Eleanor died in November 1547 and she was buried at Skipton Church. In the nineteenth century, Thomas Whitaker, author of *The History and antiquities of the deanery of Craven, in the County of York*, was given permission to enter the Clifford crypt where he saw Eleanor's deteriorating coffin. It had corroded to such an extent that he could see her skeleton and he reported that she was a 'tall and large-limbed female ... as might be expected in a daughter of Charles Brandon and the sister of Henry the Eighth'.[2]

Henry Clifford, who had succeeded his father as 2nd Earl of Cumberland in 1542, was said to have been so distraught at the loss of his wife that he fell into a catatonic state and was feared dead. He was laid out for embalming when he suddenly regained his senses. He was placed in a warm bed, given cordials and food and soon recovered his strength. He would survive his wife by another twenty-three years, dying on 8 January 1570.

Margaret's childhood is poorly recorded. It is likely that following her mother's death she was brought up in her father's household, where she would have pursued her education. We have no record of her intellectual abilities, although it is likely that she was provided with a first-rate humanist education by her well-educated father.

Like her Grey cousins, Margaret's royal blood and proximity to the throne meant that she soon became a person of interest for schemers. In 1552, during the reign of Edward VI, John Dudley, Earl of Northumberland, sought the then twelve-year-old Margaret's hand for his youngest son, Lord Guildford Dudley, the future husband of Lady Jane Grey. Cumberland turned down the offer, claiming that Margaret was already betrothed, but the wily Northumberland was not to be denied. He turned instead to the king, who wrote a letter to Earl Henry on Northumberland's behalf, 'desiring him to grow to some good end forthwith in the matter of marriage between the L. Guildford Dudley and his daughter'.[3]

News of the prospective marriage soon circulated and it was feared that Northumberland was making a pass at the crown. In August that year, Mrs Elizabeth Huggins, a servant of Anne Stanhope, Duchess of Somerset, paid a visit to Sir William Stafford at Rochford. During supper, Huggins complained about the death of her former master, Protector Somerset, the blame for which she placed firmly at the feet of Northumberland. Furthermore, she reported on the rumours of the proposed marriage of Guildford Dudley to 'my lord of Cumberland's daughter, and that the King's Majesty should devise the marriage'.[4] Then, with a 'stout gesture', she declared, 'Have at the Crown with your leave.'[5] Sir William Stafford reported her outburst to the Privy Council and Huggins was examined at the Tower. When she was asked about her claims of the marriage, she reported that she had heard it spoken of in London and that the king had arranged it. She had told Stafford the news at supper because she was 'glad thereof' and she firmly denied having said 'have at the Crown...', protesting that she had never meant any evil.[6]

The marriage never materialised, but after Lady Jane Grey's marriage to Guildford Dudley in 1553 Northumberland's thoughts turned once again to Cumberland's now thirteen-year-old daughter. He proposed that she marry his brother Sir Andrew Dudley, master of the wardrobe. This time Earl Henry agreed, and on 8 June a warrant was issued to allow Sir Andrew Dudley to take silks and jewels from the wardrobe for use in the service. King Edward's death on 6 July put an end to the marriage scheme, however, and Earl Henry threw his support behind Queen Mary when she ascended the throne.[7]

An Unhappy Marriage

Lady Margaret became one of Queen Mary's ladies-in-waiting. Her first recorded public appearance was at the queen's wedding to Prince Philip of Spain, which took place on Wednesday 25 July 1554 at Winchester Cathedral. During the blessing of the rings, Philip placed three handfuls of gold on the Bible beside them and Margaret, seeing this, opened the queen's purse while Mary placed the gold inside.[8]

The following year it was Margaret's turn to marry. Her husband was Henry Stanley, Lord Strange, the eldest son of Edward Stanley, 3rd Earl of Derby. Strange was born in 1531 and was aged twenty-four at the time of marriage, nine years older than his bride. The marriage was celebrated on 12 February 1555 at the King's Chapel at Whitehall. It was a grand affair, attended by the king and queen and celebrated with a great banquet, jousts and a 'tourney on horseback with swords'.[9] After supper, King Philip took part in the *Juego de Canas*, a Spanish sport in which combatants on horseback attempt to hit one another with canes, followed by a masque and a sumptuous banquet.[10]

Margaret and Lord Strange set up house at Bidston in Wirral, which had been granted to them by the Earl of Derby. The marriage would prove an unhappy but fruitful one, with Margaret giving birth to four children: Edward, Ferdinando, William and Francis. Both Edward and Francis died young, but Ferdinando and William would succeed their father as 5th and 6th earls of Derby respectively. Sometime after 1558 Margaret, Lord Strange and their growing family moved from Bidston and took up residence at Gaddesden in Hertfordshire.

The couple spent most of their time at court, with Margaret continuing to serve as a lady-in-waiting under Elizabeth I. Elizabeth did not bear the same ill will towards Margaret that she did to the Grey sisters, probably because she was far down the order of succession, and treated her well. In August 1564, Margaret is recorded as accompanying the queen on a visit to King's College, Cambridge, and she bore the queen's train when the queen visited the chapel.[11] She bore the queen's train again at Christmas 1565 when the queen attended the church services at Whitehall.[12] There are records of Margaret giving and receiving New Year's gifts from the queen in 1561, 1572, 1573, 1578 and 1579.

At home, however, Margaret and Lord Strange's relationship became strained over their financial difficulties. Both were spendthrifts and careless with money. According to the deposition of one of Margaret's gentlewomen, a Mrs Calfhill, Margaret spent some £600 a year but only received an annuity of £90 from her husband, which was tardily paid.[13] As a lady of the royal blood, Margaret no doubt wanted to live in a style befitting her rank and she was often forced to lend money to do so. As a result, she was constantly in debt and hounded by creditors for much of her life.

In 1567, Lord Strange made some accusations against Margaret that led to Mrs Calfhill being interviewed by the Privy Council. Her answers offer insight into episodes of Margaret's life and her money troubles. Mrs Calfhill was a widowed Irish woman whom Margaret had enticed over to England to enter her service in 1558. Mrs Calfhill had duly travelled over and found a heavily pregnant Margaret at Bidston and 'after much persuasion' had agreed to serve her.[14] Margaret and Mrs Calfhill had then travelled on to Knowsley where Margaret wished to give birth to her firstborn, Edward. She was penniless and asked Mrs Calfhill to lend her some money. Mrs Calfhill agreed to lend her £80 but foolishly divulged that she had a further £300 held by her friends in London if Margaret required it. Margaret was in such financial straits that Mrs Calfhill was even forced to provide her with some of her own belongings for use during her delivery.

After her confinement and churching, Margaret travelled to London to attend the newly crowned Queen Elizabeth at court. Lord Strange had not paid her annuity and she asked Mrs Calfhill to lend her the £300 to buy sumptuous clothes and jewels with which to attend court. On learning of Margaret's financial difficulties, Queen Elizabeth provided her with lodgings at court to help alleviate her costs, but her debts continued to spiral. The kindly Mrs Calfhill, who was reluctantly placed in charge of keeping Margaret's books, was not paid her wages in all her nine years of service except for £18 that was paid out of the £300 she had lent Margaret. Once the £300 was spent, Margaret tasked Mrs Calfhill with lending money, jewels and wares on her own credit with her friends standing as guarantors for payment. After six years of service, Mrs Calfhill attempted to leave and retire to the country, but Margaret and Lord Strange refused her request.[15]

The couple were forced to sell much of Margaret's Suffolk inheritance, inherited through her mother, to cover her debts. Before 1567, Strange sold some £1,500 worth of property.[16] Lord Strange, however, was as much to blame for the debt as Margaret. He was careless with money and his father, the Earl of Derby, even took the precaution of entailing his lands in trust on his other sons to prevent him from selling them.[17]

Following '[d]ivers breaches after divers reconciliations', things came to a head in 1567 when Strange broke up the household, citing his inability to pay its costs, and left Margaret and their children at Gaddesden.[18] In a letter to Secretary Cecil, Margaret outlined her grievances against her husband. She complained that Lord Strange had kept £100 of her share from the sale of her lands, which she had intended to use to pay her debts. Strange had also borrowed £8,000 from her father, Cumberland, but had sold or given away the property that he had promised the earl as collateral in order to not have to repay it. He had attempted to convince Margaret to sell her jewels and when she refused he had sold all the plate at Gaddesden and kept the money for himself. He had even offered Ms Newton, one of Margaret's servants, £200 to spy on Margaret, but the loyal servant refused. He cruelly threatened to send their children away if she went to court and he had been trying to goad her into breaking up the house first.[19] He was also unfaithful to her, having a mistress, Jane Halsall, with whom he fathered more children.

The two did not divorce, but Lord Strange took up residence with his mistress while Margaret returned to court or lived in one of her properties. She was at court in 1570 when her father, Cumberland, died. After the death of Lady Eleanor, Cumberland had married again and had two sons, Margaret's half-brothers George and Francis. George, as the eldest son, now became 3rd Earl of Cumberland. Queen Elizabeth wrote to the Earl of Derby and to Lord Strange requesting that Margaret remain in her service. She noted how grieved Margaret was at her father's death and told them that she had granted her permission to sell some of her lands to cover her debts. She was later forced to write again to Lord Strange, telling him to refrain from appropriating any of the money to pay his own debts.[20]

Strange's father, the Earl of Derby, died in 1572 and Strange succeeded him as 4th earl. Margaret and Derbys' eldest surviving son and heir, Ferdinando, now became Lord Strange, the title of the heir to the Derby patrimony. The year before, Queen Elizabeth had requested that Ferdinando be sent to court and he had become a squire in the royal household. The suspicious queen had no doubt wanted to keep him close in case he became a figure of intrigue as a legitimate male heir to the crown.

'A poor wretched abandoned Lady'

The death of Margaret's cousin Mary Grey in 1578 made her heir presumptive to Elizabeth I according to Henry VIII's will, and it was now Margaret's turn to feel the enmity of her royal cousin. She was still in favour at the beginning of 1579 and she is recorded as being given a New Year's gift of a 'train gown of tawny velvet' by the queen.[21] Then, in late August, Margaret was suddenly arrested and 'lodged in the house of a gentleman in London'.[22]

The Spanish ambassador, Bernardino de Mendoza, reports that Margaret had been arrested for discussing the rumoured arrival of Francis of Valois, the brother of Charles IX of France, with whom the queen was discussing marriage. The country was divided over the match and it was met with strong opposition from the queen's favourite, Robert Dudley. Margaret was against it as well, as it meant the possibility of the queen having an heir, although this was unlikely in truth as Elizabeth was then aged forty-five. Mendoza notes that a certain weight was given to what Margaret said as she was a claimant to the throne.[23]

Three days later, Mendoza reported that Margaret had also been charged with using witchcraft to determine the date of the queen's death. Mendoza notes that she had not yet been put in the Tower, although this had been ordered, and that her accomplices had been arrested.[24] The wizard that Margaret was said to have employed to predict the queen's death was the famous physician Dr Randall, who was arrested along with her. Randall was duly arraigned and, after professing Margaret's guilt, executed. Whether or not Randall told the truth is unknown – he was likely coerced into a false confession.

In a letter to Sir Francis Walsingham, then the queen's secretary, Margaret protested her innocence, stating that she suffered from chronic rheumatism and toothache and that she had been recommended the services of Dr Randall, who had a cure for her ailments 'by applying of outwards things'.[25] She had employed his services from May until August that year and had found some relief from his practices. She further complained that her creditors still hounded her for money even while under house arrest and she requested that Elizabeth allow her to sell some of her property to pay them. The queen, however, did not grant this request until June 1582 and the following year Margaret sold lands, possibly for a lease of twenty years, for £1,768.[26]

Margaret remained under house arrest for the next few years. She found a friend in the form of Sir Christopher Hatton, the queen's vice chamberlain, who was her instrument in securing the queen's favour and the only person at court who showed her compassion. In her letters, Margaret describes herself as a 'poor wretched abandoned lady' and affectionately calls Hatton 'the rock I build on'.[27]

Sometime before September 1583, Hatton was able to secure her release, although she remained out of favour with the queen. In a letter she thanked Hatton for the liberty he had gained her but complained of her poor health and poverty. She suffered from periodic fainting and 'overcomings', she said, and was often at death's door.[28] She wished to be moved to a property of her kinsman Thomas Seckford, the queen's master of requests, in Clerkenwell, where she hoped to have better air. The property was unfinished, she

Lady Margaret Clifford, Countess of Derby

remarked, and the area had recently been hit by the plague so she would be looking for a house in Highgate for the time being.

Another letter, dated 26 September 1583, is written by Margaret from Clerkenwell, suggesting that Hatton was able to fulfil her request. Hatton was even able to orchestrate a meeting between the queen and Margaret when the queen passed by Clerkenwell on her way to Oatlands Palace. This filled Margaret with renewed hope that she may receive the queen's forgiveness and she asked Hatton to once again intercede on her behalf so that 'I may come to the kissing of her Highness' hand'.[29]

Margaret never succeeded in her wish to return to the queen's favour. By 1587 she had moved to a house in Isleworth whence she wrote a desperate letter to the queen, thanking her for the 'accustomed benignity and rare goodness' she had shown her and once again begged her forgiveness.[30]

The Earl of Derby died in 1593 and Margaret was among the mourners at his funeral held at Ormskirk in Lancashire. Margaret's affection for her husband is debateable but the fact that she attended suggests that some feeling or sense of duty remained. Derby was succeeded by their eldest surviving son, Ferdinando, who became the 5th Earl. Ferdinando had married Alice Spencer, the youngest daughter of Sir John Spencer of Althorpe, and had by her three daughters. He was a poet and a great patron of the arts, supporting a Company of Players known as 'Strange's Men' which became 'Derby's Men' from 1593 and may have at one time included William Shakespeare. As a legitimate male heir of Henry VII, Ferdinando became the focus of a Catholic plot to overthrow the queen, but he revealed all. He predeceased his mother on 16 April 1594 and was succeeded to the earldom by his younger brother, William Stanley. Rumours circulating at the time said that he had died by witchcraft when in his last illness a wax image in his likeness was discovered in his chamber with some of his hair twisted through its belly.

Margaret eventually bought Seckford's house at Clerkenwell where she died, aged fifty-six, on 29 September 1596. She was buried in St Edmund's Chapel at Westminster Abbey.[31] Margaret's claim to the throne devolved on the eldest daughter of Ferdinando Stanley. Her name was Anne Stanley and she had been born in 1580. Her claim was never taken seriously and she never entertained any designs on the throne. When Elizabeth died in 1603, it was James VI of Scotland, the son of Mary, Queen of Scots, whom the queen chose as her successor, ending the years of confusion wrought by Henry VIII's legacy.

20

Mary, Queen of Scots

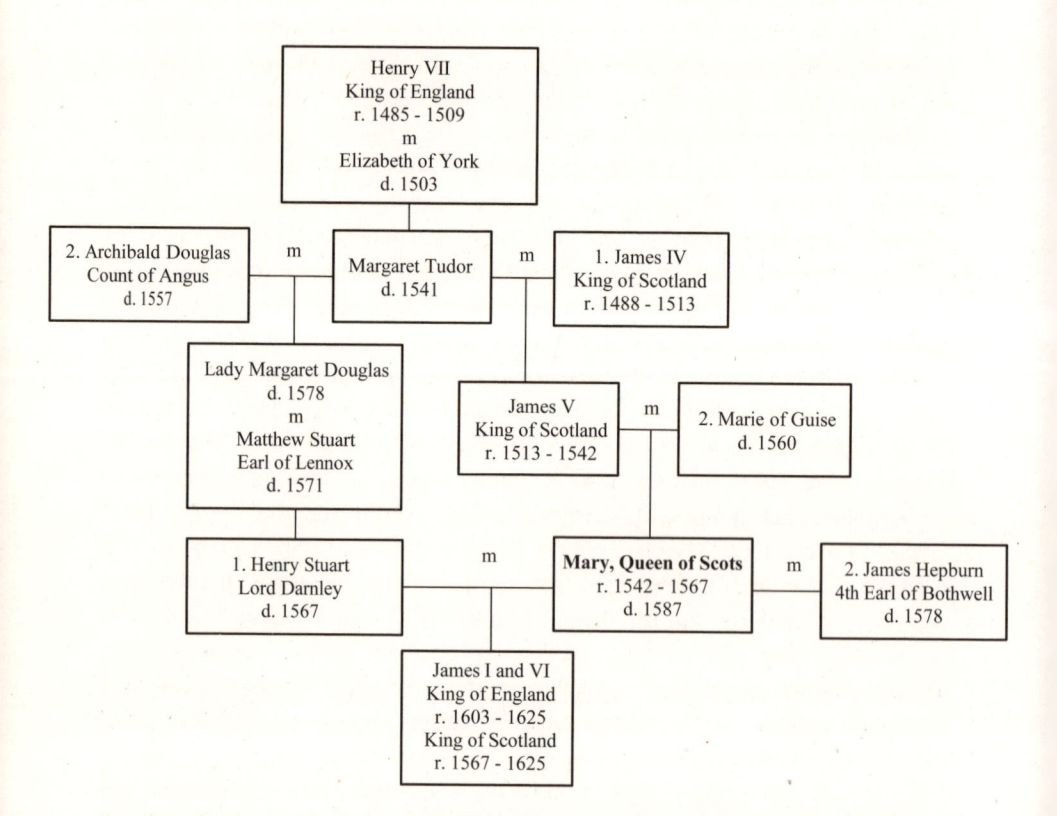

```
                    Henry VII
                  King of England
                   r. 1485 - 1509
                         m
                  Elizabeth of York
                      d. 1503
```

- 2. Archibald Douglas, Count of Angus, d. 1557 — m — Margaret Tudor, d. 1541 — m — 1. James IV, King of Scotland, r. 1488 - 1513
- Lady Margaret Douglas, d. 1578, m Matthew Stuart, Earl of Lennox, d. 1571
- James V, King of Scotland, r. 1513 - 1542 — m — 2. Marie of Guise, d. 1560
- 1. Henry Stuart, Lord Darnley, d. 1567 — m — **Mary, Queen of Scots, r. 1542 - 1567, d. 1587** — m — 2. James Hepburn, 4th Earl of Bothwell, d. 1578
- James I and VI, King of England, r. 1603 - 1625, King of Scotland, r. 1567 - 1625

On the afternoon of 7 February 1587, George Talbot, Earl of Shrewsbury and Henry Grey, Earl of Kent were conducted to the chamber of Mary Stuart, former Queen of Scotland, Queen Dowager of France and hereditary heiress presumptive to the English throne, at Fotheringhay Castle in Northamptonshire. There, in Mary's presence, they read aloud the warrant for her execution. Mary greeted their words with surprising alacrity. She had been a prisoner in England for almost nineteen years, three times the length of her reign in Scotland, and she welcomed the news that God was to finally end her long suffering. When she asked when the sentence was to be carried out, however, the reply came as a shock: eight o'clock tomorrow morning. Mary protested that this did not give her enough time to settle her affairs, but her entreaties fell on deaf ears.

That night, as she prepared for death, Mary must have reflected on her tragic life and the events that had brought her, a crowned queen, to such a terrible conclusion.

Scotland

Mary Stuart, better known to history as Mary, Queen of Scots, was the third and only surviving child of King James V of Scotland and his second queen, Marie of Guise. Her claim to the English throne derived from her paternal grandmother, Margaret Tudor, the eldest daughter of Henry VII and eldest sister of Henry VIII. The Tudor and Stuart lines had become interwoven in 1503 when Margaret married King James IV of Scotland in order to secure the Treaty of Perpetual Peace between the two nations. Margaret and James would have six children during their ten-year marriage but the only child to survive infancy was Mary's father, James V, who was born at Linlithgow Palace in April 1512.

The Treaty of Perpetual Peace did not long survive the accession of the boisterous Henry VIII. In 1513, Henry invaded France and James IV, in accordance with the provisions of the Auld Alliance, the ancient treaty of mutual aid between Scotland and France against England of 1295, entered Northumberland at the head of an army. He was killed while fighting at the disastrous Battle of Flodden on 9 September and the seventeen-month-old James V duly succeeded to the throne. His long minority was plagued by troubles from his ambitious nobles, who fought to control him, and from his grasping uncle Henry VIII, who hoped to conquer Scotland or reassert England's overlordship over it.

In 1537, James V married Madeleine, the daughter of the French king Francis I, in order to renew the Auld Alliance, but the new queen died shortly after her arrival in Scotland. The following year he married a French noblewoman, Marie of Guise, of the powerful and ambitious Guise family. The couple had two sons, Henry and Robert, but both died in short succession in 1541.

That same year, Henry VIII arranged a conference between the two kings to take place at York. James, at the advice of his nobles, decided not to attend. In 1542, the furious Henry VIII dispatched an army into Scotland and the Scots were heavily defeated at the Battle of Solway Moss on 24 November. James, who was awaiting news of the battle, retired in dudgeon. He went to see his heavily pregnant queen at Linlithgow Palace before retiring to the royal palace at Falkland, where he fell sick with grief and retired to his deathbed. On 8 December a messenger delivered him the happy news that Marie of Guise had given birth to an heir. James asked whether it was a boy or girl and when he was told the latter he sighed, 'Adieu, farewell, it came with a lass, and it will pass with a lass.'[1] This was a nod to the fact that the Stuart dynasty had started in the female line when Margery Bruce, the daughter of Robert the Bruce, had married Walter Stewart in 1318. James turned his back on his nobles and faced the wall. He would die a few days later, on 14 December, aged just thirty.

Birth and Early Life

James V's premature death saw the newborn Mary become Queen of Scotland at just six days old. Another long minority was inevitable and the regency was contested between two parties, one that supported an alliance with England and another that supported the Auld Alliance with France. These parties had a religious dimension. Like other countries in Europe, Scotland had been infiltrated by the opinions of Martin Luther and had found many converts. The Catholics supported the alliance with France while the Protestants supported one with England. The Catholic party was headed by Queen Dowager Marie of Guise, and Cardinal David Beaton, Archbishop of St Andrews, while the Protestant party was headed by James Hamilton, Earl of Arran, a grandson of King James III of Scotland and heir presumptive to the Scottish throne. The Protestants had their way and Arran was appointed regent on 22 December.

Henry VIII, meanwhile, spotted an opportunity to unite the two countries by marrying his five-year-old son, Edward, Prince of Wales, the future Edward VI, to Mary. In order to achieve this he released some of the captives taken at the Battle of Solway Moss and tasked them with using their influence to bring about the marriage. Arran, being pro-English and Protestant, was easily persuaded and he sent ambassadors into England. The marriage was agreed on 1 July 1543 in the Treaty of Greenwich, in which it was stipulated that Edward would marry Mary when she turned ten in 1552.

Mary spent the first few months of her life at Linlithgow Palace under the care of her mother and her nurse, Janet Sinclair. There were rumours circulating that Mary was a weak and sickly child who had been born premature. On 22 March, Sir Ralph Sadler, Henry VIII's ambassador in Scotland, was shown Mary naked in her nursery to quell the rumours. 'I assure your majesty,' he reported to King Henry, 'it is as goodly a child as I have seen of her age, and as like to live, with the grace of God.'[2]

Marie of Guise and Cardinal Beaton were determined to overthrow the Treaty of Greenwich and they were in contact with Francis I, King of France, who sent over Matthew Stuart, Earl of Lennox, the half-brother of Arran who had been living in exile in France, to act as a rival to the regent. Cardinal Beaton and Lennox laid siege to Linlithgow in order to gain custody of Mary, and Arran was forced to come to terms. On 26 July, Mary was moved behind the stouter walls of Stirling Castle and placed under the care of four barons. The vacillating Arran, described by Sadler as being of 'weak spirit, and fainthearted', then changed sides and became Catholic, destroying King Henry's hopes for the marriage.[3] At ten o'clock on the morning of Sunday 9 September, Mary was crowned in the Chapel Royal of Stirling Castle. Sadler, in a letter to Henry VIII, reports that it was done 'with such solemnity as they do use in this country, which is not very costly'.[4]

The Scottish Parliament repudiated the Treaty of Greenwich and in May 1544 a furious Henry VIII dispatched Edward Seymour, Earl of Hertford and the future Protector Somerset, into Scotland at the head of an army. Mary was briskly taken north to the safety of Dunkeld Castle while Hertford razed Edinburgh and harried the countryside before withdrawing to England. Another English army was sent in 1545 but suffered defeat at the Battle of Ancrum Moor.

Henry VIII died in January 1547 and, as we have seen, his will bypassed Mary, the next in blood after Princess Elizabeth according to the rules of primogeniture. It was likely that Henry had hoped to use Mary's claim to the crown as leverage for the marriage. Hertford, now Protector Somerset, pursued the war against Scotland and he defeated the Scots at the Battle of Pinkie on 10 September 1547. As a result, Arran and the council dispatched Mary to the safety of Inchmahome Priory, located on a small island in the Lake of Menteith, while they appealed to King Henri II of France for help. Henri sent a force of 6,000 men who landed in June 1548 and, joining forces with Arran, laid siege to the English at their newly erected fort at Haddington. While the siege was underway, Parliament convened at Haddington Abbey where the terms of French help were discussed. King Henri requested that Mary be sent into the safety of France where she would be brought up and married to his son, the Dauphin Francis. Parliament agreed and in July the five-year-old Mary was taken to Dumbarton where she bade her mother an emotional goodbye, in what must have been a harrowing experience for such a young child. She was taken on board the king's galley under the keeping of Monsieur de Brézé, Seneschal of Normandy, who had been appointed by King Henri to escort her to France. She would not set foot in her native kingdom for another twelve years.

France

In August, Mary arrived safely at the little port of Roscoff in Brittany. After resting a few days, she commenced her journey towards the palace of Saint-Germain-en-Laye, near Paris, where she arrived in October. There she met her future husband, the Dauphin Francis, for the first time. Francis, thirteen months Mary's junior, was a sickly and weak child who was not destined to live long. The two are reported to have gotten on well immediately, 'as if they had known one another for a long time'.[5]

Mary was educated alongside Francis and his sisters, Elizabeth and Claude, in the royal nursery. Although Mary was a queen regnant in her own right she was educated in accordance with her role as a French queen consort. She was taught the French language but not Scots, English or any of the classical languages.[6] Most fatefully, she was brought up in the Roman Catholic religion.

In 1550, peace was settled between England, Scotland and France, and Marie of Guise used the opportunity to pay a visit to France to see her daughter. She landed at Dieppe on 18 September and stayed in France for about a year before bidding Mary a fond farewell at Fontainebleau. It would prove to be the last time that they saw each other. Before she departed, Marie of Guise placed Mary in the keeping of her uncle Charles of Guise, Cardinal of Lorraine. The cardinal appointed one Madame Parois as her governess, who proved a hard taskmaster. It was under Parois' governance that Mary began to finally study classical languages.[7] When Mary turned eleven in December 1553 she was declared to be of age and provided with her own independent household. She now ruled Scotland, and with her new powers she appointed Marie of Guise as regent in place of Arran.

In 1557, Francis, Duke of Guise, another of Mary's uncles, won back Calais, which had been in the hands of the English since the time of Edward III. As a result, the Guises enjoyed great favour and influence and they pressed King Henri to conclude Mary's marriage to Francis. The pair were duly betrothed on 19 April 1558 in the great hall of the Louvre in the presence of King Henri, Queen Catherine de' Medici and members of the nobility. The service was conducted by the Cardinal of Lorraine and was afterwards celebrated with a great ball.[8] The actual wedding ceremony took place four days later on Sunday 24 April at Notre-Dame Cathedral, when Mary was fifteen. After the wedding celebrations, Mary and Francis retired to Villers-Côterèts where they spent three months together happily presiding over their court until Francis was called away to fight against Spain.

On 17 November 1558, Queen Mary I of England died and Elizabeth I ascended the throne. The pope had never recognised Henry VIII's divorce from Catherine of Aragon and Elizabeth was thus, according to Catholic law, illegitimate and the Catholics saw Mary as England's true queen. As such, King Henri declared Mary to be Queen of England and he compelled her and Francis to add the arms of England to those of France and Scotland. This move angered Elizabeth and occasioned the ill feelings that she forever bore her Scottish cousin.

Then, in July 1559, King Henri was killed while taking part in a joust and the Dauphin Francis took his father's throne. The sixteen-year-old Mary was now Queen of France.

Queen and Widow

Mary was not crowned alongside Francis at his coronation, held at Rheims Cathedral on 18 September, as she was already an anointed sovereign. As a queen consort, Mary did not wield any acknowledged power, but in reality she controlled the weak king and the Guises controlled the king through her. After the coronation, Francis's doctors recommended that the sickly king spend the winter in Blois where he and Mary passed the time hunting.

Marie of Guise died on 10 June 1560 and months later Mary suffered another tragic loss, one which would change the course of her life. In November, King Francis fell ill at Orléans with what was said to be an ear infection but was likely a brain tumour.[9] Mary stayed at his bedside and dutifully tended to him. He passed away on 5 December, leaving Mary a widow just shy of eighteen years old. Francis was succeeded by his younger brother, the ten-year-old Charles IX, while the queen dowager, Catherine de' Medici, became regent.

As French custom dictated, Mary spent forty days in mourning in a darkened room lit only by candle light. On 15 January 1561 she emerged and attended a Requiem Mass for her husband. Mary was now relegated to the role of queen dowager and found herself without a place in the new order of things. As regent, Catherine de' Medici put an end to the Guise ascendancy and treated Mary poorly, reputedly bearing a grudge as Mary had once made a joke about Catherine's descent from merchants. With her husband dead and her role of queen consort finished, Mary decided to return to Scotland.

Return to Scotland

Mary arrived at the Port of Leith, near Edinburgh, on 19 August 1561. She arrived earlier than expected and it was only the boom of cannon fire from the galleys that awoke the people to her arrival. The commons of Edinburgh flocked to the port to catch sight of their tall, beautiful, red-haired young queen. Due to her early arrival, Holyroodhouse had not yet been fitted out for her reception. She remained in Leith until evening, and then proceeded to the palace in the company of her half-brother Lord James Stuart, an illegitimate son of James V who would play a decisive role in her future. That night bonfires were lit in the streets while a band played softly and chanted psalms outside Mary's window. The nobility hastened to pay their respects to their queen and the rest of the week was spent in joyous celebration.

Soon, the subject of religion loomed large. Mary had been absent from Scotland for twelve years, and things had changed. It had experienced its own religious reformation and, on 3 August 1560, Parliament had declared it to be a Protestant country. Mary's Catholicism was a cause for concern, but when negotiating her return she had promised not to alter the country's religion. She did, however, reserve the right to have Mass said in the chapel of Holyroodhouse for her and her Catholic attendants. When Mary accordingly ordered that Mass be said at Holyrood the people took umbrage and, gathering at the palace, cried out that the priests should die. It was only the actions of Lord James, who took station at the chapel door, that allowed the service to continue unmolested. The following day Mary issued a proclamation in which she sought to allay the people's fears by reiterating that she would not change the country's religion.

As well as in matters of faith, Mary also showed herself to be conciliatory in her choice of government. She appointed twelve members to form her Privy Council, most of them Protestant. Her chief advisers were Lord James, who later became Earl of Moray, and William Maitland of Lethington. On 2 September Mary made a state entry into Edinburgh and dined at the castle. She then went on a progress around the country and was greeted everywhere with joy and acclamation, although the people did not fail to demonstrate the new religious leanings of the country in the many pageants held in her honour.

Elizabeth I

Mary's main goal was to have herself recognised as heir presumptive to the English throne. Her Catholicism stood in the way, as did the fact that, according to English common law, she could not inherit English land as she had not been born in England. Soon after her return to Scotland, Mary sent Secretary Maitland to talk with Queen Elizabeth I about cementing peace between the two nations. This peace, she suggested, could best be attained if Elizabeth recognised her as heiress presumptive to the English throne by way of an Act of Parliament. Elizabeth admitted that she preferred Mary's claim to that of all others but said she could not recognise it. If she gave Mary the succession 'she should quite cut off her own security, and in her life-time lay her own winding sheet (shroud) before her eyes, yea, make her own grave while she liveth and looketh on'.[10] There were still a large number of Catholics in England whom Elizabeth feared may plot to place Mary on the throne if she were named heir. Undeterred, Mary continued to push for recognition as Elizabeth's heir. In 1562, Mary and Elizabeth agreed to meet in person at York, but Elizabeth pulled out. Although there were further attempts at hosting a conference the two would never meet.

Darnley Marriage

Since the death of Francis II, Mary had been approached by many suitors. The subject of her marriage was one of great concern for Queen Elizabeth. If Mary were to marry a Catholic prince there was the frightening possibility that they would aid her in making good her claim to the English throne. Elizabeth thus settled on a policy of preventing a foreign marriage at all costs, and determined on a carrot-and-stick approach. Mary, still hoping to be recognised as heir, allowed Elizabeth a say in the identity of her next husband. Elizabeth suggested that Mary marry her own favourite, Robert Dudley. Mary thought the match beneath her, but in September 1564 she sent an ambassador, Sir James Melville, to England to discuss the matter. Melville did not believe that Elizabeth, who perhaps was in love with Dudley, was sincere in her offer.

Then, in February 1565, a more attractive suitor arrived in Scotland. This was the nineteen-year-old Henry Stewart, Duke of Albany, better known as Lord Darnley. Darnley was Mary's cousin and himself a grandson of Margaret Tudor. After the death of James IV, Margaret Tudor had married the Scotsman Archibald Douglas, Count of Angus, by whom she had a daughter, Lady Margaret Douglas. Lady Margaret Douglas had been brought up in England and she had married Matthew Stuart, Earl of Lennox, the half-brother of the Earl of Arran. Darnley, their eldest child, had been born and brought up in England as his father had been deprived of his estates in Scotland. This gave Darnley a claim to the English throne which some may have considered superior to Mary's. Unlike Mary, he was not considered an alien, having been born in England, although he, his mother and his siblings had also been passed over by the terms of Henry VIII's will.

In June 1563, Elizabeth had asked Mary to restore Lennox to his estates, which the Scots queen duly did. The Lennoxes secretly hoped for Darnley to marry Mary, and when Lennox arrived in Scotland in September 1564 he requested that Darnley be allowed to join him. Elizabeth, no doubt aware of the plans, agreed. Melville suggests that Elizabeth allowed Darnley to travel to Scotland in order to block the Dudley marriage, which she feared may actually come to pass.

Mary met Darnley for the first time at Wemyss Castle. She quite smitten by the handsome and courteous nineteen-year-old, gushing to Melville that 'he was the lustiest and best proportioned long man that she had seen'.[11] Mary herself was around six foot tall and the height of a prospective spouse was a cause of concern. Mary decided to marry Darnley for both political and personal reasons – she fell in love with him. Elizabeth was furious when she learned of the marriage plans and ordered Darnley to return to court. She also dispatched her ambassador, Sir Nicholas Throckmorton, to try and prevent the marriage; if this failed, he was to provoke the Protestant Scottish lords into rebelling.

Mary's half-brother Lord James Stuart, now Earl of Moray, also opposed the marriage as it would mean a weakening of his influence. He plotted with the Earl of Arran and others to seize Mary and Darnley while they travelled between Perth and Callander and send Darnley into England. The plot was disclosed, and Mary and Darnley managed to reach Callander House in safety. Mary now decided to hasten the marriage before any more opposition arose, and she and Darnley married on 29 July 1565 in the royal chapel at Holyroodhouse. At the ceremony, Mary wore a black mourning gown and large hood, which she had become accustomed to wearing since the death of King Francis. Darnley placed three rings on Mary's finger, including an exquisite diamond ring, and once the ceremony was complete she remained to hear Mass while Darnley, a Protestant, diplomatically absented himself. Now that Mary had taken a new husband, the period of mourning over her last husband was finally over and she cast off her black clothes for those more suitable for such an occasion. At noon the following day, Darnley was proclaimed king at Edinburgh. Tellingly, the only voice that was raised in his favour was that of his father, Lennox.

Soon after the wedding, Moray, Arran and some other protestant lords rebelled. They raised an army in Ayr and marched on Edinburgh, but the citizens were unwilling to support them so they retreated to Dumfries where they solicited help from England. Mary and Darnley pursued them with a force and the rebels were obliged to flee over the border to Carlisle where they sought an audience with Queen Elizabeth, who refused to help. Mary was elated. She had successfully overcome all obstacles to her marriage. All was not well, though, for Mary would soon discover that her husband was not all he was cracked up to be.

In the weeks after the marriage, Darnley began to show his true colours. He was vain, ambitious and a drunkard. He aspired to the 'crown matrimonial', which would make him the queen's equal and secure him the throne if she died. Mary, however, would not grant him the title 'until she know how well he is worthy to enjoy such a sovereignty'.[12] Their differences did not prevent them from performing their matrimonial duties, however, and Mary was soon pregnant.

Rizzio's Murder

David Rizzio was an Italian musician and a favourite of Queen Mary. He had been born in Piedmont, Italy, in 1534, the son of a poor nobleman who made his living by teaching music. Rizzio had been sent to the court of the Duke of Savoy in Nice at a young age, and in 1564 he had travelled to Scotland in the entourage of a Savoyard ambassador. A talented singer and musician, Rizzio soon caught Mary's attention as she needed a bass voice for her choir. She made him her valet de chambre and soon after he was her French Secretary. Rizzio held a great influence over the queen, and those who wished to secure her favour were forced to apply through him. Rizzio had befriended Darnley on his arrival in Scotland and had supported the marriage, but Darnley later became jealous of Rizzio's intimacy with the queen. Mary spent more time in Rizzio's company than with her husband, playing cards with him until early in the morning. There were rumours that Rizzio was in fact the father of Mary's child and had supported the queen in her decision not to grant Darnley the crown matrimonial.

Rizzio's influence over Mary made him many enemies among the Scottish nobility. Chief among them were Patrick, Lord Ruthven and James Douglas, Earl of Morton, along with Moray and the other exiled lords, who secretly plotted his destruction. The conspirators approached Darnley and promised him the crown matrimonial if he would assist them in disposing of Rizzio. Once Darnley had been granted it, he was to allow Moray and the other exiled lords to return to Scotland and reinstate them in their lands and titles. The ambitious Darnley was more than happy to be rid of his hated enemy and a date of Saturday 9 March 1566 was fixed upon for carrying out the deed. That evening, Mary, then six months pregnant, was having supper in her cabinet, a small room that enjoined her apartments in Holyroodhouse. She was accompanied by the Countess of Argyll, Lord Robert Stuart, Arthur Erskine, the ill-fated Rizzio and a few other attendants.

The Earl of Morton, Lord Lindsay and others, dressed 'in warlike manner', entered the palace grounds and took station at the gates to prevent anyone from escaping or offering assistance.[13] Ruthven, meanwhile, was concealed within Darnley's chamber, located directly below Mary's and connected via a private staircase. A little later, Darnley entered the room by this staircase, leaving the door ajar, and smugly took station beside the unsuspecting queen.

Moments later, Ruthven entered and, pointing at Rizzio, announced that he must speak with him. The frightened Rizzio instinctively took cover behind Mary and clutched at her skirts. Mary spun around on her husband and asked incredulously if he had a part in this, which he vehemently denied. She demanded that Ruthven leave under pain of treason and offered to have Rizzio tried in Parliament if he had given any offence, but Ruthven was intent on seizing his prey. Mary's servants attempted to apprehend him but Ruthven unsheathed his sword and warned them off. More assailants then entered the room and in the ensuing scuffle the table was overturned. Rizzio was apprehended, dragged to the top of the staircase and stabbed fifty-six times. His body was afterwards robbed of its jewels and then launched down the stairs.

Afterwards, the terrified and pregnant Mary was held prisoner in her chamber while Darnley wielded the royal power. The day after, Moray and the other exiled lords returned to Edinburgh. On the Monday the lords requested that Mary ratify an agreement that no harm was to come to them for their role in the conspiracy. Mary promised to sign them in the morning and they departed into the town. Once they had left, Mary convinced the weak and vacillating Darnley that it was in their best interest to flee to Dunbar. At one o'clock the following morning, he and Mary escaped via a back door. They were met by Arthur Erskine, who had horses at the ready, and rode to the safety of Dunbar.

The Assassination of Darnley

At Dunbar, Mary summoned her loyal earls, lords and barons to come to her aid and many answered the call. In order to divide and conquer her opponents, she opted to forgive and restore the exiled lords who had not been present at the murder, including Moray. Those who were present, including Ruthven and Morton, fled to England and swore revenge on Darnley for having double-crossed them. Ruthven, however, would never get to enact his vengeance. He was sickly and his illness finally got the better of him at Newcastle on 13 June.

On 18 March, Mary and Darnley entered Edinburgh at the head of an army. In a meeting of the Privy Council, Darnley professed his innocence in the murder and declared that he had only consented to the return of the exiled lords. Mary naively believed Darnley, but the conspirators sent her two bonds, signed by Darnley, which proved him to have been fully complicit in the murder.

On Wednesday 19 June, Mary gave birth to the future James VI of Scotland and I of England at Edinburgh Castle. Later that day, Darnley came to see his newborn son for the first time. Mary used it as an opportunity to prove that the child was his and not Rizzio's. 'God has given you and me a son, begotten by none but you!' she exclaimed. However, she couldn't resist throwing in a barb: 'And I am desirous that all here, both ladies and others, bear witness; for he is so much your own son, that I fear it will be the worse for him hereafter!'[14]

The people of Scotland rejoiced at the birth of an heir apparent and 500 bonfires were lit in the streets of Edinburgh. The glad tidings were transmitted to England by Melville, and Queen Elizabeth, who was dancing after supper at Greenwich Palace when she was told the news, suddenly turned sour and complained that 'the Queen of Scotland was lighter of a fair son, and that she was but a barren stock'.[15] When Melville spoke to her the next day, the queen had composed herself sufficiently to hide her disappointment and agree to be godmother to the child.

The birth of baby James did not mend his parents' fractured relationship. Darnley sulked over having not been granted the crown matrimonial and the nobility failing to pay him the respect that was his due. Mary, for her part, tried to make the best of a bad situation. She treated her husband with dignity and did not blame him for the murder of Rizzio, although she secretly feared that he may be conniving with the nobility to lay another plot against her. One day, Darnley threatened to depart for France and even had a ship at the ready. Summoning him before the Privy Council to explain his reasons, Mary tenderly took his hand and asked him if she had done anything to offend him while the nobles promised that if they had likewise done anything they were ready to make amends. Darnley denied that he had any plans of leaving and admitted that the queen had given him no cause for offence. In October the queen went to Jedburgh to hold some courts of assize while Darnley prowled around his father's castle at Glasgow.

During Mary's time at Jedburgh, she paid a visit to James Hepburn, 4th Earl of Bothwell, at Hermitage Castle. The earl had been badly injured when dealing with border rebels in his capacity as Lieutenant of the Borders, and Mary, on being apprised of his wounds, had travelled some 50 miles there and back to see him. She was accompanied by Moray and spent a few hours in Bothwell's presence before returning to Jedburgh.

In November she travelled on to Edinburgh in order to attend the baptism of baby James. Along the way, she stopped off at Craigmillar Castle, not far from Edinburgh. There, the earls of Moray, Huntly, Argyll, the now recovered Earl of Bothwell and Secretary Maitland discussed in secret the best way of securing the return of Rizzio's murderers. Their best bet, they reasoned, was to offer to secure the divorce of the queen and the detested Darnley in return for the murderers' pardon. They approached Mary and found her willing, although she stipulated that the divorce must be carried out legally and not in any way impair her son's claim to the throne. They promised that the divorce would be approved by Parliament, but in reality they were planning on murdering Darnley and entered into a bond to do so. One of the chief instigators was Bothwell, who aspired to become Mary's husband and one day rule the country as king.

On 17 December, Mary attended the baptism of baby James in the chapel of Stirling Castle. Darnley was present but he did not attend the ceremony. In the New Year he removed to his father's castle at Glasgow where he fell ill with what was said to be smallpox but was more likely to have been syphilis.[16] Mary sent her physician to attend him and at the end of the month she travelled to see him herself. Mary convinced Darnley to return with her to Craigmillar but he opted instead to take up residence at the Kirk o'Field, a small house located on the outskirts of Edinburgh. Mary attended her husband often at the house and she slept some nights in the rooms below. Some form of reconciliation took place between them. Finally, on the night of 9 February, Mary left his company to attend a masque at Holyroodhouse. As she mounted her horse in the yard, she noted that the face of Paris, a former valet of the Earl of Bothwell, was tarred by gunpowder. 'Jesu, Paris, how begrimed you are!' she exclaimed, prompting the boy to turn scarlet.[17] The significance of his appearance did not cross Mary's mind and she departed in ignorance.

At about two o'clock the following morning, 10 February 1567, the house of Kirk o'Field was suddenly blown to pieces in a huge ball of fire. The explosion was so great that nothing remained of the house. '[N]ot a stone above another, but all carried far away or dashed in dross to the very ground-stone', Mary later remarked.[18] Darnley's lifeless corpse was discovered under a tree in the yard, where it had been flung by the force of the explosion. Near him was the body of his page, William Taylor, who had been sleeping in the same room. According to some reports, Darnley had been strangled beforehand and the explosion was planned to hide the crime. Darnley's assailants had secreted gunpowder in the cellar of the house, had lit it and then escaped through a door in the yard which skirted the town walls.

Bothwell

Popular suspicion for the crime fell squarely on the Earl of Bothwell. Placards intimating his guilt appeared on the Tollbooth at Edinburgh. The Earl of Lennox, Darnley's father, demanded that he be tried for the crime and Bothwell was put on trial on 12 April. Fortunately for Bothwell, he was tried by his fellow conspirators and found not guilty.

Shortly after the sham trial, Bothwell held a meeting with some of the nobles at Ainslie's Tavern in Edinburgh where he announced his intention of marrying the queen. The nobles, won over by the promise of reward, agreed and signed a bond, known as the 'Ainslie Bond' after the tavern, to confirm it. Mary, meanwhile, paid a visit to see baby James at Stirling; it was the last time that she ever saw him. As she rode back to Edinburgh on 24 April she was suddenly ambushed by Bothwell and a force of 700–800 armed men. Bothwell forcibly took hold of the reins of Mary's horse and led her away to Dunbar Castle. She was held prisoner for twelve days, during which he solicited her hand in marriage. Bothwell professed to love her and said that he had many enemies who wished him harm and that the only way that he could guarantee his safety was by becoming her husband. He promised that he would not seek to be king and would serve her for the rest of their days. He then produced the Ainslie Bond, at which point Mary agreed to marry him.

Bothwell was already married to the sister of the Earl of Huntly so his first move was to secure a divorce, which was granted on 3 May. On 15 May, he and Mary were married at the Chapel Royal at Holyroodhouse. Unlike her previous marriages, it was conducted according to the rites of Bothwell's Protestant faith – a strange concession from a devoutly Catholic queen. The wedding was thinly attended and was not celebrated with the usual pomp and ceremony of a royal wedding. According to the French ambassador, du Croc, Mary was in a dejected mood in the days following the wedding. When he asked her what was wrong, she replied, 'If you see me melancholy, it is because I do not choose to be cheerful, because I never will be so, and wish for nothing but death.'[19]

It was not long before Bothwell's arrogance began to make him enemies and a group known as the Confederate Lords plotted to overthrow him. They claimed that Mary and Bothwell had been in love before Darnley's murder and that she had been complicit in the assassination of Darnley in order that she might marry him. Her visit to the injured Bothwell at Hermitage Castle was cited as proof of their love, while her subsequent kidnapping by Bothwell and coercion into marriage was said to have been fabricated in order to wash Mary's hands of any involvement in Darnley's death. The question of Mary's involvement in the plot to kill Darnley is the great question of her life and reign and one that is still highly debated. As we shall see, her enemies would later produce a collection of letters, love sonnets and marriage contracts known as the 'Casket Letters' that were purported to have been written between Mary and Bothwell before and after Darnley's death, proving her guilt. The authenticity of the Casket Letters is dubious but Mary's guilt would go some way to explaining her confusing behaviour in the wake of Darnley's death. Historian John Guy suggests that Mary was not involved in the plot to kill Darnley and was not yet romantically involved with Bothwell but during her captivity she was somehow won over by him.[20]

Mary summoned the southern nobles to assemble at Melrose in order to lead an expedition in the borders. It was rumoured that the expedition was a ruse for Mary and Bothwell to lead an army to Stirling and take possession of baby James. The summons was not met with the enthusiasm expected and Mary and Bothwell left Edinburgh and took residence at Borthwick Castle. On 10 June they found themselves suddenly surrounded by the Confederate Lords. Bothwell, realising that the castle would not withstand a siege, abandoned the queen and escaped via a secret postern gate and took refuge at Haddington. The following night, Mary, dressed in men's clothes and riding on horseback, fled the castle. She was reunited with Bothwell and the two rode for Dunbar where they summoned their supporters. The Confederate Lords, meanwhile, entered Edinburgh and raised their own forces. The two sides met on 15 June at the Battle of Carberry Hill, near Inveresk.

The Confederates had with them a flag which depicted Darnley's body under the tree where it was discovered, with Prince James kneeling at his side and the words 'Judge and revenge my cause, O Lord'. No battle took place. Ambassador du Croc travelled between both armies in an attempt to secure peace but none could be agreed. Bothwell then sent an offer of single combat against any of the nobles who claimed that he had killed Darnley. The offer was accepted but the challengers who stepped forward were all of a lower rank than the earl and he would not fight them. As night descended, and with the desertion of many of her men, Mary eventually agreed to hand herself over to the lords if Bothwell was allowed to escape. This was agreed, Mary and Bothwell said their goodbyes, and he retreated to Dunbar.

Mary was conveyed to the Confederate Lords' camp where she was treated as a prisoner. She was taken to Edinburgh and as she was led through the streets the pressing mass of people heckled and jeered at her. She was lodged in the house of the provost, the Confederate flag mockingly displayed outside her window. That night she purportedly wrote a letter to Bothwell in which she professed her love for him, stated that she only sent him away for his safety and that she would never abandon him. This letter was betrayed to the Confederates and they had Mary conducted to the islet fortress of Lochleven under the care of Sir Robert Douglas, there to be imprisoned indefinitely.

Mary would never see Bothwell again. He fled to the Shetland Islands, where he was pursued by the Confederate Lords, and succeeded in escaping from there to Norway. There, he was arrested and held as a prisoner by Frederick II, King of Denmark and Norway for ten years, dying in 1578.

The Loss of a Throne

With power now firmly in the hands of the Confederate Lords, they decided to force Mary to abdicate the throne in favour of her son. James was heir apparent and his young age – he was only thirteen months old – promised another long minority in which they could hold power. His youth also meant that they could bring him up in the Protestant religion and therefore protect the fledgling Scottish Reformation. On 24 July, Mary was compelled to sign three documents in which she abdicated the throne in favour of James, made Moray regent, and arranged a regency council to act until Moray, then in France, returned to Scotland. This done, James was crowned as King James VI on 29 July at Stirling Castle. When Moray returned in August, he was duly installed as regent.

Mary spent almost a year at Lochleven. On 25 March 1568 a plot was hatched to free her when George Douglas, the elder son of Mary's captors, fell in love with Mary and decided to help her escape. A laundress was conveyed across the loch to the castle, bringing with her some fresh clothes for Mary. When she was admitted into Mary's presence the two women changed clothes and the ex-queen, her face concealed behind a veil, departed from the castle and climbed aboard the boat to convey her back across the lake. The oarsmen set off but when the mysterious passenger refused to reveal her face one of them attempted to remove her veil. Mary held her hand up to stop them and the sight of her smooth white hands revealed her to be the queen. Mary demanded that the oarsmen take her ashore but they opted to take her back to the castle.

George Douglas was sent away by his parents but remained in the vicinity of the castle. He continued to plot to free the queen and in conjunction with his brother, William Douglas, planned to get her out on Sunday 2 May. Every night the castle gate was locked when Lord Douglas and his household went to supper, Lord Douglas always placing the keys beside him on the table. On the night of 2 May, William Douglas bore a plate of food to his father and managed to place a napkin over the keys and steal them away. He fetched Mary and they exited the castle, locking the gate behind them. They climbed into a boat and rowed for the shore. The queen let off a signal by displaying a white veil with a red tassel and her adherents appeared. She was placed upon a horse and then rode for Niddry Castle. After resting for a few hours she continued to Hamilton Castle, where she was acknowledged as queen by John Hamilton, Archbishop of St Andrews and others. Mary once again summoned those loyal to her and her strength was swelled to 6,000 followers. She was going to reclaim her throne.

News of Mary's escape soon reached Moray and he raised an army of 4,000 men. Mary left Hamilton for Dumbarton and as her army moved down the coast near Glasgow it was intercepted by Moray. The Battle of Langside, fought on 13 May 1568, was a devastating defeat for the queen. The battle lasted just three quarters of an hour and only 150 of her men were killed. Mary, fearing capture, rode with a few nobles and attendants for England, where she hoped to secure Elizabeth's aid in reclaiming her throne. During the 125-mile journey Mary's attendants attempted to dissuade her from trusting the unscrupulous Elizabeth and urged her instead to go to France, but Mary was adamant. It was the biggest mistake she would make in her life. And she'd made some.

The Westminster Conference

Before entering England, Mary stopped off at Dundrennan Abbey close to the English border, from where she sent a message to the governor of Carlisle Castle requesting asylum. The governor, Lord Scrope, was then absent from the castle but his deputy, Sir Richard Lowther, agreed to send word to Queen Elizabeth to ascertain her wishes. Mary could not afford to wait for permission and on 16 May she crossed the Solway Firth in a fishing boat and arrived at Workington in Cumberland (now Cumbria). From there she was taken to Cockermouth where she was met by Lowther and escorted to Carlisle. She was treated as a guest at first, being allowed to hunt and to watch her servants play football, but soon she was kept like a prisoner.

Mary, hoping that Elizabeth would help her reclaim her kingdom or allow her to pass to the continent where she could seek the aid of the French or Spanish king, requested an audience with the queen, but Elizabeth refused to see her until she was satisfied that Mary was in no way responsible for the murder of Darnley. For Elizabeth, Mary's presence in England was fraught with danger as the Catholics in England might attempt a rising in Mary's name and depose her. If she allowed her to pass to France or Spain and Mary succeeded in taking the Scottish throne with French or Spanish assistance, she might restore Catholicism in Scotland.

Elizabeth suggested that she arbitrate a conference between Mary and her rebellious subjects to settle the matter. At first, Mary refused. She was Queen of Scotland and she did not recognise the authority of an English court. Elizabeth replied that it would not be Mary who was put on trial but her enemies. In mid-July, Mary was removed from Carlisle to Bolton Castle in order to further distance her from her friends in Scotland and she was left with little choice but to agree to the conference, which began at York on 8 October. Moray was summoned to appear and he duly attended, along with Morton, Adam Bothwell, Bishop of Orkney, Robert, Abbot of Dunfermline and Lord Lindsay. Moray produced his trump card – the Casket

Letters. These incriminating letters were said to have been seized from one of Bothwell's servants, George Dalgleish, when he had attempted to smuggle them out of Edinburgh Castle shortly after the Battle of Carberry Hill.

With this new development, the conference was moved to Westminster where Elizabeth could keep a closer eye on proceedings. It reopened on 25 November and Moray produced the letters for examination. Mary, of course, denied their validity but her appeals to inspect them were tellingly denied, as was her request to speak in person before the queen or the commissioners. Elizabeth offered a compromise: Mary could grant her crown to her son and then remain in England for the rest of her life. Mary would not consider such a move, which would not only lose her the crown but also paint her as guilty of Darnley's murder. Elizabeth dissolved the conference on 10 January and announced that no evidence had been supplied to condemn Moray and his party, while also admitting that insufficient evidence had been produced to cause her to 'conceive or take any evil opinion' of Mary.[21] Moray was allowed to return to Scotland while Mary remained under house arrest in England.

A Captive Queen

Mary remained under house arrest for the rest of her life. She was passed from castle to castle, spending most of her captivity in Sheffield. She was allowed to retain a household, which she funded with her French dowry, while her keeper, George Talbot, Earl of Shrewsbury, met the costs of the household's food bill, supplemented by a small allowance given by Elizabeth. She was allowed to have visitors, although under strict supervision, but she was in constant communication with her friends and allies via secret messengers. As the years went on her health declined and she developed a crippling rheumatism, for which she was taken once a year to the healing baths at Buxton. In 1584 she was removed from Shrewsbury's care and placed under that of the elderly Sir Ralph Sadler before being transferred into the harsher keeping of Sir Amyas Paulet.

Throughout this time, Mary tried in vain to negotiate her release with Elizabeth. From 1581 there were intermittent discussions about associating her as a joint sovereign of Scotland with her son, but these hopes were dashed by the Treaty of Berwick, agreed between England and Scotland in July 1586. King James sent Mary a letter in which he refused to associate her in the government and hurtfully divulged that he recognised her only as queen mother, not as queen. She had been abandoned by her own son.

Throughout her captivity, Mary would become the subject and fellow conspirator of numerous Catholic plots and intrigues against Elizabeth. By 1586, she despaired of ever attaining her freedom and realised that her only chance was by means of a Catholic rising. The plot that cost Mary her life is known as the Babington Plot after one of its ringleaders, Anthony Babington.

Mary, Queen of Scots

The conspirators sought to murder Elizabeth and restore Mary to the throne with the help of a Spanish invasion force.

Sir Francis Walsingham, Queen Elizabeth's unscrupulous secretary and spymaster, discovered the existence of the plot via his network of informants but decided to let it play out in the hope that Mary would incriminate herself. On 6 July, Babington wrote a letter to Mary that used cipher to describe the plot. It was conveyed into Chartley Castle in Staffordshire, where she then resided, via a small wooden box concealed in a barrel of beer. The letter was intercepted by Walsingham's agents, copied and deciphered before being allowed to continue to its destination. Mary's letter in response, in which she endorsed the killing of Elizabeth, was likewise intercepted. Soon after, Walsingham had Babington and the others conspirators arrested.

Mary was blissfully unaware of the fate of the conspirators. She was removed from Chartley under the pretence of going on a hunt. On the road she was approached by a company of horsemen. Her two secretaries, who had been responsible for writing her response to Babington, were arrested and she was confined at the nearby house of Tixall. There she remained for two weeks while her secretaries were interrogated, her rooms at Chartley ransacked and her personal papers and ciphers seized for any incriminating evidence. In late September, she was transferred to Fotheringhay Castle in Northamptonshire where she was put on trial for treason before a specially appointed commission and found guilty. Parliament called for Mary's immediate execution but Elizabeth was reluctant to sign the death warrant. In December King James sent an embassy to England, headed by the Master of Gray, in the hopes of saving his mother's life, but Gray secretly told Elizabeth to go ahead with the execution. On 1 February 1587, Elizabeth finally succumbed to her ministers' wishes. On the 7th, the earls of Kent and Shrewsbury delivered the warrant to Mary at Fotheringhay and told her that she was to be executed at eight o'clock the following morning. Mary spent the last night of her life writing her will, penning letters to her Guise relations and dishing out her possessions to her servants. She attempted to get some uneasy sleep and when morning came the earls of Kent and Shrewsbury and the sheriff of Northamptonshire knocked on her door and found her at prayer. When she had finished, she was conducted to the Great Hall where her sentence was to be enacted.

A scaffold, 2 feet high and 12 feet in length, had been erected in the hall and covered in a black cloth. Upon it was a stool, a cushion and a block that was also draped in black. The forty-four-year-old Mary entered the hall dressed in a fine gown of black velvet, with a crucifix and Bible in her hand and her train borne by a servant. She ascended the scaffold and was seated upon the stool. The commission for the execution was read aloud, during which Mary sat 'with as cheerful a countenance as if it had been a pardon from her Majesty for her life'.[22] She was then approached by Doctor Richard Fletcher, Dean of Peterborough, who tried in vain to convert her to the Protestant faith. 'Mr Dean, I am settled in the ancient Catholic Roman religion, and mind to spend my blood in defence of it,' she calmly replied.[23]

Then the dean, kneeling on the stairs of the scaffold, began to pray. Mary aklso began fervently to pray in Latin, sliding off the stool to her knees. Once the dean ceased his prayers Mary began to pray in English for her son and even for Queen Elizabeth, wishing her a prosperous future. She kissed the crucifix and, making the sign of the cross, prayed Jesus to forgive her sins. Once she had finished, the executioners asked for her forgiveness and she granted it. Her ladies helped her to her feet and removed all her clothes except her kirtle and petticoat. A cloth was placed around her eyes and then she knelt on the cushion, where she recited a psalm. She afterwards felt for the block and placed her head over it. Stretching out her arms, she cried, '*In manus tuas, Domine.*'[24] One of the executioners stayed her with his hand while the other swung the axe twice, severing her head from her body by all but a small piece of gristle. This being cut, the executioner held her head aloft and cried, 'God save the Queen.'[25] As the executioner held her head the wig and cap that covered her head fell to the floor, revealing the remains of her short, grey hair, aged prematurely by the stresses of her long captivity.

Mary had wished her body to be taken to France, but even this small concession was ignored and she was instead buried in Peterborough Cathedral. When King James VI became King James I of England he had his mother exhumed and reinterred with honour at Westminster Abbey. So ended the tragic life of Mary, Queen of Scots.

21

Henry Frederick, Prince of Wales

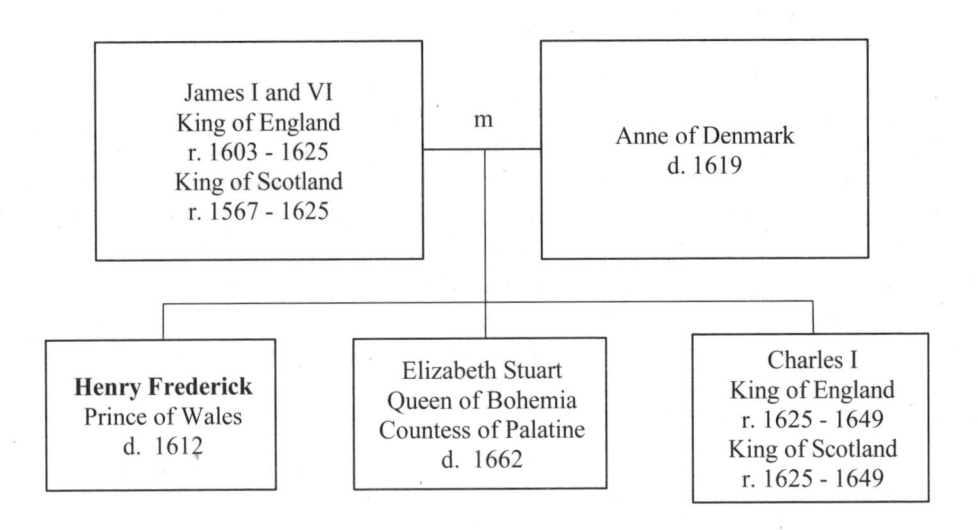

```
┌─────────────────────┐         ┌─────────────────────┐
│   James I and VI    │         │                     │
│   King of England   │    m    │   Anne of Denmark   │
│    r. 1603 - 1625   │─────────│       d. 1619       │
│   King of Scotland  │         │                     │
│    r. 1567 - 1625   │         │                     │
└─────────────────────┘         └─────────────────────┘

┌──────────────────┐   ┌──────────────────────┐   ┌─────────────────────┐
│ Henry Frederick  │   │   Elizabeth Stuart   │   │      Charles I      │
│ Prince of Wales  │   │   Queen of Bohemia   │   │   King of England   │
│     d. 1612      │   │ Countess of Palatine │   │    r. 1625 - 1649   │
│                  │   │       d. 1662        │   │   King of Scotland  │
│                  │   │                      │   │    r. 1625 - 1649   │
└──────────────────┘   └──────────────────────┘   └─────────────────────┘
```

At the Christmas festivities of 1609, fifteen-year-old Henry Frederick, Prince of Wales, eldest son of King James I of England and VI of Scotland and his queen, Anne of Denmark, challenged the knights of Great Britain to take part in a tournament known as the 'Barriers'. Henry issued the challenge in the presence chamber at Whitehall Palace before the king, queen and the whole court, dressed in the guise of Meliades, Lord of the Isles, an ancient title due to the firstborn son of Scotland, to the accompaniment of drums and trumpet. The youthful prince, we are told, wished to prove his valour in battle so that 'the world might know what a brave prince they were likely to enjoy'.[1] Sadly, Great Britain was to never see what a brave prince Henry was. A few years later he died of typhoid fever, aged just eighteen, to the great regret of the people.

Birth and Early Life

Henry Frederick, Prince of Wales, was the eldest son of King James I of England and VI of Scotland and his queen, Anne of Denmark. He was born at around three in the morning on Tuesday 19 February 1594 at Stirling Castle in Scotland.[2]

King James was delighted at the birth of a son who not only secured his dynastic position in Scotland but also made him a more attractive prospect in England. James had been hereditary heir apparent to England since his mother, Mary, Queen of Scots, had been executed in 1587 but the ageing Queen Elizabeth I refused to recognise him as her heir. James, however, was a much more palatable prospect than his mother. He was male and, more importantly, a Protestant.

Henry Frederick was not baptised for more than six months after his birth in order that ambassadors from England, France, Denmark and the Low Countries could attend. The baptism was a sumptuous affair, which necessitated the rebuilding of the Chapel Royal at Stirling to accommodate everybody. The ceremony had originally been planned for 28 August but it was delayed due to the late arrival of the English ambassador, Robert Radcliffe, Earl of Sussex. Two days later, Henry was baptised and named in honour of his grandfathers Henry Stuart, Lord Darnley and Frederick II, King of Denmark.

After the ceremony had been performed, King James retired to the great hall of the castle where Ludovick Stuart, 2nd Duke of Lennox presented the infant to the proud father, who then dubbed him a knight. Henry was then touched with a spur by John Erskine, 2nd Earl of Mar, after which the king held the ducal crown over his head. David Lindsay, Lord Lyon King of Arms then proclaimed him 'the right excellent, high, and magnanimous Henry Frederick, by the Grace of God, Knight and Baron of Renfrew, Lord of the Isles, Earl of Carrick, Duke of Rothesay, Prince and Great Steward of Scotland'.[3] These constituted the titles of the Scottish heir to the throne.

Once the christening was over, Henry was placed under the guardianship of John Erskine, Earl of Mar and he spent the first nine years of his life behind the walls of Stirling Castle. King James had himself been brought up at Stirling by Mar's father and mother, Countess Annabella, and he had been educated alongside the current earl. This outraged the maternal instincts of Queen Anne, who wished to raise Henry herself. She pleaded with James to be granted custody of their son but James feared that Henry might fall into the hands of some of the turbulent Scottish nobles and be used as a weapon against him, as he had been against his own mother. This drove Queen Anne to plot with Mar's enemies, and in 1595 a plan was hatched to abduct Henry from Stirling Castle. James, who was engaged in his favourite pastime of hunting at Falkland Palace at the time, was forewarned of the plot and he quickly rode to the queen at Holyrood House and nipped it in the bud. Anne had to be content with paying a visit to her son, James remaining adamant that the boy was to remain under Mar's care. Although relations between Anne and James were strained, she continued in her primary public function and produced several more children, two of whom would survive infancy. On 15 August 1596 she gave birth to a daughter, Elizabeth Stuart, later Queen of Bohemia, and another son, the sickly Charles Stuart, future King Charles I, was born on 19 November 1600.

When Henry reached the age of five, James appointed Adam Newton, later Dean of Durham, as his tutor. Soon after, he was moved from the keeping of women to that of men. Mar remained his governor while Sir David Murray, knight, was appointed First Gentleman of the Bedchamber. Henry followed the educational programme as set out by King James in the *Basilicon Doron*, a treatise the king had written for his son in 1599. Henry should, the king noted, 'study to know well your own craft, which is to rule your people'.[4] He recommended a practical programme that would provide Henry with only the tools he needed to perform his office and advised against accruing knowledge for knowledge's sake. He should gain a basic understanding of all the 'crafts' of the people so as to be able to control them.[5] He should 'delight in reading, and seeking the knowledge of all lawful things' but he should only do so in his spare time and only as much as will help him dispense his office.[6] He should study the scriptures and the laws of the land and be well versed in the authentic histories and chronicles of his own country, as well as those of foreign nations, which would serve him in his discourses with ambassadors and strangers.[7] He should have a general knowledge of the liberal arts and sciences but not enough to be a 'passe-master' in any of them,[8] 'for that cannot but distract you from the points of your calling'.[9] By the age of seven, Henry 'began to delight in more active and manly exercises, learning to ride, sing, dance, leap, shoot at archery, and in pieces [guns], to toss his pike, &c'.[10]

Heir to the English Throne

The uncertainty over the English succession and the plight of his mother caused King James to espouse the theory of the Divine Right of Kings. According to this theory, the king was God's representative on Earth and was accountable to God alone. The crown thus devolved by indefeasible hereditary right, that is, by primogeniture. It was God's choice who was to sit upon the throne and the rightful heir could not be denied his birthright in any circumstances. James outlined this in his treatise *The Trew Law of Free Monarchies* in which he declares, 'At the very moment of the expiring of the king reigning, the nearest and lawful heir entreth in his place: And so to refuse him, or intrude another, is ... to expel and put out their righteous king.'[11]

In December 1602, the sixty-nine-year-old Queen Elizabeth I suddenly fell ill. At the end of January 1603 she was moved from Westminster to Richmond Palace, where she grew steadily worse. Then, as she lay on her deathbed on 23 March, she finally named her successor. She had lost the ability to speak when the chief counsellors filed into her chamber and asked her if she wished for James to succeed her. She put her hand to her head, as if signifying a crown, which they understood as her giving her assent.

She slipped away early in the morning of 24 March after a remarkable reign of forty-four years and four months. Between nine and ten o'clock that morning, Sir Robert Carey took to horse and rode hastily for Edinburgh to be the first to inform James of his accession. He reached Holyrood Palace on the night of 26 March, bloodied and bruised after falling from his horse, where he delivered the joyful news to the king. Soon after, a letter arrived from the Privy Council of England advising James of his succession and he began preparations to ride into England. After the confusion wrought by Henry VIII's succession statutes and will, James's accession restored the throne to the rightful hereditary line and it once again devolved by primogeniture.

James departed from Edinburgh on 5 April and began the journey south to take possession of his new kingdom. Queen Anne and their three children did not accompany the king but remained behind in Scotland. Anne was to join her husband in twenty days' time while Henry was to remain in the safety of Stirling. Before he left, James wrote a letter to Henry in which he warned him not to let the news of his father's accession go to his head, 'for a king's son and heir was ye before, and no more are ye yet'.[12]

With the king absent from Scotland, Queen Anne spotted an opportunity of finally gaining custody of Henry. The boy's governor, the Earl of Mar, had accompanied the king to England and had left Henry in the charge of Mar's mother, the aged Countess Annabella. One day a pregnant Queen Anne suddenly appeared before Stirling Castle and demanded custody of her son. The countess refused, causing the queen such anguish that she developed a fever and suffered a miscarriage.

When word reached James, he sent Mar back to Scotland but soon after dispatched the Earl of Lennox with a warrant to place the prince under his mother's care. This being done, Anne, Henry and his sister Elizabeth departed for England on 2 June, while the sickly Charles remained behind. They stopped off at various towns, cities and manors en route to London where they were richly entertained with banquets, masques and pageants. They met the king on 27 June at Easton Neston, Northamptonshire and proceeded to Windsor Castle where they celebrated the Feast of St George on 2 July. This was the nine-year-old Henry's first public appearance in England and he was invested with the Order of the Garter. Once the ceremony had been performed, he was presented to the queen dressed in his robes. Henry's deportment garnered the praise of those present, including Charles Howard, Earl of Nottingham and Henry Howard, Earl of Northampton, who admired 'his quick witty answers, princely carriage, and reverend performing his obeisance at the altar; all which seemed very strange unto them ... considering his tender age'.[13]

The king's state entry into London had to be postponed due to an outbreak of plague. Henry and his little sister Elizabeth were removed to the safety of Oatlands Palace in Surrey and were not present at their parents' joint coronation at Westminster Abbey on 25 July. Henry and Elizabeth were provided with their own household, overseen by Sir Thomas Chaloner, which initially consisted of seventy servants but which had increased to 141 by the end of the year.

By March 1604 the plague had subsided and the prince attended his father and mother for the postponed state entry into London. At the Tower, Henry was presented with a minature ship with a keel measuring 25 feet in length and 12 foot in breadth. It had been built by Phineas Pett, the master shipwright at Woolwich Dockyard, who had been commissioned to construct the ship by the Lord Admiral for the prince 'to disport himself in above London Bridge, and to acquaint his Grace with shipping and the manner of that element'.[14] The next day James, Anne and Henry departed from the Tower and went in procession through London to Westminster. At the Cross at Cheapside the king, queen and prince were each presented with a cup of gold in the name of the mayor and the city.

On 22 March, Henry was taken aboard his new ship in the company of the Lord High Admiral and the Earl of Worcester. He sailed down to Paul's Wharf where he christened the ship the *Disdain* with a large bowl of wine. Henry was so impressed with the ship that he made Pett one of his servants. Thus began a love affair with the navy which lasted for the rest of Henry's short life.

Henry, as heir apparent, accompanied the king and queen on several royal visits and ceremonies. He joined them on a visit to Oxford University in August 1605 where he was matriculated at Magdalen College. He also took part in the celebrations held in honour of the state visit of his uncle Christian IV, King of Denmark, in July 1606. Henry met his uncle at Tilbury Hope and no doubt delighted in Christian's huge warship, the *Admiral*, which weighed some 1,500 tons. Its beakhead, stern and galleries were gilded with gold and it had a large armament of cannon.

Henry was present at the hunts, masques and processions that were held in the Danish king's honour and participated in a joust on 5 August where he reportedly 'showed himself in his armour, being gallantly mounted, and a heart as powerful as any, though that his youth denied strength'.[15] Before returning home, King Christian gave Henry with his best warship, *the Vice-Admiral*, worth £2,500, as well as a rapier and hanger (a short hunting sword) worth 2,000 marks.

The Gunpowder Plot

Henry's participation in royal ceremonies saw him placed in great danger in November 1605 with the discovery of the Gunpowder Plot. Robert Catesby and eleven other Catholic gentlemen plotted to blow up Westminster Palace when Parliament opened on 5 November in order to murder King James, Queen Anne, Prince Henry and all others present and set up the young Princess Elizabeth as a puppet queen. In order to carry out their design, the conspirators had rented a cellar that ran under the Parliament Chamber that they filled with barrels of gunpowder, leaving the infamous Guy Fawkes to light the fuse. As the time drew near, one of the conspirators, Francis Tresham, sent a letter of warning to his brother-in-law William Parker, Lord Monteagle, advising him to keep away from the palace on the day of the opening of Parliament. Monteagle turned the letter over to the Privy Council and on the night of 4 November the cellar was discovered, primed and ready. Fawkes was arrested and tortured at the Tower and eventually hung, drawn and quartered; Catesby was killed resisting arrest and the others conspirators were placed on trial and executed. (There are of course several conspiracy theories about the conspiracy; this brief resumé may not be the whole truth.)

Character

As Henry grew towards manhood he cut a very different figure to his father. He was tall and broad shouldered, with a big nose, cloven chin and dark hair while James was of middling height, overweight, with a thin beard, large roving eyes and a tongue too big for his mouth. While King James was bookish and intelligent, Henry showed a greater inclination towards physical activity. The *Basilicon Doron* had highlighted the importance of exercise for the 'banishing of idleness ... [and] for making ... [the] body able and durable for travel, which is very necessary for a king'.[16] James recommended running, leaping, wrestling, fencing, dancing, tennis and archery, but he particularly emphasised activities on horseback, 'for it becommeth a prince best of any man, to be a fair and good horseman'.[17] James had advocated games that required the use of weapons while on horseback such as the tilt, the ring and James's personal favourite pastime of hunting. Hunting, he remarked, resembled war and made a man hardy and skilful at riding in different terrains.[18] Henry performed these activities with such grace that his reputation spread far and wide. It was said that the people of other countries would scarcely have believed his reputation if it were not backed up by the word of their own countrymen who had witnessed him in action.

The prince's predilection for exercise meant that his studies suffered. He plied the books for just two hours a day and spent the rest of his free time playing sports. '[H]e is never idle,' the French ambassador la Boderie reported in 1606.[19] By 1607, the prince's lack of interest in his studies began to concern James. The *Basilicon Doron* had decreed that he should only learn what was practical for the execution of his role as king, but James later changed his mind and for the next three years had the prince focus more on his studies. It seems to have worked as the prince delivered an oration in Latin in which he discussed the importance of a liberal education for a prince, which he presented to his father as a New Year's gift in 1609.[20]

Henry Frederick, Prince of Wales

Henry differed from James in other ways. He did not share his father's love of hunting or his penchant for drinking or swearing. The prince is said to never have uttered a swearword and he kept swear jars at his palaces at Richmond, Nonsuch and St James's and used the money collected to feed the poor. While James showed little interest in the running of government, Henry showed a precocious interest in both foreign and home affairs. He often asked probing questions from which he is said to have developed a considerable insight into state affairs. In religion he was Protestant but with Puritan inclinations and he was said to hate popery to death, something that the abortive Gunpowder Plot no doubt helped strengthen. He was an avid attendant at church services and delighted in listening to long sermons. This devoutness and hatred of popery excited the minds of the Protestants who believed him to have been sent by God to destroy Catholic idolatry. While King James preferred peace to war and the book to the sword, Henry was of a martial character. He was immensely popular as a result and the king became increasingly jealous of him.

The prince's interest in the navy continued to develop. In 1607 he was presented with a model ship by Phineas Pett and in August 1608 he paid the first of many visits to the royal dockyard at Woolwich. On his arrival he was greeted by a salute of thirty-one cannon, which he witnessed from the poop deck of the *Anne Royal*. Phineas Pett then took him on a tour of the dockyard where he saw the keel, stem and stern of his own ship, the *Princes Royal*, which was then under construction in the yard.

Henry later went to inspect the mount from which the cannon had fired the salute. He requested that the salute be fired again, but as Pett was reluctant to put the prince in any danger, he opted to watch it from the safety of his barge. He lifted his handkerchief as a signal and the cannon were discharged, much to his delight. The prince was fond of Phineas Pett, and lent his support when the shipwright was accused of misdemeanours and abuses in his role as a naval officer. In May 1609 the prince and king attended a hearing at Woolwich where the accusations against Pett were proven false. The prince, in a high voice, shouted, 'Where be now these perjured fellows that dare thus abuse his Majesty with these false informations, do they not worthily deserve hanging?'[21]

At the Christmas festivities of 1609, the now fifteen-year-old Henry made his challenge to the knights of Great Britain. The challenge was accepted and took place on Epiphany, 6 January 1610, at the Banqueting House at Whitehall. The prince had six assistants, known as the 'Assailants', while his opponents, the 'Defendants', had fifty-six members. Each of the prince's Assailants took on eight Defendants and fought two rounds, one with a pike and one with a sword. The prince fought admirably for his age, giving and receiving thirty-two pushes of pikes and 360 sword strokes.[22] After the tournament had finished, the scores were totted up and prizes given.

Prince of Wales

When Henry reached the age of sixteen he began to gently push his father to be created Prince of Wales, Earl of Chester and Duke of Cornwall. James agreed and the ceremony was arranged to take place on Monday 4 June 1610. That morning, Henry and King James embarked from Whitehall aboard a barge to Westminster Bridge. King James proceeded to Westminster Palace while Henry went to the Court of Wards to prepare for the ceremony.

When everything was set, Henry was led in procession to the White Chamber where the ceremony was to take place. First came the heralds and officers of arms, followed by twenty-five Knights of the Bath, whom the king had created the day before, dressed in purple satin robes lined with white taffeta. They were followed by the Garter King of Arms who carried the letters patent for Henry's creation. Next came the Earl of Sussex with the prince's robes, the Earl of Cumberland with the sword, the Earl of Rutland the ring, the Earl of Derby the rod, and the Earl of Shrewsbury the cap and coronet. The prince, bareheaded and supported by the earls of Nottingham and Northampton, entered the chamber and approached the throne, bowed three times and knelt upon a pillow before the king. Salisbury read the letters patent and the king placed the robes upon him, girted him with the sword, invested him with the rod and ring and then placed the cap and coronet on his head. The prince rose and James took him by the hand and kissed him. He was then led by the earls of Suffolk and Worcester to take his seat on the left-hand side of the king's throne.

After the ceremony, they returned to Whitehall and the prince dined in the Great Hall. He was seated with many of the great lords while the newly created Knights of the Bath were placed at a table to his left. The following day a masque was performed in which Henry's mother, sister and brother Charles, who had arrived in England in 1604 and been created Duke of York in 1605, took part. The third day was celebrated with jousts, fireworks and a mock naval battle upon the Thames.

In September, the royal family attended the launch of the *Princes Royal* at Woolwich. Henry stood upon the poop deck ready to christen the ship but, embarrassingly, the ship became wedged between the dock gates and refused to budge. When it became apparent that the vessel would not be freed anytime soon, the king, queen and other spectators returned in indignation to Greenwich. Henry later went to Greenwich but returned early in the morning, braving a heavy storm to see the ship finally launched when the tide came in at 3 a.m. This time it slipped into the river effortlessly and the delighted prince, gulping down some of the wine and emptying the rest upon the deck, declared the vessel to be named the *Princes Royal*.

Now that Henry had been made Prince of Wales, Earl of Chester and Duke of Cornwall, he reorganised and enlarged his household. He retained the services of his governor, Thomas Chaloner, who became his chamberlain while Sir David Murray was made a groom of the stool. His former tutor Adam Newton became his secretary. Newcomers included Sir Charles Cornwallis, who was made lord treasurer and who later wrote some tracts on the prince, and John Holles, who was made comptroller. Henry took his new responsibilities seriously and acted 'more like a grave, wise and ancient counsellor, surveying, disposing, and dispatching his affairs, then so young and great a prince'.[23] He personally drew up the rules governing the household. These included the provisions that all members of the household were to receive the sacrament at least four times a year on pain of losing their job, that the principal officers were not to accept bribes and that no strangers were to be lodged in or near the prince's house.

The prince now became the subject of complex marriage negotiations with foreign powers. In 1611, offers came from the dukes of Savoy and Tuscany and the King of Spain. The Spanish match was soon off the table when it emerged that the king's eldest daughter was already destined for the hand of the French king, Louis XIII. King James played the other two against each other in order to receive the highest dowry. The prince did not involve himself in the negotiations but he was against the Tuscan match, and though he preferred the idea of the Savoyard match he was against marrying a Catholic, saying that 'two religions should never lie in his bed'.[4] In 1612 the French also threw their hat into the ring and proposed a marriage between Louis XIII's second sister, Christine, and the prince.

Princess Elizabeth proved a much less complex problem than the prince. She was destined to marry Frederick V, the Elector Palatine. Prince Henry was greatly in favour of this marriage as the young elector was a Protestant. He did all in his power to promote the marriage, entertaining and throwing his support behind the Count of Hanau, who was sent to England in 1612 to arrange it.

A Death Recorded in Detail

In the summer of 1612, the prince accompanied his father on a progress around the kingdom that terminated at Woodstock, where the prince held 'one of the greatest and best ordered feasts as ever was seen'.[25] After this he returned to Richmond to prepare for the expected arrival of the Elector Palatine, who was due to marry Elizabeth.

The prince started displaying the first signs of the typhoid fever that would shortly take his life. Sir Charles Cornwallis noted that his face had become paler, thinner and longer and that he often complained of a headache.[26] He was prone to sudden bouts of fainting and would have to be revived with strong spirits. The once active prince became listless and lethargic, not rising to walk the fields in the early morning as was his usual custom but lying in until nine o'clock.

On 10 October the prince managed to rouse himself from his sickbed to visit Whitehall for the celebration of Elector Frederick's arrival. He tried his best to conceal his illness and on 24 October played tennis outside in just a shirt. The next day he developed a fever and went to St James's to recuperate. Soon, he was stricken with a great thirst that would not abate and his eyes became sensitive to candlelight. Over the next twelve days he grew steadily worse, his physicians disagreeing on how best to treat him. One physician suggested bleeding him while he still had the strength but the others preferred to continue administering cordials.

At first the prince was able to rise in the morning and play at cards but by 29 October he was fully confined to his bed. On 1 November he was bled, which (apparently) helped ease his symptoms and gave renewed hope to the king, queen and princess when they visited him later that day. But the fever returned with a vengeance and the following night he called out for his clothes and rapier in his delirium. On 3 November, his physicians shaved his head and applied pigeons and cupping glasses to little effect. His fever worsened and he became restless, singing in his sleep and attempting to jump out of bed. Even more bizzarely, the next day a chicken, cloven at the back, was applied to his feet. The king came to visit his dying son that day, but he was warned not to see him in his current state for the grief it would cause him. The king departed, never to see his son again.

On 5 November, the king was notified that the prince was unlikely to survive. George Abbot, Archbishop of Canterbury prepared Henry for death and as the end drew near Sir David Murray came to see his ailing friend. The prince struggled to speak but managed to task his groom with the burning of some personal letters stored in a cabinet in his room. The captive Sir Walter Raleigh, a prisoner in the Tower of London and a friend of the prince, sent him a cordial which was administered in desperation, but which only eased his symptoms for a little while. The prince held on until the evening of 6 November when he slipped away, aged just eighteen.

The prince, said to be 'the flower of his house, the glory of his country, and the admiration of all strangers', was deeply mourned by the royal family and the public.[27] He was laid to rest in Westminster Abbey on Monday 7 December. The twelve-year-old Prince Charles, now heir apparent to the throne, acted as chief mourner.

22

Sophia, Electress of Hanover

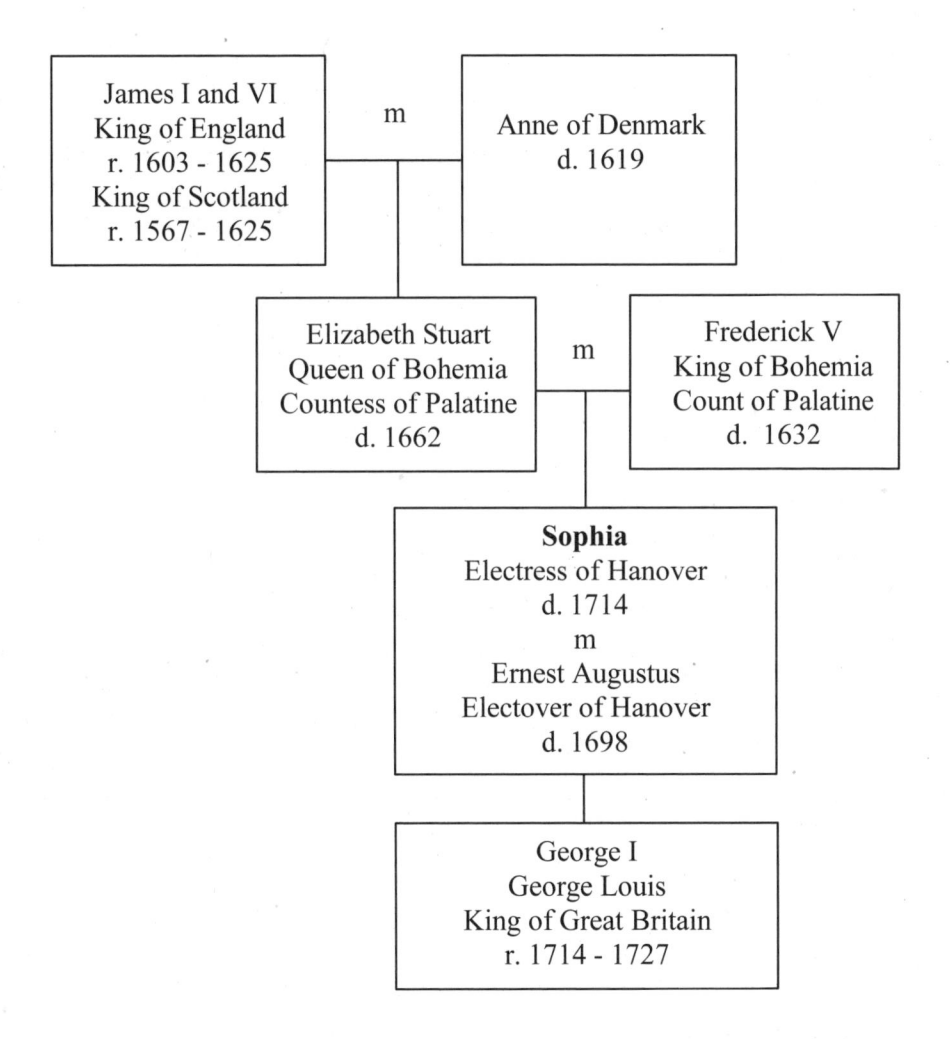

```
┌─────────────────────┐       ┌─────────────────────┐
│   James I and VI    │   m   │   Anne of Denmark   │
│  King of England    ├───────┤       d. 1619       │
│    r. 1603 - 1625   │       │                     │
│  King of Scotland   │       └─────────────────────┘
│    r. 1567 - 1625   │
└─────────────────────┘
              │
    ┌─────────────────────┐       ┌─────────────────────┐
    │  Elizabeth Stuart   │   m   │    Frederick V      │
    │  Queen of Bohemia   ├───────┤  King of Bohemia    │
    │ Countess of Palatine│       │  Count of Palatine  │
    │       d. 1662       │       │       d. 1632       │
    └─────────────────────┘       └─────────────────────┘
                        │
              ┌─────────────────────┐
              │       Sophia        │
              │ Electress of Hanover│
              │       d. 1714       │
              │          m          │
              │   Ernest Augustus   │
              │ Electover of Hanover│
              │       d. 1698       │
              └─────────────────────┘
                        │
              ┌─────────────────────┐
              │      George I       │
              │    George Louis     │
              │ King of Great Britain│
              │    r. 1714 - 1727   │
              └─────────────────────┘
```

On the evening of 8 June 1714, the eighty-three-year-old Sophia, Electress of Hanover, heir presumptive to the thrones of Great Britain, was taking one of her daily strolls in her gardens at Herrenhausen Palace in Hanover, Germany. She was in animated conversation with her granddaughter-in-law Caroline of Ansbach and one of her ladies-in-waiting when it started to rain. The three women made a dash for cover. Sophia collapsed and died.

A little under two months later, on 1 August, Queen Anne of Great Britain passed away. The elderly Sophia had missed out on becoming queen by just two months. It was her son George who succeeded to the throne in her place as George I, ushering in the beginning of the Hanoverian dynasty.

Birth and Early Life

Princess Sophia, Electress of Hanover was the twelfth child and fifth daughter of Frederick V, Elector Palatine and his wife, Elizabeth Stuart, the only daughter of King James I. She was declared heiress presumptive of the childless Queen Anne as her nearest Protestant heir in the Act of Settlement (1701).

The premature death of Henry Frederick, Prince of Wales did not hinder the plans for Princess Elizabeth's marriage to Elector Frederick and the couple were married in the chapel at Whitehall Palace on Valentine's Day, 14 February 1613. Two months later, Elizabeth and her new husband crossed over to Heidelberg, the capital of the Palatinate, and took up residence at the castle. In August 1619, the Protestant people of the Kingdom of Bohemia (now the Czech Republic) deposed their Catholic king, Ferdinand of Styria, and offered the Protestant Frederick the poisoned chalice of its crown.

Frederick rashly accepted the offer against the advice of his father-in-law, King James I, and he and Elizabeth rode to Prague where they were crowned King and Queen of Bohemia in November 1619. Ferdinand of Styria, in the meantime, had been elected Holy Roman Emperor after the death of his predecessor and was determined on reclaiming Bohemia. He defeated the Bohemians at the Battle of White Mountain, just outside of Prague, on 8 November 1620. Frederick and Elizabeth were forced to flee Bohemia and took refuge at The Hague in Holland under the hospitality of the stadtholder, Maurice, Prince of Orange. Emperor Ferdinand exiled Frederick on 21 January 1621 and forfeited him of the Palatinate and his status as an elector, a title which allowed him to have a vote in the election of a new emperor.

This was the beginning of the European conflict known as the Thirty Years War (1618–1648), which included Denmark, Sweden and France and did not end until the Peace of Westphalia was signed on 24 October 1648. Elizabeth remained at The Hague throughout the war while her husband sought in vain to reclaim the Palatinate. She bore a total of thirteen children. The eldest, Frederick Henry, was born in 1614 but drowned in 1629. Charles Louis, their second son and heir apparent after the death of Frederick Henry, was born in 1618. There followed Elizabeth (1618), Rupert (1619), Maurice (1621), Louise Hollandine (1622), Louis (1623), Edward (1625), Henrietta Maria (1626), John (1627) and Charlotte (1628).

Princess Sophia, their twelfth child and last daughter, was born on 14 October 1630, to little fanfare. Her parents even struggled to find her a name as all the kings and princes of repute had already lent their names to the couple's other children. They instead adopted a policy of casting lots and the winning name was 'Sophia'. Sadly, Sophia never got to know her father for he died when she was two, having never recovered the Palatinate.

We are fortunate that Sophia wrote a memoir which documents the first fifty years of her life and reveals her to have been a clever, insightful and witty woman. Soon after her birth, she tells us, she was sent to Leiden to be brought up and educated along with her brothers and sisters while her mother, whom Sophia notes was more interested in the society of her pet monkeys and dogs than that of her own children, remained at The Hague. Sophia's governess was the elderly Madame de Ples, who had been governess to her father. De Ples was assisted by her two God-fearing daughters, whose appearance, Sophia remarks, 'was frightful enough to terrify little children'.[1] They raised Sophia as a Protestant, 'to love God and fear the Devil', instilling in her the 'good' doctrine of Calvin.[2]

Her day-to-day life was governed by a rigid timetable. She awoke at 7 a.m. and was immediately dispatched to Marie de Quat, one of de Ples's aforementioned daughters, who made her pray and read the Bible. She was then made to read *Pibrac's Precepts for the Guidance of Man* while de Quat brushed her teeth. '[H]er grimaces during this performance are more firmly fixed in my memory than the lessons which she tried to teach,' Sophia recalls.[3] She was then changed and at 8:30 a.m. she began her formal lessons. She was relieved when 10 a.m. came around and she could enjoy an hour of dancing. Dinner was served at 11 a.m., after which she was allowed to rest until 2 p.m. when she began the afternoon's lessons. She supped at 6 p.m. and went to bed at 8.30 p.m., after having said her prayers and read some chapters from the Bible.

As her siblings grew older, they left the nursery at Leiden. The boys went to make their way in the world while her three surviving sisters, Elizabeth, Louise and Henrietta Maria, moved to The Hague to be with their mother. Eventually, only Sophia and her youngest brother, the 'handsome' but sickly Gustav, the thirteenth and final child born of Elizabeth and Frederick, remained.[4] Gustav died at the age of eight on 9 January 1641 and her mother had Sophia removed to The Hague.

The ten-year-old Sophia was in awe of the bustling activity of the court. She spent her time teasing people and hiding from her new governess, an old maid named Galen, whom she detested. She was once again in the society of her three elder sisters who, she admits, were 'all handsomer and more accomplished than myself'.[5] Her eldest sister, Elizabeth, was beautiful and scholarly and a friend of the French philosopher René Descartes. She was prone to being lost in deep thought and suffered the occasional embarrassment of a red nose for which her sisters cruelly mocked her. Louise Hollandine, the second eldest, was artistic and amiable but neglected to take care of herself. 'One would have said that her clothes had been thrown on her,' Sophia muses.[6] The sandy blonde hair of the third sister, Henrietta Maria, differentiated her from the other two sisters whose hair was jet black. She excelled at needlework and preserving and would often bestow her creations upon a grateful Sophia. Elizabeth and Louise were tasked by their mother with moulding Sophia's manners and behaviour and they did such a good job that Sophia tells us she was 'even more commended for conduct than for beauty'.[7] Sophia draws us a portrait of herself at this time. Her hair was light brown and naturally curling, her stature short but her figure good and, although she had been brought up in relative poverty, she had the bearing of a princess.[8]

In 1642, Henrietta Maria, the queen of King Charles I, brought their eldest daughter, Mary, the Princess Royal, to The Hague to begin her new life as the wife of William II, Prince of Orange. The queen also sought to pawn her jewels and raise funds and men for the civil war that was about to erupt in England between King Charles and Parliament. Sophia, who was twelve months older than Princess Mary, was chosen to accompany the princess.

As Sophia grew older, people began to consider her as a possible bride for her cousin Charles, Prince of Wales, the eldest son of Charles I and Queen Henrietta Maria and the future King Charles II. The main promoter of the marriage was William, Lord Craven, Elizabeth's devoted friend and benefactor. Prince Charles came to The Hague in 1648 but he was in no position to consider marriage. The civil war in England had gone from bad to worse for the Royalists and King Charles I was being held prisoner at Carisbrooke Castle on the Isle of Wight. He was executed in January 1649 and England became a Commonwealth. This, however, did not prevent the exiled Charles from playing on Sophia's hopes for his own ends. He met her one day on the promenade at Vorhoeit and paid her many compliments, stating that she was more beautiful than his mistress, Lucy Walter, and that he hoped to see her soon in England. She afterwards discovered that he had been put up to it by two of his friends in order to induce her to get money from Lord Craven. Sophia was highly offended and did not return to the promenade the next day, although her mother, eager for the match, pressed her to do so. She complained of a corn on her foot but in reality, she confesses, she wished 'to avoid the king, having sense enough to know that the marriages of great kings are not made up by such means'.[9]

Sophia realised that there was little chance she would ever become a queen consort, and tiring of the intrigue at The Hague began to consider her future. As part of the Treaty of Westphalia (1648), the Lower Palatinate had been restored to Sophia's elder brother, Charles Louis. In 1650, Sophia, now aged twenty, left The Hague and went to stay with her brother at Heidelberg. Charles was twelve years her senior and he was extremely fond of his little sister, whom he affectionately called his daughter. Sophia likewise regarded him in the light of a father figure; indeed, she remarks, 'in point of age [he] might have been a father to me'.[10]

Sophia found herself caught in the middle of her brother's domestic quarrels. Charles had recently married Charlotte Elizabeth, the daughter of the Landgrave William V of Hesse-Cassel. Sophia was shocked when, the day after her arrival, Charlotte had confided in her that she had been forced to marry Charles, 'a jealous old man', against her will.[11] Charles, for his part, told Sophia that Charlotte had many good qualities but that she had been badly brought up and he asked Sophia to counsel her on how a person of her rank should behave. Charlotte unfortunately loved to attract attention, which made Charles jealous. He would accuse her of looking at other men, which would cause her to fly into a rage. She later became jealous herself, even alleging that Charles was having an affair with Sophia, his own sister. Charles did eventually have an affair with one of Charlotte's maids of honour, Baroness Louise von Degenfeldt, which Charlotte discovered after finding some love letters written in Latin. Charles would go on to set up home with Louise, marrying her in January 1658. Even though their relationship was difficult, however, Charles and Charlotte produced two children early in their marriage: a son, Charles, and a daughter, Elizabeth Charlotte. Sophia was made governess to the children and grew extremely close with Elizabeth Charlotte, known as Liselotte, who would later accompany her to Hanover and with whom she kept up a spirited correspondence in later life.

Marriage

By 1656 Sophia was twenty-five years old and still unmarried. Her brother's domestic issues made her increasingly unhappy and she longed to marry and escape her difficult situation. That same year, George William, Duke of Hanover and his youngest brother, Ernest Augustus of the House of Brunswick–Lüneburg, paid a visit to Heidelberg en route for Venice. This was not a social visit; George had come with the intention of seeking Sophia's hand in marriage.

The pleasure-loving and extravagant George found the idea of marriage intolerable but he had been cajoled into the unthinkable act by his subjects in return for an increase in his revenues. His brother, Ernest, had met Sophia on a previous visit to Heidelberg when the two had danced and duetted on guitar and he had recommended her as a suitable bride. George wooed Sophia, plying her with compliments, and eventually asked her permission to approach Elector Charles about marrying her. 'My answer was not that of a heroine of romance,' Sophia confesses, 'for I unhesitatingly said "yes".'[12] Charles assented, agreements were signed and George and Ernest moved on to Venice. There, George threw himself with abandon into the pleasures of women, drink and gambling. His letters to Sophia became colder in sentiment and the inveterate bachelor soon began to regret having ever agreed to the marriage. Not wanting to break his promise, however, he came up with a deal – Sophia would marry Ernest instead. To make the match more appealing, George promised never to marry and when he died Ernest or his and Sophia's heirs would succeed him as Duke of Hanover.

Ernest readily agreed but this plan was opposed by their brother John Frederick. There were four brothers in the House of Brunswick–Lüneburg. The eldest was Christian Lewis, followed by George William, John Frederick and Ernest Augustus. On their father's death the duchy of Brunswick-Lüneburg had been divided into the duchies of Celle and Hanover, and Christian Lewis, as the senior brother, had been given the choice of the two, with the remainder going to George as next in age. Christian had chosen Celle, the richer of the pair, and Hanover went to George. John Frederick and Ernest Augustus were not granted an inheritance but if Christian or George were to die without heirs then Frederick and Ernest stood to inherit one of the duchies in order of seniority. John Frederick unsurprisingly resented this new agreement that Ernest, who was lower down in the pecking order than him, would inherit instead of him if George were to die.

George continued undeterred with his plans and he communicated them to Heidelberg. Elector Charles and Sophia assented to the change. Sophia does not reveal her thoughts on this episode in her memoir but states that she only wished for a good establishment of her own and if that was achieved by the hand of a younger brother or an elder was a matter of indifference. Sophia and Ernest were married at Heidelberg in September 1658.

The Third Wheel

After the marriage the newly-weds set up home at Hanover. What had been purely a business match soon blossomed into one of love. Sophia fell deeply for Ernest and she pined for him when he was absent on his frequent trips to Italy. Ernest in turn loved his wife but this did not stop him from having mistresses, a fact to which Sophia seems to have turned a blind eye.

To Sophia's horror, she soon discovered that there were three people in their marriage. George and Ernest were extremely close and he often joined them in their activities such as playing cards, hunting and walking. 'I formed as it were the third person in this union,' she relates, 'in which, alas! the numbers were unequal.'[13] In a tragicomical twist, George fell in love with Sophia and regretted having given her up. One day, when George was ill in bed, Sophia, perched beside his bed, pointed out that he must wish that he was in Venice. No, he declared, he did not wish to be anywhere else when Sophia was at Hanover. Sophia laughed and quoted the words of a song: 'When one cannot have what one wants, one must want what one has.'[14] Ernest, who was present in the room perusing a book, overheard the end of the conversation and he became jealous, believing that Sophia had only married him as she couldn't have George. When they returned to the privacy of their own apartments, he would not speak to her until he eventually confessed his fears, which she managed to disprove through her tears and entreaties. Relations between the two brothers cooled but remained amiable, and they continued to go on trips to Italy together.

On 7 June 1660, Sophia's first child, George Louis, the future King George I, was born to the great joy of the people.[15] A few months later Sophia saw her mother, Elizabeth, at Rotterdam for what would prove to be the last time. Elizabeth was about to retire to England which, following the Restoration that year, was now ruled by her nephew King Charles II. Elizabeth's retirement in England was not of long duration. She died on 13 February 1662 and was buried at Westminster Abbey in the same vault as her beloved brother, Henry Frederick.

In December 1661, an opportunity arose for Sophia to quit Hanover and Duke George's suffocating presence. By the terms of the Treaty of Westphalia, it was agreed that the bishopric of Osnabrück, some 45 miles in length and 25 in breadth, would alternate between a Catholic and Protestant ruler. The Protestant bishop was to be appointed by the House of Brunswick and Ernest's father had earmarked him for the role. In December the Catholic bishop died and Ernest succeeded him as the next Protestant heir. Sophia, who was 'considered an unnecessary appendage in this ecclesiastical ceremony', did not attend Ernest's inauguration into the bishopric in September 1662.[16] The couple afterwards took up residence at the castle of Iburg.

In 1664, Ernest convinced Sophia to accompany him on a tour of Italy. Sophia visited Venice, Loretto, Rome and Florence. She was decidedly unimpressed with her husband's precious Venice, whose canals and the cries of the gondoliers she found to be melancholy. When Sophia and Ernest returned to Iburg in 1665 they learned of the death of Ernest's eldest brother, Christian Lewis, Duke of Celle. The duke had no heirs, and according to their father's will John Frederick would now inherit one of the duchies. As eldest son, George had the option of choosing which of the two duchies he wished to have, but as he was absent at the time the wily John Frederick seized Celle for himself. Ernest supported Duke George in the ensuing quarrel and raised an army to help him press his rights, but John, fearing a civil war, eventually agreed to abide by the terms of the will. George took Celle and John settled for Hanover.

The Problem of Duke George

Ernest and Sophia could now look forward to one day inheriting Celle if Duke George continued to adhere to his promise of not marrying. The vacillating duke, however, had fallen for the charms of Madame Eleanore d'Olbreuse, the ambitious daughter of an exiled French Huguenot who served as a lady-in-waiting of the Princess of Taranto. At George's request,

Eleanore joined Sophia's household. Sophia found her pleasing at first. 'She was grave and dignified in manner. Her face was beautiful, her figure tall and commanding,' Sophia states.[17] George wished to marry Eleanore but he was unable to do so due to the terms of the renunciation. He instead formed what Sophia terms an 'anti-contract of marriage', whereby he pledged himself to Eleanore for ever, as if they were married, and granted her a yearly pension of 2,000 crowns.[18] As this preserved their own rights, Sophia and Ernest gladly assented to the contract.

Sophia's enthusiasm for Eleanore soon waned. She wished to be known as Duchess of Celle but she had to be satisfied with the title of Madame de Harburg after the property that George had granted her as her dowry. Eleanore soon fell pregnant and there were troubling rumours that if she had a son then the duke would marry her officially and thereby legitimate the child as his successor. Fortunately, the child proved to be a daughter named Sophia Dorothea, born in September 1666, later the repudiated and imprisoned wife of King George I.

Sophia, meanwhile, gave birth to more children. A second son, Frederick Augustus, had been born at Hanover on 8 October 1661. In 1666 she gave birth to twins, one of whom passed away, and the surviving child was named Maximilian William.[19] On 12 October 1668, she gave birth to her only daughter, her beloved Sophia Charlotte, whom she affectionately called Figuelotte. On 13 October 1669 another son, Charles Philip, was born, followed by Christian in 1671 and their last child, Ernest Augustus, in 1674.

Relations between Ernest and Duke George remained cordial until the thorny subject of marriage once again arose. George wished to marry his daughter, Sophia Charlotte, to Augustus Frederick, the son of Anthony Ulric, the younger brother and heir of Duke Rudolph of Brunswick–Wolfenbüttel. Sophia Charlotte's illegitimacy was a stumbling block and Anthony pressed George and Eleanore to marry in order to legitimate her. Duke George promised Ernest that if he were allowed to marry Eleanore his children would not inherit his rank or possessions and that Eleanor would only become Countess of Wilhelmsburg and their children counts and countesses of the same. Ernest and Sophia reluctantly agreed, but with the provision that the Diet, army and ministers of Celle should confirm Ernest's position as heir and, in the event that Eleanore had any more children, the people of Celle were to swear an oath of allegiance to him.

While these articles were being forwarded for the Holy Roman Emperor's ratification, Duke George and Ernest and Sophia's eldest son, the fifteen-year-old George Louis, went to war against France. George Louis acquitted himself so valiantly in the war that Emperor Leopold I afterwards sent him a laudatory letter.

On their return home in 1676, Duke George married Eleanore. Shortly after, he began to renege on his promises. Eleanore was granted the honour of being prayed for in church, a distinction only reserved for a duchess, while people began to address her as 'Highness'.[20] When Eleanore once again became pregnant, Ernest demanded that the people of Celle pay him homage as per the agreement, but George, with the assistance of his wily chancellor Schutz, managed to avoid doing so. The chancellor also succeeded in stealing the emperor's decree that the Chamber of Spires was not to receive any lawsuits against Ernest's claims. The duke's next child proved to be another daughter, who was stillborn.

Sophia Dorothea's proposed husband, Augustus Frederick, was killed at the siege of Philipsburg that same year. Thoughts now turned to a marriage between George Louis and Sophia Dorothea, which would mend relations between Ernest and Duke George and secure the succession to Celle. Sophia, who looked down on Eleanore's inferior birth, was not keen on the idea. She preferred a match between George Louis and a daughter of Duke John Frederick, who had married Benedicta, one of Sophia's nieces, in 1668 and by whom he had several daughters.

In December 1679, Sophia was visiting her dying eldest sister, Elizabeth, who had become Abbess of Herford, when she received the unexpected news that John Frederick had died. As John had no male heirs, the Duchy of Hanover passed to Ernest Augustus. Sophia paid her last respects to her fading sister and then made haste to Osnabrück where she was met by her husband. His first words to her were, 'I am glad it was not I who died.'[21] This may at first seem callous but it was prompted by Ernest's fears over his children's future if he were to predecease his brothers.

Ernest and Sophia took up residence in their new capital of Hanover. This piece of good fortune meant that they now stood to inherit the entire duchy of Brunswick–Lüneburg when George died. Ernest wished to be at peace with Duke George in order to guard the succession of Celle, and he gave his blessing for Eleanore to be granted the title of Duchess of Celle on the condition that Emperor Leopold was to draw up a new contract regarding the succession, in the event that the new duchess should have a son.

Heiress Presumptive

Sophia's memoirs sadly come to an end in the year 1681, when she was fifty years old. The death of her sister, Abbess Elizabeth, followed shortly after by her brother, Charles Lewis, Elector of Palatine, see them end on a dour note and with the author anticipating that she would soon die herself. Yet Sophia would live for another thirty-three years. The last stage of her life would see her unexpectedly become heiress presumptive to the throne of Great Britain and lead to the rise of the Hanoverian dynasty.

Before there was any hint of a throne, Ernest Augustus had pretensions of making Hanover into the ninth electorate of the Empire. This would give Ernest membership of the Electoral College and the right to elect the next emperor. In order to effect this Ernest needed to consolidate all of the Brunswick–Lüneburg lands into the hands of one individual instead of splitting it between sons. As part of the plan he renewed discussions for the marriage of George Louis and Sophia Dorothea, which, through Sophia's influence, was eventually agreed and celebrated at Celle on 22 November 1682. Unfortunately, Ernest's plans for the succession served to disrupt family relations. His younger sons, who now stood to lose out, were naturally averse to them. Their second son, Frederick Augustus, fell out with Ernest, and Sophia was caught in the middle. Sophia loved her children and the family arguments stung her. 'I cry about it all night long,' she stated in a letter, 'for one child is as dear to me as another; I am the mother of them all, and I grieve most for those who are unhappy.'[22] Frederick was exiled and joined in the Great Turkish War in support of the emperor. He was killed in battle in 1691, as was Charles Philip, who had also enlisted. After the death of Frederick, Maximilian and his younger brother Christian also rebelled against their father. Maximilian was aided by Frederick III, Elector of Brandenburg, and a plot was unmasked by Sophia's daughter, Sophia Charlotte, now the wife of Frederick III, with the result that Maximilian was banished from Hanover and was forced to renounce his claim to the inheritance. Christian joined the Imperial Army and died in 1703. Their last son, Ernest Augustus, became Duke of York and Albany and Bishop of Osnabrück during the reign of George I. He died in 1728.

Meanwhile, in England, the Glorious Revolution of 1688 (so called as it was achieved without the spilling of blood) opened up the distant possibility that Sophia or her heirs may one day inherit the thrones of Great Britain and Ireland. The Stuarts had been restored to the throne in 1660 when Charles, Prince of Wales was crowned as King Charles II. Charles married Catherine of Braganza in May 1662 but the couple never had any children who survived infancy and his younger brother James, Duke of York and Albany remained his heir presumptive throughout his reign, eventually succeeded him as King James II in 1685.

King James had married twice. His first wife was Anne Hyde, the daughter of Charles II's favourite minister, Edward Hyde. She produced two daughters, Princesses Mary and Anne, who would rule England as Queen Mary II and Queen Anne respectively. In 1677, Mary married William III of Orange, the son of the William II of Orange who had married Mary Stuart, the Princess Royal and daughter of Charles I, thus making William a claimant to the throne himself, while Anne married Prince George of Denmark in 1683. However, in 1669, James, 'touched in conscience', fatefully decided to convert to Catholicism, a decision that would have huge repercussions for his dynasty, the succession and the country.[23] Anne Hyde died in 1671 and two years later James made the unpopular decision to marry the Catholic Mary of Modena. There were fears that if James was to become king he would restore

Catholicism, and an unsuccessful attempt was made by Parliament to bar him from the throne during the Exclusion Crisis (1679–81).

Surprisingly, when King Charles died on 6 February 1685, James ascended the throne without any trouble. At the commencement of his reign he promised to defend the established Anglican Church, but he wished to enforce religious toleration so that Catholics were free to practise their religion. The king's introduction of the Declaration of Indulgence, which removed the penal laws against Catholics and Nonconformists, met with the opposition of the Anglican Church and a protest signed by seven bishops, including William Sancroft, Archbishop of Canterbury. The outraged king had them thrown into the Tower and they were brought for trial before the King's Bench on charges of seditious libel but were found not guilty. Meanwhile, several Protestant noblemen invited William III of Orange, as husband of James's daughter Princess Mary, to come at the head of an army and seize the throne.

At the eleventh hour, Queen Mary of Modena, who had thus far failed to produce a living heir, bore James a son (10 June 1688). He was named James Francis Edward Stuart and he was recognised, although never officially created, as Prince of Wales. There were rumours circulating that a supposititious child had been smuggled into the queen's bedchamber during the birth at St James's Palace via a warming pan in order to foist a Catholic heir on the country. William of Orange, meanwhile, accepted the invitation and landed at Torbay on 5 November 1688 with an army of 14,000 men. James, bereft of support, sent Queen Mary and their newborn prince into France. Soon after, James threw the Great Seal into the Thames and then left to join his wife and son at the court of King Louis XIV of France.

With James gone, a Convention Parliament, comprising the House of Commons and House of Lords, met in January 1689 to determine who was to be the next monarch. It was declared that James had abdicated the throne and it was now vacant, thereby terminating the old line of succession. Instead of offering the crown to a new dynasty, however, they turned to the nearest Protestant heir of James: his daughter Princess Mary. She refused to rule without her husband, William of Orange, and on 13 February Parliament bestowed the throne jointly on them as King William III and Queen Mary II, with the executive power invested solely in William. This was later enshrined in the Bill of Rights in December.

The Bill of Rights delineated the order of succession which, while still hereditary, now became subject to limitation by Parliament. The bill excluded James II and his son from the throne and invested it in the persons of William and Mary. The throne was to remain with the survivor of the pair and then pass on to any children of Princess Mary, she being higher in the order of succession than William. In the event that Mary had no children, Princess Anne was to succeed, followed by her own children. If Anne had no surviving children, the throne was to pass to any children of King William born of another wife.

More importantly for Sophia, the Bill of Rights excluded Roman Catholics or anyone who was married to a Roman Catholic from ascending the throne. In the case of a Catholic heir the people were to be absolved of their allegiance and the crown was to pass to the next Protestant heir as if they were dead.

This invited the possibility that Sophia herself would one day become queen of Great Britain. At the time of the bill's creation, Queen Mary and Princess Anne were both childless; if they and William died without heirs then Sophia qualified as the next Protestant claimant. Only two of Sophia's elder siblings had produced any children. Charles Louis had a Protestant son but he had died in 1685 without an heir while his daughter Liselotte had married the Duke of Orléans and turned Catholic. Edward, the only other brother to have children, had also turned Catholic and although he had several descendants they, too, were of the Catholic faith. Of Sophia's sisters only Louise Hollandine still lived, and she was also disqualified as she had converted to Catholicism and become Abbess of Maubuisson. Sophia's chances, however, were dealt a blow when on 24 July 1689 Princess Anne gave birth to a son, William, Duke of Gloucester.

While these events were playing out in England, Ernest continued his plans to have Hanover made into an electorate. This was finally granted by Emperor Leopold I in December 1692 in exchange for money and a force of 6,000 men to fight in the Great Turkish War, but opposition from the other electors meant that the new elector was not granted his seat in the Electoral College until after Ernest's death in 1708.

Two years later, a scandal erupted at the Hanoverian court when it was discovered that Sophia Dorothea, wife of George Louis, was having an affair with Count Philip von Königsmarck, a general in the Hanoverian army. George Louis proved a cold and distant husband and was often away fighting on military campaigns, and the lonely Sophia Dorothea had fallen head over heels for the dashing Swedish soldier. Then, in 1694, von Königsmarck disappeared mysteriously while going to pay Sophia a visit. It is likely that he was murdered by palace officers and his body thrown into the River Leine. Sophia was afterwards placed under house arrest in the castle of Ahlden in Celle, where she remained for the last thirty-two years of her life, dying in 1726. George Louis had many mistresses but he never married again and he never had a queen consort when he became king.

Sophia's world was turned upside down when Ernest fell ill. She stayed at his side, nursing him and keeping him company until he died in January 1698, after which George Louis, as their eldest son, succeeded to the electorate.

After Ernest's death Sophia spent most of her time at Herrenhausen Palace, located a mile and a half from Hanover, which her husband had left her in his will. Here she held her court and whiled away one or two hours a day walking in its elegant gardens and listening to the songs of her nightingales. She was often accompanied by her friend Gottfried Wilhelm Leibniz, a famous philosopher and mathematician, and the two would have philosophical discussions as well as chatting about current events.

The question of the English succession was often a hot topic. Queen Mary had died of smallpox in December 1694, aged thirty-two, and, as per the Bill of Rights, William III retained the throne as sole monarch. William and Mary had no children and the early death of Anne's son William, Duke of Gloucester on 30 July 1700 necessitated a reordering of the succession.

In the Act of Settlement (1701), Sophia, as the nearest Protestant in blood, was recognised as third in line to the throne, following King William and Princess Anne. This was to the prejudice of over fifty descendants of the Stuarts who had a better hereditary claim.[24] The Act of Settlement states that 'the most excellent Princess Sophia, Electress and Duchess Dowager of Hanover, daughter of the most excellent Princess Elizabeth, late queen of Bohemia, daughter of our late sovereign lord King James I, of happy memory, be and is hereby declared to be the next in succession, in the Protestant line ... and the heirs of her body, being Protestants'.[25] This Act also declared that whoever came to the throne must be in communion with the Church of England. The Earl of Macclesfield was sent to Hanover to deliver a copy of the Act to Sophia and to invest Elector George Louis as a member of the Order of the Garter.

King William died on 8 March 1702 after reigning on his own for seven years and he was succeeded by Queen Anne. Anne was thirty-seven years old at the time of her accession and she had been married to George of Denmark, the son of King Frederick III of Denmark and his queen, Sophia Amelia, a sister of the dukes of Brunswick–Lüneburg, since 1683. Anne gave birth to a total of probably nineteen children, the last in 1700, but most were stillborn or died in infancy; an experience difficult to imagine. This meant that by the Act of Settlement the seventy-one-year-old Sophia or her eldest son George Louis could one day look forward to inheriting the throne. Due to her advanced age and the fact that Queen Anne was still young, Sophia's chances of one day becoming queen were remote. The Act of Union (1707) of Scotland and England saw Anne become the first Queen of Great Britain and also confirmed Sophia as heir presumptive.

Further tragedy was to befall Sophia. Her daughter Sophia Charlotte, who had become Queen of Prussia after marrying King Frederick I, died in 1705 while paying her mother a visit. Later that year her brother-in-law Duke George of Celle also died, and Celle passed to the Elector George Louis, finally unifying Celle and Hanover under one ruler. The year was also to see happier events with the marriage of George Augustus, Elector George's son and the future George II, to Caroline of Ansbach. In 1707 Caroline gave birth to her eldest son, Frederick Louis, the future Prince of Wales.

Uncrowned

George Augustus had been created Duke of Cambridge by the English Parliament in 1706, a distinction which gave him the right to a seat in the House of Lords, but Queen Anne refused to allow him to attend Parliament. When Anne fell ill in 1714 there were fresh calls for a member of the Hanoverian dynasty to come to England. Queen Anne was enraged and she wrote to Sophia, Elector George and Prince George Augustus, jealously stating that she would never allow a member of the dynasty to come to England while she lived. These letters caused Sophia some distress and she asked that they be copied and sent to her friends in England. The next day, 7 June, an illness confined Sophia to her bed, but she had recovered her energy the next day. Sophia was walking in her gardens at Herrenhausen at about 6 p.m. on 8 June with Caroline of Ansbach and a lady-in-waiting when it suddenly started to rain. She rushed to find some cover but she collapsed and expired shortly after in her daughter-in-law's arms, aged eighty-three. Samuel Molyneux, who has written an account of Sophia's last days, attributes her death to the heartbreak caused by the letters.[26] Sophia was buried in the chapel at the palace of Hanover.

Queen Anne survived Sophia by less than two months and died on 1 August. She was succeeded by Elector George Louis, who reigned as King George I; the Hanoverian dynasty begins.

23

James Francis Edward Stuart

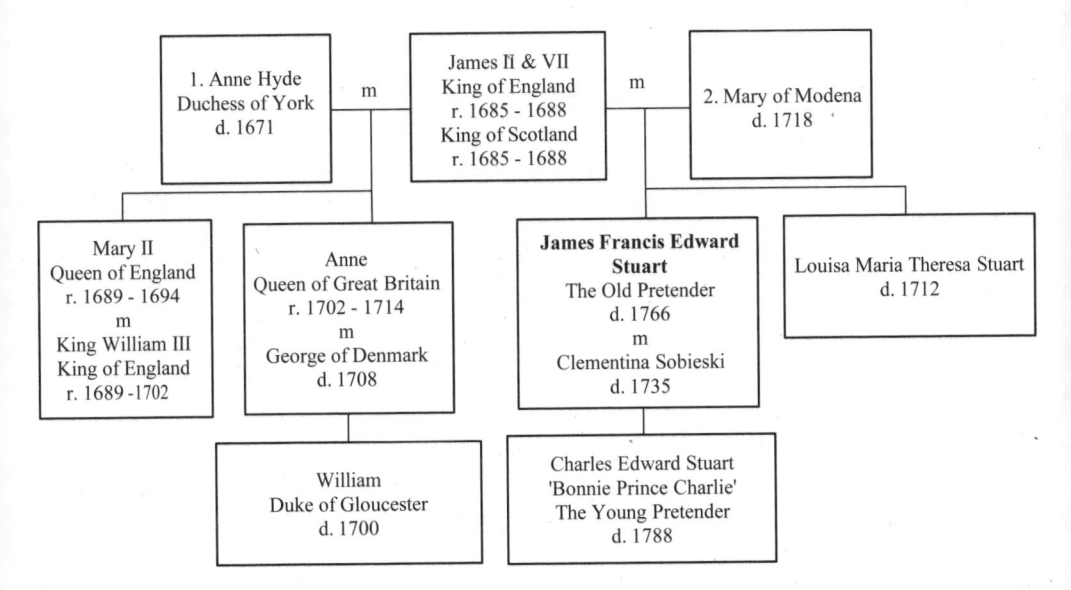

```
┌─────────────────┐     ┌─────────────────┐     ┌─────────────────┐
│ 1. Anne Hyde    │  m  │ James II & VII  │  m  │ 2. Mary of Modena│
│ Duchess of York │─────│ King of England │─────│    d. 1718       │
│    d. 1671      │     │  r. 1685 - 1688 │     │                  │
└─────────────────┘     │ King of Scotland│     └─────────────────┘
                        │  r. 1685 - 1688 │
                        └─────────────────┘
```

Mary II	Anne	**James Francis Edward Stuart**	Louisa Maria Theresa Stuart
Queen of England	Queen of Great Britain	The Old Pretender	d. 1712
r. 1689 - 1694	r. 1702 - 1714	d. 1766	
m	m	m	
King William III	George of Denmark	Clementina Sobieski	
King of England	d. 1708	d. 1735	
r. 1689 -1702			

William	Charles Edward Stuart
Duke of Gloucester	'Bonnie Prince Charlie'
d. 1700	The Young Pretender
	d. 1788

At around eight o'clock on the morning of Sunday 10 June 1688, Queen Mary of Modena, the wife of King James II, went into labour at St James's Palace, London. The king was immediately sent for and messengers dispatched to those the king wished to bear witness to the birth.

Mrs Wilks, the midwife, readied the queen's bed and, as the queen was cold, a warming pan full of hot coal was slipped under the covers. Once everything was set, the queen climbed inside.

The witnesses to the birth began to arrive. Many of them had been called out of church, it being Trinity Sunday, or rushed over from Whitehall Palace. These included the Queen Dowager, Catherine of Braganza, and her ladies, the queen's ladies, the royal physicians and eighteen members of the Privy Council. All in all there were over forty-two individuals present with a good mixture of both Catholics and Protestants.

The queen's modesty was covered by the large bed canopy, which was drawn tightly around her, and only Mrs Wilks and an underdresser were permitted entrance. The Queen Dowager, along with Catherine, Lady Sunderland, Lady Roscommon and Mrs Labadie, the dry nurse, sat near to the queen's side of the bed while the other witnesses congregated around it. The queen cried out in such pain during the birth that the Earl of Peterborough was forced to cover his ears. After one final push, at around ten o'clock, it was announced that the baby had been born. Frighteningly, the baby did not utter a cry and the queen feared that the infant was dead. Mrs Wilks assured her that it was not dead and asked if she could cut the umbilical cord. The queen was averse to her doing so in case it proved dangerous to herself, but Mrs Wilks once again reassured her and the queen consented. Then, to the queen's relief, the infant wailed.

In a pre-planned move, Mrs Wilks tugged on the coat of Lady Sunderland to indicate that the child was a boy, and Lady Sunderland then touched her head to signify this to the king. Mrs Wilks swaddled the baby and then handed him to Mrs Labadie, who immediately took him into the adjoining small bedchamber. She was followed by the king and members of the Privy Council, who found her sat before the fire, cradling the infant on her lap. King James, still unconvinced, demanded to know what sex it was and Mrs Labadie responded that it was what he desired.[1] Mrs Labadie unwrapped the cloth so that the king could see the baby's nakedness and he was afterwards shown to all the members of the Privy Council. The baby was undoubtedly male, and the residue of the birth proved that he had just been born.

Shortly after, Mrs Wilks entered the room. She cut the remainder of the umbilical cord still attached to the baby beyond the ligature and dripped three drops of fresh blood on to a spoon. Mrs Labadie then mixed the blood with black cherry water and fed it to the child, a supposed remedy against the 'convulsions' that had claimed the lives of some of the queen's previous children.[2] The baby was later washed and clothed and named James Francis Edward Stuart. Seemingly against all odds, England had a new male heir to the throne.

At two o'clock that afternoon, the Tower ordinance was discharged and church bells rang out across London in celebration. Unfortunately, the king and queen's euphoria was not shared by many of their Protestant subjects. Scandalous rumours circulated that the queen had not been pregnant at all and that a child had been introduced into the bed via the warming pan in order to ensure a Catholic was heir to the throne. Just under five months later, William III of Orange invaded England as James II's rule collapsed and baby James and the queen were carted off to France for their safety. They were later joined by the king while James's Protestant daughter, Mary II, and her husband, William III of Orange, were consecrated joint King and Queen of England in his place. King James died in 1701, never to regain his throne, and it would fall to James Francis, the rightful heir according to the rules of primogeniture, to try and win it back.

Birth and Early Life

James Francis Edward Stuart, also known as James III, the Old Pretender and the Chevalier de St George, was the only son and heir of King James II of England and VII of Scotland and his second wife, Queen Mary of Modena.

James Francis Edward Stuart

King James ascended the throne at the death of his elder brother, Charles II, in February 1685. There were fears that the king, who had converted to Catholicism in 1669, would attempt to enforce popery on the country, and at the beginning of the reign James had sort to allay these fears by promising the Privy Council and then his first parliament that he would defend and maintain the church and preserve the government in church and state as it was established by law.[3]

The reign of Charles II had seen the introduction of the so called 'Clarendon Code', a series of laws which penalised Nonconformists, and the Test Act of 1673, which prevented anyone from taking civil and military office who did not first receive the sacrament according to the rites of the Church of England and renounce transubstantiation. This last Act was aimed squarely at Catholics and meant that they could not enjoy any political office. Although James had promised to retain the church and laws, he was determined to remove the Clarendon Code and Test Act so that Catholics and Nonconformists could enjoy liberty of conscience and practise their religion. James, however, found Parliament obdurate and unwilling to repeal the laws and in April 1687 he used his dispensing powers to issue the Declaration of Indulgence, which suspended both the Clarendon Code and the Test Act.

The Protestant people grumbled but they were comforted by the knowledge that when James, already in his early fifties, died he would be succeeded by his Protestant heir presumptive, Mary Stuart, Princess of Orange, born of his first marriage, who would undo all of James's pro-Catholic policies. Then, on 1 January 1688, it was suddenly announced that Queen Mary was pregnant. On the 15th of that same month a day of thanksgiving was held at St James's Church. The news was greeted by raised eyebrows. '[I]t is strange to see,' Lord Clarendon notes in his diary, 'how the Queen's great belly is every where ridiculed, as if scarce any body believes it to be true.'[4] Although Queen Mary was only twenty-nine years old, she had not been with child for nearly five years and people assumed that her childbearing days were over. Furthermore, the Protestants feared that if the queen was indeed pregnant and had a son then he would be brought up as a Roman Catholic and, ascending the throne to the prejudice of his Protestant half-sisters, continue his father's religious policies.

This was, of course, anathema to the Protestant population and they began to suspect that a plot was afoot to place a suppositious Catholic heir on the throne, a belief that was shared by Princess Mary and her younger sister, Princess Anne, who would both be replaced in the line of succession if the child was a boy. Suspicions were raised by the confident boasts of the Catholic bishops that the child would be a son and heightened by the air of secrecy that was said to surround the pregnant queen. She was not dressed as usual by her servants and even Princess Anne was not allowed to feel her belly and satisfy herself of the truth. At Easter, the queen was rumoured to have suffered a miscarriage but she afterwards continued pregnant.[5]

The queen had originally reckoned on two dates as the time of the baby's conception. Her first date of reckoning was Tuesday 6 September 1687, when the king had visited her when she was taking in the rejuvenating waters at Bath. The second date was a month later when she had come from Bath to join the king at Windsor. Believing the latter to be the correct date, she planned on lying-in at Windsor from 14 June and preparations were made for the delivery at the castle. Then, late on the night of 9 June, she unexpectedly travelled from Whitehall to St James's Palace where she gave birth the following morning. The king's enemies cried foul – that the queen had suddenly changed her date of reckoning in order to prevent Princess Anne, who was at Bath recovering from a miscarriage, from being present; that only Catholic ladies had witnessed the birth and that no one had seen the contents of the warming pan placed under the covers for the queen's comfort. It was whispered that the queen had never been pregnant and that a child had been concealed within the warming pan and, after a pretended labour, had been presented as the king's son and heir. '[T]is possible it may be her child,' Princess Anne acknowledged in a letter to Princess Mary, 'but where one believes it, a thousand do not.'[6]

It was touch and go whether baby James would live. Princess Mary reported to her sister in a letter dated 9 July that the infant had been ill the previous three or four days. '[I]f he has been so bad as some people say, I believe it will not be long before he is an angel in heaven,' she states.[7] Astonishingly, the king's physicians had recommended baby James not be fed milk, which was said to have caused the queen's previous children to die of convulsions, and he was instead given a diet of water gruel – a mixture of barley flour, water and sugar – which unsurprisingly made him ill.[8] Later that month he was removed to Richmond Palace in order to take in fresh air but when this failed to rejuvenate him it was finally agreed to give him a wetnurse. The lady chosen for this task was the wife of a tile maker from Richmond. '[S]he came in her cloth petticoat and waistcoat, and old shoes and no stockings,' John Ellis stated in a letter, 'but she is now rigged by degrees ... a 100*l*. per annum is already settled upon her.'[9] The prince went from strength to strength and, to the horror of the Protestants, he soon recovered.

Events, meanwhile, hurtled towards their disastrous conclusion. Shortly before the prince's birth, King James had reissued the Declaration of Indulgence and ordered it to be read in all parish churches. This was opposed by seven bishops, including William Sancroft, Archbishop of Canterbury, who drew up a petition that declared the king's use of the dispensing power to be illegal. The bishops were arrested and tried before the King's Bench for seditious libel. The arrest and trial of the seven bishops caused great excitement in the kingdom, and when they were acquitted of the charges on 30 June the people celebrated in the streets and lit bonfires at night.

The day that the bishops were acquitted, some of the nobility invited William III of Orange to come to England with an army. Prince William, himself a descendant of Charles I through Charles's daughter Mary, the Princess Royal, was not being offered the crown at this stage but he may have seen it as the natural outcome of armed intervention. William was at war with France and hoped to have the power of England on his side if he became king, and so he began to prepare for an invasion.

On 15 October, baby James was baptised as James Francis Edward in the chapel at St James's. The pope stood as his godfather, represented by the Papal Nuncio, while Queen Dowager Catherine stood as godmother.[10] With rumours circulating that Prince William was poised to invade the country, James thought it wise to address the uncertainty surrounding the prince's birth. He summoned a council on 22 October where those who had been present at the birth were asked to give depositions of what had occurred. James noted that 'by particular providence scarce any prince was ever born, where there were so many persons present'.[11] Forty-two individuals took oath that they had witnessed the arrival of baby James. Twenty-eight of these were Protestant and fourteen Catholic, which dispels the myth that only Catholics were present at the birth. These proofs were enrolled in Chancery and the king had them published, but his enemies took little heed of them. According to Bishop Burnet, who wrote an account of the time, the depositions only served to strengthen the belief that the child was supposititious.[12]

Prince William landed at Torbay on 5 November and King James sent his baby son to the safety of Portsmouth in the keeping of Lord Dartmouth so that he could be conveyed on a yacht to France should the need arise. On 1 December James sent the order to depart but Dartmouth would not do so without the approval of Parliament, warning that it could have dire consequences for the king: 'I beg leave to advise you ... that sending away the Prince of Wales, without the consent of the nation ... I dread will be of fatal consequence to your person, crown, and dignity, and all your people will (too probably) grow so much concerned at this your great mistrust, as to throw off their bounded allegiance to you.'[13] The prince was duly taken in a coach back to Whitehall by the Lord and Lady Powis.

As Prince William made his way through the country, James found himself bereft of support. Much of his army deserted and even Princess Anne fled from London. James now resolved on sending both the queen and prince to France and on the windy and rainy night of 9 December, Queen Mary crossed the Thames to Lambeth in secret with the prince, Mrs Labadie, the Comte de Lauzun and a few attendants. The coach that was to conduct them to Gravesend was delayed and the queen and prince were forced to take shelter under the walls of an old church in order to shield them from the weather. The queen's eyes darted nervously to the lights of the city, hoping that they would not be discovered. After a tense hour, the coach finally arrived and the party reached Gravesend where they were taken aboard a yacht and arrived safely at Calais the following day. Mary waited at Calais for the arrival of King James, who had promised to join them within twenty-four hours, but she received the frightening news that the king had been caught while attempting to escape and had been taken back to London. Mary decided to send the prince to Paris and then return to England to aid her husband, but she was persuaded by those around her to continue her journey. Louis XIV, King of France sent coaches to bring mother and son to the palace of Saint-Germain-en-Laye, where they arrived on 28 December.

King James, meanwhile, had been taken to a house at Rochester where Prince William had ordered him to be thinly guarded to permit his escape. In the early hours of 23 December, James secretly took ship to France. The family were reunited at Saint-Germain, which Louis bestowed upon them as their residence and where they constituted their court. King Louis treated them well and granted them an allowance of 50,000 livres per month, which was conveyed to the palace on an iron cart. Their numbers were swelled by exiles from England. These supporters were known as 'Jacobites', Jacobus being the Latin name for James.

In England, the king was declared to have vacated the throne and Prince William and Princess Mary, who came over to England on 12 February 1689, were crowned as joint monarchs. Two months after his arrival in France, King James travelled to Ireland, which was holding out against King William under the loyal Catholic the Duke of Tyrconnel. On 1 July 1690 James was defeated at the Battle of the Boyne and was forced to once again return to France, where he would spend the remainder of his life in religious devotion. On 28 June 1691, Queen Mary gave birth to a daughter, Louisa Maria Theresa, giving the lie to the claim that she could not bear a child. Louisa died of smallpox on 18 April 1712, aged twenty.

The Nine Years War against France, which England joined in 1702, was brought to an end by the Treaty of Ryswick in 1697. By its terms King Louis recognised William as king and promised not to aid James in retaking the throne, but the French king refused to evict James and his family from Saint-Germain. Somewhat surprisingly, King William handed King James an olive branch. Queen Mary II had died in 1694, and as William had no children he offered to make James Francis Edward his heir if the prince was sent into England and brought up in the Protestant religion. The idea of their son being brought up Protestant was too much to bear for the zealous Catholics James and Anne, and they blankly refused.

King James died on 16 September 1701 after suffering two strokes. The thirteen-year-old Prince James went to see his father on his deathbed and the dying king made him promise to adhere to the Catholic religion, to be obedient to his mother and to be grateful to the King of France. King Louis promised James that he would recognise the prince as King of England, Ireland and Scotland. Louis was true to his word, and once the old king was dead he had Prince James proclaimed as King James III of Great Britain outside the gate of Saint-Germain in direct contravention of the Treaty of Ryswick. The English Parliament responded by issuing the Act for the

Attainder of the Pretended Prince of Wales of High Treason, which passed the sentence of death on young James in addition to attainting him. The Act also stipulated that any person who had contact with or sent money to James or his adherents was guilty of high treason and would suffer the same fate.

King Louis provided for the education of the thirteen-year-old James. The young man had already studied the Classics, and Louis now provided him with tutors to teach him the 'masculine accomplishments' of navigation and fortification.[14] James was highly intelligent and was later reported to have spoken many European languages and to have had a mastery of navigation.

Just over six months after the death of James II, William III died. As stipulated in the Act of Settlement, he was succeeded by James's half-sister Queen Anne. This gave the Jacobites some hope that Anne, who had by now lost all of her children and would likely never produce an heir, would seek to overturn the Act of Settlement in favour of James. These hopes were to be disappointed, but in 1707 an opportunity arose to place James on the throne by force.

The '08

Queen Anne had continued the policy of her predecessor and declared war on France and Spain in what became known as the War of the Spanish Succession. On 16 January 1707, the Act of Union was passed by the English and Scottish parliaments, uniting England and Scotland under the name of Great Britain. The union was unpopular and many of the Scottish people resented being made subordinate to their ancient enemy. This provided fertile ground for an invasion of Scotland in the name of James, and King Louis began to canvas support in the country. Much of the Scottish nobility promised their support, but only if the prince took command in person.

By March 1708, King Louis had assembled a fleet of thirty-five ships at Dunkirk under the command of the Comte de Forbin and an army of 6,000 men. Accompanying the army was the now nineteen-year-old James, filled with the optimism of youth. He had developed into a tall and slender young man who bore some resemblance to his uncle Charles II. He was amiable, but the years of hardship had taken their toll on him. 'He is always cheerful but seldom merry,' notes Mr Lesly, the Protestant chaplain to his household, 'thoughtful but not dejected, and bears his misfortunes with a visible magnanimity of spirit.'[15] Like his father, James was a devoted Catholic but he also followed his father's principles of religious toleration and promised that if he became king he would allow freedom of conscience.

Before James departed, Louis presented to him a sword with a hilt studded with diamonds. 'Adieu!' he said, 'The best wish I can make you is, that I may never see your face again.'[16] The expedition met with disaster from the start. James developed measles and the resultant fever delayed the fleet's departure and allowed the English to send a fleet of thirty-eight men-of-war under the command of Sir George Byng to blockade the French outside Dunkirk. The Comte de Forbin was also unenthusiastic about the expedition, which he believed would be a failure, but when the English fleet was forced to retire due to strong winds King Louis forced him to set sail. The winds prevented the fleet from moving and they had to anchor among the shoals of Newport Pitts, where they spent the night being battered by gale-force winds. James's conduct impressed de Forbin. '[Y]oung as he was,' de Forbin wrote, '[James] faced the danger with a courage and coolness beyond his years.'[17]

They left Newport on the night of 19 March and on the 23rd they arrived at the mouth of the Firth of Forth and anchored off the Isle of May. The fleet's objective was to take Edinburgh Castle, after which James would be crowned as King James VIII of Scotland. They lit fires and fired their cannon as a pre-arranged signal to their accomplices on land but, ominously, nobody responded. That night they heard the distinct boom of cannon to the south and in the morning they were greeted with the sight of Byng's English fleet some 4 leagues away.

The French were anchored in a bay and in order to escape they were forced to bear down on the English as if to engage them and then veer off. A single English vessel pursued them and aimed for James's ship, the *Mars*, which so alarmed the prince's adherents that they recommended that he go aboard one of the frigates and make his way to his friends at Wemyss Castle in Fifeshire. The young prince was persuaded by their counsel but de Forbin refused, stating that the prince was perfectly safe on board, that King Louis had personally entrusted him with the prince's care and that he had been told to look after him as if he were the King of France himself. De Forbin's advice was sound as the English ship soon turned its attention to another of the ships, the *Salisbury*, which it proceeded to take. By the next day they had lost sight of the English and de Forbin decided to head for Inverness, but contrary winds and the lack of a local pilot to guide them forced the fleet back to Dunkirk. The expedition had failed.

The '15

Back in France, and with his prospects at a low ebb, James joined the French army in Flanders. He saw action at the battles of Oudenarde (11 July 1708) and Malplaquet (11 September 1709). Although both were defeats for the French. James was commended for his courage and bravery in the battles, which increased his popularity and reputation in France.

Meanwhile, his prospects were beginning to look up in England. In 1710, one Doctor Henry Sacheverell preached and printed a sermon against the Glorious Revolution and the following March he was impeached by Parliament. This act enraged the public and saw an end to the Whig supremacy in Parliament and the ascent of the Tories. Unfortunately for

James, the Tories wished to bring an end to the war and by the terms of the resultant Treaty of Utrecht, signed on 11 April 1713, James was sent into exile from France. James broke up his household at Saint-Germain and found refuge at Bar-le-Duc in Lorraine under the patronage of its duke, Leopold.

The following year (1714), Queen Anne died and George Louis, Elector of Hanover succeeded her as King George I, the first king of the Hanoverian dynasty. James once again sought the aid of King Louis but his steadfast ally died on 1 September and with him went the prospect of another French invasion. Louis was succeeded by his grandson Louis XV, who was only five years old, and the former king's nephew Philip, Duke of Orléans was appointed as regent. Duke Philip was in no position to aid James. Louis XV was a sickly child and if he were to die then Philip was next in line to the throne. Philip, however, had competition in the form of Louis XIV's grandson Philip V of Spain, and he thus planned on forming an alliance with England in case King Philip was to make his own bid for the throne.

While James and his court deliberated over their next move they received word from Scotland that John Erskine, 6th Earl of Mar, had rebelled in James's name in the Highlands. Mar had been among the commissioners responsible for the Act of Union and he had served as Secretary of State for Scotland under Queen Anne, but he had been snubbed by King George I on the latter's accession and now he wanted revenge. Donning a disguise, Mar travelled from London to Braemar in Scotland where, under the pretence of being a hunting party, he summoned the Highland chiefs and announced his plan to restore James to his rightful inheritance. On 6 September 1715, Mar raised his standard at Aboyne and declared James as King of England, Scotland and Wales. Ominously, the gilt ball on the top of the standard dropped off, something that was considered a bad omen by the superstitious Highlanders. Undaunted, Mar continued south to Perth, swelling his numbers along the way to 10,000, and set up camp. James was duly invited to come over to Scotland and take charge of the army.

George I sent John Campbell, Duke of Argyll with an army into Scotland and the duke took up station at Stirling Castle. Mar was slow to act, but on 13 November he encountered Argyll's army at the Battle of Sherriffmuir, near Dunblane. The fight was indecisive and was only ended by the coming of night. When Argyll awoke the following morning, he found that Mar had retreated to Perth to await the expected arrival of James.

James finally arrived at Peterhead on 22 December when he stepped for the first and last time onto the shores of his family's ancient hereditary kingdom. He met the Earl of Mar at Fetteresso and Mar had him proclaimed king at the gates of the house. Illness kept James confined at Fetteresso for a few days but once he had recovered he made his way towards Perth. On 5 January 1716 he entered Dundee on horseback, flanked by Mar on his right and George Keith, Earl Marischal on his left. He spent an hour in the marketplace where the joyful inhabitants greeted him and kissed his hand. The next day he travelled to Scone, the ancient coronation site of the Scottish kings. He entered Perth on 9 January to the joy of the Highlanders and inspected the army before returning to Scone. Joy soon turned into disappointment. The Highlanders were not impressed by the sullen and withdrawn figure that James cut. Years of hardship and misfortune had made him cold and overly serious and he never smiled. He spoke even less than he smiled, and when he did so he failed to clearly convey his thoughts. He did not venture to ingratiate himself with the men, to watch them handle their arms and exercise, or inspire them to fight for his cause. As a result, the Highlanders 'began to despise him', and 'some asked if he could speak'.[18]

By the end of January, word arrived that Argyll was about to march from Stirling. The Highlanders, although not inspired by James, were still resolved to fight but Mar advised a tactical retreat. James held a council of war on 29 January to discuss their options but was himself inclined to agree with Mar. At the end of the meeting, a few of the chiefs held a secret council where it was revealed that some of the soldiers were planning to make peace with Argyll and hand James over to him. James therefore resolved to flee, and the decision was announced to the army the next day. The army retreated across the frozen Tay to Dundee and thence north to Montrose. Some of James's adherents counselled that he should go back to France and await a more opportune moment to assert his rights. England had not risen in his name, no foreign aid had arrived and the English army were hot on their heels. James was reluctant, but it was pointed out that the army had the best chance of survival if James was to leave it. James agreed and on the evening of 4 February he boarded a small French vessel in the harbour along with Mar and some other Jacobites. The Highlanders, meanwhile, were left under the command of General Alexander Gordon and marched to Aberdeen before breaking up and going their separate ways.

James landed at Gravelines and then went to see his mother at Saint-Germain. It would be the last time that he saw her as Mary of Modena died in May 1718. James requested an interview with the regent Philip to request his aid, but Philip was eager for him to return to Lorraine and James had no choice but to pack up his belongings. This time, however, he found that the Duke of Lorraine was unable to offer him asylum and he was forced to take refuge in the papal state of Avignon. Pope Clement XI was more than happy to give refuge to the exiled Stuart whose father had lost his throne due to his devotion to the Catholic faith and who represented an opportunity to one day restore Catholicism to Great Britain and Ireland.

Plots and Marriage

In January 1717, France, England and Holland formed a Triple Alliance against Spain. Taking advantage of their temporary alliance, the English pushed the regent Philip to have James removed from Avignon. In February, James reluctantly crossed the Alps and headed for Rome. He was made welcome by Pope Clement, who granted James the use of Urbino Palace for his court and provided him with a pension of 12,000 scudi.

In 1718, a plot to restore James was set in train by Cardinal Giulio Alberoni, the guileful first minister of King Philip V of Spain. As part of the terms of the Treaty of Utrecht, King Philip V had ceded the Spanish-held lands in Italy to Emperor Charles VI, but Spain was eager to get them back. In June, the Spanish invaded and conquered Sicily. As a result, England, France, Holland and the Holy Roman Emperor entered into a Quadruple Alliance against Spain. England sent Admiral Byng, who had thwarted the invasion of 1708, into the Mediterranean where he defeated a Spanish fleet off the coast of Cape Passaro. Alberoni then turned his attention to England. He conspired with James Butler, Duke of Ormond and King Charles XII of Sweden to attack England, but the latter's death in December 1718 removed Sweden from the equation. A two-pronged attack was planned instead. The Duke of Ormonde and an army of 5,000 Spanish were to land in England while George Keith, Earl Marischal was to make for the Hebrides simultaneously and once again raise the Highlanders in James's name.

While Alberoni's plot was taking shape, James was in negotiations for the hand of Princess Clementina Sobieski, a granddaughter of John III, King of Poland. Since his return from Scotland, James's friends had pushed for him to marry and produce an heir. In early 1718, James sent Charles Wogan, a gentleman from Ireland, to Ohlau in Silesia to solicit the girl's hand. Wogan found the princess, then aged sixteen, to be highly enthusiastic at the prospect. Clementina, by a strange coincidence, had delighted in being called Queen of England by her friends when she was a girl, and it remained an affectionate nickname for her at court. Now Wogan offered her the chance of making an imaginary title a real one.[19] The marriage was agreed and the princess brought with her a large and much-needed dowry of 900,000 French livres.[20] James and his new wife were to meet at Bologna and there celebrate their marriage, but on his arrival James received some disastrous news. Clementina and her mother had been seized at Innsbruck in Austria. There they were being held in confinement in a convent on the orders of Emperor Charles.

The English, having caught wind of the marriage, had pressed the emperor to do what he could to prevent Clementina from reaching Italy. James sent Wogan to Innsbruck to see if he could effect her release, and as he waited for news he was invited to come to Madrid to join the Spanish invasion force. In order to hide his intentions from enemy spies, James announced that he was going to Bologna to meet the princess and he sent Mar and others to act as a decoy while he secretly took ship at Nettuno. Mar and the other decoys were arrested at Voghera and taken to the castle of Milan, but when it was discovered that James was not among them they were released. James reached the port of Rosas on 9 March 1719 after braving sea storms and suffering from a fever which kept him confined in the house of the 'master of the ship' at Marseilles for a period of three days.[21] He proceeded to Madrid, where he met King Charles III of Spain and his queen and took up residence at the palace of Buen Retiro. On 17 April he travelled to Corunna to await the arrival of the Spanish fleet from Cadiz, but as with all the Jacobite plots, this one, too, met with disaster. The fleet was scattered by a storm and was forced to return to Cadiz while the Earl Marischal, although successfully landing in Scotland, failed to raise a large Highlander host and was defeated at the Battle of Glen Shiel on 10 June.

Later Years and Death

Wogan, in the meantime, had come up with a plan to free Princess Clementina. Chatteaudeau, a gentleman usher to the princess's mother, had become friendly with the porter at the gate of the convent that served as Clementina's prison and had taken to bringing in women from the town. He noticed that the porter did not enquire into the women's identities but merely winked. On the night of 27 April, Chatteaudeau took with him a maid named Jenny to act as a decoy for the princess. Jenny was escorted to Clementina's chamber, handed the captive woman her cloak and took her place in the bed. Chatteaudeau led the princess to the gate and bade her farewell as the unsuspecting porter looked on.[22] Wogan met Clementina outside the gate and she was taken to an inn before boarding a coach. She made it safely to Bologna, where she and James were married by proxy on 9 May. James returned to Italy in August following the failed Spanish expedition and summoned Clementina to meet him at Montefiascone, where they married on 1 September. Afterwards, they returned to Rome and set up court at the Palazzo Muti. The palace, located in the Piazza di Sant' Apostoli, would remain as James's main residence until his death. The pope treated him as if he were a reigning sovereign and provided him with a company of guards who would accompany him wherever he went.

Clementina gave birth to two sons: Charles Edward Stuart, the famous 'Bonnie Prince Charlie', on 31 December 1720 and Henry Benedict Stuart, the future Cardinal York, on 6 March 1725. The marriage, however, proved unhappy. James was cold and withdrawn, always plotting his next move, and had little time for his young and vivacious wife. In December 1724 he made Colonel John Hay, a Protestant and titular Earl of Inverness, his secretary of state. Hay and his wife Marjory Murray took up residence at the palace and they came to exert a malign influence over James, much to Clementina's chagrin. She held the Hays responsible for the dismissal of Mrs Sheldon, her close confidante and nurse to Prince Charles, who was replaced by Marjory's brother James Murray, Lord Dunbar. Dunbar was a Protestant and Mrs Sheldon played upon Clementina's fears that her child would be brought up a Protestant and even claimed that Marjory was James's mistress. At the end of 1725, the dejected and petulant Clementina moved into the Convent of St Cecilia and announced that she would not return to her husband until the Hays were removed from his society.

The strained relations between James and Clementina had a detrimental effect upon James's prospects. Pope Benedict XIII threatened to stop James's pension and the English Jacobites were split over the matter. As a result, James was forced to let Hay go in 1727 and Clementina, after a two-year absence, returned to court. Before she arrived the news of the death of King George I on 11 June 1727 had caused James to head immediately to Nancy, the capital of Lorraine, to take advantage of the developing situation. None of his adherents or foreign allies offered to help him and the Duke of Lorraine was pressured into once again sending him packing. James afterwards went to Avignon but he was once again forced to return to Italy, where he was re-joined by Clementina at Bologna. James and Clementina would stay together until her death eight years later, but the couple remained unhappy. She found refuge in her religion and died of tuberculosis on 18 January 1735, being buried in the crypt of St Peter's. After her death, James became more dejected and he appeared little in public. He spent his mornings in prayer near her tomb and then retired to his closet, only appearing for dinner, where he spoke little before returning to his closet.

Jacobite hopes were now becoming centred on the rising sun of Charles Edward Stuart. In 1744, the twenty-three-year-old Charles was to head a new invasion of England in conjunction with Louis XV of France. James agreed that if the invasion was successful then Charles would act as regent of the three kingdoms until the time of his own arrival. Charles travelled to Paris incognito and then went to Gravelines, where the invasion fleet was amassing under Marshal Maurice de Saxe, Count of Saxony. The English had caught wind of the plot and sent Sir John Norris at the head of a fleet to intercept it while the French, on their retreat, were hit by a storm which wrecked many of their ships. Charles returned to Paris and, finding no further assistance from King Louis, rashly fitted out his own expedition the following year in the hope of inspiring the Highlanders and English Jacobites by his sudden arrival. He raised funds by pawning his mother's jewels and taking out loans with which he brought guns, broadswords and field pieces. He also leased the *Elizabeth*, a French man-of-war, and a brig, the *Doutelle*, to convey him and his supplies to Scotland.

Charles first notified James of his intent in a letter in which he explained his reasons for fitting out an expedition. 'Your Majesty cannot disapprove a son's following the example of his father. You yourself did the like in the year 15,' he reasoned. 'But the circumstances now are indeed very different, by being much more encouraging, there being a certainty of succeeding with the least help.'[23] He had not told his father of his plan, he revealed, in case James 'might have thought what I had a mind to do, to be rash; and so have absolutely forbid my proceedings'.[24]

Charles landed at Eriskay on 23 July 1745 and marched south, recruiting many Highlanders to his cause. He took Edinburgh on 17 September and then proceeded south towards England, defeating the army of Sir John Cope at the Battle of Prestonpans on 21 September. From there he took Carlisle and then proceeded to Derby where disagreements between his generals, a lack of English recruits and an approaching English army forced him to turn back.

James, meanwhile, sent into France his younger son, Henry Benedict, who was eager to join his brother. The capture of Edinburgh and defeat of Cope had convinced King Louis to fit out an expedition from Dunkirk with Henry at its head, but this was called off when word arrived of Charles's retreat from Derby. Charles was defeated at the Battle of Culloden, near Inverness, on 16 April 1746 and fled the battlefield. James was clueless as to the fate of his fugitive son until Charles's sudden arrival at Roscoff in Brittany. The young man received a hero's welcome in Paris but he was not granted the help he sought from King Louis. He instead tried his luck in Spain, but after securing an audience with King Ferdinand he was told that the king could not offer him help at that time. He returned indignantly to Paris, where he was greeted with the news that Henry Benedict was to become a cardinal at Rome. Henry had long harboured dreams of entering the church but he had put them aside for his family's cause. Now, believing that cause to be hopeless, he had notified James of his desire. James did not tell Charles until shortly before Henry's creation as cardinal in order to prevent him from creating any obstacles as he and Henry had foreseen that he might not approve. Charles was indeed furious, but there was little he could do.

Further disappointment was to come. The Treaty of Aix-la-Chapelle, agreed on 18 October 1748, between England, France and the Netherlands, led to Charles's dismissal from France. He wandered from place to place, wasted away by drink and loose living, until his father's death.

James himself remained at Rome for the rest of his life, never seeing his dynasty restored to its rightful inheritance. Illness confined him to bed for the last five years of his life until he died on 1 January 1766 at the age of seventy-seven. He was buried in the crypt of St Peter's Basilica beside Clementina.

Charles returned to Rome after James's death but he was not recognised as Charles III by the pope and had to settle for the title of Duke of Albany. In April 1772, he married Princess Louisa of Stolberg. Like his parents' marriage, it proved unhappy. It produced no children and the two separated in 1784. Charles had an illegitimate daughter, Charlotte, by his mistress Clementina Walkinshaw and he had her legitimated and made his heir. She nursed him until his death on 30 January 1788, but died herself the following year. Cardinal Henry passed away in 1807, and he and Charles, who had been refused burial at St Peter's, were laid to rest beside their father. The Stuart line became extinct with the death of Charles Edward, Charlotte's only son, in 1854.

24

Frederick Louis, Prince of Wales

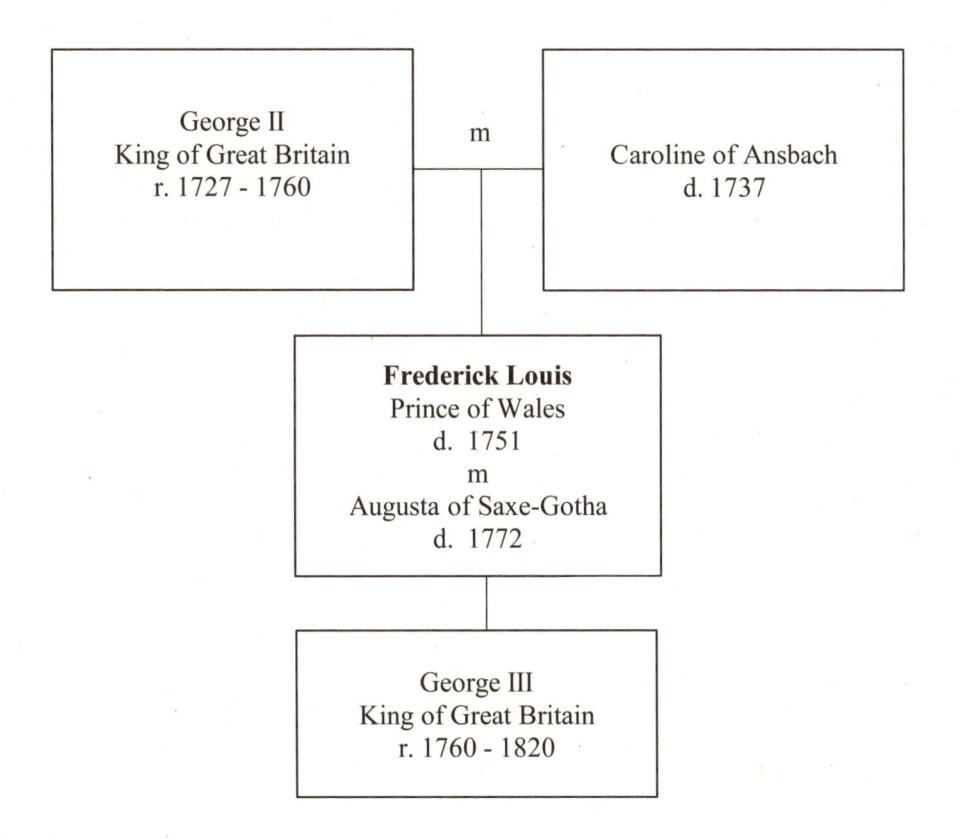

```
┌─────────────────────┐       ┌─────────────────────┐
│    George II        │       │  Caroline of Ansbach│
│ King of Great Britain│──m──│       d. 1737       │
│   r. 1727 - 1760    │       │                     │
└─────────────────────┘       └─────────────────────┘
              │
      ┌───────────────────┐
      │  Frederick Louis  │
      │  Prince of Wales  │
      │     d. 1751       │
      │       m           │
      │Augusta of Saxe-Gotha│
      │     d. 1772       │
      └───────────────────┘
              │
      ┌───────────────────┐
      │    George III     │
      │King of Great Britain│
      │   r. 1760 - 1820  │
      └───────────────────┘
```

'[M]y dear first-born is the greatest ass and the greatest liar, and the greatest *canaille*, and the greatest beast in the whole world, and ... I most heartily wish he was out of it.'[1] These were the venomous words spoken by Queen Caroline of Ansbach, the wife of King George II, to describe their eldest son and heir, Frederick Louis, Prince of Wales, in 1737. The prince had recently defied his parent's order that his pregnant wife, Augusta, Princess of Wales, give birth to a potential heir to the crown under their roof at Hampton Court Palace. The king and queen distrusted and disliked their son so much that they even thought him incapable of producing a child and feared that he planned to deceive them and the country by introducing a suppositious child who would one day become King of England. When Augusta went into labour, Frederick secreted her away at St James's Palace where she gave birth to a baby daughter. The king and queen were furious when they discovered their son's insolence, but the sex and size of the child reassured them that the baby was in fact the prince's. Even so, this did not stop them from throwing the new parents and child out of the royal palaces and out of royal favour.

Birth and Early Life

Frederick Louis, Prince of Wales, the eldest son of George II and Queen Caroline of Ansbach, was born at Herrenhausen Palace, just outside the city of Hanover, on 20 January 1707. At the time of his birth Frederick was fourth in line to the throne following his great-grandmother Sophia, Electress of Hanover, his grandfather the Elector George Louis and his father, George Augustus, Electoral Prince of Hanover and Duke of Cambridge.

There is little record of Frederick's early life, which he spent at Herrenhausen with his father, mother and grandfather, but we know it was a far from happy existence. Georges senior and junior bore a mutual hatred for one another, the source of which is unrecorded but may stem from the younger George's resentment at the treatment of his mother, Sophia Dorothea, whom George had kept in confinement since her affair with Count Philip von Königsmarck, or from the elder George's dislike of a son born from his hated wife. Whatever the case, this animosity between father and son would become a hereditary trait in the family and one that was inherited by George II, Frederick Louis, Frederick's son George III, and George III's eldest son, George IV. It was only Frederick's early death that prevented his relationship with George III from following the same pattern.

From as early as 1712, there were discussions about Frederick marrying his cousin Wilhelmina, the Princess Royal of Prussia. Wilhelmina was the eldest daughter of King Frederick William I of Prussia and George I's daughter Sophia Dorothea. Frederick was keen on the idea from the start. 'My little admirer began, even at that time, to send me presents,' Wilhelmina recounts in her memoirs, 'and no post-day passed without these princesses corresponding about the future union of their children.'[2]

Both Electress Sophia and Queen Anne died in 1714 and as per the terms of the Act of Settlement, Elector George Louis became King George I of Great Britain. George Augustus, now Prince of Wales and heir to the throne, accompanied the new king to England, followed a month later by Princess Caroline and Frederick's three sisters, Anne, Amelia and Caroline. King George, however, decreed that the seven-year-old Frederick was to remain behind at Hanover to act as a representative of the family. He would not see his parents for another fourteen years, a fact that no doubt contributed to their difficult relationship.

Lady Mary Wortley Montagu, who visited the Hanoverian court in November 1716, has left us a picture of the then nine-year-old Fredrick in a letter she penned to Elizabeth Hervey, Countess of Bristol. She spoke with Frederick for some time, she tells us, and was impressed with what she saw and heard. 'I am extremely pleased that I can tell you, without either flattery or partiality, that our young prince has all the accomplishments that it is possible to have at his age, with an air of sprightliness and understanding, and something so very engaging and easy in his behaviour, that he needs not the advantage of his rank to appear charming,' she earnestly relates. 'I was surprised at the quickness and politeness that appeared in every thing he said; joined to a person perfectly agreeable, and the fine fair hair of the princess.'[3]

Unfortunately, the young Frederick was corrupted by the dissolute Hanoverian court, where he picked up the vices of drinking and gambling and the family predilection for mistresses. Horace Walpole, the son of Sir Robert Walpole, tells us in his diary that beauty was not a prerequisite of these mistresses.[4] Frederick's first mistress, the "elderly' Madame d'Elitz, 'had a thousand lovers' and listed among her conquests both Frederick's father and grandfather.[5]

In 1720, the marriage between Frederick and Princess Wilhelmina once again came under discussion and it was agreed that a double marriage should take place, with Frederick's sister Amelia marrying Frederick, Prince Royal of Prussia, the future Frederick 'the Great'. In October 1724, King George I, during one of his many visits to Hanover, travelled to Berlin to satisfy himself of the truth of rumours that Wilhelmina was plain and extremely deformed. He examined her 'from head to foot' by candlelight, not speaking a word and for what must have felt like an eternity to the poor girl.[6] Satisfied that the rumours were false, he agreed to a treaty of alliance and the double marriage, but the treaty was never signed. The death of George I in June 1727 finally put paid to it as George II bore a mutual hatred for King Frederick and was dead set against the match.

On 22 October 1727, George Augustus was crowned as King George II of Great Britain and Ireland at Westminster. Frederick, now heir apparent to the throne, was not present and he remained at Hanover where awaiting a summons by his parents. The jealous king did not want his eldest son to be present in England for fear that he might become a beacon for the opposition and undermine the governance of the realm. King George, when himself Prince of Wales, had formed such a court of opposition at Leicester House and had proved the bane of his father.

Frederick remained at Hanover for another eighteen months. King George ignored the calls of Parliament and the people to bring him over and it took a rash move on Frederick's part to finally cause George to summon him. Frederick was still besotted with the idea of marrying Princess Wilhelmina, and in a deliberate act of defiance he sent a messenger to his aunt Queen Sophia of Prussia to notify her of his intention to come secretly to Berlin and marry the princess without his father's knowledge. The delighted queen made the mistake of revealing the plan to the English ambassador at Berlin, who glumly informed her that he was duty bound to inform King George. George was furious at his son's duplicity and was convinced by Sir Robert Walpole, his Prime Minister, to send immediately for the prince to come to England where he could be kept under royal supervision.

England

Frederick arrived in England on 7 December 1728 to a sombre welcome. No one greeted him on his arrival and he was forced to make his way from Whitechapel to St James's Palace aboard a common hackney carriage. He entered the queen's apartments via a back staircase and saw his parents and siblings for the first time in fourteen years. He now had a little brother, the seven-year-old William Augustus, Duke of Cumberland, whom he had never met and who was the apple of his parent's eye.

Things began well. The Countess of Bristol, in a letter penned to her husband on 7 January 1729, describes the prince as 'the most agreeable young man it is possible to imagine, without being the least handsome; his person little, but very well made and genteel; a liveliness in his eyes that is indescribable, and the most obliging address that can be conceived'. His crowning glory, she states, was the duty and regard that he paid towards the king and queen, who were equally fond of their son. She finished her letter with the wish that 'Pray God long to continue it'.[7] Unfortunately, God had other plans and relations soon became strained between parents and son. George refused to pay the debts the prince incurred during his time at Hanover and would only grant him an income of £24,000 per annum from the Civil List, even though Parliament had set aside £100,000 for him. Frederick was created Prince of Wales and Earl of Chester on 8 January 1729 but he was not granted his own establishment and he was forced to live under his parent's supervision at St James's. Frederick fought fire with fire. He rashly accepted the proposal of the shrewd Sarah Churchill, Duchess of Marlborough, who offered him the hand of her granddaughter Lady Diana Spencer and an accompanying dowry of £100,000. The wedding was set to take place at the duchess's lodge at Richmond Park, but it came to the attention of Walpole, who notified the king. The marriage was prevented but the episode served to strain relations with his parents further.

The king's fear that Frederick would become a centre of opposition created a self-fulfilling prophecy as Frederick was forced to turn to the opposition to borrow money and fight his battles in Parliament. He befriended George Bubb Dodington, a vain and wealthy politician whose overriding ambition in life was to secure himself a peerage. Dodington had originally been a disciple of Walpole, but when the latter refused to grant him a peerage he latched on to the prince as his best means of achieving it. He acted as his chief adviser and moneylender and shared in the extravagant prince's debaucheries involving women and gambling. Once, on seeing Dodington pass by his window at Kensington Palace, the prince remarked to his secretary, 'That man is reckoned one of the most sensible men in England, yet with all his parts, I have just nicked him out of five thousand pounds.'[8]

Lord Hervey

Frederick was unfortunate enough to get on the wrong side of John, Lord Hervey, the effeminate son of John Hervey, Earl of Bristol and his wife Elizabeth. The two were firm friends at first but they fell out when Frederick stole Lord Hervey's mistress, Anne Vane, a maid of honour of the queen, and got her pregnant. Anne gave birth to an illegitimate son, Fritz-Frederick Vane, in 1732.

Lord Hervey served as vice-chamberlain to the king's household and was a close confidant of Queen Caroline. The two shared a mutual hatred of Frederick, and it is from Lord Hervey's memoirs that we derive much of our information about him. This, of course, gives us a largely partisan and negative view which must be treated with caution.

Princess Augusta

Frederick was frustrated when in 1733 the king announced that Anne, the Princess Royal, was to marry William, Prince of Orange and be granted a large marriage jointure. Frederick was now twenty-six years old, still unmarried and heavily in debt. He believed that as heir apparent to the throne he should be married first. In 1734, Frederick demanded an audience with the king in which he made three requests: to lead an army in the Rhine, to have his income increased to help pay his debts, and to have a suitable marriage arranged by the king. The king refused his first request outright but agreed to consider the other two.[9]

The king reluctantly gave Frederick some money towards his debts and when he paid a visit to Hanover in 1735 he selected a bride for the prince in the form of the sixteen-year-old Princess Augusta, daughter of Frederick II, Duke of Saxe-Gotha. In 1736, Lord Delaware was sent to demand the hand of the princess. The marriage was agreed and on Sunday 25 April the new Princess of Wales, now seventeen, arrived at Greenwich to little pomp and ceremony. Frederick immediately repaired to Greenwich where he conversed with his new bride in German for several hours. The prince was delighted by his bride-to-be and the following day he took her for a romantic trip down the Thames to the Tower and back aboard his barge to the accompaniment of musicians. The couple afterwards dined 'in public', seated before an open window in the palace where people could catch a glimpse of their future king and queen.[10] On Tuesday 27 April, the day of the marriage, Augusta was conducted to St James's Palace. The princess was an hour late and, on entering the drawing room, 'threw herself all along on the floor first at the King's and then at the queen's feet', in a display that served to calm the haughty king's temper.[11] Later, Frederick and Augusta ate dinner with his younger brother the Duke of Cumberland and the princesses in his apartments. Unfortunately, petty questions over precedence disturbed proceedings – the prince ordered his siblings to sit on stools and not to be served on the knee as was custom but the princesses, jealous of their royal station, refused to sit until they were given armed chairs and were served by their own servants.[12] The marriage itself took place at 9 p.m. in the Chapel Royal at St James's. The couple were then seen to bed, the prince wearing a nightgown 'of silver stuff' and a cap 'of the finest lace.'[13] Members of the nobility were herded through the bedchamber to see the couple sat upright in bed, surrounded by the royal family, before they were left alone to consummate the marriage.

In his memoirs, Lord Hervey describes Princess Augusta as tall and ungainly, with an ordinary air 'which no trappings could cover or exalt'.[14] The queen saw her as a mere puppet of her son and thought her harmless and stupid.[15] Augusta was still childish and the footguards and sentinels of Kensington Palace would laugh at her habit of dressing a 'great jointed baby' doll by the window.[16] Princess Caroline eventually warned Augusta not to dress the doll so publicly so that she did not suffer ridicule.

Shortly after the wedding, King George went to Hanover to be with his mistress and left the queen to act as regent in his absence, a role that Frederick considered should have been his as heir apparent. In December, the king was making preparations to return to England when a great storm broke out at sea. It was believed that he had already set sail and had been caught in the storm and lost. This was not true, but it seemed for a moment that Frederick might come into his inheritance. Soon, word reached England that the king was safe. Once the storm abated, he was thought to have then set sail. Unexpectedly, another storm raged and it was again supposed that the king had been lost. Fears were heightened when one ship of the king's fleet arrived, its masts cut, and its crew reported that the king had indeed set sail and that they did not know what had happened to him. Then, on the 26th, the queen received a letter from the king reporting that he had managed to limp back to port. He finally arrived in England in early January.

Money Problems

If Frederick believed that the king would now grant him his own establishment and finally increase his revenues to £100,000, he was to be disappointed. The king reluctantly agreed to up his revenue from £24,000 to £50,000 but he would not provide him with an establishment or even grant Augusta a jointure as Princess of Wales. The opposition, led by William Pulteney, pressed the prince to raise the matter in Parliament. The king was ill with a fever and piles at the time and Lord Hervey makes the unlikely suggestion that the prince hoped it would cause the king such anguish as to finish him off. On Monday 21 February, the day before the question of Frederick's revenue was to be brought before the Commons, the king sent members of the Cabinet Council to confirm the prince's allowance and to provide Augusta with a jointure in order to prevent the matter being raised. Frederick listened to the proposal but declared that the matter was now out of his hands.

On Tuesday 22 February, Pulteney brought the motion before the Commons in an eloquent speech. He acknowledged that the prince's allowance had only been given tacitly at the time that the Civil List was granted but that it was generally understood that he was to receive £100,000, the same amount the king had himself received as Prince of Wales. Walpole then rose from his seat and spoke of the king's attempts at making a settlement the day before and the prince's haughty response. He pointed out that the allowance for the members of the royal family had been left to the king's discretion and that Parliament had no right to dictate how his majesty should distribute it. When it came to the vote, the prince lost by just thirty votes (234 to 204) and when it was brought before the House of Lords the next day it was defeated by sixty-three votes.

Exile

The king and queen, elated by their unexpected victory, wished to throw their disobedient son out of St James's Palace but they were dissuaded by Walpole's warning that such an act would cause him to form a rival court. Frederick remained at St James's and continued to attend the drawing rooms, to dine with his parents and to attend levees (events where monarchs could be approached by invited subjects). The king would not acknowledge Frederick's presence and passed him by as if he were a ghost, while Queen Caroline would grant him her hand as was custom but would not utter a word to him.

The final breach between Frederick and his parents was occasioned by the birth of his and Augusta's first child. On 5 July 1737, Frederick announced that Augusta was pregnant and that she was to give birth in October. The king and queen, blinded by hate, came up with the preposterous theory that Frederick was unable to reproduce and that he planned to deceive them and the country with someone else's child. To prevent this, the queen vied to be there when the child was born. '[A]t her labour I positively will be, let her lie-in where she will,' she announced to Lord Hervey, 'for she cannot be brought to bed as quick as one can blow one's nose, and I will be sure it is her child.'[17] King George ordered that the birth take place at Hampton Court, where he was then residing, but Frederick had no desire for his parents to be present when the child was born. He had in fact lied about the due date and on the evening of 31 July the princess went into labour shortly after dining with the king and queen. Frederick secretly ordered a coach to be made ready to transport her to St James's and she was carried down the stairs and into the waiting vehicle, the prince rallying her with the cry of 'Courage! Courage! *Ah, quelle sottise*!' when she pleaded to remain at Hampton Court.[18] They made the palace by 10 p.m. but it was not set up for the birth of a child and the princess was put to bed in between two tablecloths. Forty-five minutes later she gave birth to a little girl, named Augusta, whom Lord Hervey spitefully calls a 'little rat of a girl, about the bigness of a good large toothpick-case'.[19]

The king and queen were roused with the news that Augusta was in labour – at St James's. The queen quickly got changed and arrived at the palace at 4 a.m. She found Frederick in Augusta's antechamber, where he kissed her hand and cheek and announced the birth of their daughter. The astonished queen was led into the princess's bedchamber where she was shown the newborn baby. The queen was incensed at the prince's actions but was nonetheless convinced of the child's genuineness. 'Well, upon my honour, I no more doubt this poor little bit of a thing is the princess's child ... if, instead of this poor, little, ugly she-mouse, there had been a brave, large, fat, jolly boy, I should not have been cured of my suspicions,' she told Lord Hervey.[20] King George and Queen Caroline decided to use the prince's insolence towards them as a reason to expel him from St James's. A letter was penned and signed by the king, approved by the Cabinet Council and delivered to the prince on 10 September. In the letter the king berated Frederick for concealing the princess's pregnancy for so long and for endangering both Augusta and the baby by moving them to St James's. He declared, 'My pleasure, therefore, is that you and all your family remove from St James's as soon as ever the safety and convenience of the princess will permit.'[21] When Frederick heard the message he 'changed colour several times' but remained civil and told the messengers to tell the king that he was sorry for what had happened.[22] Orders were given to the peers and privy counsellors that they should not visit the prince and that if they did so they would no longer be welcome at court.

On Monday 12 September, Frederick, Augusta and baby Augusta moved into Kew House. The plight of the ousted couple garnered the sympathy of the people. When Frederick attended the play *Cato* in London he was applauded on his entrance as was custom, but when the titular character uttered the lines 'When vice prevails, and impious men bear sway, the post of honour is a private station,' the audience huzzaed him.[23] The prince played upon this sympathy, giving printed copies of the king's letter of eviction to the mayor and aldermen of London at an audience at Carlton House. The king and the prince both had their letters published to give their side of the story.

Frederick leased Norfolk House in St James's Square, London, where he formed his court of opposition. In November, the prince received news of the queen having fallen mortally ill. Queen Caroline complained of pain in her

Frederick Louis, Prince of Wales

stomach and bowels, caused by a rupture to her womb occasioned by the birth of her last child, Louisa, in 1724. The king was aware of the rupture but the queen, fearing that it would lessen her hold over him, refused to speak of it and it had been brushed under the royal carpet. The pain would occasionally flare up and the king would press her to see a surgeon but he eventually agreed to never raise the subject again.[24]

On Friday 11 November, the prince went to Carlton House in Pall Mall to be near the queen but the king forbade him from seeing her, believing that the prince only wished to play the part of the caring and dutiful son. The prince, nevertheless, sent daily messengers to St James's to inquire into his mother's health and as her condition worsened these 'ravens', as the queen called them, became more frequent visitors.[25] Lord Hervey, always seeking to portray the prince in a bad light, said that the prince would wait up all night at Carlton House hoping to hear news of her death. 'Well, sure we shall soon have good news,' he would say, 'she cannot hold out much longer.'[26] He attributes the source of this information to those close to the prince, but Hervey, who himself relates that he was always ready to 'give the prince a slap', is not to be trusted.[27] The prince's thoughts cannot be known but it is likely that he was genuinely concerned about his mother.

The king eventually revealed the queen's ailment to his surgeons and she was put under the knife. Unfortunately, it proved too late. She died on the night of Sunday 20 November and was buried a month later at Westminster Abbey. The prince was never reconciled to his mother and he did not attend her funeral.

Princess Augusta, meanwhile, continued to bear children. Their first son, George, the future George III, was born on 24 May 1738 at Norfolk House. There followed Edward Augustus in 1739, Elizabeth Caroline in 1740, William Henry in 1743 and Henry Frederick in 1745.

Frederick and the opposition found their chance to bring down Walpole in the conflict with Spain known as the War of Jenkins' Ear. Walpole was committed to peace but the people cried out for war. He was finally made to acquiesce to their wishes in 1739, but with the war going badly the prime minister was forced to resign in 1742. He was created Earl of Orford and died in 1745.

After Walpole's resignation, Frederick was advised to write a submissive letter to the king and they were reconciled, with the prince finally granted his coveted £100,000 annual allowance. Alas, the reconciliation proved superficial. When the War of Jenkins' Ear developed into the War of the Austrian Succession, Frederick requested to be given command of the army but was overlooked in favour of his brother the Duke of Cumberland. He was also denied a military role in 1745 when Bonnie Prince Charlie invaded England. As the royal army besieged Carlisle, Frederick had to content himself with throwing cherry plums at a pastry model of the castle that he had ordered to be made for dessert.

Death

In the last few years of his life, Frederick assumed that the ageing George II was nearing the end of his days and began to ponder the policies he would pursue as king. He was not provided with the opportunity to put these policies into practice. On 5 March 1751, the forty-four-year-old prince developed a pleurisy but recovered enough to attend the king at the House of Lords on the 12th. The prince, dressed in his ceremonial robes, was extremely hot and when he afterwards went to Carlton House he exchanged them for a lighter frock. He then proceeded to Kew where he spent a few hours walking in the gardens. On his return to Carlton House that evening, he reclined upon a couch beside an open window for three hours and caught a chill. The next day he was worse and complained of a pain in his side. He was attended by three doctors and a surgeon who bled him twice and opened blisters on his back and legs. On the 15th he had 'a plentiful evacuation' of his bowels and seemed to be on the mend, but he soon grew worse.[28] On the night of the 20th, the prince had a violent fit of coughing. One of the doctors remarked optimistically to the prince that since he had brought up all the phlegm he might sleep soundly the rest of the night. Another of the doctors, on leaving the room, confessed, 'Here is something I don't like.'[29]

The prince's coughing fit continued until about quarter to ten when he suddenly placed a hand on his stomach and announced, '*Je sens la mort*' or 'I feel death.'[30] Pavonarius, the prince's valet-de-chambre, who was holding him in a reclining position, felt his body shiver and shouted out, 'Good God! The prince is going!'[31] Augusta, dutifully sat at the foot of the bed, bolted upright and grabbed a candle but by the time she reached his side the prince had expired. Consumed by grief, she refused to accept that he was dead and remained at his side until six in the morning when her ladies finally convinced her to retire to bed. By eight she was up again, burning the prince's private papers and correspondence.

As soon as Frederick died, Lord North was sent to notify the king. King George was playing at cards when he received the news. He immediately went to Lady Yarmouth and, turning ghostly pale, said simply, '*Il est mort!*'[32] The following morning Frederick's body was opened up and an abscess was discovered in his side that had reportedly burst and killed him. The abscess was thought to have been the result of the impact of a tennis ball that had struck him in the side some three years before, or a fall that he had had that summer which had caused him some pain afterwards. It is more likely that he died of the less fanciful pneumonia.

King George seems to have been deeply affected by the prince's death, although Horace Walpole suggests that he enjoyed playing the role of 'the tender grandfather' to his little grandchildren.[33] This act, Walpole notes, soon turned genuine. He went to see Augusta on 31 March and spurned his chair of state to sit with the princess upon a couch where he embraced her and let out his emotions.

While King George had thus far shown more regard for his son in death than in life, he did not attend the funeral, held on 13 April. The funeral was not characterised by the usual pomp and ceremony. Bubb Dodington in his diary notes that other than the pallbearers and attendants of the chief mourner there were no English lords or bishops present but only one Irish lord, two sons of two Irish dukes, one baron's son and two privy counsellors, including Dodington himself. Edward Seymour, 8th Duke of Somerset, acted as chief mourner, notwithstanding, Dodington points out, 'the flourishing state of the royal family'.[34] The prince's body, and his bowels housed in a separate box covered in red velvet, had been placed in his apartments in the House of Lords and were guarded by his gentlemen of the bedchamber.

At seven o'clock the procession began. The weather was rainy and the mourners were not given any cover as they made their way from the House of Lords to Westminster Abbey, where they entered the Henry VII Chapel through the south-east door and laid the prince to rest in the vault beside his mother without anthem or organ. Once the shock was over, King George returned to his usual dislike of his son, saying spitefully, 'This has been a fatal year to my family! I lost my eldest son – but I am glad of it.'[35]

25

Frederick, Duke of York and Albany

```
                George III          m    Charlotte of Mecklenburg-
              King of Great Britain        Strelitz
                r. 1760 - 1820                d. 1818
```

George IV	Frederick	William IV	Edward
King of Great Britain	Duke of York and Albany	King of Great Britain	Duke of Kent
r. 1820 - 1830	d. 1827	r. 1830 - 1837	d. 1820
m	m	m	m
Caroline of Brunswick-Wolfenbuttel	Frederica Charlotte Ulrica	Adelaide of Saxe-Meiningen	Victoria of Saxe-Coburg
d. 1821	d. 1820	d. 1849	d. 1861

Charlotte Augusta
d. 1817

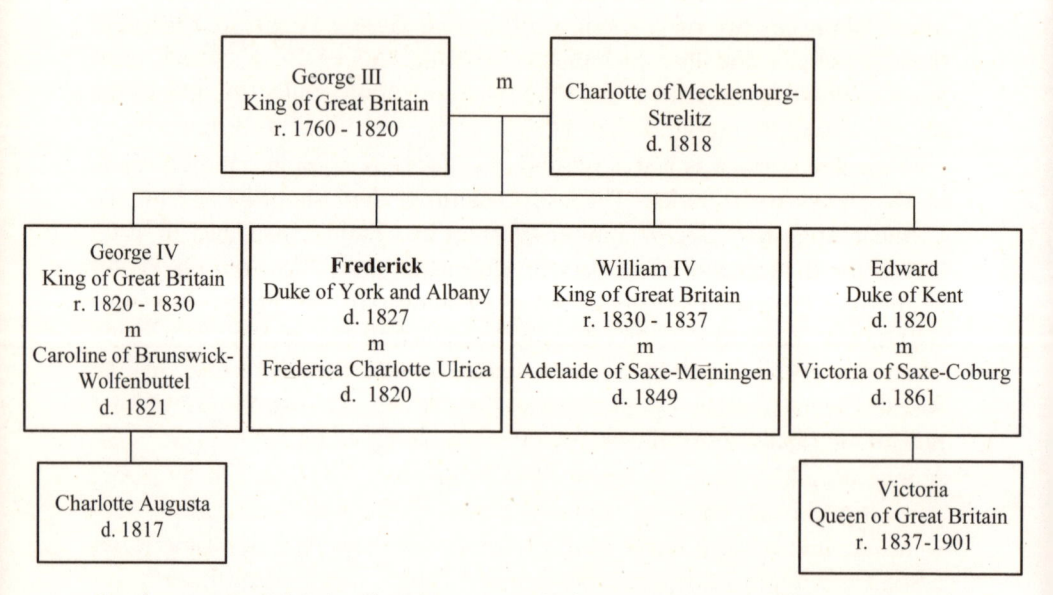

Victoria
Queen of Great Britain
r. 1837-1901

On the evening of 8 April 1834, a crowd of spectators gathered at St James's Park to watch as a statue of the late Frederick, Duke of York and Albany, was hoisted up to top the new monument erected in his memory. The statue, secured by slings and chains wrapped around its arms and raised by a windlass, ascended the 94-foot column with ease. Once it had reached its destination it was affixed to the pedestal and soldered into place. Just over two weeks later, on Wednesday 23 April, the Duke of York's monument was unveiled to the public in a ceremony that cost a shilling per head to attend.

The monument had been commissioned to commemorate the public services of the Duke of York in his role as Commander-in-Chief of the British Army. Frederick was responsible for reforming the British Army, and it was these great reforms that were said to have secured the victory against Napoleon. But today Frederick is best remembered as the likely candidate for the incompetent 'Grand Old Duke of York' immortalised in the nursery rhyme.

Birth and Early Life

Frederick, Duke of York and Albany, the second son of King George III and Queen Charlotte of Mecklenburg-Strelitz, was born at Buckingham House at around ten o'clock on the morning of 16 August 1763.[1] On 14 September, he was baptised by the venerable Dr Thomas Secker, Archbishop of Canterbury and bestowed with the name Frederick in honour of his grandfather Frederick Louis, Prince of Wales.

At the time of Frederick's birth, George III had been king of Great Britain for nearly three years, having ascended the throne on 25 October 1760 on the death of George II. George III had married Princess Charlotte of Mecklenburg-Strelitz on 8 October 1761 and George Augustus Frederick, their eldest son and heir and the future King George IV, had been born ten months later on 12 August 1762. Just over a year later, Frederick, the obligatory spare, entered the world.

When Frederick was just seven months old he was granted the bishopric of Osnabrück by his father. The last occupant of the bishopric, the Catholic Clement Augustus, Elector and Archbishop of Cologne, had died in 1761 and as per the terms of the Treaty of Westphalia it was down to George III to choose a Protestant successor from the Hanoverian line. Frederick was, of course, too young to take up office and remained in England.

The proximity in age between George and Frederick meant that the two brothers were brought up and educated together, and they formed a close bond that lasted the rest of their lives. They were at first placed in the nursery, superintended by Lady Charlotte Finch, and when they reached the age of seven or eight they took up residence at Kew to begin their education. They were put under the governorship of Robert D'Arcy, Earl of Holdernesse, while Dr William Markham, the former head of Westminster School, was made preceptor, assisted by Revd Cyril Jackson of Christ Church, Oxford, as sub-preceptor. The boys studied modern languages, the Classics, mathematics and the sciences. Frederick was not as intellectually gifted as his brother; Charles Greville, a contemporary and friend of Frederick, notes in his diary that Frederick was not particularly clever but that he was blessed with a justness of understanding that was absent in his brothers.[2] He was more practically inclined and as a child he delighted in having two of his attendants hold to the height of his mouth a garter which he would then run at and leap over in a single bound. When they were not studying, Frederick and George played single-wicket cricket, fenced and learned how to ride a horse, with Frederick excelling at each activity. Their father, whose love of agriculture earned him the nickname of 'Farmer George', granted them a patch of land at Kew which they tended and used to grow wheat. When it was ready, they harvested the wheat and took it to a mill to be made into bread.

From an early age Frederick developed a predilection for the military, infused in him when he accompanied his father to military drills. The king was happy to cultivate his son's military enthusiasm, importing the latest foreign works on the military craft from the polytechnic schools of France and Prussia and placing him under the tuition of General Smith, one of the most celebrated engineers of the time. In the gardens at Kew, Frederick and

General Smith would recreate the legendary battles of the Prussian king, Frederick II or Frederick 'the Great', during the Seven Years War (1756–1763), including the Battle of Prague, and Frederick would act the part of his namesake general.[3]

As the boys grew older they developed a rebellious streak. The Earl of Holdernesse fell ill in 1774 and he spent some time away in France to recuperate. On his return in 1775 he found that the boys' minds had been prejudiced against him by their sub-preceptor, Jackson, and they disobeyed his commands and mocked him to his face. Frederick was said to be the worst offender. Horace Walpole records in his journal that he once asked Holdernesse if Frederick had behaved as badly as Prince George. 'Oh!' exclaimed the earl, 'Prince Frederick has gone the farthest, and has been the instrument to inflame his brother.'[4] Holdernesse resigned his post in 1776 and was replaced by Lord Bruce, while Markham and Jackson made way for Dr Richard Hurd, Bishop of Lichfield and Revd William Arnold. Lord Bruce's tenure as governor proved short, and he was soon replaced by George, Duke of Montagu.

When Frederick reached the age of seventeen, George III decided to send him to Hanover to complete his military education in Germany. On 1 November 1780 he was made a colonel in the army by brevet and at the end of the month he said a tearful goodbye to his family at Buckingham House. Prince George was reported to have been so overwhelmed at losing his childhood companion that he 'stood in a state of entire insensibility, totally unable to speak, or to express the concern he felt so strongly'.[5]

Frederick landed at Ostend in Flanders on 2 January 1781 and proceeded to Hanover. After a few weeks' stay he travelled to Brunswick where he was tutored for a time by his uncle Charles William Ferdinand, Duke of Brunswick, a famous Prussian general and veteran of the Seven Years War. During his time in Germany he visited the court of his hero, Frederick the Great, and he joined the king in reviewing the famous Prussian troops. In 1784 he travelled to Vienna where he met Emperor Joseph II and reviewed the Imperial Army, which he did not believe to be up to the same standard as the Prussian troops.

King George, meanwhile, continued to bestow honours on Frederick. On 23 March 1782 he was made colonel of the 2nd Regiment of Horse Grenadiers and on 22 November that same year he was made a major-general. On 27 November 1784, having reached the age of twenty-one, he was created Duke of York and Albany and Earl of Ulster. In January 1785 he was made one of the lords of the regency of Hanover and a member of the Supreme Council. He was also involved in the formation of the League of Princes along with Frederick the Great, this being established to counter the pretentions of Emperor Joseph II to exchange Bavaria for the Austrian Netherlands.[6]

Unfortunately, Frederick's time at the debauched German courts had an adverse effect on his character. He fell under the spell of one Baron

Seltenheim, who introduced him to the pleasures of gambling. Frederick was soon removed from Seltenheim's society but the damage was done. Gambling would remain a constant companion in his life.

Return to England

After an absence of nearly seven years, Frederick returned to England in August 1787. He landed at Dover and headed straight for Windsor, where he was reunited with the king, queen and his sisters. King George and Queen Charlotte had by now completed their family of fifteen children, of which eight boys and five daughters still lived. Of most interest to us are their third son, William, Duke of Clarence, the future King William IV, born in 1765, and their fourth son, Edward, Duke of Kent, born in 1767, the father of Queen Victoria.

The following day, the Prince of Wales arrived from Brighton. Unfortunately, the 'hereditary curse' which death had spared Frederick Louis and George III was inherited by the king and his eldest son. Denied any role in government, the prince had plunged headfirst in to a life of pleasure and debauchery. His uncle Henry Frederick, Duke of Cumberland had introduced him to the intoxications of wine, women and gambling, and he soon racked up heavy debts. He had a succession of mistresses and in 1785 he had secretly married Maria Fitzherbert, a Catholic widower six years his senior. This was in direct contravention of the Royal Marriages Act of 1772, which forbade any of the descendants of George II under the age of twenty-five from marrying without the king's permission. More troubling for the king was the prince's support of the opposition as a way of undermining his father and achieving his own aims. Prince George was a close friend and confidant of the Whig leader, Charles James Fox, who shared in his debaucheries and fought his battles over his income in Parliament.

To the king's horror, Frederick now fell under his brother's spell. He often stayed at the prince's residence, Carlton House, in Pall Mall and he was 'initiated into all the extravagances and debaucheries of this most *virtuous* metropolis'.[7] '[T]he Prince has taught the Duke to drink in the most liberal and copious way,' notes a contemporary, 'and the Duke in return has been equally successful in teaching his brother to lose his money at all sorts of play – Quinze, Hazard, &c. – to the amount as we are told, of very large sums.'[8] Frederick's visits to his parents at Windsor became less frequent. Then, in November 1788, the fifty-year-old George III suffered his first attack of 'insanity'. It was not known whether the king's affliction would be temporary or permanent and it was decided that in the meantime a regent must be appointed. Parliament assembled in December to address the issue and Fox and the opposition claimed that it was Prince George's right as an heir apparent of full age to be made regent and exercise the executive power without limitation. This was controverted by Prime Minister William Pitt the Younger who, afraid that George would dismiss him if he came to power, said that it was the right of Parliament to choose the regent and define his powers. On 15 December, Frederick rose in the House of Lords in a bid to put an end to the question and denied that the prince had made any claim of right to the regency. The prince, Frederick remarked, 'understood the sacred principles which seated the house of Brunswick on the British throne' – that is, not to assume any power not derived by Parliament.[9] Pitt's solution was to propose a limited regency in which the prince was not allowed to grant peerages, office or pension while the king's person was to be placed under the care of the queen. On 23 January, Frederick, his brother the Duke of Cumberland and fifty-five peers entered a protest on the journals against these restrictions, but Prince George, seeing little choice, accepted them. However, on 20 February 1780, before the resultant Regency Bill could pass, the king recovered his senses.

Colonel Lennox

In May that year Frederick took part in his infamous duel with Charles Lennox, a lieutenant-colonel of the Coldstream Guards. The inflammatory incident had occurred when the Prince of Wales had been insulted by three masked individuals at a masquerade. Frederick, who was present at the event, believed that Lt Colonel Lennox was one of the individuals involved. He called the colonel a coward and a disgrace to his profession and demanded that he remove his mask but 'Lennox' refused to do so. Later, as reported in the newspapers, Frederick claimed that in his presence words had been made use of to Colonel Lennox at Daubigny's Club 'that no Gentlemen ought to submit to' – that Lennox had been insulted and had not responded. This would seem to have been a matter for Lennox, not the Duke. But Lennox was a member of the Prince's regiment and once the matter had been discussed before the other soldiers, it became, arguably, a matter of regimental honour. Lennnox denied hearing anything. (It is possible that it was Frederick himself who had made the insult.) On 15 May 1789, Lennox confronted Frederick at a field day for the Coldstream Guards and asked him if the duke had said 'that he had put up with language unfit for any gentleman to hear'.[10]

Lennox was forced to write to the members of Daubigny's asking for anyone who had heard this supposed remark to come forward. Receiving no satisfactory reply, he demanded that Frederick rescind the accusation. Frederick refused and Lennox sent another letter offering to settle the matter by a duel. The proud Frederick did not hide behind his royal rank but readily agreed. Early in the morning of 26 May he snuck out of Carlton House for Wimbledon Common, where the duel was set to take place. In order to hide the fact from his brother, he left his hat on the table and borrowed one from a member of the prince's household. When Frederick and Lennox met on the common, a distance of 12 paces was measured between them. A signal was given for them to fire and Lennox eagerly discharged his pistol. The ball grazed Frederick's wig and removed one of its curls, but he remained calm and composed. Lennox realised that Frederick had not fired his pistol and he demanded to know why. Lord Rawdon, who acted as Frederick's second, explained that the duke had only come to give Lennox satisfaction and that he had no desire to fight. Lennox commanded him to fire but to no avail. If he was not satisfied, Frederick remarked, he could fire again, but the honourable Lennox did not wish to fire on somebody who would not defend themselves and the duel ended. Once knowledge of the duel was noised abroad, Frederick was praised for his bravery and conduct in refusing to return fire.

Marriage

In January 1791, a treaty of alliance was cemented between the courts of England and Prussia, to be sealed by the marriage of Frederick to Princess Frederica Charlotte Ulrica Catherina, the granddaughter of Frederick the Great and Princess Royal of Prussia. Frederica had caught Frederick's eye during his time at the Prussian court. On the evening of 29 September 1791, Frederick married the diminutive Frederica in the White Hall at Charlottenburg Palace in Berlin. The newlyweds set off for England in October, but as they passed through France their carriage was swarmed by a revolutionary mob who attempted to deface the royal arms on the panels and were only prevented from doing so with great difficulty.[11] The couple landed at Dover on 21 November and they were married again, this time in the presence of the royal family, in the saloon at Buckingham House on the evening of the 23rd. Fredrick was dressed in his regimentals while Frederica wore a white satin dress with tassels, fringed with gold and diamonds, completed with a headdress of white feathers and three pins given to her by the king.[12] Lord Malmesbury noted in his diary that Frederica was 'far from handsome, but lively, sensible, and very tractable'.[13] If only 10 per cent of the fondness the couple then had for one another remained, he reasoned, it would be more than enough to make an excellent household. Frederick was granted £18,000 a year by Parliament to support his new wife, which, combined with his other funds gave him a total income of £37,000 a year.[14]

The marriage began well but relations later cooled. Frederica was unable to have children and she began to spend much of her time at Oatlands Palace, which Frederick bought from the Duke of Newcastle shortly after the wedding, and where she took great pleasure in her forty dogs, monkeys and parrots. Frederick would visit Oatlands on the weekends and the couple would hold parties until Monday, when Frederick would return to London.

French Revolutionary War

In February 1793, Revolutionary France declared war on England and Holland before invading the latter. The French were already at war with Austria and Prussia, and they had succeeded in defeating the Austrians at the Battle of Jemappes (6 November 1792) and conquering the Austrian part of the Netherlands (Belgium). It was decided that an army would be sent to assist the Dutch in collaboration with the Austrians and Prussians. The twenty-nine-year-old Frederick, although inexperienced at war, was appointed commander of the English army at the king's request. On 25 February he took ship at Greenwich in the presence of the king and members of the royal family, landing at Hellevoetsluis on 4 March. Two weeks later, on 18 March, the Austrians under Prince Josias of Saxe-Coburg succeeded in defeating the French at the Battle of Neerwinden, driving them out of Belgium and back into France.

The allies, including the English, Austrians, Prussians and Dutch, then convened at Antwerp. They entered France and Frederick took command of the siege of Valenciennes, one of the French border fortresses. Valenciennes capitulated on 28 July and Frederick and Coburg were conducted by the city magistrates through the town to the Grand Place. As they rode through the streets, women clapped their hands from the windows of the houses and shouted '*Vive le Roi*' and 'God save the King' at Frederick.[15] Flushed by this success, Frederick received orders from the cabinet to lay siege to Dunkirk. Frederick was averse to splitting from Coburg, who requested his help in besieging Le Quesnoy, but he had little choice but to follow orders and in August he headed for Dunkirk. He succeeded in forcing the French from their camp at Ghyvelde, and defeating a sally by the French from Dunkirk he took up position before the town. He was let down by the late arrival of the heavy artillery needed to conduct the siege and of a promised English naval fleet that was to have cooperated with the army, while Field Marshal Freytag, who formed the duke's covering army, was defeated at Hondschoote, causing Frederick ignominiously to retreat.[16] The defeat at Dunkirk was a turning point in the war and the French, their numbers now swelled, were on the offensive and in many places caused the allies to retreat. The year's campaign was brought to an end by the onset of winter.

In February 1794, Frederick travelled to England to plan the next campaign with the war cabinet. He returned to the continent in early March, and this time the allies were to be co-ordinated by Emperor Francis II with the intention of marching on Paris. The allies assembled at Cateau on 16 April and three days later they laid siege to Landrecies, which capitulated on the 29th. The allies then moved to attack the French in five columns and force them from the Low Countries. Frederick's column took Lannoy, Roubaix and Mouvaux but he found himself exposed to great danger when he was forced to send two battalions to Tourcoing, where his men were under attack by the French. This left Frederick's right flank open and he was soon assaulted by the French in the front and rear, only reaching the safety of a division of Austrians under General Otto after a struggle.

The plan having failed, the allies reconvened at Tournai where, on 22 May, they were attacked by a French army under General Pichegru. The French were repulsed but the allies afterwards lost a succession of key towns and cities. On 26 June the Austrians suffered a decisive defeat at the Battle of Fleurus, which cleared the way for the French to retake Belgium. Frederick, who had been at Tournai, was forced to retreat to Antwerp and then into Holland. On 15 September he was driven over the River Meuse by the advancing French as far as Nijmegen and in October he was forced to cross the River Waal. Back in England, the blame for the misfortunes of the army was placed squarely on Frederick's shoulders and Pitt called for his recall and replacement. King George protested in vain that they had been let down by the other allied powers, but he eventually gave way and Frederick returned to England on 6 December. In April 1795, the English army returned home and Holland was conquered by the French. Holland, along with Belgium, became the Republic of Batavia.

Commander-in-Chief of the British Army

On the duke's return he was consoled for his loss of office by being created Commander-in-Chief of the British Army, taking the post on 18 February 1795. He would hold this office for the rest of his life, except between the years 1809 and 1811, during which time he carried out sweeping reforms of the army. Frederick's first-hand experience in the French Revolutionary Wars had shown him the deficiencies and abuses prevalent in the internal organisation of the army and of the poor training of its officers. His first objective was to put a check on the ancient system of purchasing commissions in the army, whereby a boy fresh from college could be made a field officer without having any prior experience or knowledge, to the detriment of more seasoned hands. Frederick made it mandatory that any officer must first serve an allotted time in his current rank before being able to purchase a commission. Another innovation he made was to create the first military schools in England to provide training for officers. Prior to this, anyone who was interested in learning the art of war would have to travel to one of the great military schools in Germany. In 1799, Frederick established the Royal Military College at High Wycombe, Buckinghamshire, which in 1813 moved to Sandhurst where it still operates today.

Frederick did not overlook the lot of the common soldier. He reformed the uniform for something much more comfortable and practical, increased wages and improved discipline. He ensured that any complaints from common soldiers against officers would be investigated and prohibited the use of the cane. Frederick also established charitable foundations, including the Royal Military Asylum in Chelsea, to educate the orphans of British soldiers killed in the Napoleonic Wars. After the defeat of Napoleon at Waterloo in 1815, the House of Commons voted to thank Frederick 'for his continual, effectual, and unremitting attention to the duties of his office, for a period of more than twenty years, during which time the army has improved in discipline and in science to an extent unknown before; and, under Providence, risen to the height of military glory'.[17]

Holland Campaign, 1799

In the summer of 1799, the English government planned an invasion of Holland in concert with Russia. It was hoped that the arrival of the troops would cause the Dutch to rise against their French masters and restore the House of Orange. On 13 September, Frederick landed at Helder and amassing his forces convened an army of around 33,000 men, including 17,000 Russians. On 19 September the allies led a concerted attack on the French near the city of Alkmaar in four columns, but they were let down by the unruly and rash Russian division, which commenced hostilities two hours early. The Russians succeeded in dislodging the French from Bergen but were systematically defeated while sacking the town, with many of them killed or captured. Although the other allied divisions enjoyed some success, the defeat of the Russians eventually forced them to retreat.

On 2 October, Frederick led another attack. This was much more successful and Bergen, Egmond aan Zee and Alkmaar were captured. On 6 October, Frederick led an assault in the hope of capturing Haarlem. The Russians once again acted precipitately by attacking Castricum and were driven back with considerable loss, while the other three columns were unable to effect any meaningful victories. The battle thus proved indecisive and Frederick afterwards summoned a council of war, which advised him that their position was untenable and that they should retreat. The army left its new gains and retreated north, pursued by the enemy.

Winter was coming, supplies were low and the Dutch had not risen as was hoped, with the result that Frederick offered a truce. This was agreed in the Convention of Alkmaar on 18 October, by which terms the army was allowed to depart for home in exchange for 8,000 French and Dutch prisoners held in England. Frederick arrived back in Yarmouth on 3 November, closing his unspectacular career as a general.[18] Frederick is often thought to be the subject of the children's nursery rhyme 'The Grand Old Duke of York', who marched his 10,000 men up a hill and back down again, for his lacklustre performance as general during the French Revolutionary Wars. Other candidates have been suggested, such as Richard, Duke of York after his defeat and death at the Battle of Wakefield. While it is true that both of Frederick's campaigns had been failures, he was not entirely to blame. He was certainly limited by his inexperience as a general but he also had to work with allies who did not always act with one mind and purpose and, particularly in the 1799 campaign, he was continuously let down by them. Frederick, according to a contemporary, 'displayed many of the qualities of an able general, and nobly supported that high character for daring and dauntless courage which is the patrimony of his house'.[19]

Mary Anne Clarke Scandal

While Frederick did not shine as a general, he was admired in his capacity as Commander-in-Chief. Then, in 1809, he was accused of corruption by his ex-mistress, Mary Anne Clarke. Frederick had begun a relationship with Mary Anne around 1803. Her origins are obscure, as are the particulars of how the two first met, but he soon gifted her a grand house in Gloucester Place, Chelsea, and a country house in Weybridge, near to Oatlands, where he kept her in great state and comfort. Mary Anne was intelligent, shrewd and avaricious, and she soon realised that she could enrich herself by taking backhanders from army officers with the promise of using her influence with the duke to secure them promotions. Frederick ended the affair in 1806, granting Mary an annuity of £400 per annum, and took a new mistress. The dejected Mary was approached by three men: Gwillym Lloyd Wardle, an ex-colonel in the Welsh Fusiliers and now MP for Okehampton; Major Thomas Dodd, secretary to the Duke of Kent; and James Glenie, a former lieutenant of artillery. Together, they entered into a conspiracy to rob the duke of his command.

At a session of parliament held on 27 January 1809, Wardle brought charges of corruption against Frederick before the Commons, accusing him of 'abuse, with regard to promotions, exchanges, and appointments to commissions in the army, and staff of the army, and in raising Levies for the Army'.[20] He gave evidence of Mary Anne's dealings, which he said were carried out with the duke's approval. The matter was brought before a committee and Mary Anne acted as chief witness. The duke wrote a letter to the Speaker, declaring his innocence and washing his hands of any knowledge or suspicion of the transactions. He finished by declaring that 'if, upon such testimony as has been adduced against me, the House of Commons can think my innocence questionable, I claim of their justice, that I shall not be condemned without trial, nor be deprived of the benefit and protection which is afforded to every British subject, by those sanctions, under which alone evidence is received in the ordinary administration of the law.'[21]

The duke was found innocent of the charges by a majority of eighty-two votes, but he was deemed guilty in the court of popular opinion. He had little choice but to resign his office as Commander-in-Chief.

The Regency

In 1810, Frederick's sister Princess Amelia died and the grief caused King George III to fall ill once again. As in 1788, the question of the regent's power was discussed in Parliament but this time the Regency Act was passed and Prince George was installed in office in early 1811. He was granted limited powers for the first year in the hope that the king would recover, but when it became apparent that this would not happen the prince was granted full powers. The king remained ill for the last nine years of his life in a period known as 'the Regency', in which he was once again placed under the care of the queen, for which she received an annuity of £10,000. One of the Prince Regent's first moves was to reappoint Frederick as Commander-in-Chief of the British Army.

Heir Presumptive

Ever since his birth, Frederick had been second in line to the throne. Then, in 1795, Prince George had married his cousin, Princess Caroline of Brunswick. The marriage proved unhappy and after the birth of their only child and heir, Princess Charlotte Augusta, on 7 January 1796, they went their separate ways. The birth of the princess saw Frederick demoted to third in line to the throne and there seemed little chance of him one day becoming king.

The popular Princess Charlotte married Prince Leopold of Saxe-Coburg in 1816, and in November the following year she gave birth to a stillborn child. To the great sorrow of the nation, Charlotte followed the infant to the grave. Frederick was distraught at his niece's death but one small consolation was the fact that he was once again second in line to the throne.

The princess's untimely death sparked off a succession crisis. Remarkably, of the thirteen children of George III that survived to adulthood, only Prince George had produced a child, in whom all the hopes of the continuance of the dynasty were bound up. Now that Princess Charlotte was dead that future looked uncertain. As such, it was now deemed expedient to affect some marriages among the younger members of the royal family in the hopes of procuring an heir.[22] In 1818, the third son, William, Duke of Clarence, was married to Adelaide of Saxe-Meiningen while Edward, Duke of Kent, the third son, married Victoria, the sister of the Prince of Saxe-Coburg. The move proved successful when the following year a daughter Alexandrina Victoria, the future Queen Victoria, was born to the Duke of Kent on 24 May.

The next few years witnessed a number of deaths in the ageing royal family which resulted in major shifts in the order of succession. The first death was that of Queen Charlotte, who died on 17 November 1818. Following her death, Frederick assumed the role of king's guardian for which he was granted £10,000 a year by Parliament.[23] Then, on 23 January 1820, the Duke of Kent passed away unexpectedly from a fever at Sidmouth, making his daughter, the infant Princess Victoria, fourth in line to the throne. Six days later, amid preparations for Kent's funeral, Frederick received word that King George had taken a turn for the worse. He made a beeline for Windsor where he witnessed the passing of the king, after a then record-breaking reign of fifty-nine years, from pneumonia. Frederick duly acted as chief mourner at the king's funeral, which took place at St George's Chapel at Windsor on Ash Wednesday.[24] With the death of the old king, Prince George now became King George IV and Frederick, as the next senior male in the royal line, became heir presumptive to the throne. For a brief moment after the old king's death it even looked as if Frederick might become king – Prince George had been ill with pleurisy but he fortunately recovered.

Sadly, as if the losses were not already enough, in early August Frederick was notified that Frederica, Duchess of York had come down with tuberculosis. Frederick, who was then at London, made a dash for Oatlands. The duchess died in Frederick's presence on 6 August. While the two had largely lived apart, Frederick had loved Frederica and he deeply mourned her death. She was buried, at her request, in a vault at St Nicholas's Church at Weybridge on Monday 14 August. The day before her funeral, her coffin was laid in state in the dining room at Oatlands for people to pay their final respects and again until just after midday on the day of the funeral. For the final hour before the procession began at 3 p.m., Frederick sat at the head of the coffin. On exiting Oatlands he burst into tears, which deeply affected all present. The procession to the church then began, headed by four mutes on horseback, and followed by a selection of poor boys and girls whom the duchess had supported. This was followed by Frederick's state carriage draped in black and occupied by Sir Thomas Stepney, who carried the duchess's coronet. Next came the hearse itself, pulled by six of the duchess's iron-grey horses, then the carriage containing Frederick, who acted as chief mourner. Once the service had been carried out, Frederica's coffin was led out of the church in procession and into the external entrance to the vault, where her remains were deposited.

Last Years and Death

During the last few years of his life, Frederick began to show signs of declining health. In June 1826 he took a turn for the worse after returning from the races at Ascot. He suffered from dropsy (edema), a build-up of fluid in his legs, and mobility became difficult. He sought a change of air at Brompton and then Brighton, where his condition worsened, but on making a slight recovery he proceeded to London and stayed at the Duke of Rutland's house in Arlington Street where he grew worse. Although he was convinced he would recover, he had the Bishop of London secretly brought in to administer the Sacrament while he still retained control of his senses. In September he was tapped by his physician, Mr Macgregor, producing 22 pints of water from his legs, but the water soon returned and his legs grew worse. Throughout his illness he continued to attend to his official business as Commander-in-Chief and spent his time reading and receiving visits from the king, his friends and other members of the royal family.

By the end of December he had lost his appetite, but his spirits remained high and he still believed that he was going to get better. On 27 December he saw the king for the final time, and the following day he once again received the Sacrament from the Bishop of London. His health continued to decline, his vision failed and he suffered from bouts of fainting, spasms and delirium. On 4 January 1827 he called to his side his companions Colonel Stephenson and Sir Herbert and whispered to them, 'I am now dying.'[25] He held out until 9.20 p.m. on Friday 5 January, when he passed away peacefully in his great armchair dressed in a grey dressing-gown, 'his head inclined against the side of the chair, hands lying before him, and looking as if he were in a deep and quiet sleep'.[26] He was sixty-three. The devastated king arranged his funeral, which took place at Windsor on 20 January. The king had wished the funeral to be a magnificent affair and was disappointed with its execution. The weather at the event was bitterly cold and many attendees contracted colds, including the Bishop of Lincoln, who died of his illness.

After his death the press savaged the duke's reputation, deriding his expensive habits and his addiction to gambling while reviving the story of the Mary Anne Clark scandal of 1809. The press soon realised that the public held a genuine affection for the duke, however, and began to print articles praising his public services and his private merits.[27] It was in his capacity as Commander in Chief that Frederick shone, and this was how his contemporaries chose to remember him, erecting his column in St James's Park in 1834.

George IV outlived his younger brother by a little over three years, passing away on 26 June 1830. He was succeeded by his third brother, William, Duke of Clarence, who reigned as King William IV. William died on 20 June 1837 and, having no surviving legitimate children, was succeeded by his niece Alexandrina Victoria, daughter of the deceased Duke of Kent, by way of representation. She was crowned as Queen Victoria on 28 June 1838.

26

The Rules of Succession Today

Queen Victoria reigned for a period of nearly sixty-four years, dying on 22 January 1901. She had married Prince Albert of Saxe-Coburg in 1840 and had nine children by him. Her eldest son, Albert Edward, Prince of Wales, was born on 9 November 1841. Prince Albert was, until recently, the longest-serving Prince of Wales, holding the title for almost sixty years. He ascended the throne upon the death of Queen Victoria and changed his regnal name to King Edward VII. King Edward was married to Alexandra of Schleswig-Holstein, a daughter of the King of Denmark. Their eldest son and heir, Albert Victor, Duke of Clarence, was born in 1864 but died in May 1890 and never became heir apparent to the throne. Edward's second son, George Frederick Ernest Albert, was Edward's eventual successor at his death on 6 May 1910 and reigned as King George V.

George V had married Mary of Teck in 1893 and had by her six children. The eldest, a son named Edward, Prince of Wales, succeeded his father on 20 January 1936 as King Edward VIII. Edward's reign proved remarkably short and he was never crowned. He chose to abdicate less than eleven months later, on 11 December, as he wished to marry the American socialite and divorcée Wallis Simpson.

The throne thus devolved on his brother Frederick Arthur George, who reigned as King George VI. A few years later he married Elizabeth Angela Marguerite and the couple had two daughters, Elizabeth and Margaret. Elizabeth succeeded her father as Queen Elizabeth II on 6 February 1952. Queen Elizabeth married Prince Philip in 1947 and just under a year later she gave birth to their first child, Prince Charles. Queen Elizabeth died on 8 September 2022 after a record-breaking reign of seventy years and was succeeded by Prince Charles, who became King Charles III. Charles is himself a record holder, having held the title of Prince of Wales for seventy years, beating the previous record held by Edward VII.

Charles's eldest son, William, Prince of Wales and Duke of Cambridge, born by his first wife Lady Diana Spencer, is heir apparent at the time of writing. Prince William married Kate Middleton in 2011 and their eldest child, Prince George, born on 22 July 2013, became third in line. As George was born after 28 October 2011, he is the first member of the royal family to be affected by the recent Succession to the Crown Act, which was introduced in 2013. This Act, the latest change to the rules of succession, has done away with the outdated male bias that has no place in twenty-first-century society.

Now it is the eldest child of the monarch that is heir apparent, regardless of gender. As Prince George is male we will likely not see the succession of an elder daughter over that of a younger son until the next generation, and even then only if George marries and his first child is a daughter. Its effects, however, can be seen in the positions of George's two younger siblings – Princess Charlotte, born on 2 May 2015 and Prince Louis, born on 23 April 2018. Princess Charlotte is fourth in line and the first female in history whose place in the succession is not superseded by a younger brother.

While the Succession to the Crown Act has done away with male-preference primogeniture, it has not done away with the provision that disqualifies a Catholic from the throne. A monarch may now marry a Roman Catholic, but they must be an Anglican themselves and in communion with the Church of England. It is hoped by many that one day this archaic rule may also be overturned, bringing the rules of succession fully in line with modern ways of thinking.

Notes

Abbreviations

CCR: Calendar of Close Rolls
CPR: Calendar of Patent Rolls

Introduction: The setting Sun

1. Thomas Birch, *The life of Henry, Prince of Wales, eldest son of King James I* (London: A. Millar, 1760), p. 405; Anon, *A True Accompt Of the Most Triumphant, and Royal Accomplishment of the Baptism of the Most Excellent, Right High, and Mighty Prince, Henry Frederick, By the Grace of God, Prince of Scotland, and now Prince of Wales* (Edinburgh: Printed by John Reid, for Alexander Ogston stationer, 1687), p. 1.
2. *Ibid*, p. 1; John Nichols, *The progresses, processions, and magnificent festivities, of King James the First, his royal consort, family and court* (London: J.B. Nichols, 1828), Vol ii, p. 504.
3. Birch, *The life of Henry, Prince of Wales*, p. 405.
4. *Memoirs of Robert Cary Earl of Monmouth*, ed. G. H. Powell (London: Alexander Moring, limited, the De La More Press, 1905), p. 90.
5. Birch, *The life of Henry, Prince of Wales*, p. 406; Williamson, *The Myth of the Conqueror*, p. 1.
6. *The Oxford Guide to the English Language* (London: Guild Publishing, 1985), p. 369.
7. Robert Blackburn, *King and Country: Monarchy and the future king Charles III* (London: Politico's Publishing, LTD, 2006), p. 150.

1 Robert II, Duke of Normandy

1. William Aird, *Robert Curthose: Duke of Normandy, c. 1050–1134* (Woodbridge: Boydell Press, 2008), pp. 26–8.
2. Nicholas Orme, *From Childhood to Chivalry* (London: Methuen, 1984), p. 18; Charles Wendall David, *Robert Curthose, Duke of Normandy* (London: Harvard University Press, 1920), p. 6.
3. *Ibid*, p. 20.
4. Emily Zack Tabuteau, *The Role of Law in the Succession to Normandy*, in ed. Robert B. Patterson, *The Haskins Society Journal*, Vol 3 (London: Hambledon Press, 1991), p. 150.
5. N. J. Higham, *Death of Anglo-Saxon England* (Stroud: Sutton Publishing, 1997), p.xiii.

6. See, for instance, Charles Wendall David, p.18. Catherine Lack suggests Robert may have been made duke in 1075 at the time when William fell ill at Bonneville. Lack, Catherine, *Conqueror's Son* (Stroud: Sutton Publishing, 2007), p. 20.
7. *William of Malmesbury's Chronicles of the Kings of England*, trans. J. A Giles (London: H. G. Bohn, 1847), p. 420.
8. *The Ecclesiastical History of England and Normandy*, trans. Thomas Forrester (London: H. G. Bohn, 1853), Vol ii, p. 172.
9. *William of Malmesbury's Chronicles of the Kings of England*, p. 420.
10. *The Ecclesiastical History of England and Normandy*, Vol ii, p. 173.
11. J. C. Holt, *Politics and Property in Early Medieval England*, in ed. J.C. Holt, *Colonial England 1066 – 1215* (London: Hambledon Press, 1997), p. 120.
12. *Ecclesiastical History of England and Normandy*, Vol iii, p. 72.
13. *William of Malmesbury's Chronicles of the Kings of England*, p. 333.
14. August Charles Krey, *The First Crusade* (Princeton: Princeton University Press, 1921), p. 127.
15. *The Gesta Tancredi of Ralph of Caen*, trans. Bernard S. Bachrach and David S. Bachrach (Aldershot: Ashgate Publishing, 2005), p. 84.
16. *William of Malmesbury's Chronicles of the Kings of England*, p. 421.
17. *Ecclesiastical History of England and Normandy*, Vol iii, p. 278.
18. *Henry of Huntingdon: The History of the English People 1000 – 1154*, trans. Diana Greenway (Oxford: Oxford University Press, 2009), p. 51.
19. William Aird, *Robert Curthose, Duke of Normandy, c. 1050–1134* (Woodbridge: Boydell Press, 2008), p. 282.
20. *William of Malmesbury's Chronicles of the Kings of England*, p. 423.

2 William Aetheling

1. *The Life of King Edward the Confessor*, trans. Frank Barlow (London: Thomas Nelson and Sons, 1962), p. 76.
2. Kate Norgate, *England under the Angevin Kings*, Vol 1 (London: Macmillan and Co., 1887), p. 1.
3. *William of Malmesbury's Chronicles of the Kings of England*, p. 455.
4. Judith A. Green, *Henry I* (Cambridge: Cambridge University Press, 2009), p. 75.
5. *William of Malmesbury's Chronicles of the Kings of England*, p. 448.
6. Mary Anne Everett Green, *Lives of the Princesses of England from the Norman Conquest* (London: Henry Colburn, 1849), Vol i, p. 84.
7. *Henry of Huntingdon: The History of the English People 1000 – 1154*, p. 101.
8. *The History of the Norman People (Wace's Roman de Rou)*, trans. Glyn S. Burgess (Woodbridge: Boydell, 2004), pp. 205–6.
9. RRAN, p. 107.
10. *Ecclesiastical History of England and Normandy*, Vol iii, p. 474.
11. *Ibid*, p. 485.
12. *William of Malmesbury's Chronicles of the Kings of England*, p. 455.
13. *Ibid*, p. 456.
14. *Ecclesiastical History of England and Normandy*, Vol iv, p. 35.
15. *Ibid*, p. 35.
16. *Ibid*, p. 36.
17. *Ibid*, p. 40.
18. *Ibid*, p. 37.

3 Empress Matilda

1. *The Anglo-Saxon Chronicle*, trans. Rev J. Ingram (London: Longman, Hurst, Rees, Orme and Brown, 1823), pp. 367–368.
2. Marjorie Chibnall, *The Empress Matilda* (Oxford: Blackwell Publishers LTD, 1999), p. 9.
3. *Henry of Huntingdon: The History of the English People 1000 – 1154*, p. 52.
4. *The Church Historians of England*, trans. Joseph Stevenson (London: Seelys, 1858), Vol v, Part 1, p. 11.
5. Lynsey Wood, *The very next blood of the king*, in eds. Ana Maria, S. A. Rodrigues, Manuela Santos Silva, Jonathan Spangler, *Dynastic Change* (Abingdon: Routledge, 2020), p. 22.
6. *Ibid*, p. 24.
7. *The Chronicle of Florence of Worcester*, trans. Thomas Forrester (London: H. G. Bohun, 1854), p. 269.
8. *Gesta Stephani*, trans. K. R. Potter (London: Thomas Nelson and Sons, 1955), p. 64.
9. *William of Malmesbury's Chronicles of the Kings of England*, p. 519.
10. *Ibid*, p. 520.
11. The Church Historians of England, trans. Joseph Stevenson (London: Seelys, 1856), Vol iv – Part 2, p. 413.
12. *Ibid*, Vol v, Part 1, p. 93.
13. *William of Malmesbury's Chronicles of the Kings of England*, p. 522.
14. *Ibid*, p. 528.
15. *The Chronicle of Florence of Worcester*, p. 284.
16. *Ibid*, p. 284.
17. *Notes and Queries*, Vol 168, no. 9, pp. 155–6.
18. *Ibid*, p. 156

4 Eustace, Count of Boulogne

1. *Henry of Huntingdon: The History of the English People 1000 – 1154*, p. 89.
2. *Oxford Dictionary of National Biography*, Eustace, count of Boulogne.
3. *The Anglo Saxon Chronicle*, p. 372.
4. *William of Malmesbury's Chronicles of the Kings of England*, p. 522.
5. *The Church Historians of England*, Vol v, Part 1, p. 127.
6. Elizabeth Hallam, *Plantagenet Chronicles* (Surrey: Tiger Books, 1995), p. 48.
7. *Ibid*, p. 48.
8. Edmund King, *King Stephen* (Newhaven and London: Yale University Press, 2012), p. 238.
9. *Gesta Stephani*, p. 138.
10. *The Anglo Saxon Chronicle*, p. 372.
11. *Henry of Huntingdon: The History of the English People 1000 – 1154*, p. 92.
12. *Gesta Stephani*, p. 138.
13. *Ibid*, p. 158.

5 Henry the Young King

1. W. H. Hutton, *S. Thomas of Canterbury* (London: David Nutt, 1899), p. 14.
2. *Ibid*, p. 14.
3. *The Church Historians of England*, Vol iv, Part 2, p. 778.
4. *Ibid*, Vol iv, part 2, p. 484.
5. *The Annals of Roger de Hoveden*, ed. Henry T. Riley (London: H. G. Bohn, 1853), Vol i, p. 383.
6. *Ibid*, Vol i, p. 388.
7. *Ibid*, Vol i, p. 412.
8. *Ibid*, Vol i, p. 490.
9. *History of William Marshal*, trans. A. J Holden, S. Gregory and D. Couch (London: Anglo-Norman Texts Society, 2002–6), Vol i, p. 133.
10. *The Annals of Roger de Hoveden*, Vol ii, p. 21.
11. *Ibid*, Vol ii, p. 23.

6 Arthur, Duke of Brittany

1. *History of William Marshal*, trans. A. J Holden, S. Gregory and D. Couch (London: Anglo-Norman Texts Society, 2002–6), Vol ii, p. 95.
2. *Ibid*, p. 95.
3. *Gesta Regis Henrici Secundi Benedicti Abbatis*, ed. William Stubbs (London: Longmans, Green, Reader and Dyer, 1867), Vol i, p. 358.
4. *The Church Historians of England*, Vol v, Part 1, p. 151; *The Annals of Roger de Hoveden*, Vol ii, p. 56.
5. *The Annals of Roger de Hoveden*, Vol ii, p. 165.
6. *Ibid*, Vol ii, p. 165.
7. *Ibid*, Vol ii, p. 297.
8. J. A. Everard, *Brittany and the Angevins* (Cambridge: Cambridge University Press, 2000), p. 165.
9. *The Annals of Roger de Hoveden*, Vol ii, p. 456.
10. F. W. Maitland, *The Constitutional History of England* (Cambridge: University Press, 1950), , p.99.
11. *The Annals of Roger de Hoveden*, Vol ii, p. 481.
12. *Roger of Wendover's Flowers of History*, trans. J. A. Giles (London: H. G. Bohn, 1849), Vol ii, p. 188.
13. *Ibid*, p. 188.
14. Thomas Duffus Hardy, *A Description of The Patent Rolls In The Tower of London* (London: G. Eyre and A. Spottiswoode, 1835), p. 23.
15. *Roger of Wendover's Flowers of History*, Vol ii, p. 204.
16. *Ibid*, Vol ii, p. 204.
17. Thomas Duffus Hardy, *A Description of The Patent Rolls In The Tower of London*, p. 37.
18. *Roger of Wendover's Flowers of History*, Vol ii, p. 205.
19. Kate Norgate, *John Lackland* (London: Macmillan And Co., Limited, 1902), p. 91.
20. Stephen Church, *King John: England, Magna Carta and the Making of a Tyrant* (London: Macmillan, 2015), p. 110.
21. *Ibid*, pp. 109–10.
22. Wood, *The very next blood of the king*, p. 25.

Notes

7 Edward of Woodstock, the Black Prince

1. *The Chronicle of Froissart: Translated Out of French by Sir John Bourchier [and] Lord Berners, annis 1523–5* (London: David Nutt, 1901), Vol i, p. 300.
2. *Ibid*, p. 300.
3. *Froissart Chronicles*, ed. Geoffrey Brereton (Middlesex: Penguin Books, 1968), p. 92.
4. CPR, *1334–38*, p. 243.
5. There is some doubt as to whether Simon Burley really acted as the Black Prince's tutor. Nicholas Orme notes that the tradition that he did so only surfaced in the sixteenth century, pp. 20-1.
6. CCR, *1333–37*, p. 523.
7. CPR, *1338–40*, p. 112.
8. *Adæ Murimuth Continuatio Chronicarum: Robertus de Avesbury de Gestis Mirabilibus Regis Edwardi Terti*, ed. Edward Maunde Thompson (London: Spottiswoode, 1889), p. 204.
9. W. Mark Ormrod, *Edward III* (London: Yale University Press, 2013), pp. 278–9.
10. W. J. Ashley, *Edward III & his Wars, 1327–1360: Extracts from the Chronicles of Froissart, Jehan le Bel, Knighton, Adam of Murimuth, Robert of Avesbury, the Chronicle of Lanercost, the State Papers, & other contemporary records* (London: David Nutt, 1887), p. 104.
11. *The Chronicle of Geoffrey le Baker*, trans. David Preest (Woodbridge: The Boydell Press, 2012), p. 74.
12. *Ibid*, p. 74.
13. *Knighton's Chronicle, 1337 – 1396*, trans. G. H. Martin (Oxford: Oxford University Press, 1995), p. 197; *The Chronicle of Geoffrey le Baker*, p. 74.
14. *Holinshed's Chronicles of England, Scotland and Ireland* (London: J. Johnson [etc], 1807–8), Vol ii, pp. 648–9.
15. *Adæ Murimuth Continuatio Chronicarum*, p. 445.
16. *The Chronicle of Geoffrey le Baker*, p. 120.
17. *Ibid*, p. 130.
18. *Syllabus (In English) of the documents relating to England and other kingdoms contained in the collection known as "Rymer's Foedera"*, ed. Thomas Duffy Hardy (London: Longmans, Green & Co., 1869–85), Vol i, p. 387.
19. Richard Barber, *Edward, Prince of Wales and Aquitaine* (Suffolk: The Boydell Press, 1978), p. 172.
20. Richard Barber, *Life & Campaigns of the Black Prince* (Suffolk: Boydell Press, 1986), p. 105.
21. *The Chronicle of Froissart: Translated Out of French by Sir John Bourchier [and] Lord Berners, annis 1523–5* (London: David Nutt, 1901), Vol ii, pp. 355–356.
22. *Oxford Dictionary of National Biography*, Edward [Edward of Woodstock; known as the Black Prince]
23. *The Chronicle of Froissart*, Vol ii, p. 211.
24. *Knighton's Chronicle*, p. 199.

8 Roger Mortimer, 4th Earl of March

1. *The Wigmore Chronicle 1066 to 1377*, trans. Paul Martin Remfry (United Kingdom: Castle Studies Research & Publishing, 2013), pp. 97–8.
2. *Ibid*, p. 98.
3. *Chronicon Adæ de Usk, A.D. 1377 – 1404*, ed. Edward Maunde Thompson (London: John Murray, 1876), p. 128.

4. Charles Hopkinson and Martin Speight, *The Mortimers: Lords of the March* (Logaston: Logaston Press, 2013), pp. 116–17.
5. *The Chronica Maiora of Thomas Walsingham (1376 – 1422)*, trans. David Preest (Woodbridge: The Boydell Press, 2005), pp. 186–7.
6. CPR, *1381–85*, p. 184.
7. Ibid, p. 377.
8. *Rymer's Foedera*, Vol ii, p. 501.
9. CPR, *1381–85*, pp. 345 + 452.
10. *The Westminster Chronicle, 1381 – 1394*, trans. L. C. Hector and Barbara F. Harvey (Oxford: Oxford University Press, 1982), p. 195.
11. Michael Bennett, *Edward III's Entail and the Succession to the Crown, 1376–1471* in *The English Historical Review*, Vol 113, No. 452 (June 1998), p. 583.
12. David J. Seipp, *How to Get Rid of a King: Lawyering the Revolution of 1399* in Catharine MacMillan and Charlotte Smith, eds., *Challenges to Authority and the Recognition of Rights* (Cambridge: Cambridge University Press, 2018), p. 62.
13. W. Mark Ormrod, *Edward III* (London: Yale University Press, 2013), pp. 564–5.
14. Seipp, *How To Get Rid of a King*, p. 63.
15. W. Mark Ormrod, *The DNA of Richard III: False Paternity and the Royal Succession in Later Medieval England* in eds. Joanna Martin and Rob Lutton, *Nottingham Medieval Studies*, 60 (2016), pp. 195–7.
16. *Continuatio Eulogii*, trans. Chris Given-Wilson (Oxford: Oxford University Press, 2019), p. 55.
17. Ian Mortimer, *Medieval Intrigue* (London: Continuum International Publishing Group, 2010), pp. 263–4.
18. Ibid, pp. 268–72.
19. *The Chronica Maiora of Thomas Walsingham (1376 – 1422)*, p. 268.
20. CPR, *1391–96*, p. 375.
21. J. T. Gilbert, *History of the Viceroys of Ireland* (Dublin: James Duffy, 1865), p. 274.
22. *Chronicon Adæ de Usk, A.D. 1377 – 1404*, p. 125.
23. Ibid, p. 125.
24. Ibid, p. 126.

9 Edmund Mortimer, 5th Earl of March

1. Chris Given-Wilson, *Chronicles of the Revolution 1397 – 1400* (Manchester: Manchester University Press, 2008), p.171.
2. Ibid, p. 186.
3. CPR, *1399–1401*, p. 380.
4. Henry Ellis, *Original Letters Illustrative of English History*, 2nd series (London: Harding And Lepard, Pall Mall East, 1827), Vol i, p. 25.
5. *Holinshed's Chronicles of England, Scotland and Ireland*, Vol iii, p. 33.
6. CPR, *1405–08*, p. 276.
7. Mortimer Levine, *Tudor Dynastic Problems 1460–1571* (London: George Allen & Unwin LTD, 1973), pp. 19–20.
8. CPR, *1408–13*, p. 149.
9. CCR, *1413–19*, p. 98.
10. *The Chronica Maiora of Thomas Walsingham (1376 – 1422)*, p. 404.
11. *Chronicles of London*, ed. Charles Lethbridge Kingsford (Oxford: Oxford Clarendon Press, 1905), p. 283.
12. Ibid, p. 283.

Notes

13. K. H. Vickers, *Humphrey Duke of Gloucester* (London: A. Constable and Company, Limited, 1907), p. 123.
14. CPR, *1422–29*, p. 96.
15. *The Historical Collections of a citizen of London in the fifteenth century*, ed. James Gairdner (Westminster: Camden Society, 1876), p. 158.

10 Richard, Duke of York

1. P. A. Johnson, *Duke Richard of York 1411 – 1460* (Oxford: Clarendon Press, 1988), p. 1.
2. *Rymer's Foedera*, Vol ii, p. 589.
3. Johnson, *Duke Richard of York 1411 – 1460*, p. 1.
4. David Grummitt, *A Short History of the Wars of the Roses* (London: I. B. Tauris & Co., Ltd, 2013), p. 28.
5. CPR, *1429–36*, p. 38.
6. *Rymer's Foedera*, Vol ii, p. 648.
7. CPR, *1429–36*, p. 207.
8. *Hall's Chronicle*, ed. Henry Ellis (London: J. Johnson [etc], 1809), p. 181.
9. *Ibid*, p. 187.
10. *Ibid*, p. 208.
11. CPR, *1446–52*, p. 185.
12. *Three Fifteenth-Century Chronicles*, ed. James Gairdner (London: The Camden Society, 1880), p. 97.
13. *The Paston Letters 1422 – 1509*, ed. James Gairdner (Birmingham: 1872), Vol i, p. 83.
14. *Ibid*, p. lx.
15. *Ibid*, p. lxi.
16. *Ibid*, p. 84.
17. *Ibid*, p. lxxiii.
18. *The New Chronicles of England and France by Robert Fabyan*, ed. Henry Ellis (London: F. C. and J. Rivington et al, 1811), p. 627.
19. *Rymer's Foedera*, Vol ii, p. 585.
20. Elizabeth Hallam, *The Wars of the Roses* (Surrey: Bramley Books, 1997), p. 214.
21. *Ibid*, p. 216.
22. Edith Thompson, *The Wars of York and Lancaster 1450 – 1485* (London: David Nutt, 1892), p. 46.
23. *The Paston Letters 1422 – 1509*, Vol i, p. 408.
24. Thompson, *The Wars of York and Lancaster 1450 – 1485*, p. 66.
25. *Ibid*, p. 68.
26. *Holinshed's Chronicles of England, Scotland and Ireland*, Vol iii, p. 269.

11 Edward of Lancaster

1. *The Brut or The Chronicles of England*, ed. Friedrich W. D. Brie (London: Early English Text Society, 1906), part 1, p. 521
2. Matthew Lewis, *The Wars of the Roses: The Key Players in the Struggle for Supremacy* (Stroud: Amberley Publishing, 2015), p. 49.
3. *The Paston Letters*, Vol i, p. 378.
4. *Ibid*, p. CXvii.
5. Thompson, *The Wars of York and Lancaster 1450 – 1485*, p. 71.
6. *Ibid*, p.72.

7. *The Historical Collections of a citizen of London in the fifteenth century*, p. 212.
8. *Ibid*, p. 214.
9. *The Chronicles of the White Rose of York*, ed. J. A. Giles (London: James Bohn, 1845), pp. 7–8.
10. David Grummit, *A Short History of the Wars of the Roses*, p. 71.
11. *The Chronicles of the White Rose of York*, p. 108.
12. *Ibid*, p. 106.
13. *Hall's Chronicle*, p. 286.
14. *Histoire of the arrival of Edward IV in England and the finall recouerye of his kingdomes from Henry VI*, ed. John Bruce (London: Camden Society, 1838), p. 10.
15. *Ibid*, p. 29.
16. *Ibid*, p. 29.
17. *Hall's Chronicle*, p. 300.
18. *The New Chronicles of England and France by Robert Fabyan*, p. 662.
19. *Hall's Chronicle*, p. 301.
20. *Ibid*, p. 301.
21. *Ibid*, p. 301.
22. Thompson, *The Wars of York and Lancaster 1450 – 1485*, p. 118.
23. *The Chronicles of the White Rose of York*, p. 84.
24. *Histoire of the arrival of Edward IV*, p. 38.

12 Edward V

1. CPR, 1467–77, p. 283.
2. *Holinshed's Chronicles of England, Scotland and Ireland*, Vol iii, p. 300.
3. *Ibid*, Vol iii, p. 300; Michael Hicks, *Edward V* (Stroud: Tempus Publishing, 2003), p. 54.
4. *Histoire of the arrival of Edward IV*, p. 17.
5. *Rymer's Foedera*, Vol ii, p. 702.
6. CPR, 1467–77, p. 283.
7. *Ibid*, p. 401.
8. *A Collection of ordinances and regulations for the government of the royal household*, ed. John Nichols (London: Society of Antiquaries, 1790), p. 27.
9. *Ibid*, p. 28.
10. *Ibid*, p. 29.
11. *Ibid*, p. 28.
12. *Ibid*, p. 28.
13. *The New Chronicles of England and France by Robert Fabyan*, p. 668.
14. *Ingulph's Chronicle of the Abbey of Croyland*, ed. Henry T. Riley (London: Bohn, 1854), p. 487.
15. *Ibid*, pp. 487–88.
16. *Ibid*, p. 487.
17. *Three Books of Polydore Vergil's English History*, ed. Henry Ellis (London: Camden Society, 1844), p. 175.
18. Dominic Mancini, *The Usurpation of Richard III*, trans. C. A. J. Armstrong (Gloucester: Alan Sutton Publishing, 1989), p. 93.
19. David Baldwin, *Richard III* (Stroud: Amberley Publishing, 2013), pp. 96–9.
20. Dominic Mancini, *The Usurpation of Richard III*, trans. C. A. J. Armstrong (Gloucester: Alan Sutton Publishing, 1989), p. 93.
21. A. H. Thomas and I. D. Thornley (eds), *Great Chronicle of London* (1938, reprinted Gloucester, 1983), pp. 234, 236-7, quoted in Keith Dockray and

Notes

Peter Hammond (eds), *Richard III From Contemporary Chronicles, Letters & Records* (London: Fonthill Media Limited, 2016), p. 71.
22. Thomas More, *The History of King Richard The Third*, trans. George M. Logan (Indiana: Indiana University Press, 2005), pp. 97 – 101.
23. See, for instance, the excellent synthesis of evidence by Annette Carson in *Richard III: The Maligned King* (Stroud: The History Press, 2008).

13 Edward of Middleham

1. Peter Hammond, *The Children of Richard III* (London: Fonthill Media, 2018), p. 18.
2. *CPR, 1476–85*, p. 512.
3. *Ibid*, p. 67.
4. *Ibid*, p. 403.
5. Robert Davies, *Extracts From the Municipal Records of the City of York During the Reigns of Edward IV, Edward V and Richard III* (London: J.B. Nichols and Son, 1843), pp. 281–2.
6. *Three Books of Polydore Vergil's English History*, p. 190.
7. Davies, *Extracts From the Municipal Records of the City of York*, p. 282.
8. Horrox, Rosemary and P. W. Hammond (eds.), *The British Library Harleian Manuscript 433* (Gloucester: Alan Sutton Publishing for The Richard III Society, 1979), Vol i, p. 83.
9. *Ingulph's Chronicle*, p. 495.
10. *Ibid*, p. 496.
11. *Ibid*, p. 497.

14 John de la Pole, Earl of Lincoln

1. George Edward Cokayne, *Complete Peerage* (London: George Bell and Sons, 1893), Vol iv, p. 93.
2. *CPR 1467–77*, p. 96.
3. Wendy E. A. Moorhen, 'The Career of John de la Pole, Earl of Lincoln' in ed. Anne F. Sutton, *The Ricardian*, Vol 13 (2003), p. 342.
4. Anne F. Sutton and Livia Visser-Fuchs, *The Royal Funerals of The House of York at Windsor* (London: Richard III Society, 2005), p. 17.
5. James Gairdner, *Letters and Papers illustrative of the reigns of Richard III and Henry VII* (London: Green, Longman, and Roberts, 1861), Vol i, p. 10.
6. George Edward Cokayne, *Complete Peerage* (London: George Bell and Sons, 1893), Vol iv, p. 93.
7. *CPR, 1476–85*, p. 388.
8. Keith Dockray and Peter Hammond, *Richard III From Contemporary Chronicles, Letters & Records* (London: Fonthill Media Limited, 2013), p. 59.
9. *Ibid*, p. 90.
10. Matthew Lewis, *Richard III* (Stroud: Amberley Publishing, 2018), p. 367.
11. A. F. Pollard, *The Reign of Henry VII From Contemporary Sources* (London: Longmans, Green And Co., 1913), Vol i, p. 12.
12. *Joannis Lelandi Antiquarii de rebus britannicis collectanea*, ed. Thomas Hearnii (London: Jo Richardson, 1770), Vol iv, p. 185.
13. *CPR, 1485–94*, p. 106.
14. *Ibid*, p. 107.
15. *Hall's Chronicle*, p. 429.

16. Bernard André, *The Life of Henry VII*, trans. Daniel Hobbins (New York: Italica Press, 2011), p. 45.
17. *Hall's Chronicle*, p. 432.
18. A. F. Pollard, *The Reign of Henry VII From Contemporary Sources*, Vol i, p. 51.
19. *Hall's Chronicle*, p. 433.
20. *Ibid*, p. 434.

15 Arthur Tudor

1. *Joannis Lelandi Antiquarii de rebus britannicis collectanea*, ed. Thomas Hearnii (London: Jo Richardson, 1770), Vol iv, pp. 204–207.
2. *Hall's Chronicle*, p. 425.
3. *Joannis Lelandi Antiquarii de rebus britannicis collectanea*, Vol iv, p. 204.
4. *Ibid*, Vol iv, p. 204.
5. CPR, 1485–94, P. 152.
6. W. Campbell, *Materials for a History of the Reign of Henry VII* (London: Longman & Co. etc, 1873–7), Vol ii, p. 349.
7. *Ibid*, Vol ii, p. 115.
8. *Joannis Lelandi Antiquarii de rebus britannicis collectanea*, Vol iv, p. 250.
9. *Ibid*, Vol iv, pp. 250–253.
10. Bernard André, *The Life of Henry VII*, p. 39.
11. *Ibid*, p. 39.
12. Aysha Pollnitz, *Princely Education in Early Modern Britain* (Cambridge: Cambridge University Press, 2015), p. 40.
13. *Ibid*, p. 30.
14. *Calendar of Letters, Despatches, And State Papers, Relating to the negotiations between England and Spain: Henry VII 1485 – 1509*, ed. G. A. Bergenroth (London: Longman, Green, Longman & Roberts, 1862), Vol i, p. 11.
15. *Hall's Chronicle*, p. 491.
16. *Calendar of Letters, Despatches, And State Papers, Relating to the negotiations between England and Spain: Henry VII 1485 – 1509*, Vol i, p. 213.
17. Mary Anne Everett Wood, ed., *Letters of Royal and Illustrious Ladies of Great Britain* (London: Henry Colburn, 1846), Vol i, pp. 121–2.
18. *Calendar of Letters, Despatches, And State Papers, Relating to the negotiations between England and Spain: Henry VII 1485 – 1509*, Vol i, p. 264.
19. *Joannis Lelandi Antiquarii de rebus britannicis collectanea*, Vol v, p. 355.
20. *Letters of Henry VIII, 1526–29*, ed. Tim Coates (London: The Stationary Office, 2001), p. 170.
21. *Hall's Chronicle*, p. 425.
22. *Joannis Lelandi Antiquarii de rebus britannicis collectanea*, Vol v, p. 374.
23. *Ibid*, Vol v, p. 374.
24. *Ibid*, Vol v, p. 381.
25. Eric Ives, *Tudor Dynastic Problems Revisited* in Historical Research 81 (2008), pp. 259–263.

16 Lady Jane Grey

1. Mary Anne Everett Wood, *Letters of Royal and Illustrious Ladies of Great Britain*, Vol iii, p. 278.

Notes

2. Eric Ives, *Lady Jane Grey: A Tudor Mystery* (Chichester: Wiley-Blackwell, 2011), p. 36.
3. Aysha Pollnitz, *Princely Education in Early Modern Britain* (Cambridge: Cambridge University Press, 2015), p. 219.
4. *Holinshed's Chronicles of England, Scotland and Ireland*, Vol iv, p. 25.
5. *The Catechism of Thomas Becon*, ed. John Ayre (Cambridge: University Press, 1844), p. 424.
6. Agnes Strickland, *Lives of the Tudor and Stuart Princesses* (London: George Bell & Sons, 1907), pp. 61–2.
7. *Ibid*, p. 62.
8. *A Collection of State Papers Relating to Affairs in the Reigns of King Henry VIII, King Edward VI, Queen Mary and Queen Elizabeth*, ed. Samuel Haynes (London: William Bowyer, 1740), p. 78.
9. *Ibid*, p. 78.
10. *Ibid*, p. 76.
11. Roger Ascham, *Schoolmaster* (London: Cassell and Company, 1909), p. 40.
12. *Ibid*, p. 40.
13. *Ibid*, p. 40.
14. *Ibid*, p. 40.
15. *Ibid*, p. 41.
16. Strickland, *Lives of the Tudor and Stuart Princesses*, p. 74.
17. John Strype, *Historical Collections of the Life and Acts of John Aylmer* (Oxford: Clarendon Press, 1821), p. 196.
18. *Ibid*, p. 196.
19. Strickland, *Lives of the Tudor and Stuart Princesses*, p. 74.
20. *The Acts and Monuments of John Foxe*, ed. Rev. Stephen Reed Cattley (London: R. B. Seeley and W. Burnside, 1837–9), Vol viii, p. 700.
21. *Ibid*, Vol viii, p. 700.
22. *The Vita Mariae Angliae Reginae of Robert Wingfield of Brantham*, trans. Diarmaid Macculloch, in *Camden Miscellany 28* (London: Royal Historical Society, 1984), p. 249.
23. Alison Plowden, *Lady Jane Grey: Nine Days Queen* (Stroud: Sutton Publishing, 2003), p. 97.
24. *The Chronicle of Queen Jane and of two years of Queen Mary*, ed. John Gough Nichols (London: Camden Society, 1850), p. 110.
25. Alison Plowden, *Lady Jane Grey: Nine Days Queen* (Stroud: Sutton Publishing, 2003), p. 99.
26. *Holinshed's Chronicles of England, Scotland and Ireland*, Vol iii, p. 1067.
27. *Ibid*, p. 1068.
28. *The Chronicle of Queen Jane and of two years of Queen Mary*, p. 8.
29. *The Vita Mariae Angliae*, p. 266.
30. *The Chronicle of Queen Jane and of two years of Queen Mary*, p. 25.
31. *Ibid*, p. 25.
32. *Ibid*, p. 25.
33. *Ibid*, p. 25.
34. *Ibid*, p. 32.
35. *Memoirs and Remains of Lady Jane Grey*, ed. Nicholas Harris Nicolas (London: Henry Colburn and Richard Bentley, 1831), p. 48.
36. *The Acts and Monuments of John Foxe*, Vol vi, p. 422.
37. *Memoirs and Remains of Lady Jane Grey*, pp. 57–58.
38. *The Chronicle of Queen Jane and of two years of Queen Mary*, p. 56.
39. *Ibid*, p. 57.

40. *Ibid*, p. 59.
41. *Ibid*, p. 59.
42. *Ibid*, p. 59.

17 Lady Catherine Grey, Countess of Hertford

1. Richard Davey, *The Sisters of Lady Jane Grey* (London: Chapman And Hall, LTD, 1911), p. 83.
2. Retha M Warnicke, *Women of the English Renaissance and Reformation* (London: Greenwood Press, 1983), p. 99.
3. Thomas Fuller, *The History of the Worthies of England* (London: Thomas Tegg, 1840), Vol ii, p. 227.
4. William Camden, *The History of the Most Renowned and Victorious Princess Elizabeth, Late Queen of England* (London: R. Bentley, 1688), p. 70.
5. Leanda De Lisle, *The Sisters who would be Queen* (London: HarperPress, 2009), pp. 232–3.
6. Theresa Lewis, *Lives of the Friends and Contemporaries of Lord Chancellor Clarendon* (London: John Murray, 1852), Vol iii, p. 192.
7. *Oxford Dictionary of National Biography*, 'Mary I (1516 – 1558), queen of England and Ireland'.
8. Camden, *The History of the Most Renowned and Victorious Princess Elizabeth, Late Queen of England*, p. 54.
9. *Calendar of Letters and State Papers relating to English Affairs: preserved principally in the Archives of Simancas: Elizabeth 1558–1567*, ed. Martin A.S. Hume (London: Eyre and Spottiswoode, 1892), Vol i, p. 45.
10. Strickland, *Lives of the Tudor and Stuart Princesses*, p. 123.
11. Leanda De Lisle, *The Sisters who would be Queen* (London: HarperPress, 2009), p. 196.
12. *Calendar of Letters and State Papers relating to English Affairs: preserved principally in the Archives of Simancas: Elizabeth 1558–1567*, Vol i, p. 122.
13. *CSP, 1559–60*, p. 2.
14. *Ibid*, p. 2.
15. Lewis, *Lives of the Friends and Contemporaries of Lord Chancellor Clarendon*, Vol iii, p. 184.
16. *Ibid*, Vol iii, p. 194.
17. *Ibid*, Vol iii, p. 194.
18. Strickland, *Lives of the Tudor and Stuart Princesses*, p. 128.
19. Lewis, *Lives of the Friends and Contemporaries of Lord Chancellor Clarendon*, Vol iii, p. 200.
20. *Ibid*, Vol iii, p. 200.
21. *Calendar of Letters and State Papers relating to English Affairs: preserved principally in the Archives of Simancas: Elizabeth 1558–1567*, Vol i, p. 216.
22. Strickland, *Lives of the Tudor and Stuart Princesses*, p. 140.
23. *Notes and Queries*, Eighth Series, Vol vii, p. 342.
24. Henry Ellis, *Original Letters Illustrative of English History*, 2nd series (London: Harding And Lepard, Pall Mall East, 1827), Vol ii, p. 279.
25. *Ibid*, Vol ii, pp. 281–2.
26. *Ibid*, Vol ii, p. 283.
27. George Harbin, *The Hereditary Right of the Crown of England Asserted* (London: G. James, 1713), p. xli.

28. Ellis, *Original Letters Illustrative of English History*, 2nd series, Vol ii, p. 289.
29. *Ibid*, Vol ii, p. 290.
30. *Ibid*, Vol ii, p. 290.
31. *Ibid*, Vol ii, p. 290.

18 Lady Mary Grey

1. Davey, *The Sisters of Lady Jane Grey*, p. 291.
2. Warnicke, *Women of the English Renaissance and Reformation*, p. 99.
3. *Oxford Dictionary of National Biography*, Lady Mary Keyes [née Grey].
4. Leanda De Lisle, 'The Tudor Dwarf Princess', p.2. [Accessed 15/07/2023]
5. John William Burgon, *The Life and Times of Sir Thomas Gresham* (London: Robert Jennings, 1839–44), Vol ii, p. 389.
6. *Archaeologia Cantiana*, Vol 21 (London: Kent Archaeological Society, 1895), p. 246.
7. Ellis, *Original Letters Illustrative of English History*, 2nd series, Vol ii, p. 299.
8. Burgon, *The Life and Times of Sir Thomas Gresham*, Vol ii, p. 389.
9. *Ibid*, Vol ii, p. 388.
10. *Ibid*, Vol ii, p. 388.
11. Ellis, *Original Letters Illustrative of English History*, Vol ii, p. 310.
12. Burgon, *The Life and Times of Sir Thomas Gresham*, Vol ii, 393–4.
13. *Ibid*, Vol ii, p. 402.
14. *Ibid*, Vol ii, p. 403.
15. Strickland, *Lives of the Tudor and Stuart Princesses*, p. 179.
16. Burgon, *The Life and Times of Sir Thomas Gresham*, Vol ii, p. 410.
17. Davey, *The Sisters of Lady Jane Grey*, p. 285.
18. John Nichols, *Progresses and Public Processions of Queen Elizabeth* (London: John Nichols and Son, 1823), Vol ii, pp. 65–81.
19. *Notes and Queries*, Eighth Series, Vol vi, p. 302.
20. *Ibid*, Vol vi, p. 302.
21. *Ibid*, Vol vi, p. 303.
22. Leanda De Lisle, *The Sisters who would be Queen* (London: HarperPress, 2009), pp. 290–91.

19 Lady Margaret Clifford, Countess of Derby

1. Edward Quillinan, *Carmina Brugesiana: Domestic Poems* (Geneva: W. Fick, 1822), p. 41.
2. Thomas Dunham Whitaker, *The History and antiquities of the deanery of Craven, in the county of York* (London: Nichols, 1805), p. 313.
3. John Gough Nichols, *Literary Remains of King Edward the Sixth* (London: Roxburghe Club, 1857), Vol i, p. clxv.
4. *Ibid*, clxvii.
5. *Ibid*, clxvii.
6. *Ibid*, clxvii.
7. *Ibid*, cxcii-iii.
8. *Chronicle of Queen Jane and of two years of Queen Mary*, p. 169.
9. *The diary of Henry Machyn*, ed. John Gough Nichols (London: Camden Society, 1848), p. 82.
10. *Ibid* p. 82.
11. Nichols, *Progresses and Public Processions of Queen Elizabeth*, Vol i, p. 163.

12. *Ibid*, Vol i, p. 199.
13. *CSP, Addenda, 1566–79*, p. 43.
14. *Ibid*, p. 42.
15. *Ibid*, pp. 42–44.
16. Barry Coward, *The Stanleys, Lord Stanleys and Earl of Derby 1385 – 1672* (Manchester: Cheltenham Society, 1983), p. 31.
17. *Oxford Dictionary of National Biography*, Henry Stanley, fourth earl of Derby.
18. *CSP, Addenda, 1566–79*, p. 33.
19. *Ibid*, pp. 33–4.
20. Strickland, *Lives of the Tudor and Stuart Princesses*, p. 191.
21. Nichols, *Progresses and Public Processions of Queen Elizabeth*, Vol ii, p. 249.
22. *Calendar of Letters and State Papers relating to English Affairs: preserved principally in the Archives of Simancas: Elizabeth 1558–1567*, Vol ii, p. 692.
23. *Ibid*, Vol ii, p. 692.
24. *Ibid*, vol ii, p. 693.
25. Sir Harris Nicolas, *Memoirs of the life and times of Sir Christopher Hatton, K. G., Vice-Chamberlain and Lord Chancellor to Queen Elizabeth* (London: Richard Bentley, 1847), p. 146.
26. Coward, *The Stanleys, Lord Stanleys and Earl of Derby 1385 – 1672*, p. 32.
27. Nicolas, *Memoirs of the life and times of Sir Christopher Hatton*, p. 148.
28. *Ibid*, p. 148.
29. *Ibid*, p. 347.
30. *Ibid*, p. 150.
31. Edward Quillinan, *Carmina Brugesiana: Domestic Poems* (Geneva: W. Fick, 1822), p. 41.

20 Mary, Queen of Scots

1. Robert Lindesay, *The History of Scotland* (Edinburgh: Mr. Baskett and Company, 1728), p. 176.
2. *The State Papers and Letters of Sir Ralph Sadler*, ed. Arthur Clifford (London: T. Cadell etc, 1809), Vol i, p. 88.
3. *The Hamilton Papers*, ed. Joseph Bain (Edinburgh: H. M. General Register House, 1890), Vol ii, p. 3.
4. *The State Papers and Letters of Sir Ralph Sadler*, Vol i, p. 289.
5. Jane T. Stoddart, *The Girlhood of Mary, Queen of Scots* (London: Hodder and Stoughton, 1908), p. 20.
6. Pollnitz, *Princely Education in Early Modern Britain*, p. 211.
7. *Ibid*, p. 212.
8. Jane T. Stoddart, *The Girlhood of Mary, Queen of Scots* (London: Hodder and Stoughton, 1908), p. 142.
9. John Guy, *My Heart is My Own: The Life of Mary, Queen of Scots* (London: Fourth Estate, 2009), p. 119.
10. Camden, *The History of the Most Renowned and Victorious Princess Elizabeth, Late Queen of England*, p. 54.
11. Sir James Melville, *Memoirs of His Own Life* (Edinburgh: The Bannatyne Club, 1827), p. 134.
12. Robert S. Rait, *Mary, Queen of Scots, 1542 – 1587* (London: David Nutt, 1900), p. 70.
13. Robert Keith, *History of the affairs of Church and State in Scotland*, ed. John Parker Lawson, Vol ii (Edinburgh: Spottiswoode Society, 1845), p. 414.

Notes

14. John Maxwell Herries, *Historical Memoirs of the reign of Mary Queen of Scots*, ed. Robert Pitcairn (Edinburgh: Abbotsford Club, 1836), p. 79.
15. Sir James Melville, *Memoirs of His Own Life*, p. 159.
16. Antonia Fraser, *Mary Queen of Scots* (London: Weidenfeld & Nicholson, 2015), p. 350.
17. Claude Nau, *The History of Mary Stewart*, ed. Joseph Stevenson (Edinburgh, William Paterson, 1883), p. 34.
18. Rait, *Mary, Queen of Scots, 1542 – 1587*, p. 110.
19. *Ibid*, p. 121.
20. John Guy, *My Heart Is My Own: The Life of Mary, Queen of Scots* (London: Fourth Estate, 2009), p. 330.
21. Rait, Mary, *Queen of Scots, 1542–1587*, p. 160.
22. Ellis, *Original Letters Illustrative of English History*, 2nd series, Vol iii, p. 115.
23. *Ibid*, Vol iii, p. 115.
24. *Ibid*, Vol iii, p. 117.
25. *Ibid*, Vol iii, p. 117.

21 Henry Frederick, Prince of Wales

1. *A collection of scarce and valuable tracts*, ed. Walter Scott (London: T. Cadell etc, 1809), Vol ii, p. 228.
2. Birch, *The life of Henry, Prince of Wales*, p. 1.
3. *A collection of scarce and valuable tracts*, p. 177.
4. *The Workes of the most high and mightie prince, Iames, by the grace of God, king of Great Britaine, France and Ireland, defender of the faith, &c.*, ed. James, Bishop of Winton (London: Robert Barker and John Hill, 1616), p. 175.
5. *Ibid*, p. 175.
6. *Ibid*, p. 175.
7. *Ibid*, pp. 175–77.
8. *Ibid*, p. 177.
9. *Ibid*, p. 177.
10. *A collection of scarce and valuable tracts*, p. 227.
11. *The Workes of the most high and mightie prince, Iames*, p. 209.
12. Nichols, John, *The progresses, processions, and magnificent festivities, of King James the First*, Vol i, p. 147.
13. John Stow, *Annales, or a generall chronicle of England* (London: Richardi Meighen, 1631), p. 826.
14. *The Autobiography of Phineas Pett*, ed. W. G. Perrin (London: Navy Records Society, 1918), p. 21.
15. John Nichols, *The progresses, processions, and magnificent festivities, of King James the First*, Vol ii, p. 80.
16. *The Workes of the most high and mightie prince, Iames*, p. 185.
17. *Ibid*, p. 185.
18. *Ibid*, pp. 185–6.
19. Thomas Birch, *The life of Henry, Prince of Wales*, p. 76.
20. Pollnitz, *Princely Education in Early Modern Britain*, pp. 348–9.
21. *The Autobiography of Phineas Pett*, p. 62.
22. *A collection of scarce and valuable tracts*, p. 229.
23. *Ibid*, p. 230.
24. Samuel R. Gardiner, *History of England from the Accession of James I to the Outbreak of Civil War* (London: Longmans, Green and Co., 1883), Vol ii, p. 157.

25. *A collection of scarce and valuable tracts*, p. 232
26. *Ibid*, p. 231.
27. Thomas Birch, *The life of Henry, Prince of Wales*, p. 405.

22 Sophia, Electress of Hanover

1. *Memoirs of Sophia, Electress of Hanover, 1630–1680*, ed. H. Forester (London: Richard Bentley & Son, 1888), p. 4.
2. *Ibid*, p. 4.
3. *Ibid*, p. 5.
4. *Ibid*, p. 8.
5. *Ibid*, p. 9.
6. *Ibid*, p. 15.
7. *Ibid*, p. 18.
8. *Ibid*, p. 17.
9. *Ibid*, p. 24.
10. *Ibid*, p. 51.
11. *Ibid*, p. 38.
12. *Ibid*, p. 56.
13. *Ibid*, p. 89.
14. Robert S. Rait, *Five Stuart Princesses: Margaret of Scotland, Elizabeth of Bohemia, Mary of Orange, Henrietta of Orleans, Sophia of Hanover* (Westminster: Archibald Constable & Co., LTD, 1902), p. 304.
15. *Memoirs of Sophia, Electress of Hanover*, p. 93.
16. *Ibid*, p. 99.
17. *Ibid*, p. 150.
18. *Ibid*, p. 152.
19. *Ibid*, p. 155.
20. *Ibid*, p. 185.
21. *Ibid*, p. 253.
22. Adolphus William Ward, *The Electress Sophia and the Hanoverian Succession* (London: Longmans, Green, and Co., 1909), p. 201.
23. *The Life of King James The Second*, ed. Rev. S. Clarke (London: Longman, Hurst, Rees, Orme and Brown, 1816), Vol i, p. 440.
24. Vernon Bogdanor, *The Monarchy and the Constitution* (Oxford: Oxford University Press, 1997), p. 7.
25. Hutton Webster (ed.), *Historical Source Book* (London: D C. Heath And Company, 1920), p. 60.
26. William Coxe, *Memoirs of the Duke of Marlborough*, ed. John Wade, Vol iii (London: George Bell & Sons, 1889), p. 361.

23 James Francis Edward Stuart

1. *The several declarations toghether [sic] with the several depositions made in council on Monday October 22. 1688. concerning the birth of the Prince of Wales*, p. 43.
2. *Ibid*, p. 85.
3. Gilbert Burnet, *Bishop Burnet's History of His Own Time* (London: J Nunn, 1818), Vol ii, pp. 239–40.

Notes

4. *The Correspondence of Henry Hyde, Earl of Clarendon*, ed. Samuel Weller Singer, Vol ii, p. 156.
5. Burnet, *Bishop Burnet's History of His Own Time*, Vol ii, p. 382.
6. John Dalrymple, *Memoirs of Great Britain and Ireland* (London: W. Strahan and T. Cadell, in the Strand, 1773), Vol ii, p. 304.
7. *Ibid*, Vol ii, p. 304.
8. Martin Halle, *Queen Mary of Modena her life and letters* (London: J. M. Dent & Co., 1905), p.189.
9. George Agar Ellis (ed.), *The Ellis Correspondence* (London: Henry Colburn, 1829), Vol ii, pp. 114–5.
10. *Memoirs of the Chevalier de St. George*, in ed. E. M. Goldsmid, *The Clarendon Historical Society's Reprints*, Series II, 1884–86 (Edinburgh: Privately Printed For The Society, 1886), p. 15.
11. *The Life of King James The Second*, Vol ii, p. 198.
12. Burnet, *Bishop Burnet's History of His Own Time*, Vol ii, p. 457.
13. Dalrymple, *Memoirs of Great Britain and Ireland*, Vol ii, p. 329.
14. *Memoirs of the Chevalier de St. George*, p. 30.
15. Charles Sanford Terry, *The Chevalier de St. George* (London: David Nutt, 1901), p. 175.
16. John Heneage Jesse, *Memoirs of the Pretenders and Their Adherents* (Philadelphia, J. W. Moore, 1846), p. 36.
17. Terry, *The Chevalier de St. George*, p. 136.
18. *A True Account of the Proceedings at Perth*, p. 20.
19. Charles Wogan, *Female Fortitude, Exemplify'd, in an Impartial Narrative, of the Seizure, Escape and Marriage of the Princess Clementina Sobiesky* (London: 1722), p. 3.
20. *Oxford Dictionary of National Biography*, James Francis Edward.
21. Terry, *The Chevalier de St. George*, p. 468.
22. Wogan, *Female Fortitude, Exemplify'd, in an Impartial Narrative, of the Seizure, Escape and Marriage of the Princess Clementina Sobiesky*, p. 21.
23. Lord Mahon, *History of England from the peace of Utrecht to the peace of Versailles, 1713 – 1748* (London: John Murray, 1853), p. pxvi.
24. *Ibid*, p. pxvi.

24 Frederick Louis, Prince of Wales

1. Lord Hervey, John, *Memoirs of the reign of George the Second*, ed. John Wilson Croker (London: John Murray, 1848), Vol ii, p. 472.
2. *Memoirs of Frederica Sophia Wilhelmina*, trans. Howells, William D. (Boston: James R. Osgood and company, 1877), Vol i, p. 33.
3. *The letters and works of Lady Mary Wortley Montagu*, ed. Lord Wharncliffe (London: Bohn, 1861), Vol i, p. 258.
4. Horace Walpole, *Memoirs of the Reign of King George II*, ed. Lord Holland (London: Henry Colburn, 1847), Vol i, p. 75.
5. Lord Hervey, *Memoirs of the reign of George the Second*, Vol ii, p. 126.
6. *Memoirs of Frederica Sophia Wilhelmina*, Vol i, p. 85.
7. Lord Hervey, *Memoirs of the reign of George the Second*, Vol i, p. xxxii.
8. Walpole, *Memoirs of the Reign of King George II*, Vol i, p. 77.
9. Lord Hervey, *Memoirs of the reign of George the Second*, Vol i, p. 313.
10. *Ibid*, Vol ii, p. 114.
11. *Ibid*, Vol ii, p. 114.

12. *Ibid*, Vol ii, p. 117.
13. *Ibid*, Vol ii, p. 118.
14. *Ibid*, Vol ii, p. 116.
15. *Ibid*, Vol ii, p. 132.
16. *Ibid*, Vol ii, p. 132.
17. *Ibid*, Vol ii, p. 363.
18. *Ibid*, Vol ii, p. 364.
19. *Ibid*, Vol ii, pp. 365–66.
20. *Ibid*, Vol ii, pp. 371–2.
21. *Ibid*, Vol ii, p. 428.
22. *Ibid*, Vol ii, p. 434.
23. *Ibid*, Vol ii, p. 466.
24. *Ibid*, Vol ii, pp. 206–7.
25. *Ibid*, Vol ii, p. 520.
26. *Ibid*, Vol ii, p. 521.
27. *Ibid*, Vol ii, p. 520.
28. *The Diary of the Late George Bubb Dodington*, ed. Henry Penruddocke Wyndham (Salisbury: E. Easton, 1784), p. 96.
29. Walpole, *Memoirs of the Reign of King George II*, Vol i, p. 71.
30. *Ibid*, Vol i, p. 71.
31. *Ibid*, Vol i, p. 72.
32. *Ibid*, Vol i, p. 77.
33. *Ibid*, Vol i, p. 78.
34. Dodington, *The Diary of the Late George Bubb Dodington*, p. 112.
35. Walpole, *Memoirs of the Reign of King George II*, Vol i, pp. 227–8.

25 Frederick, Duke of York

1. John Watkins, *A Biographical Memoir of Frederick, Duke of York and Albany* (London: Henry Fisher, 1827), p. 9.
2. Charles Greville, *The Greville Memoirs: A Journal of the Reigns of King George IV and King William IV*, (London: Longmans, Green, and Co., 1874 – 1903), Vol i, p. 6.
3. Robert Huish, *Authentic Memoir of his late Royal Highness Frederick, Duke of York and Albany* (London: John Williams, 1827), p. 5.
4. *The Last Journals of Horace Walpole*, ed. A. Francis Steuart (London: John Lane, 1910), Vol i, p. 556.
5. *Annual Register, 1781, Third Edition* (London: G. Robinson, 1782), p. 161.
6. John Watkins, *A Biographical Memoir of Frederick, Duke of York and Albany*, pp. 60–6.
7. *Correspondence of Charles, First Marquis Cornwallis*, ed. Charles Ross (London: John Murray, 1859), Vol i, p. 360.
8. *Ibid*, Vol i, pp. 374–5.
9. John Watkins, *A Biographical Memoir of Frederick, Duke of York and Albany*, p. 117.
10. *Ibid*, p. 135.
11. *Annual Register, 1791* (London: Printed for F. and C. Rivington, 1795), p. 48.
12. *Ibid*, p. 49.
13. Percy Fitzgerald, *The Royal Dukes and Princesses of the family of George III*, Vol ii (London: Tinsley Brothers, 1882), p. 105.

Notes

14. John Watkins, *A Biographical Memoir of Frederick, Duke of York and Albany*, p. 187.
15. Robert Huish, *Authentic Memoir of his late Royal Highness Frederick, Duke of York and Albany* (London: John Williams, 1827), p. 16.
16. *Annual Register, 1793* (London: Printed, by assignment from the executors of the late Mr. James Dodsley, 1797), p. 273.
17. John Watkins, *A Biographical Memoir of Frederick, Duke of York and Albany*, p. 480.
18. The following account has been synthesised from Terry Astley, *The Campaign in Holland, 1799* (London: W. Mitchell, 1861), pp. 2–70.
19. *Annual Register, 1827* (London: Printed for Baldwin And Cradock et al., 1828), p. 4.
20. *Stratford's Authentic Edition of the investigation of the charges brought against His Royal Highness the Duke of York*, Vol i, p. 5.
21. John Watkins, *A Biographical Memoir of Frederick, Duke of York and Albany*, p. 460.
22. *Ibid*, p.483.
23. *Ibid*, p. 488.
24. *Ibid*, p. 490.
25. Charles Greville, *The Greville Memoirs: A Journal of the Reigns of King George IV and King William IV*, Vol i, p. 87.
26. *Ibid*, Vol i, p. 85.
27. *Ibid*, Vol i, pp. 88–89.

Bibliography

Primary Sources

Anon, *A True Accompt Of the Most Triumphant, and Royal Accomplishment of the Baptism of the Most Excellent, Right High, and Mighty Prince, Henry Frederick, By the Grace of God, Prince of Scotland, and now Prince of Wales* (Edinburgh: Printed by John Reid, for Alexander Ogston stationer, 1687)

Anon, *A True Account of the Proceedings at Perth* (London: J. Baker, 1616)

Anon, *The Annual Register, 1781, Third Edition* (London: G. Robinson, 1782)

Anon, *The Annual Register, 1791* (London: Printed for F. And C. Rivington, 1795)

Anon, *The Annual Register, 1793* (London: Printed, by assignment from the executors of the late Mr. James Dodsley, 1797)

Anon, *The Annual Register, 1827* (London: Printed for Baldwin and Cradock et al., 1828)

Anon, *The several declarations toghether [sic] with the several depositions made in council on Monday October 22. 1688. concerning the birth of the Prince of Wales* (1688)

Anon, *Writings of Edward the Sixth, William Hugh, Queen Catherine Parr, Anne Askew, Lady Jane Grey, Hamilton, and Balnaves* (Philadelphia: Presbyterian Board of Publication, 1842)

Armstrong, C. A. J. (trans.), Dominic Mancini, *The Usurpation of Richard III* (Gloucester: Alan Sutton Publishing, 1989)

Ascham, Roger, *Schoolmaster* (London: Cassell and Company, 1909)

Ashley, W. J. (ed.), *Edward III & his Wars, 1327–1360: Extracts from the Chronicles of Froissart, Jehan le Bel, Knighton, Adam of Murimuth, Robert of Avesbury, the Chronicle of Lanercost, the State Papers, & other contemporary records* (London: David Nutt, 1887)

Ayre, John (ed.), *The Catechism of Thomas Becon* (Cambridge: University Press, 1844)

Bachrach, Bernard S. And Bachrach, David S. (trans.), *The Gesta Tancredi of Ralph of Caen* (Aldershot: Ashgate Publishing, 2005)

Bain, Joseph (ed.), *The Hamilton Papers*, Vol 2 (Edinburgh: H. M. General Register House, 1890)

Barber, Richard, *Life & Campaigns of the Black Prince* (Suffolk: Boydell Press, 1986)

Barlow, Frank (trans.), *The Life of King Edward the Confessor* (London: Thomas Nelson and Sons, 1962)

Bergenroth, G. A. (ed.), *Calendar of Letters, Despatches, And State Papers, Relating to the negotiations between England and Spain: Henry VII 1485 – 1509*, Vol 1 (London: Longman, Green, Longman & Roberts, 1862)

Bourchier, Sir John and Lord Berners (trans.), *The Chronicle of Froissart: Translated Out of French by Sir John Bourchier [and] Lord Berners, annis 1523-5*, Vol 2 (London: David Nutt, 1901)

Brereton, Geoffrey (ed.), *Froissart Chronicles* (Middlesex: Penguin Books, 1968)

Bibliography

Brie, Friedrich, W. D (ed.), *The Brut or The Chronicles of England*, Vol 1 (London: Early English Text Society, 1906)

Bruce, John (ed.), *Histoire of the arrival of Edward IV in England and the finall recouerye of his kingdomes from Henry VI* (London: Camden Society, 1838)

Bryant, Nigel (trans.), *The True Chronicles of Jean le Bel* (Woodbridge: The Boydell Press, 2015)

Burgess, Glyn S. (trans.), *The History of the Norman People – Wace's Roman de Rou* (Woodbridge: Boydell, 2004)

Burnet, Gilbert, *Bishop Burnet's History of His Own Time*, Vol 2 (London: J Nunn, 1818)

Burney, Fanny, *Diary and Letters of Madame D'Arblay*, Vol 4 (London: Henry Colburn, 1843)

Camden, William, *The History of the Most Renowned and Victorious Princess Elizabeth, Late Queen of England* (London: R. Bentley, 1688)

Calendar of Close Rolls, Edward III, 14 Vols, 1327–1377 (London: HMSO, 1896–1913)

Calendar of Close Rolls, Henry V, 2 Vols, 1413–1422 (London: HMSO, 1929–1932)

Calendar of the Patent Rolls, Edward III, 16 Vols, 1327–1377 (London: HMSO, 1891–1916)

Calendar of Patent Rolls, Edward IV & Henry VI, 1 Vol, 1467–1477 (London: HMSO, 1900)

Calendar of Patent Rolls, Edward IV, Edward V & Richard III, 1 Vol, 1476–1485 (London: HMSO, 1916)

Calendar of the Patent Rolls, Henry IV, 4 Vols, 1399–1413 (London: HMSO, 1903–1909)

Calendar of Patent Rolls, Henry VI, 6 Vols, 1422–1461 (London: HMSO, 1901–1910)

Calendar of Patent Rolls, Henry VII, 2 Vols, 1485–1509 (London: HMSO, 1914–1916)

Calendar of the Patent Rolls, Richard II, 6 Vols, 1377–1399 (London: HMSO, 1895–1905)

Calendar of State Papers, Domestic Series, Elizabeth, Addenda, 1566 – 1579, ed. Mary Anne Everett Green (London: Longman etc, 1871)

Campbell, W. (ed.), *Materials for a History of the Reign of Henry VII*, 2 Vols (London: Longman & Co. etc, 1873-7)

Cattley, Stephen Reed (ed.), *The Acts and Monuments of John Foxe*, 8 Vols (London: R. B. Seeley and W. Burnside, 1837–9)

Clarke, Rev. S. (ed.), *The Life of King James The Second*, 2 Vols (London: Longman, Hurst, Rees, Orme and Brown, 1816)

Clifford, Arthur (ed.), *The State Papers and Letters of Sir Ralph Sadler*, 2 Vols (London: T. Cadell etc, 1809)

Coates, Tim (ed.), *Letters of Henry VIII, 1526–29* (London: The Stationary Office, 2001)

Croker, John Wilson (ed.), John, Lord Hervey, *Memoirs of the reign of George the Second: from his accession to the death of Queen Caroline*, 2 Vols (London: John Murray, 1848)

Dalrymple, John, *Memoirs of Great Britain and Ireland*, Vol 2 (London: W. Strahan and T. Cadell, in the Strand, 1773)

Dockray, Keith (ed.), *Henry VI, Margaret of Anjou and the Wars of the Roses* (London: Fonthill Media Limited, 2016)

Dockray, Keith and Hammond, Peter (eds.), *Richard III From Contemporary Chronicles, Letters & Records* (London: Fonthill Media Limited, 2013)

Ellis, George Agar (ed.), *The Ellis Correspondence* (London: Henry Colburn, 1829)

Ellis, Henry (ed.), *Hall's Chronicle* (London: J. Johnson [etc], 1809)

Ellis, Henry (ed.), *Original Letters Illustrative of English History*, 2nd series, 4 Vols (London: Harding And Lepard, Pall Mall East, 1827)

Ellis, Henry (ed.), *The New Chronicles of England and France by Robert Fabyan* (London: F. C. And J. Rivington et al, 1811)

Ellis, Henry (ed.), *Three Books of Polydore Vergil's English History* (London: Camden Society, 1844)

Forester, H. (trans.), *Memoirs of Sophia, Electress of Hanover, 1630–1680* (London: Richard Bentley & Son, 1888)

Forrester, Thomas (trans.), *The Chronicle of Florence of Worcester* (London: H. G. Bohun, 1854)

Forrester, Thomas (trans.), *The Ecclesiastical History of England and Normandy by Ordericus Vitalis*, 4 Vols (London: H. G. Bohn, 1853)

Fuller, Thomas, *The History of the Worthies of England*, 3 Vols (London: Thomas Tegg, 1840)

Gairdner, James (ed.), *Letters and Papers illustrative of the reigns of Richard III and Henry VII*, Vol 1 (London: Green, Longman, and Roberts, 1861)

Gairdner, James (ed.), *The Historical Collections of a citizen of London in the fifteenth century* (Westminster: Camden Society, 1876)

Gairdner, James (ed.), *The Paston Letters 1422 – 1509*, Vol 1 (Birmingham: 1872)

Gairdner, James (ed.), *Three Fifteenth-Century Chronicles* (London: The Camden Society, 1880)

Giles, J. A. (ed.), *The Chronicles of The White Rose of York* (London: James Bohn, 1845)

Giles, J. A. (trans.), *Roger of Wendover's Flowers of History*, 2 Vols (London: H. G. Bohn, 1849)

Giles, J. A. (trans.), *William of Malmesbury's Chronicle of the Kings of England* (London: H. G. Bohn, 1847)

Given-Wilson, Chris (ed.), *Chronicles of the Revolution 1397 – 1400* (Manchester: Manchester University Press, 2008)

Given-Wilson, Chris (trans.), *Continuatio Eulogii* (Oxford: Oxford University Press, 2019)

Greenway, Diana (trans.), *Henry of Huntingdon: The History of the English People 1000 – 1154* (Oxford: Oxford University Press, 2009)

Greville, Charles C.F., *The Greville Memoirs: A Journal of the Reigns of King George IV and King William IV*, 3 Vols (London: Longmans, Green, and Co., 1874 – 1903)

Hallam, Elizabeth, *The Plantagenet Chronicles* (Surrey: Tiger Books, 1995)

Hallam, Elizabeth, *The Wars of the Roses* (Surrey: Bramley Books, 1997)

Hamilton, William Douglas (ed.), *A Chronicle of England during the reigns of the Tudors by Charles Wriothesley*, 2 Vols (Westminster: Camden Society, 1875–7)

Harbin, George, *The Hereditary Right of the Crown of England Asserted* (London: G. James, 1713)

Hardy, Thomas Duffus, *A Description of The Patent Rolls In The Tower of London* (London: G. Eyre and A. Spottiswoode, 1835)

Hardy, Thomas Duffy (ed.), *Syllabus (In English) of the documents relating to England and other kingdoms contained in the collection known as "Rymer's Foedera"*, 3 Vols (London: Longmans, Green & Co., 1869–85)

Haynes, Samuel (ed.) *A Collection of State Papers Relating to Affairs in the Reigns of King Henry VIII, King Edward VI, Queen Mary and Queen Elizabeth* (London: William Bowyer, 1740)

Hearnii, Thomas (ed.), *Joannis Lelandi Antiquarii de rebus britannicis collectanea*, 5 Vols (London: Jo Richardson, 1770)

Bibliography

Hector, L. C. and Harvey, Barbara, F. (trans.), *The Westminster Chronicle, 1381 – 1394* (Oxford: Oxford University Press, 1982)

Hobbins, Daniel (trans.), Bernard André, *The Life of Henry VII* (New York: Italica Press, 2011)

Holland, Lord (ed.), Walpole, Horace, *Memoirs of the Reign of King George II*, Vol I (London: Henry Colburn, 1846)

Holden, A. J., Gregory, S. and D. Couch (trans.), *History of William Marshal*, 3 Vols (London: Anglo-Norman Texts Society, 2002–6)

Holinshed, Ralph, *Holinshed's Chronicles of England, Scotland and Ireland*, 6 Vols (London: J. Johnson [etc], 1807–8)

Horrox, Rosemary and P. W. Hammond (eds.), *The British Library Harleian Manuscript 433*, Vol 1 (Gloucester: Alan Sutton Publishing for Richard III Society, 1979)

Howells, William D. (trans.), *Memoirs of Frederica Sophia Wilhelmina*, 2 Vols (Boston: James R. Osgood And Company, 1877)

Hume, Martin A.S. (ed.), *Calendar of Letters and State Papers relating to English Affairs: preserved principally in the Archives of Simancas: Elizabeth 1558–1567*, Vol 1 (London: Eyre and Spottiswoode, 1892)

Hutton, W. H. (ed.), *S. Thomas of Canterbury* (London: David Nutt, 1899)

Ingram, Rev J. (trans.), *The Anglo-Saxon Chronicle* (London: Longman, Hurst, Rees, Orme and Brown, 1823)

Ives, E. W, *Tudor Dynastic Problems Revisited*, in *Historical Research 81* (2008)

James, Bishop of Winton (ed.), *The Workes of the most high and mightie prince, Iames, by the grace of God, king of Great Britaine, France and Ireland, defender of the faith, &c.* (London: Robert Barker and John Hill, 1616)

Johnson, Charles, and Cronne, H. A. (eds.), *Regesta Regum Anglo-Normannorum 1066 – 1154*, Vol 2 (Oxford: Clarendon Press, 1913)

Kingsford, Charles Lethbridge (ed.), *Chronicles of London* (Oxford: Oxford Clarendon Press, 1905)

Krey, August C. (ed.), *The First Crusade* (Princeton: Princeton University Press, 1921)

Lawson, John Parked (ed.), Robert Keith, *History of the affairs of Church and State in Scotland*, Vol 2 (Edinburgh: Spottiswoode Society, 1845)

Lindesay, Robert, *The History of Scotland* (Edinburgh: Mr. Baskett and Company, 1728)

Logan, George M. (trans.), Thomas More, *The History of King Richard The Third* (Indiana: Indiana University Press, 2005)

Macculloch, Diarmaid (trans.), *The Vita Mariae Angliae Reginae of Robert Wingfield of Brantham*, in *Camden Miscellany 28* (London: Royal Historical Society, 1984)

Martin, G. H. (trans.), *Knighton's Chronicle, 1337 – 1396* (Oxford: Oxford University Press, 1995)

Melville, Sir James, *Memoirs of His Own Life* (Edinburgh: The Bannatyne Club, 1827)

Memoirs of the Chevalier de St. George, in Goldsmid, E. M. (ed.), *The Clarendon Historical Society's Reprints*, Series II, 1884–86 (Edinburgh: Privately Print For The Society)

Nichols, John (ed.), *A Collection of ordinances and regulations for the government of the royal household, made in diverse reigns* (London: Society of Antiquaries, 1790)

Nichols, John Gough (ed.), *Chronicle of the Grey Friars of London* (London: Camden Society, 1852)

Nichols, John Gough (ed.), *The Chronicle of Queen Jane and of two years of Queen Mary* (London: Camden Society, 1850)

Nichols, John Gough (ed.), *The Diary of Henry Machyn* (London: Camden Society, 1848)

Nicolas, Nicholas Harris (ed.), *Memoirs and Remains of Lady Jane Grey* (London: Henry Colburn and Richard Bentley, 1831)

Perrin, W. G. (trans.), *The Autobiography of Phineas Pett* (London: Navy Records Society, 1918)

Pitcairn, Robert (ed.), John Maxwell Herries, *Historical Memoirs of the reign of Mary Queen of Scots* (Edinburgh: Abbotsford Club, 1836)

Pollard, A. F. (ed.), *The Reign of Henry VII From Contemporary Sources*, Vol 1 (London: Longmans, Green And Co., 1913)

Powell, G. H. (ed.), *Memoirs of Robert Cary, Earl of Monmouth* (London: Alexander Moring, limited, The De La More Press, 1905)

Potter, K. R. (trans.), *Gesta Stephani* (London: Thomas Nelson and Sons, 1955)

Preest, David (trans.), *The Chronicle of Geoffrey le Baker* (Woodbridge: The Boydell Press, 2012)

Preest, David (trans.), *The Chronica Maiora of Thomas Walsingham 1376 – 1422* (Woodbridge: The Boydell Press, 2005)

Quillinan, Edward (ed.), *Carmina Brugesiana: Domestic Poems* (Geneva: W. Fick, 1822)

Rait, Robert S. (ed.), *Mary, Queen of Scots, 1542 – 1587* (London: David Nutt, 1900)

Remfry, Paul Martin (trans.), *The Wigmore Chronicle 1066 to 1377* (United Kingdom: Castle Studies Research & Publishing, 2013)

Riley, Henry T. (ed.), *Ingulph's Chronicle of the Abbey of Croyland* (London: Bohn, 1854)

Riley, Henry T. (trans.), *The Annals of Roger de Hoveden*, 2 Vols (London: H. G. Bohn, 1853)

Ross, Charles (ed.), *Correspondence of Charles, First Marquis Cornwallis*, 3 Vols (London: John Murray, 1859)

Scott, Walter (ed.), *A collection of scarce and valuable tracts*, Vol 2 (London: T. Cadell etc, 1809)

Singer, Samuel Weller (ed.), *The Correspondence of Henry Hyde, Earl of Clarendon* (London: H Colburn, 1828)

Steuart, A. Francis (ed.), Horace Walpole, *The Last Journals of Horace Walpole*, 2 Vols (London: John Lane, 1910)

Stevenson, Joseph (ed.), Claude Nau, *The History of Mary Stewart* (Edinburgh, William Paterson, 1883)

Stevenson, Joseph (trans.), *Scalacronica of Thomas Grey of Heton* (Edinburgh: Maitland Club, 1836)

Stevenson, Joseph (trans.), The Church Historians of England, Vol IV – Part 2 (London: Seelys, 1856)

Stevenson, Joseph (trans.), The Church Historians of England, Vol V – Part 1 (London: Seelys, 1858)

Stow, John, *Annales, or a generall chronicle of England* (London: Richardi Meighen, 1631)

Stratford's Authentic Edition of the investigation of the charges brought against His Royal Highness the Duke of York, 2 Vols (London: J. Stratford, 1809)

Stubbs, William (ed.), *Gesta Regis Henrici Secundi Benedicti Abbatis*, 2 Vols (London: Longmans, Green, Reader and Dyer, 1867)

Strype, John, *Historical Collections of the Life and Acts of John Aylmer* (Oxford: Clarendon Press, 1821)

Terry, Charles Sanford (ed.), *The Chevalier de St. George* (London: David Nutt, 1901)

Thompson, Edith (ed.), *The Wars of York and Lancaster 1450 – 1485* (London: David Nutt, 1892)

Bibliography

Thompson, Edward Maunde (ed.), *Adæ Murimuth Continuatio Chronicarum: Robertus de Avesbury de Gestis Mirabilibus Regis Edwardi Terti* (London: Spottiswoode, 1889)

Thompson, Edward Maunde (ed.), *Chronicon Adæ de Usk, A.D. 1377 – 1404* (London: John Murray, 1876)

Van Houts, Elizabeth M. C. and Love, Rosalind C. (trans.), *The Warenne (Hyde) Chronicle* (Oxford: Oxford University Press, 2013)

Wade, John (ed.), William Coxe, *Memoirs of the Duke of Marlborough*, Vol 3 (London: George Bell & Sons, 1889)

Webster, Hutton (ed.), *Historical Source Book* (London: D C. Heath And Company, 1920)

Wharncliffe, Lord (ed.), *The letters and works of Lady Mary Wortley Montagu*, Vol 1 (London: Bohn, 1861)

Wilson, Chris-Given (trans.), *Continuatio Eulogii* (Oxford: Oxford University Press, 2019)

Wogan, Charles, *Female Fortitude, Exemplify'd, in an Impartial Narrative, of the Seizure, Escape and Marriage of the Princess Clementina Sobiesky* (London: 1722)

Wood, Mary Anne Everett (ed.), *Letters of Royal and Illustrious Ladies of Great Britain*, 3 Vols (London: Henry Colburn, 1846)

Wyndham, Henry Penruddocke (ed.), Bubb Dodington, *The Diary of the Late George Bubb Dodington* (Salisbury: E. Easton, 1784)

Secondary Sources

Aird, William, M., *Robert Curthose: Duke of Normandy, c. 1050 – 1134* (Woodbridge: Boydell Press, 2008)

Archaeologia Cantiana, Volume 21 (London: Kent Archaeological Society, 1895)

Ashdown, Dulcie, M., *Tudor Cousins* (Stroud: Sutton Publishing, 2000)

Astley, Terry, *The Campaign in Holland, 1799* (London: W. Mitchell, 1861)

Baldwin, David, *Richard III* (Stroud: Amberley Publishing, 2013)

Barber, Richard, *Edward, Prince of Wales and Aquitaine* (Suffolk: The Boydell Press, 1978)

Bartlett, Robert, *Blood Royal* (Cambridge: Cambridge University Press, 2020)

Bennett, Michael, *Edward III's Entail and the Succession to the Crown, 1376 – 1471* in *The English Historical Review*, Vol 113, No. 452 (June 1998)

Birch, Thomas, *The life of Henry, Prince of Wales, eldest son of King James I* (London: A. Millar, 1760)

Blackburn, Robert, *King and Country: Monarchy and the future king Charles III* (London: Politico's Publishing, LTD, 2006)

Bogdanor, Vernon, *The Monarchy and the Constitution* (Oxford: Oxford University Press, 1997)

Bradbury, Jim, *Stephen and Matilda: The Civil War of 1139 – 53* (Stroud: Alan Sutton Publishing, 1996)

Bridge, F. Maynard, *Princes of Wales* (London: H. F. W Deane and Sons, 1922)

Burgon, John William, *The Life and Times of Sir Thomas Gresham*, 2 Vols (London: Robert Jennings, 1839–44)

Carson, Annette, *Richard III: The Maligned King* (Stroud: The History Press, 2008)

Chibnall, Marjorie, *Anglo-Norman England 1066 – 1166* (Oxford: Blackwell Publishing, 1993)

Chibnall, Majorie, *The Empress Matilda* (Oxford: Blackwell Publishers LTD, 1999)

Church, Stephen, *King John: England, Magna Carta and the Making of a Tyrant* (London: Macmillan, 2015)

Cokayne, George Edward, *Complete Peerage*, Vol 4 (London: George Bell and Sons, 1893)

Coward, Barry, *The Stanleys, Lords Stanley and Earls of Derby 1385 – 1672* (Manchester: Cheltenham Society, 1983)

Davey, Richard, *The Sisters of Lady Jane Grey* (London: Chapman And Hall, LTD, 1911)

David, Charles Wendell, *Robert Curthose, Duke of Normandy* (London: Harvard University Press, 1920)

Davies, Robert, *Extracts From the Municipal Records of the City of York During the Reigns of Edward IV, Edward V and Richard III* (London: J.B. Nichols and Son, 1843)

De Lisle, Leanda, *The Sisters who would be Queen* (London: HarperPress, 2009)

Doran, John, *The Book of the Princes of Wales* (London: Richard Bentley, 1860)

Everard, J. A, *Brittany and the Angevins* (Cambridge: Cambridge University Press, 2000)

Fitzgerald, Percy, *The Royal Dukes and Princesses of the family of George III*, Vol 2 (London: Tinsley Brothers, 1882)

Fraser, Antonia, *Mary Queen of Scots* (London: Weidenfeld & Nicholson, 2015)

Gardiner, Samuel R., *History of England from the Accession of James I to the Outbreak of Civil War*, Vol 2 (London: Longmans, Green and Co., 1895)

Gilbert, J. T, *History of the Viceroys of Ireland* (Dublin: James Duffy, 1865)

Given-Wilson, Chris, *Legitimation, Designation and Succession to the Throne in Fourteenth-century England* in Isabel Alfonso, Hugh Kennedy and Julio Escalona (eds.), *Building Legitimacy: Political Discourses and forms of Legitimation in Medieval Societies* (Leiden: Brill, 2004), p. 100.

Green, Judith A., *Henry I* (Cambridge: Cambridge University Press, 2009)

Green, Judith A., *The Government of England Under Henry I* (Cambridge: Cambridge University Press, 1986)

Green, Mary Anne Everett, *Lives of the Princesses of England from the Norman Conquest*, Vol 1 (London: Henry Colburn, 1850)

Grummitt, David, *A Short History of the Wars of the Roses* (London: I. B. Tauris & Co., Ltd, 2013)

Guy, John, *My Heart is My Own: The Life of Mary, Queen of Scots* (London: Fourth Estate, 2009)

Halle, Martin, *Queen Mary of Modena her life and letters* (London: J. M. Dent & Co., 1905)

Hammond, Peter, *The Children of Richard III* (London: Fonthill Media, 2018)

Hicks, Michael, *Edward V* (Stroud: Tempus Publishing, 2003)

Hicks, Michael, *The Wars of the Roses* (London: Yale University Press, 2010)

Higham, N. J., *The Death of Anglo-Saxon England* (Stroud: Sutton Publishing, 1997)

Holt, J. C., *Politics and Property in Early Medieval England* in J.C. Holt, (ed.), *Colonial England 1066 – 1215* (London: The Hambledon Press, 1997)

Hopkinson, Charles and Speight, Martin, *The Mortimers: Lords of the March* (Logaston: Logaston Press, 2013)

Huish, R., *Authentic Memoir of his late Royal Highness Frederick, Duke of York and Albany* (London: John Williams, 1827)

Ives, Eric, *Lady Jane Grey: A Tudor Mystery* (Chichester: Wiley-Blackwell, 2011)

Ives, Eric, *Tudor Dynastic Problems Revisited* in *Historical Research 81* (2008)

Jesse, John Heneage, *Memoirs of the Pretenders and Their Adherents* (Philadelphia, J. W. Moore, 1846)

Bibliography

Johnson, P.A, *Duke Richard of York 1411 – 1460* (Oxford: Clarendon Press, 1988)

King, Edmund, *King Stephen* (Newhaven and London: Yale University Press, 2012)

Lack, Catherine, *Conqueror's Son* (Stroud: Sutton Publishing, 2007)

Le Patourel, John, *The Norman Succession, 996 – 1135*, in *English Historical Review*, Vol 86, No. 339 (1971)

Levine, Mortimer, *Tudor Dynastic Problems 1460 – 1571* (Letchworth: The Aldine Press, 1973)

Lewis, Lady Theresa, *Lives of the Friends and Contemporaries of Lord Chancellor Clarendon*, Volume 3 (London: John Murray, 1852)

Lewis, Matthew, *The Wars of the Roses: The Key Players in the Struggle for Supremacy* (Stroud: Amberley Publishing, 2015)

Lewis, Matthew, *Richard III* (Stroud: Amberley Publishing, 2018)

Mahon, Lord, *History of England from the peace of Utrecht to the peace of Versailles, 1713 – 1748* (London: John Murray, 1853)

Maitland, F. W., *The Constitutional History of England* (Cambridge: University Press, 1950)

Moorhen, Wendy E.A., 'The Career of John de la Pole, Earl of Lincoln' in ed. Anne F. Sutton, *The Ricardian*, Vol 13 (2003)

Mortimer, Ian, *Medieval Intrigue* (London: Continuum International Publishing Group, 2010)

Nichols, John, *Progresses and Public Processions of Queen Elizabeth*, 3 Vols (London: John Nichols and Son, 1823)

Nichols, John, *The progresses, processions, and magnificent festivities, of King James the First, his royal consort, family and court*, 4 Vols (London: J.B. Nichols, 1828)

Nichols, John Gough, *Literary Remains of King Edward the Sixth*, 2 Vols (London: Roxburghe Club, 1857)

Nicolas, Sir Harris, *Memoirs of the life and times of Sir Christopher Hatton, K. G., Vice-Chamberlain and Lord Chancellor to Queen Elizabeth* (London: Richard Bentley, 1847)

Norgate, Kate, *England Under the Angevin Kings*, Vol 1 (London: Macmillan and Co., 1887)

Norgate, Kate, *John Lackland* (London: Macmillan And Co., Limited, 1902)

Notes and Queries, Eighth Series, Vol VI (London: John C. Francis, July-December 1894)

Notes and Queries, Eighth Series, Vol VII (London: John C. Francis, January – June 1895)

Notes and Queries, Vol 168, No. 9 (London: Anon, March 2, 1935)

Orme, Nicholas, *From Childhood to Chivalry* (London: Methuen, 1984)

Ormrod, W. Mark, *Edward III* (London: Yale University Press, 2013)

Ormrod, W. Mark, *The DNA of Richard III: False Paterniy and the Royal Succession* in eds. Joanna Martin and Rob Lutton, *Nottingham Medieval Studies*, 60 (2016)

Oxford Dictionary of National Biography, online edition.

Pollard, A.J., *Late Medieval England, 1399 – 1509* (Essex: Pearson Education Limited, 2000)

Pollnitz, Aysha, *Princely Education in Early Modern Britain* (Cambridge: Cambridge University Press, 2015)

Plowden, Alison, *Lady Jane Grey: Nine Days Queen* (Stroud: Sutton Publishing, 2003)

Rait, Robert S., *Five Stuart Princesses: Margaret of Scotland, Elizabeth of Bohemia, Mary of Orange, Henrietta of Orleans, Sophia of Hanover* (Westminster: Archibald Constable & Co., LTD, 1902)

Seipp, David J., *How to Get Rid of a King: Lawyering the Revolution of 1399*, in Catharine MacMillan and Charlotte Smith, eds., *Challenges to Authority and the Recognition of Rights* (Cambridge: Cambridge University Press, 2018)

Stoddart, Jane T., *The Girlhood of Mary, Queen of Scots* (London: Hodder and Stoughton, 1908)

Strickland, Agnes, *Lives of the Tudor and Stuart Princesses* (London: George Bell & Sons, 1907)

Strickland, Matthew, *Henry the Young King 1155–1183* (London: Yale University Press, 2016)

Stringer, Keith J, *The Reign of King Stephen* (London: Routledge, 1993)

Stubbs, William, *Constitutional History of England, Vol 1* (Oxford: Clarendon Press, 1883)

Strype, John, *Historical Collections of the life and acts of the Right Reverend Father in God, John Aylmer* (Oxford: Clarendon Press, 1821)

Sutton, Anne F., and Visser-Fuchs, Livia, *The Royal Funerals of The House of York at Windsor* (London: Richard III Society, 2005)

Tabuteau, Emily Zack, *The Role of Law in the Succession to Normandy*, in Robert B. Patterson (ed.), *The Haskins Society Journal*, Vol 3 (London: Hambledon Press, 1991)

Vickers, K. H, *Humphrey Duke of Gloucester* (London: A. Constable and Company, Limited, 1907)

Walters, John, *The Royal Griffin* (London: Jarrolds, 1972)

Ward, Adolphus William, *The Electress Sophia and the Hanoverian Succession* (London: Longmans, Green, and Co., 1909)

Warnicke, Retha M., *Women of the English Renaissance and Reformation* (London: Greenwood Press, 1983)

Watkins, John, *A Biographical Memoir of Frederick, Duke of York and Albany* (London: Henry Fisher, 1827)

Weir, Alison, *Britain's Royal Families* (London: Vintage, 2008)

Whitaker, Thomas Dunham, *The History and antiquities of the deanery of Craven, in the county of York* (London: Nichols, 1805)

Williams, Anne, *Some Notes and Consideration on Problems Connected with the English Royal Succession, 860–1066*, in R. Allen Brown (ed.), *Proceedings of the Battle Conference 1978* (Ipswich: The Boydell Press, 1979)

Williamson, J. W., *The Myth of the Conqueror – Prince Henry Stuart: A Study of 17th Century Personation* (New York: AMS Press, 1978)

Wood, Lynsey, *The very next blood of the king*, in Ana Maria, S. A. Rodrigues, Manuela Santos Silva, Jonathan Spangler, (eds.), *Dynastic Change* (Abingdon: Routledge, 2020)

Index

Adela, Countess of Blois 20, 32, 37, 48
Adeliza of Louvain, Queen of
    Henry I 38, 41
Anne of Denmark, Queen of
    James I 221-222, 224-225, 228, 230
Angevin Empire 56-57, 66, 68, 70, 71, 72, 73, 75, 80, 88
Anne, Queen 232, 240, 241-242, 243-244, 260
Anselm, Archbishop of
    Canterbury 29-30, 36
Arthur, Duke of Brittany 66-75
Augusta, Charlotte, Princess, daughter of George IV 280
Augusta, Princess of Wales, wife of Frederick Louis, Prince of Wales 259-60, 263-269
Augustus, Ernest, Elector of Hanover 235-242

Beaufort, Cardinal Henry 114, 116-117
Beaufort, Edmund, 2nd Duke of
    Somerset 116, 117-121, 126
Beaufort, Edmund, 4th Duke of
    Somerset 133-135
Beaufort, Henry, 3rd Duke of
    Somerset 122, 124, 129-130
Beaufort, Margaret 145
Becket, Thomas, Archbishop of
    Canterbury 46, 56-59, 60, 69, 95
Brandon, Lady Frances, Duchess of
    Suffolk 169, 173, 175, 176, 180, 181, 183, 189-190
Brandon, Lady Eleanor, Duchess of
    Cumberland 169, 195-196, 199

Calfhil, Mrs 198
Caroline of Ansbach, queen of
    George II 231, 243-244, 259-260, 261, 262, 265-267

Catherine of Aragon, wife of Arthur
    Tudor, queen of Henry VIII 158, 159-166
**Clifford, Lady Margaret, Countess of
    Derby 195-201**
Constance of Brittany 57, 67, 70-72
Constance of France, wife of Eustace of
    Boulogne 49, 56
Charles I, King of England 9, 222, 234, 240, 249
Charles II, King of England 234, 240-241, 247, 251
Charles V, King of France 90, 92-93, 94, 95
Charles VI, King of France 102, 110, 111, 114
Charles VII, King of France 111, 115-116, 117, 119, 129

David I, King of Scots 38, 41, 42-43, 51
Dodington, George Bubb 262-263, 269
Dudley, Lord Guildford, husband
    of Lady Jane Grey 174-175, 177-178, 180, 196-197
Dudley, John, Earl of
    Northumberland 168, 173-177, 189, 196-197

Edmund 'Crouchback', Earl of
    Lancaster 102-3, 105-106
Edmund, Earl of Rutland, son of
    Richard, Duke of York 113, 122, 124, 148
Edward, Earl of Warwick,
    son of George, Duke of
    Clarence 138-139, 147, 148, 150, 151-152
**Edward of Lancaster, Prince of
    Wales 120, 123-124, 125-135, 142, 144, 145**

Edward of Middleham, Prince of
    Wales   144-146, 148-149
Edward of Woodstock, the Black Prince,
    Prince of Wales   9, 76, 78-95,
    97, 99
Edward the Confessor   13-14, 28, 29,
    79, 126
Edward I   76-77, 79-80, 99, 102
Edward II   76-77, 79, 89, 95, 97
Edward III   76-77, 78-85, 88-89, 90,
    92, 94-95, 96-97, 98-100, 106,
    111, 113, 139, 145, 206
Edward IV   116, 122-124, 125, 129,
    130-135, 136-143, 144, 146,
    147-148, 151, 156, 158, 160
Edward V   10, 133, **136-143**, 148,
    157-158
Edward VI   167, 168, 170-171,
    173-174, 175, 181, 189, 190,
    196-197, 204
Edward VII   283
Edward VIII   10, 283
Eleanor of Aquitaine, queen of
    Henry II   52, 54, 55, 56, 59-60,
    68, 71, 73, 75
Elizabeth I, Queen of
    England   166-167, 171-172, 173,
    176, 178, 180, 182-188, 189-194,
    195, 197-201, 205, 206, 208-210,
    212, 217-220, 222, 223-224
Elizabeth of York, daughter of Edward
    IV   136, 143, 146, 149, 150, 151,
    156-157, 163, 164
Eustace of Boulogne   40, 43, 47-54, 56

Ferdinand II, King of Aragon   159-162,
    165
Francis II, King of France   183,
    205-207, 208, 209
Frederica, Duchess of York, wife of
    Frederick, Duke of York and
    Albany   275, 281
**Frederick, Duke of York and
    Albany**   270-282
**Frederick, Henry, Prince of
    Wales**   9-10, **221-230**, 232, 237
Frederick II, King of Prussia (the
    Great)   261, 272
Frederick V, Elector Palatine and King
    of Bohemia   229, 232-233
Fulk V, Count of Anjou   31, 32, 38-39

Gaunt, John of, Duke of
    Lancaster   84-85, 88, 91-92, 94,
    99-100, 101, 102-3, 105, 114,
    116, 123, 135, 145
Geoffrey, Count of Anjou   38-40,
    44-45, 49, 50, 51-52
Geoffrey, Count of Brittany   57, 60,
    61, 62-64, 66-67, 71
George, Duke of Clarence   122,
    131-132, 134-135, 137-138,
    141-142, 144-145, 147-149, 151,
    161, 186
George I   232, 237, 238, 239, 240,
    242-244, 253, 257, 260, 261
George II   243-244, 259-269, 273
George III   260, 267, 270-277,
    280-281
George IV   271-274, 280-282
George V   283
George VI   283
Glyndwr, Owain   107-109
Green Tree Prophecy, the   28, 29, 35,
    48, 54
Grey, Henry, Marquis of Dorset and
    Duke of Suffolk   169-173,
    175-179, 180-181, 186, 188,
    189-190
**Grey, Lady Catherine, Countess
    of Hertford**   169, 174, 178,
    180-188, 189-192, 193
Grey, Lady Jane, Queen   10, 157,
    167, **168-179**, 180-181, 189-190,
    196-197
Grey, Lady Mary   169, 180-181, 182,
    183, **189-194**, 199
Grey, Lord John   177, 186-187

Harold II, Godwinson   13, 14
Hatton, Sir Christopher   200-201
Heinrich V, Emperor   30, 36-37, 38
Henri II, King of France   183, 205-206
Henry of Blois, Bishop of
    Winchester   38, 40, 41, 42-44
Henry I   9, 12, 15, 16-17, 18-20,
    23-27, 28-35, 36-41, 46, 48, 50,
    51, 55, 64, 70
Henry II   10, 35, 39, 45-46 48, 50-54,
    55-64, 66-68, 69, 71, 120
Henry III   75-77, 79, 102, 106
Henry IV   99, 101-103, 105-109, 117,
    132, 145

Index

Henry V 106-107, 109-111, 114-115, 127
Henry VI 111-112, 114-124, 125-133, 135, 137, 142, 145, 148
Henry VII 114, 136, 141, 143, 145-146, 147, 149-154, 156-165
Henry VIII 142, 154, 157, 163, 165-167, 169-171, 173-174, 182, 185, 187, 190, 192, 195-196, 199, 201, 203-205, 209, 224
Henry of Trastamara, King of Castile 90-92
Henry, the Young King 10, **55-65**, 66-67
Hepburn, James, 4th Earl of Bothwell 212-215
Hervey, Lord John 263-267
Hundred Years War, the 80, 97, 100, 114, 131, 141

Isabella of Angoulême, 2nd queen of King John 72, 75
Isabella, Queen of Castile 159-162
Isabella of France, queen of Edward II 77, 79-80

James, Earl of Moray (Lord James) 207-208, 209-213, 216-218
James I of England, VI of Scotland 188, 201, 212-216, 218-220, 221-230, 232, 243
James II of England, VII of Scotland 240-241, 245-251
James IV, King of Scotland 160, 203, 209
James V, King of Scotland 167, 203-204, 207
Joan of Kent, 'Fair Maid of', wife of Edward of Woodstock, the Black Prince 83, 89-91, 94
John, Duke of Bedford 110-116
John, King of England 57, 59, 66-75, 99
John II, King of France 85, 86-89

Keyes, Master Thomas, husband of Lady Mary Grey 189-193

Lionel of Antwerp, Duke of Clarence 88, 94, 96-97, 99, 113-114, 123

Louis, Frederick, Prince of Wales 243, **259-269**, 271
Louis VI, King of France 31-33, 38, 40, 48
Louis VII, King of France 49, 51-52, 56, 57, 58-61, 62
Louis VIII, King of France 70, 75
Louis XI, King of France (Spider King) 129-131, 135
Louis XIII, King of France 229
Louis XIV, King of France 241, 250-253
Louis XV, King of France 253, 257-258

Malcolm III, King of Scotland 19, 24, 29, 48
Mancini, Dominic 141-142
Margaret of Anjou, queen of Henry VI 117, 120-122, 124, 125-133, 135
Margaret of France, queen of Henry, the Young King 56, 58, 59, 63
Margaret of York, Duchess of Burgundy 131, 151-152
Margaret, Saint, daughter of Edmund Ironside 14, 24, 48
Marshal, William, Earl of Pembroke 59, 61-62, 66-67, 71, 75
Mary I, Queen of England 83, 166-167, 170, 172-178, 181-182, 206
Mary II, Queen of England 240-243, 246-248, 250
Mary, Queen of Scots 9, 157, 167, 173, 182, 183, 187, 201, **202-220**, 222
Marie of Guise 173, 203-204, 206-207
Mary of Modena, queen of James II 240-241, 245-250, 254
Matilda, Empress 24, 29-30, **36-46**, 48-51
Matilda of Flanders, queen of William I 12, 15, 16, 31, 38
Matilda II, queen of Henry I 24, 25, 28-30, 36, 38, 41, 48
Matilda III, of Boulogne, queen of King Stephen 38, 42-44, 48, 49, 52, 53
Mortimer, Anne 98, 105, 110, 112, 113-114

315

Mortimer, Edmund, 5th Earl of
    March   98, 103, **104-112**, 114
Mortimer, Roger, 1st Earl of
    March   77, 79, 89, 97
**Mortimer, Roger, 4th Earl of
    March   96-103**, 104
Mortimer, Sir Edmund   107-109

Neville, Anne, queen of
    Richard III   131-132, 135, 142,
    144-146
Neville, Cecily   114, 116, 122-123
Neville, Richard, Earl of
    Warwick   120-123, 127-133,
    137-138, 144

Odo, Bishop of Bayeux   18, 20
D'Olbreuse, Eleanore   237-239

Pedro, King of Castile (the Cruel)   84,
    90-92
Pett, Phineas   225, 227
**Pole, John De La, Earl of
    Lincoln   147-154**, 156
Philip, Count of Flanders   59, 60-61,
    62-63
Philip I, King of France   12, 16, 20, 31
Philip II, King of France
    (Augustus)   62-63, 67-75
Philip VI, King of France   79, 80-83,
    85
Philippa of Clarence, daughter of Lionel
    of Antwerp   96-97, 100, 103
Philippa of Hainault, queen of
    Edward III   79, 88, 89, 94

Richard I   57, 60, 61, 62-64, 66-71, 74
Richard II   91, 94-95, 96-103,
    105-107, 117, 145
Richard III   122, 132, 134-135,
    136-137, 139-143, 144-146,
    147-151, 190
Richard, Duke of York   112, 113-124,
    126-128, 148, 149, 151
Richard, Duke of York, son of Edward
    IV   136, 138, 140, 141-143, 148
Richard of Conisburgh, Earl of
    Cambridge   104, 110, 112,
    113-114
Rizzio, David   210-213
Robert of Bellême, Earl of
    Shrewsbury   24-26, 31

Robert II, Duke of Normandy   12-27,
    29
Robert, Earl of Gloucester   27, 32, 36,
    38, 39, 40-42, 43-45, 49, 51
des Roches, William   71, 74

Seymour, Edward, Earl of Hertford,
    husband of Lady Catherine
    Grey   181-186, 188
Seymour, Lady Jane   181-182, 184-185
Sibyl of Conversano   23, 24-25
Simnel, Lambert   152-153
Sobieski, Princess Clementina, wife
    of James Francis Edward
    Stuart   255-258
**Sophia, Electress of Hanover   11,
    231-244**, 260
Stafford, Henry, Duke of
    Buckingham   139-140, 143,
    145-146, 148, 149, 157
Stanley, Ferdinando, 5th Earl of
    Derby   197, 199, 201
Stanley, Henry, 4th Earl of
    Derby   197-199, 201
Stephen, King of England   37-38,
    40-45, 47-54, 57-58, 67, 70
Stuart, Charles Edward   256-258
Stuart, Elizabeth, Queen of
    Bohemia   222, 224-225, 229,
    232-234, 237
Stuart, Henry Benedict, Cardinal
    York   256, 258
Stuart, Henry, Lord Darnley   208-215,
    217-218, 222
**Stuart, James Francis Edward   241,
    245-258**
Succession, rules of
    acquisitions   16-17
    Act of Accord (1460)   123, 127-128
    Anglo-Saxon England   13-14
    children   13, 71
    crowning during lifetime   47, 52,
        57-58, 65
    designation   13-14, 23, 54, 66, 68,
        70, 99, 103, 106, 148-149, 168
    Divine Right of Kings   223
    election   13-14, 24, 40, 42, 71, 129
    entails
        Edward I   76-77, 99
        Edward III   99-100, 102, 106
        Henry IV   108-109
        Henry VI   132

Index

exclusion crisis 241
female succession 10, 13, 24-25, 29, 35, 38, 76-77, 99, 102, 109, 145, 149, 166-167, 284
Glorious Revolution (1688) 77, 241-243, 247-250, 252
  Act of Settlement (1701) 232, 243, 251, 260
  Bill of Rights (1688) 241-243
Henry VIII's Acts of Succession 166
  First Act (1534) 166-167
  Second Act (1536) 167
  Third Act (1544) 167
Henry VIII's will 167, 170, 173, 174, 185, 187, 192, 195, 199, 205, 209, 224
oath taking/homage 32, 38, 40, 55, 58, 75
primogeniture 11, 66, 71, 76, 97, 99, 145, 149, 166, 175, 182, 205, 223-224, 246, 284
Reformation 165-167
Succession to the Crown Act (2013) 283-284
Treaty of
  Alton (1101) 24-25
  Caen (1091) 19
  Le Goulet (1200) 72
  Messina (1190) 68, 70
  Montmirail (1169) 57
  Wallingford (1153) 45, 54
Swynford, Catherine, 3rd queen of John of Gaunt 114

Theobald IV, Count of Blois 32, 34, 37

Tudor, Arthur, Prince of Wales 10, 151, **155-165**
Tudor, Margaret, queen of James IV of Scotland 157, 161, 167, 203, 209
Tudor, Mary, Queen of France, duchess of Suffolk 157, 167, 169-170, 192, 195

Victoria, Queen 273, 280, 282, 283

Walsingham, Sir Francis 200, 218-219
De Warenne, William, Earl of Surrey 24, 25
Wilhelmina, Princess Royal of Prussia 260-261
William I (the Conqueror) 12-17, 18, 24, 26, 27, 28, 33, 36, 37, 48, 59, 81
William II (Rufus) 12, 15, 16, 17, 18-20, 23, 24, 29, 37
William III 240, 241-243, 246, 248-251
William IV 273, 282
William Aetheling 9, **28-35**, 36, 37
William Clito 24-25, 26, 29, 31-33, 35, 37, 38-39
William, Duke of Gloucester, son of Queen Anne 242-243
William, George, Duke of Celle 235-239, 243
Woodville, Anthony, Earl Rivers 137, 139-140
Woodville, Elizabeth, queen of Edward IV 131, 136-137, 139, 141, 146, 148, 156, 169